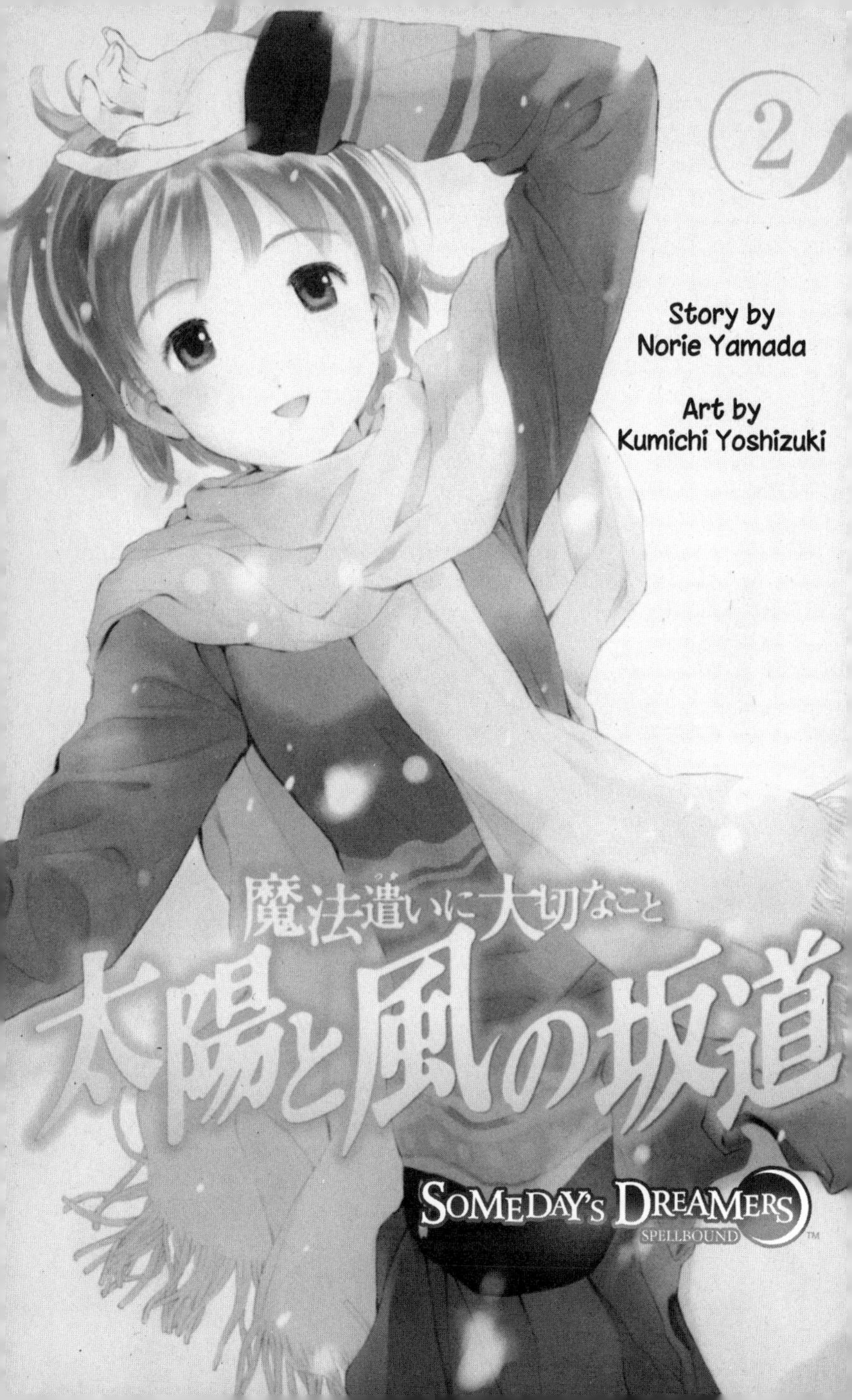
2
Story by
Norie Yamada
Art by
Kumichi Yoshizuki
魔法遣いに大切なこと
太陽と風の坂道
SOMEDAY's DREAMERS
SPELLBOUND
™

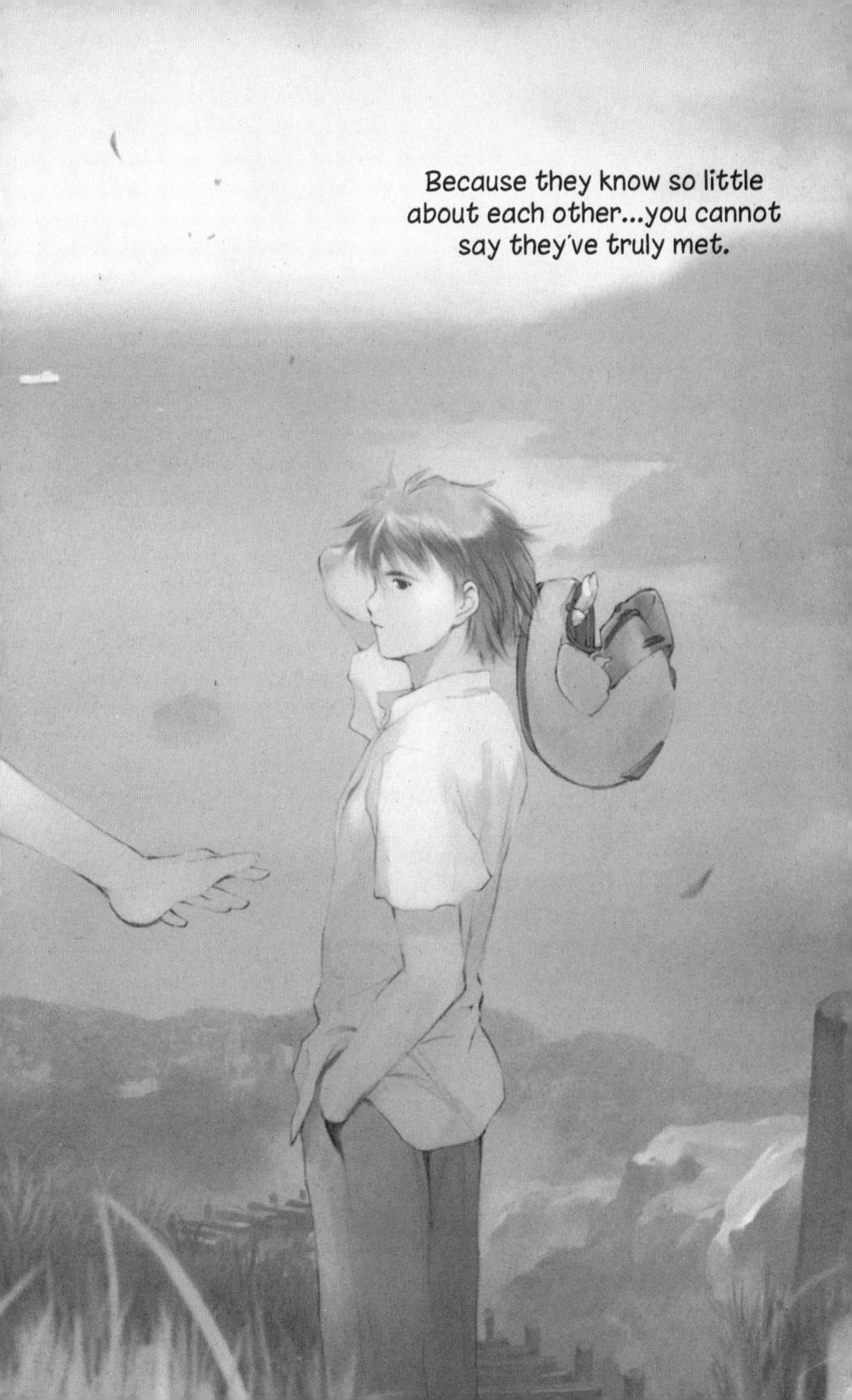
Because they know so little about each other...you cannot say they've truly met.

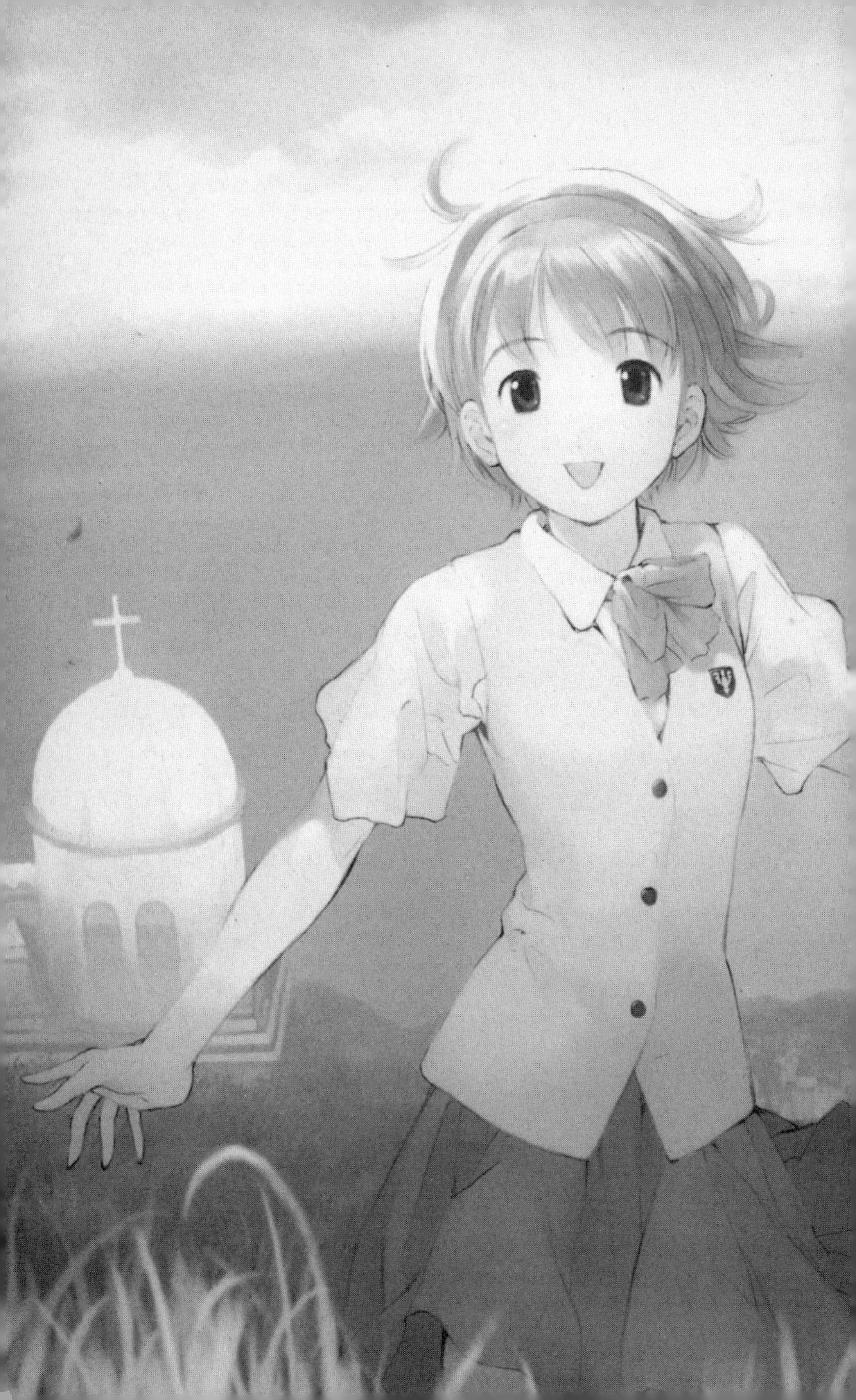

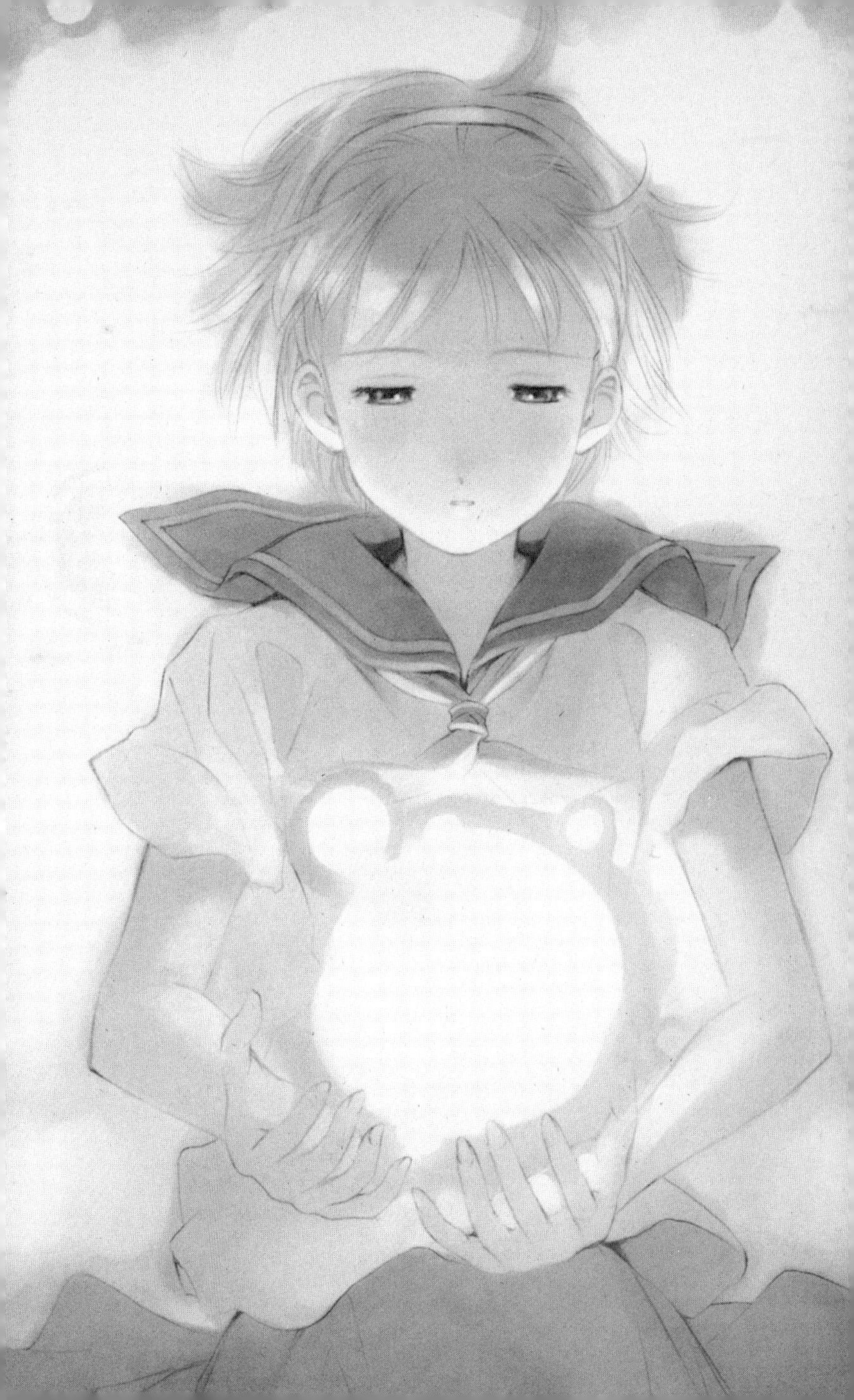

SOMEDAY'S DREAMERS
SPELLBOUND

Volume 2

Story by Norie Yamada
Art by Kumichi Yoshizuki

TOKYOPOP®

HAMBURG // LONDON // LOS ANGELES // TOKYO

Someday's Dreamers: Spellbound Vol. 2
Story By Norie Yamada
Art By Kumichi Yoshizuki

Translation - Jeremiah Bourque
English Adaptation - Hope Donovan
Retouch and Lettering - Star Print Brokers
Production Artist - Courtney Geter
Cover Design - Jose Macasocol, Jr.

Editor - Paul Morrissey
Digital Imaging Manager - Chris Buford
Pre-Production Supervisor - Erika Terriquez
Art Director - Anne Marie Horne
Production Manager - Elisabeth Brizzi
Managing Editor - Vy Nguyen
VP of Production - Ron Klamert
Editor-in-Chief - Rob Tokar
Publisher - Mike Kiley
President and C.O.O. - John Parker
C.E.O. and Chief Creative Officer - Stuart Levy

A **TOKYOPOP** Manga

TOKYOPOP Inc.
5900 Wilshire Blvd. Suite 2000
Los Angeles, CA 90036

E-mail: info@TOKYOPOP.com
Come visit us online at www.TOKYOPOP.com

MAHOUTSUKAI NI TAISETSUNA KOTO TAIYOU TO KAZE NO SAKAMICHI Volume 2 © 2004 NORIE YAMADA/KUMICHI YOSHIZUKI First published in Japan in 2004 by KADOKAWA SHOTEN PUBLISHING CO., LTD., Tokyo. English translation rights arranged with KADOKAWA SHOTEN PUBLISHING CO., LTD., Tokyo through TUTTLE–MORI AGENCY, INC., Tokyo.

ISBN: 978-1-59816-643-9

First TOKYOPOP printing: April 2007
10 9 8 7 6 5 4 3 2 1
Printed in the USA

CONTENTS:

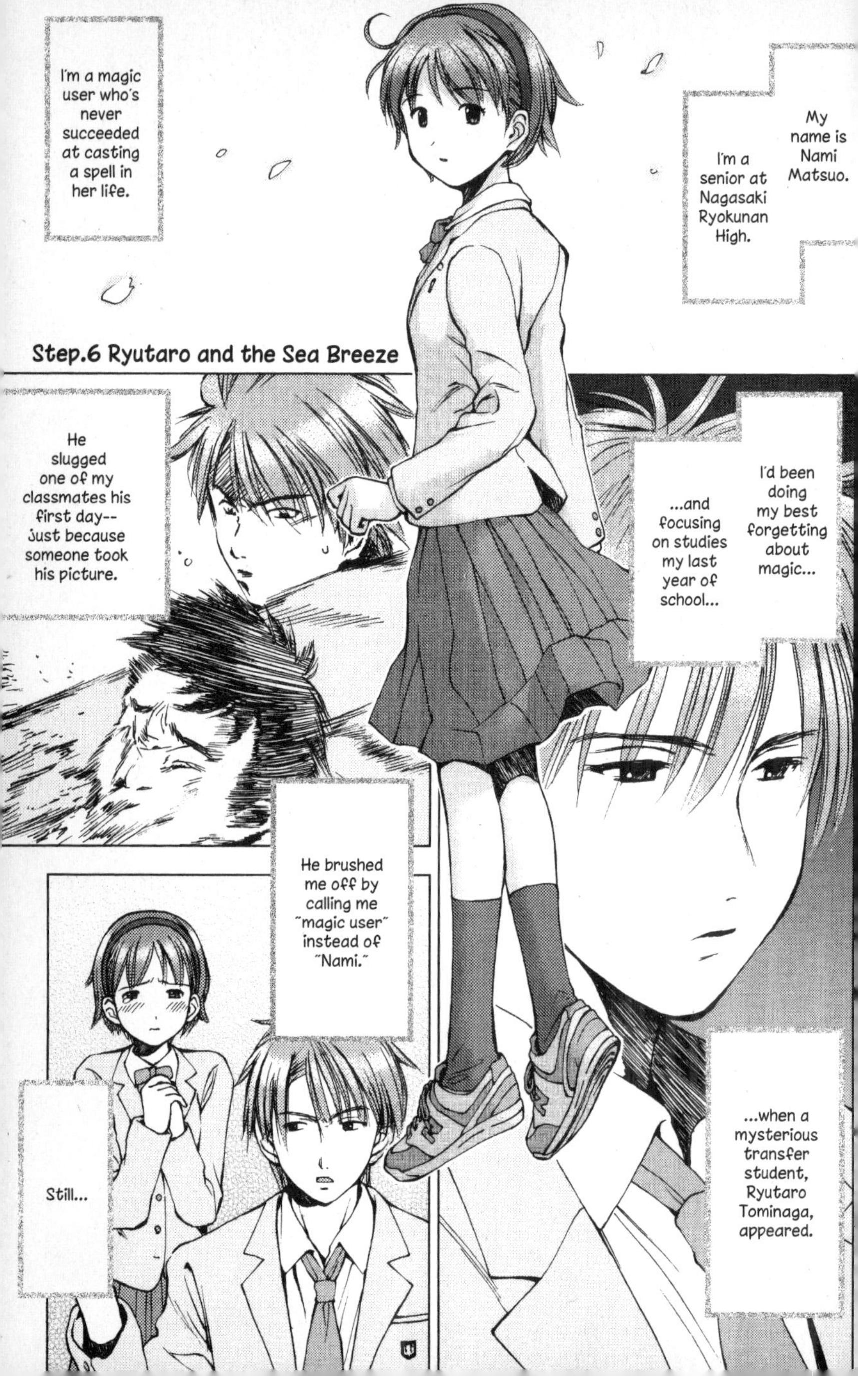
My name is Nami Matsuo.
I'm a senior at Nagasaki Ryokunan High.
I'm a magic user who's never succeeded at casting a spell in her life.
Step.6 Ryutaro and the Sea Breeze
I'd been doing my best forgetting about magic...
...and focusing on studies my last year of school...
...when a mysterious transfer student, Ryutaro Tominaga, appeared.
He slugged one of my classmates his first day--just because someone took his picture.
He brushed me off by calling me "magic user" instead of "Nami."
Still...

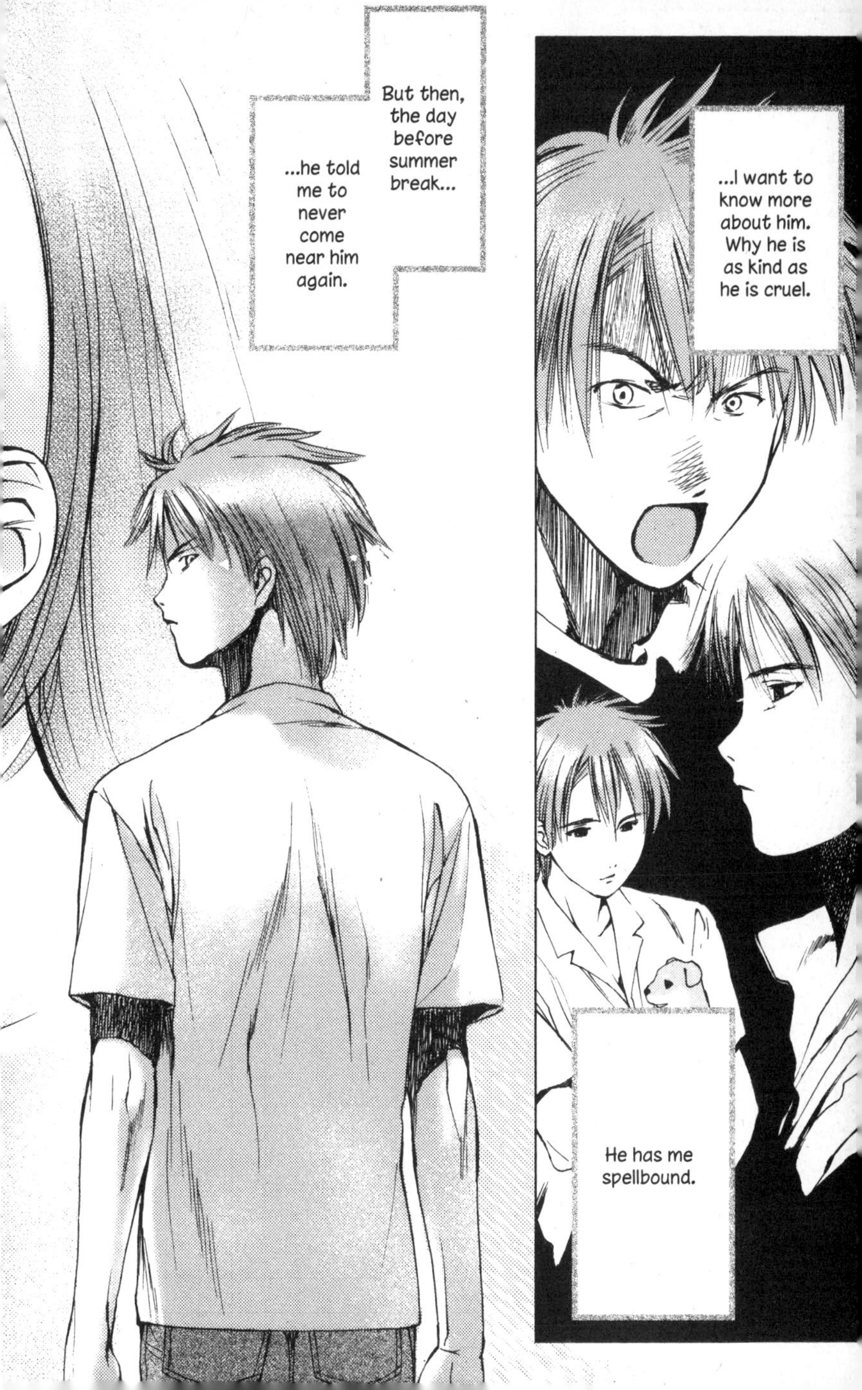
...I want to know more about him. Why he is as kind as he is cruel.
He has me spellbound.
But then, the day before summer break...
...he told me to never come near him again.

Step.6 Ryutaro and the Sea Breeze

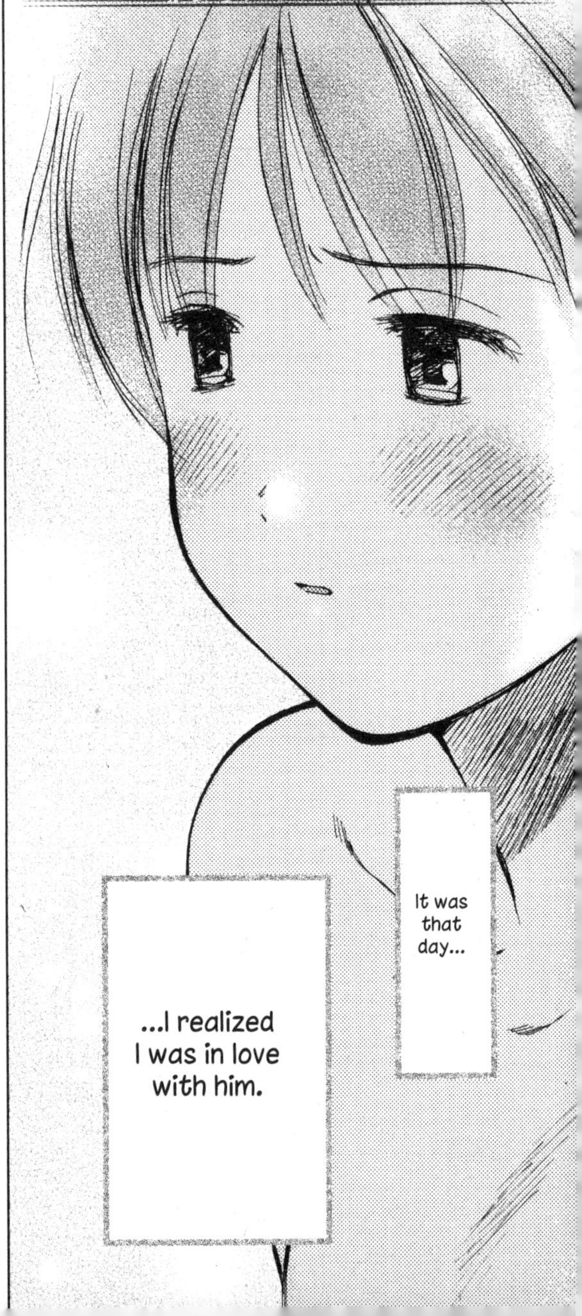
It was that day...
...I realized I was in love with him.

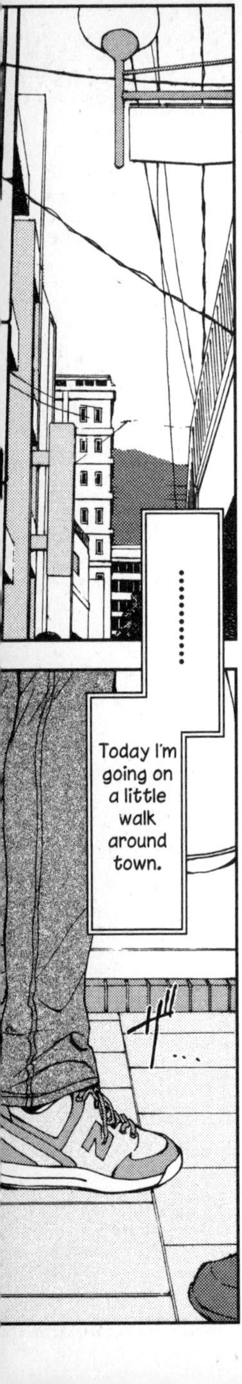
....
Today I'm going on a little walk around town.

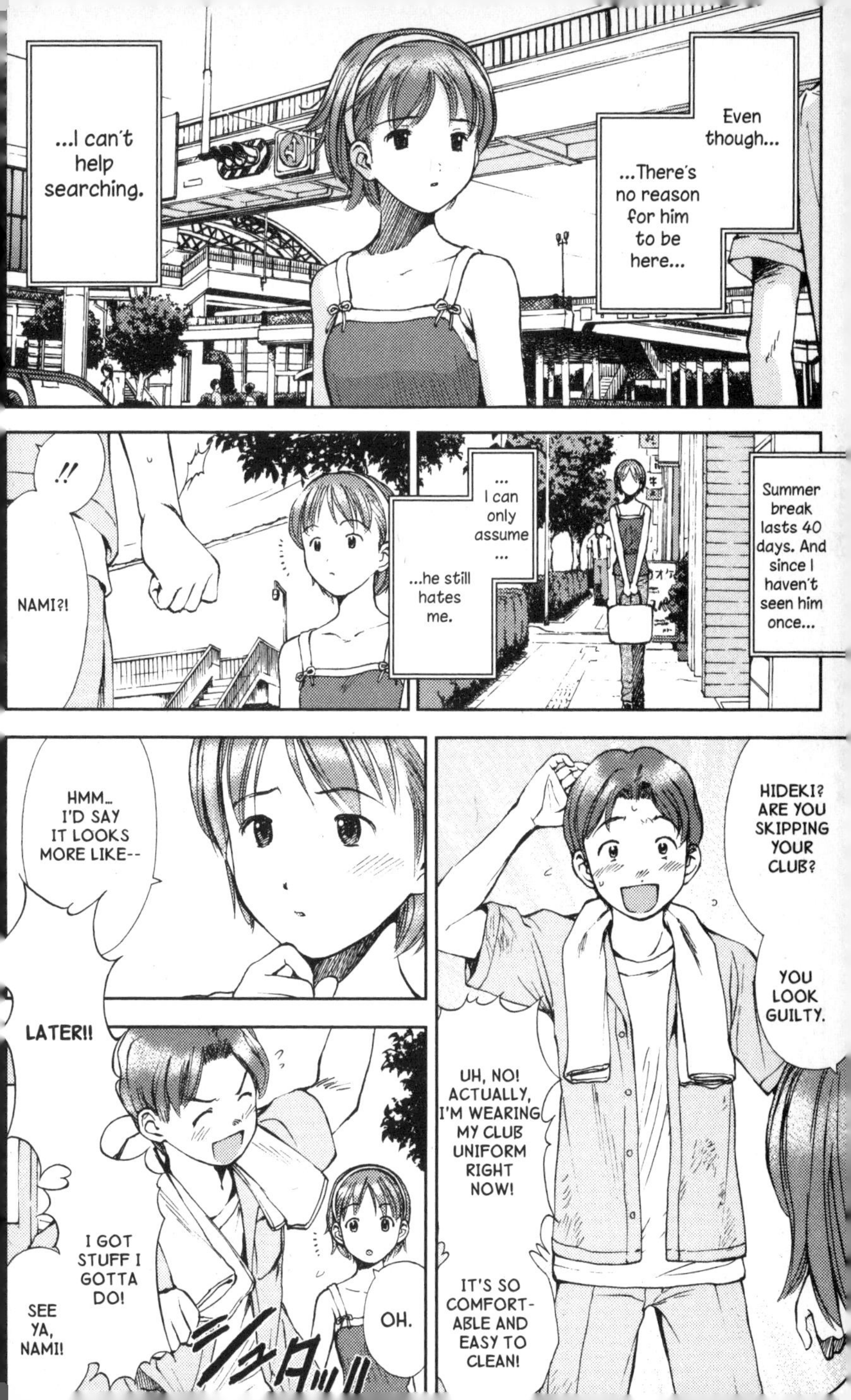
Even though...
...There's no reason for him to be here...
...I can't help searching.
Summer break lasts 40 days. And since I haven't seen him once...
...I can only assume...
...he still hates me.
!!
NAMI?!
HIDEKI? ARE YOU SKIPPING YOUR CLUB?
YOU LOOK GUILTY.
UH, NO! ACTUALLY, I'M WEARING MY CLUB UNIFORM RIGHT NOW!
IT'S SO COMFORT-ABLE AND EASY TO CLEAN!
HMM... I'D SAY IT LOOKS MORE LIKE--
LATER!!
I GOT STUFF I GOTTA DO!
SEE YA, NAMI!
OH.

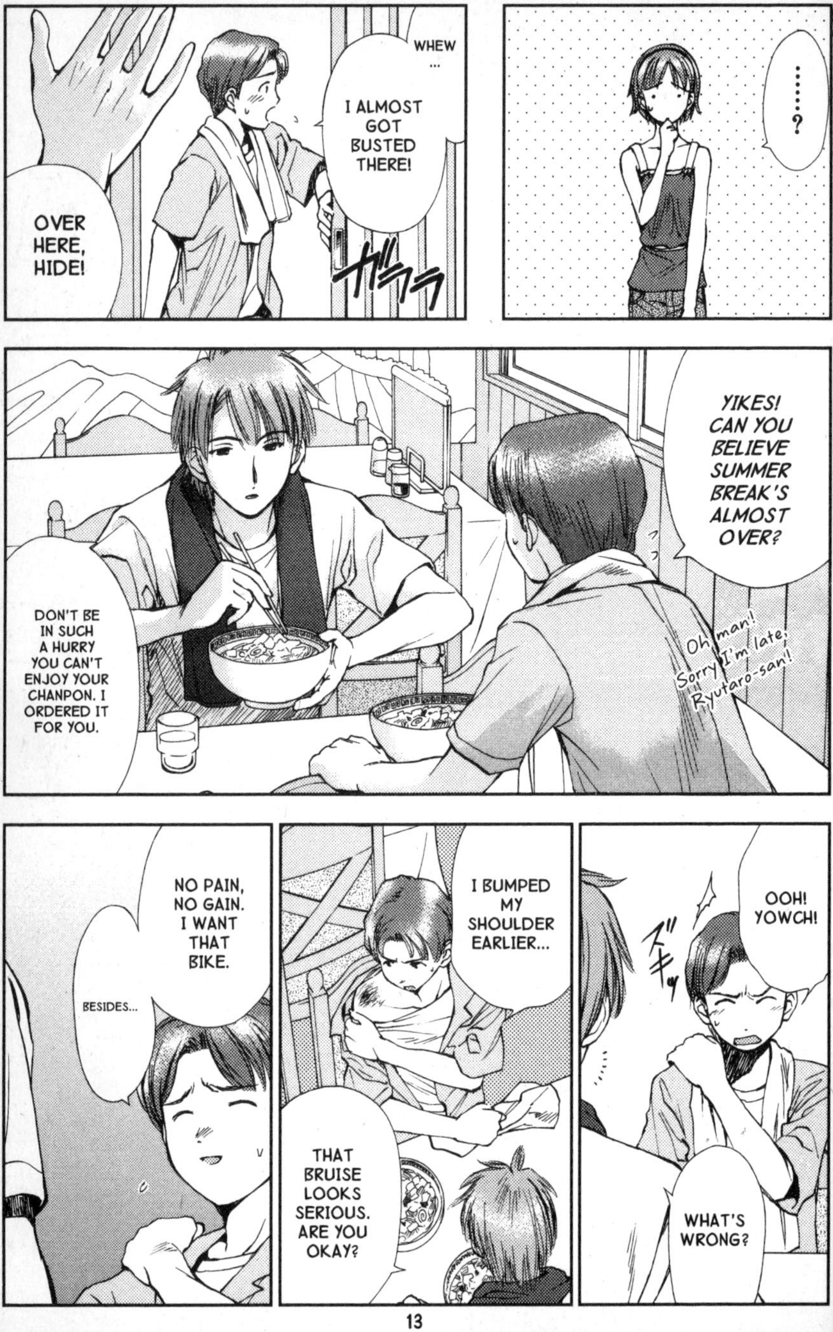
......?
WHEW ...
I ALMOST GOT BUSTED THERE!
OVER HERE, HIDE!
YIKES! CAN YOU BELIEVE SUMMER BREAK'S ALMOST OVER?
Oh man! Sorry I'm late, Ryutaro-san!
DON'T BE IN SUCH A HURRY YOU CAN'T ENJOY YOUR CHANPON. I ORDERED IT FOR YOU.
OOH! YOWCH!
WHAT'S WRONG?
I BUMPED MY SHOULDER EARLIER...
THAT BRUISE LOOKS SERIOUS. ARE YOU OKAY?
NO PAIN, NO GAIN. I WANT THAT BIKE.
BESIDES...

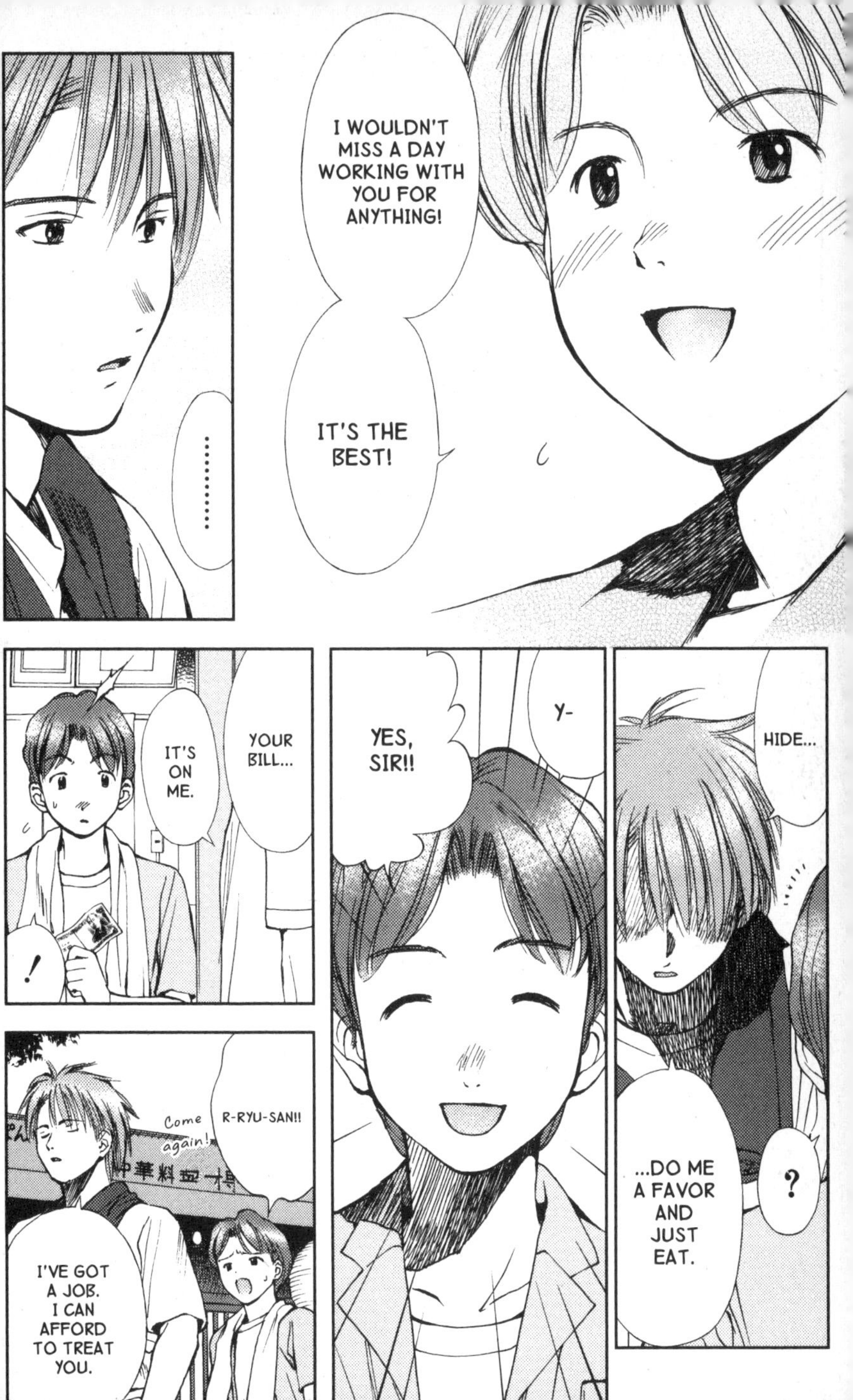
I WOULDN'T MISS A DAY WORKING WITH YOU FOR ANYTHING!
IT'S THE BEST!
......
HIDE...
?
...DO ME A FAVOR AND JUST EAT.
Y-
YES, SIR!!
YOUR BILL...
IT'S ON ME.
!
R-RYU-SAN!!
Come again!
I'VE GOT A JOB. I CAN AFFORD TO TREAT YOU.

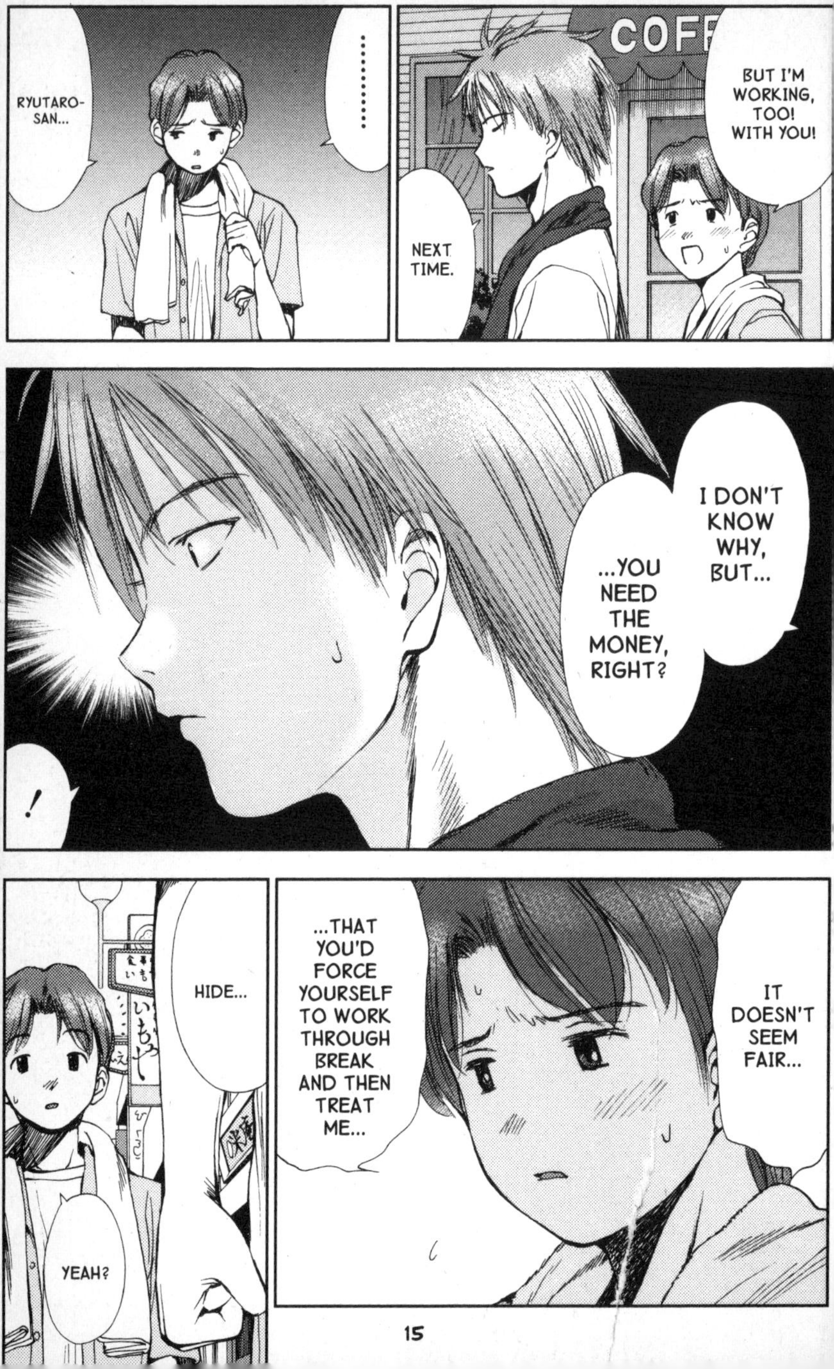
BUT I'M WORKING, TOO! WITH YOU!
NEXT TIME.
....
RYUTARO-SAN...
I DON'T KNOW WHY, BUT...
...YOU NEED THE MONEY, RIGHT?
!
IT DOESN'T SEEM FAIR...
...THAT YOU'D FORCE YOURSELF TO WORK THROUGH BREAK AND THEN TREAT ME...
HIDE...
YEAH?

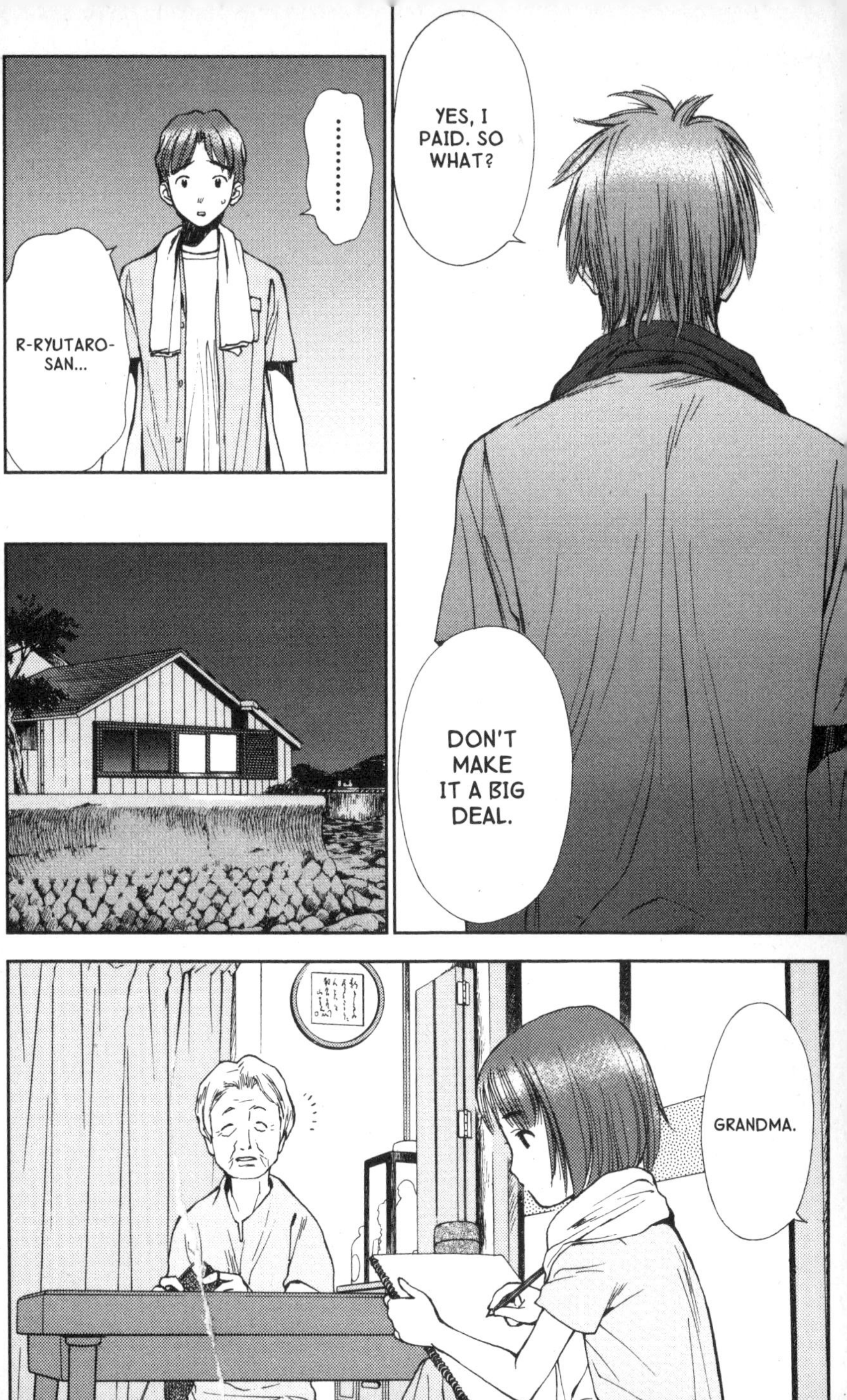
YES, I PAID. SO WHAT?
DON'T MAKE IT A BIG DEAL.
......
R-RYUTARO-SAN...
GRANDMA.

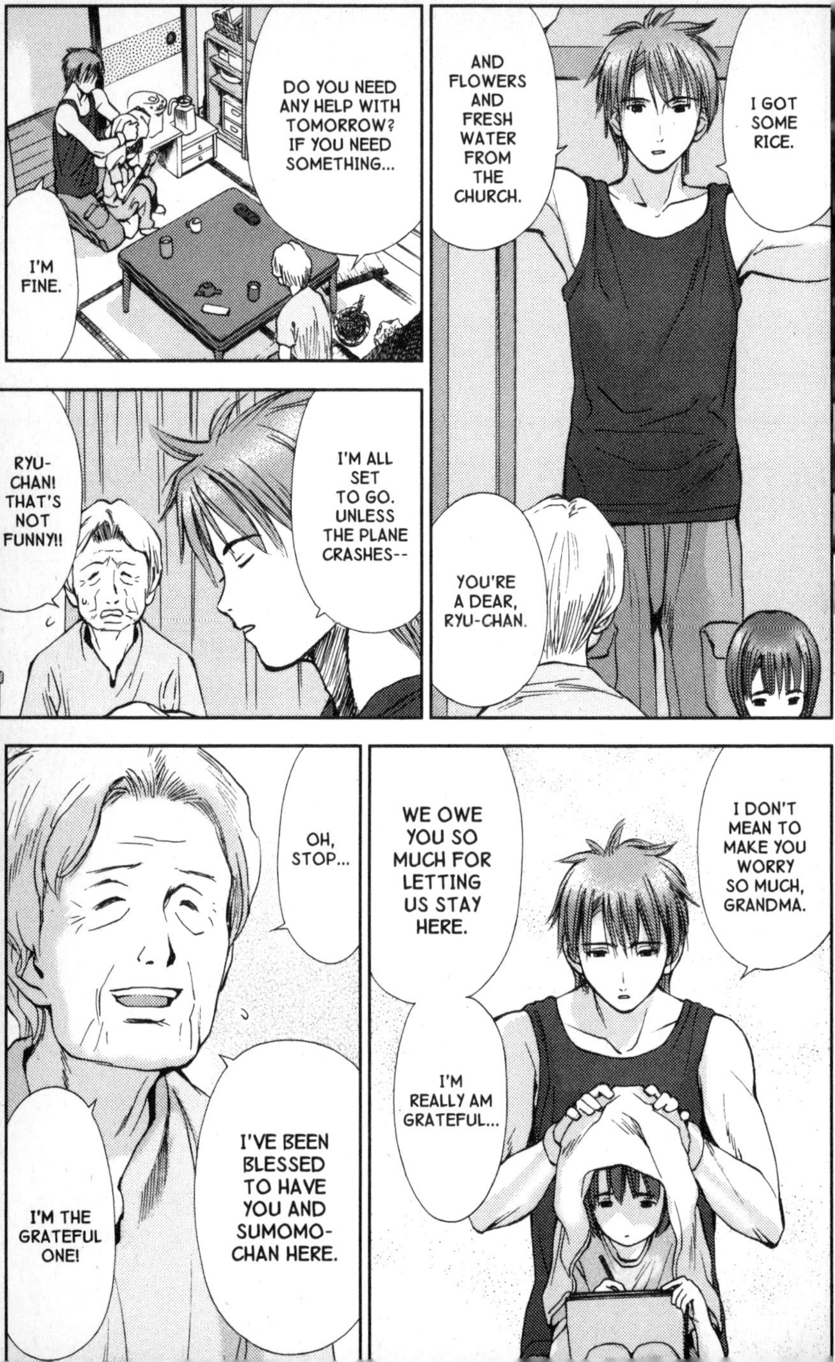
I GOT SOME RICE.
AND FLOWERS AND FRESH WATER FROM THE CHURCH.
YOU'RE A DEAR, RYU-CHAN.
DO YOU NEED ANY HELP WITH TOMORROW? IF YOU NEED SOMETHING...
I'M FINE.
I'M ALL SET TO GO. UNLESS THE PLANE CRASHES--
RYU-CHAN! THAT'S NOT FUNNY!!
I DON'T MEAN TO MAKE YOU WORRY SO MUCH, GRANDMA.
WE OWE YOU SO MUCH FOR LETTING US STAY HERE.
I'M REALLY AM GRATEFUL...
OH, STOP...
I'VE BEEN BLESSED TO HAVE YOU AND SUMOMO-CHAN HERE.
I'M THE GRATEFUL ONE!

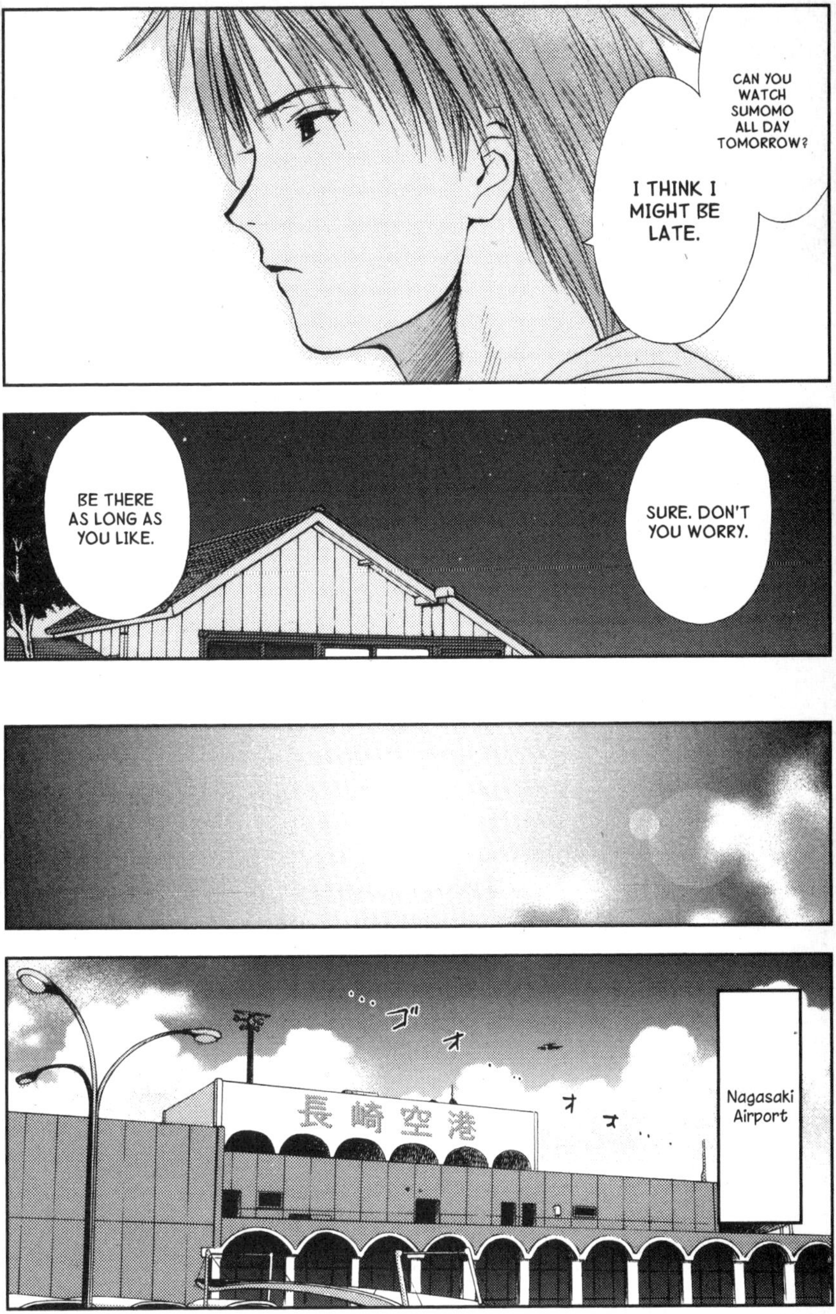
CAN YOU WATCH SUMOMO ALL DAY TOMORROW?
I THINK I MIGHT BE LATE.
SURE. DON'T YOU WORRY.
BE THERE AS LONG AS YOU LIKE.
Nagasaki Airport
ゴォォ
長崎空港

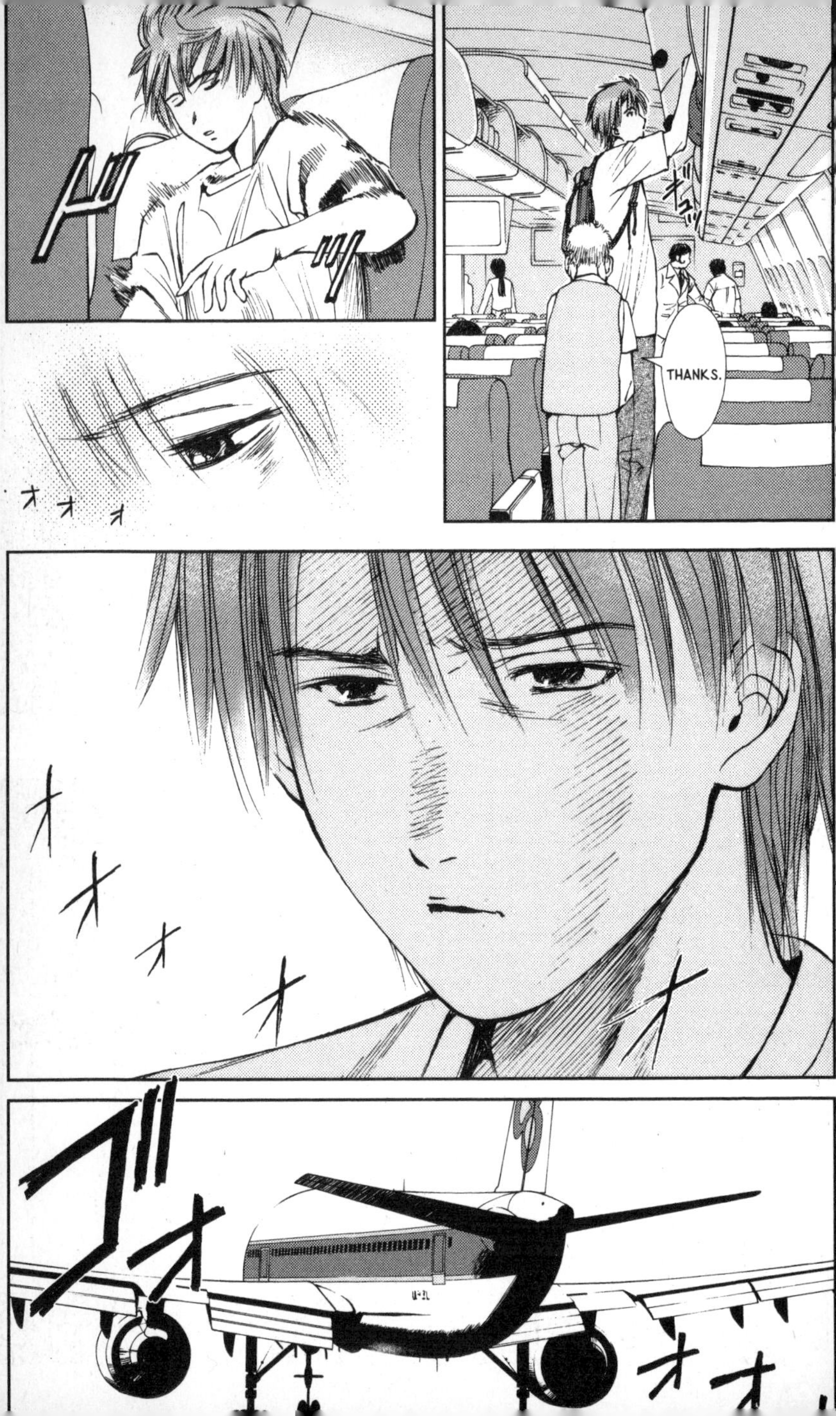
ギュッ
THANKS.
ドッ
…オオオ
ゴオ
オオ

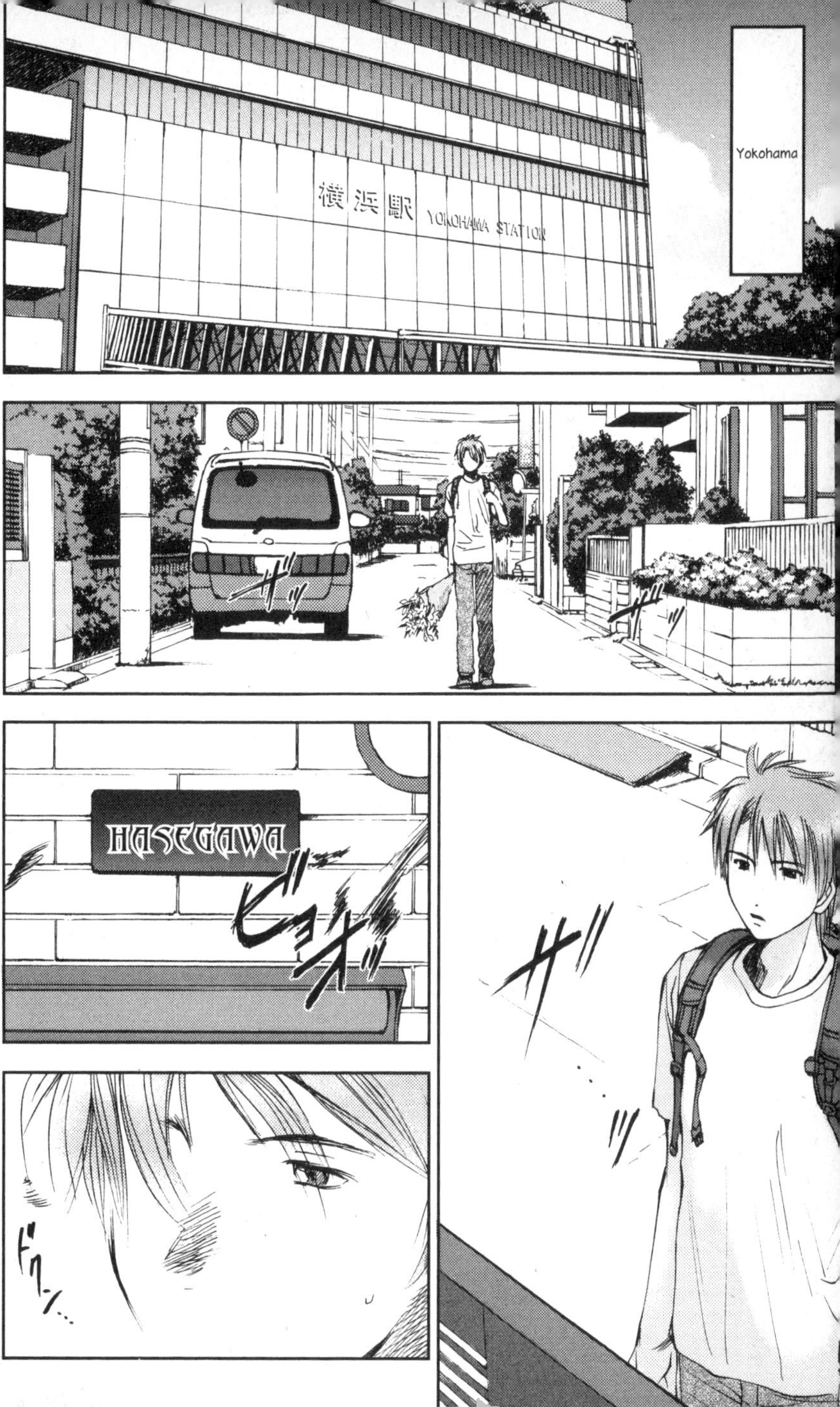
Yokohama
横浜駅 YOKOHAMA STATION
ザッ
ザッ
ザ……ッ
HASEGAWA
ビュオッ
ドクン…

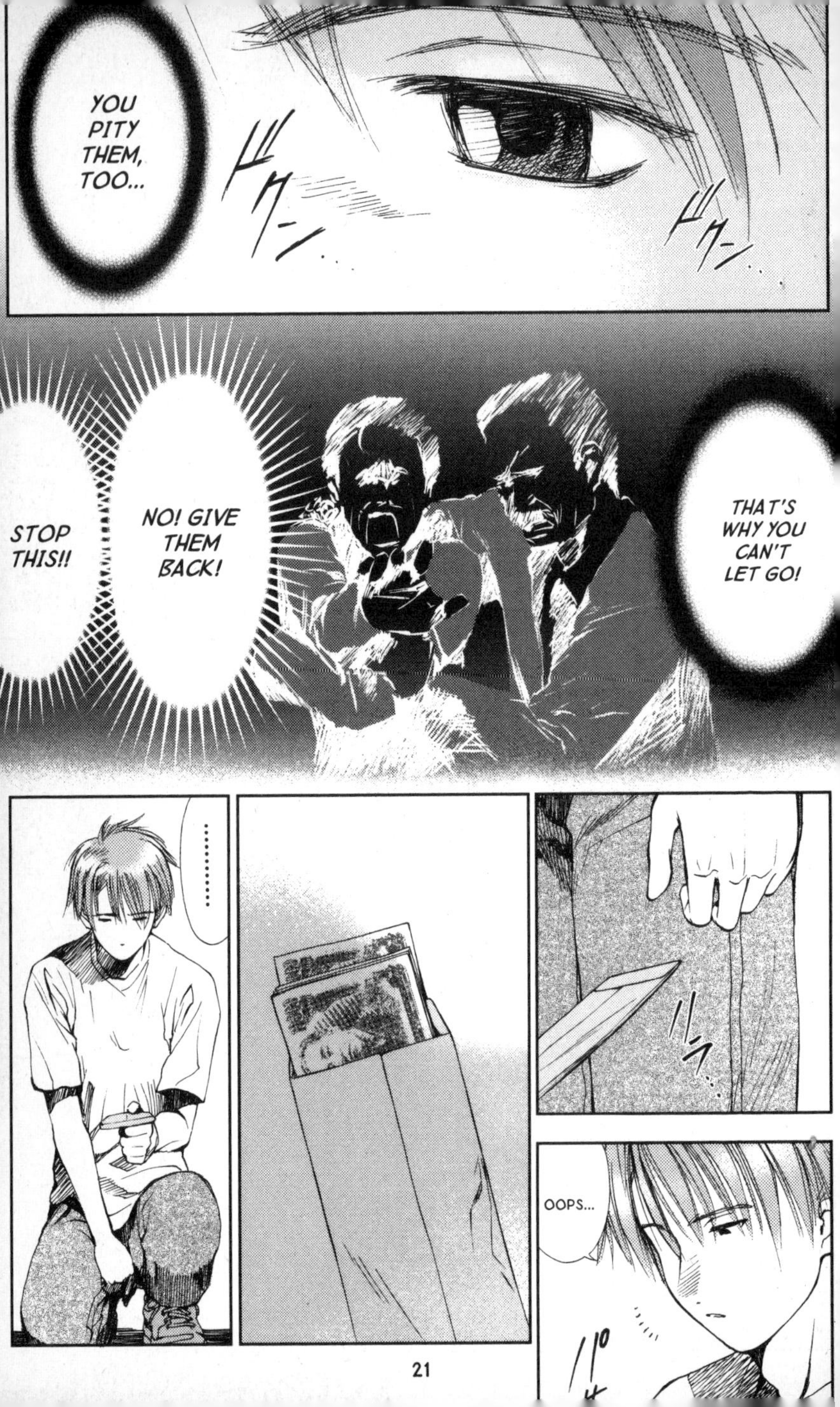
YOU PITY THEM, TOO...
THAT'S WHY YOU CAN'T LET GO!
NO! GIVE THEM BACK!
STOP THIS!!
OOPS...
....

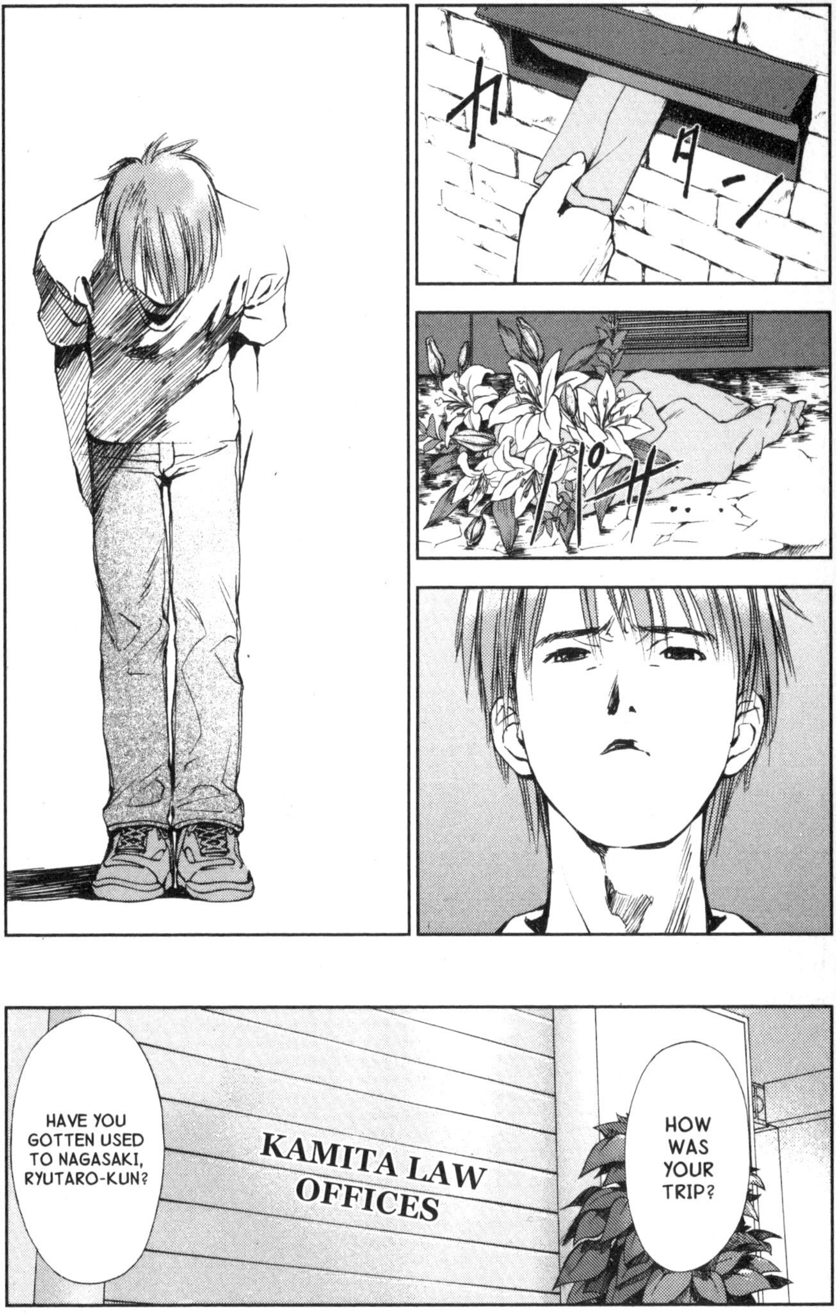
カタン
パサッ
HOW WAS YOUR TRIP?
KAMITA LAW OFFICES
HAVE YOU GOTTEN USED TO NAGASAKI, RYUTARO-KUN?

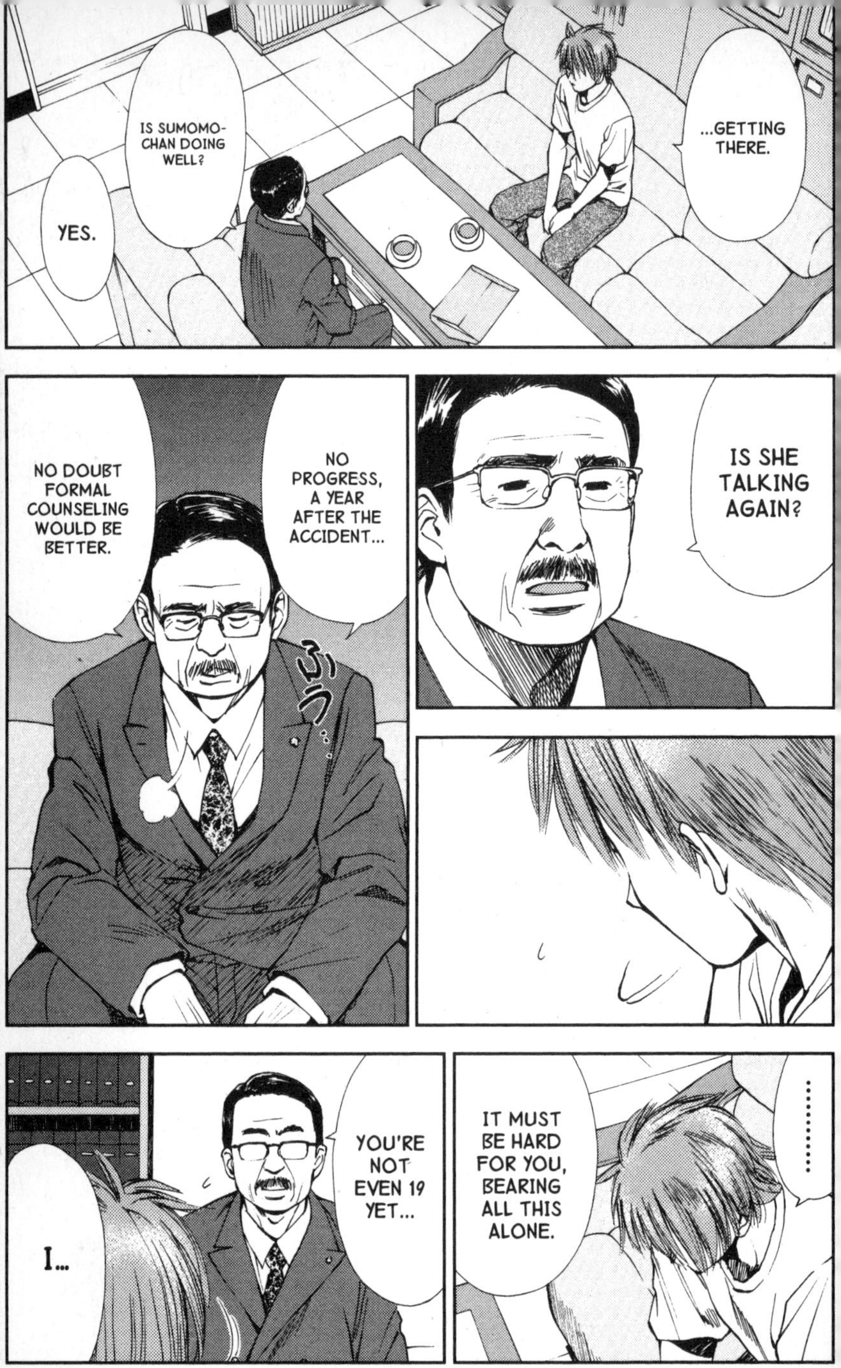
...GETTING THERE.
IS SUMOMO-CHAN DOING WELL?
YES.
IS SHE TALKING AGAIN?
NO PROGRESS, A YEAR AFTER THE ACCIDENT...
NO DOUBT FORMAL COUNSELING WOULD BE BETTER.
ふう...
....
IT MUST BE HARD FOR YOU, BEARING ALL THIS ALONE.
YOU'RE NOT EVEN 19 YET...
I...

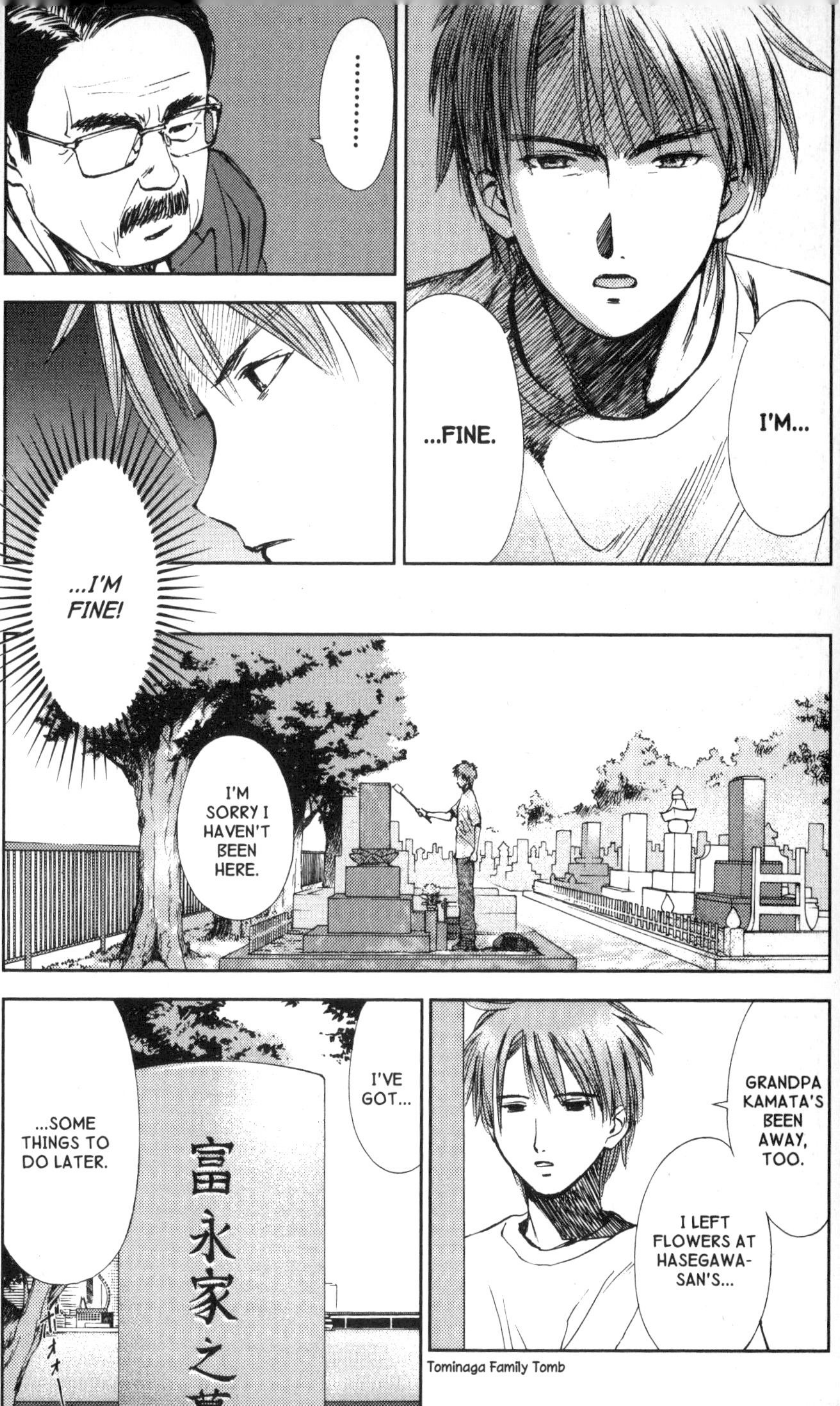
I'M...
...FINE.
......
...I'M FINE!
I'M SORRY I HAVEN'T BEEN HERE.
GRANDPA KAMATA'S BEEN AWAY, TOO.
I LEFT FLOWERS AT HASEGAWA-SAN'S...
I'VE GOT...
...SOME THINGS TO DO LATER.
富永家之
Tominaga Family Tomb

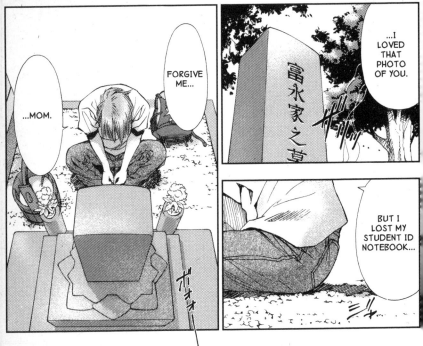

...MOM.

FORGIVE ME...

富永家之墓

...I LOVED THAT PHOTO OF YOU.

BUT I LOST MY STUDENT ID NOTEBOOK...

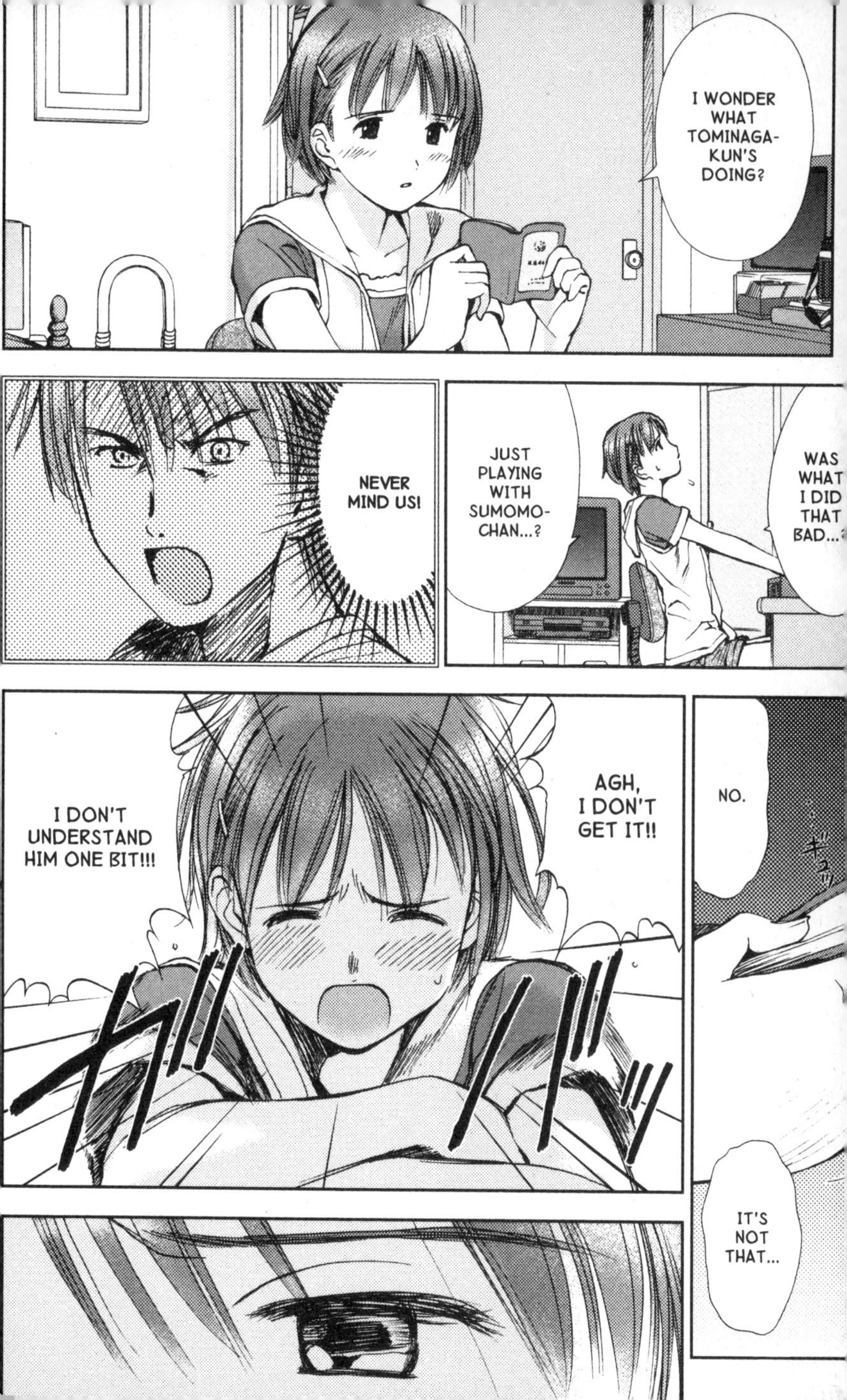
I WONDER WHAT TOMINAGA-KUN'S DOING?
WAS WHAT I DID THAT BAD...?
JUST PLAYING WITH SUMOMO-CHAN...?
NEVER MIND US!
NO.
IT'S NOT THAT...
AGH, I DON'T GET IT!!
I DON'T UNDERSTAND HIM ONE BIT!!!

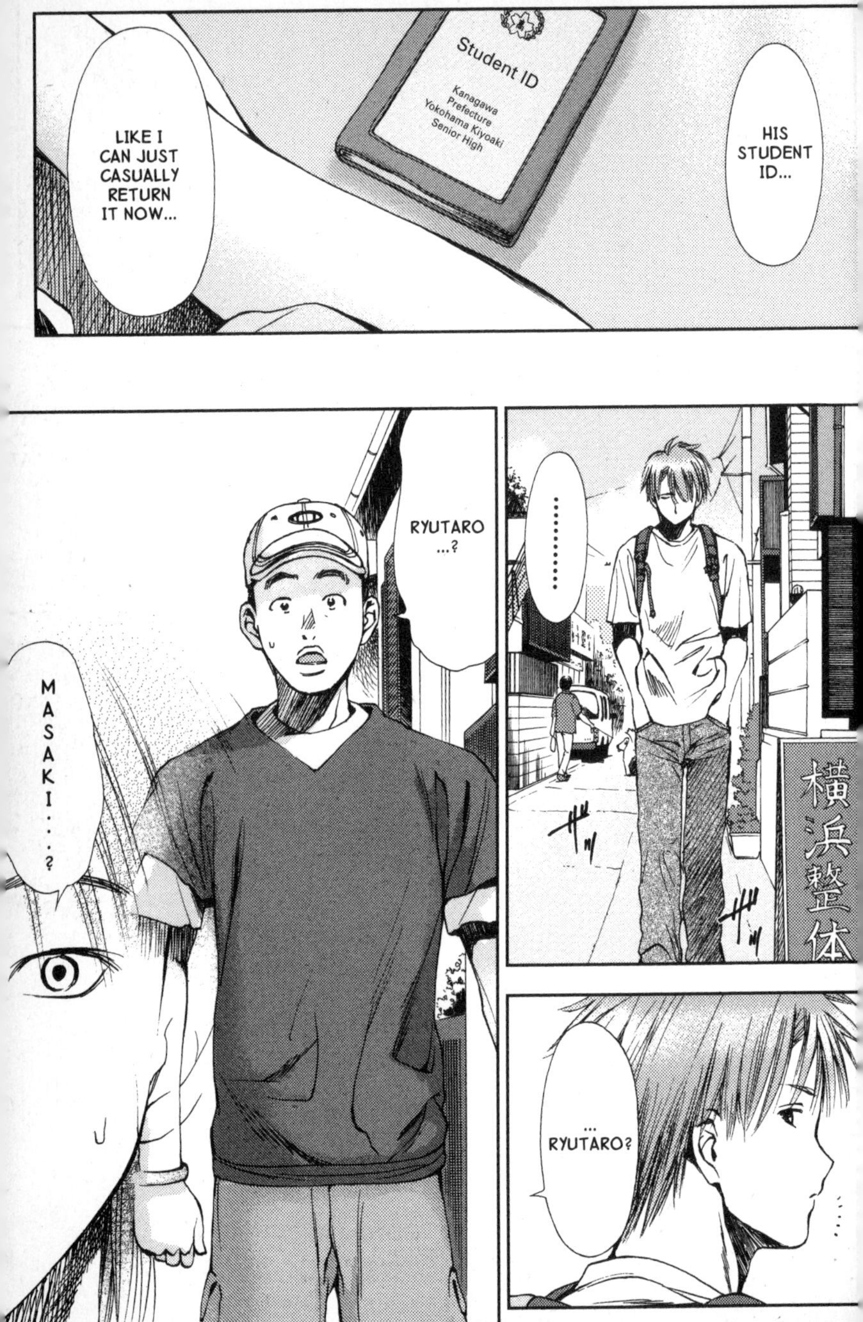
HIS STUDENT ID...
Student ID
Kanagawa Prefecture Yokohama Kiyoaki Senior High
LIKE I CAN JUST CASUALLY RETURN IT NOW...
....
横浜整体
...RYUTARO?
......
RYUTARO...?
MASAKI...?

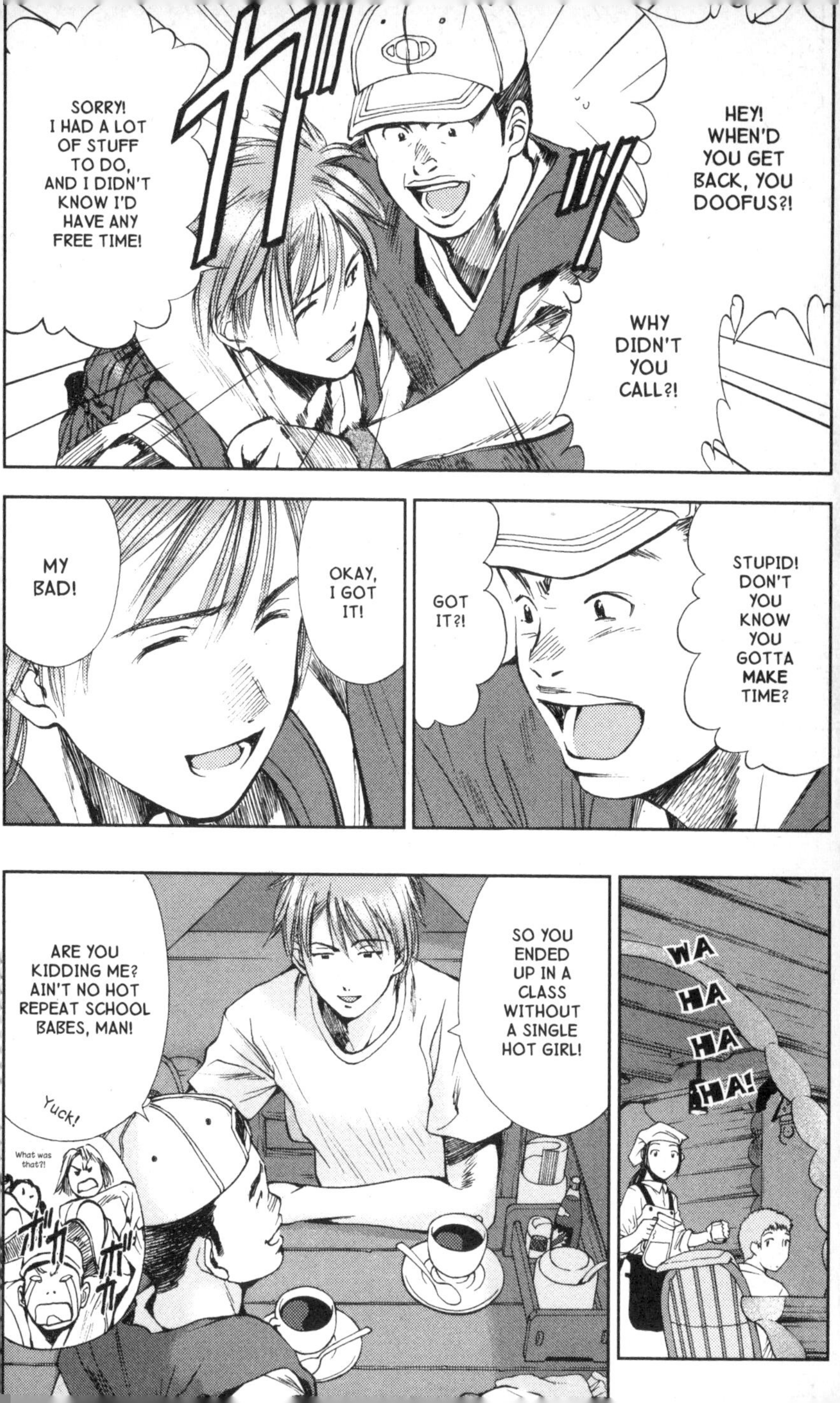
HEY! WHEN'D YOU GET BACK, YOU DOOFUS?!
WHY DIDN'T YOU CALL?!
SORRY! I HAD A LOT OF STUFF TO DO, AND I DIDN'T KNOW I'D HAVE ANY FREE TIME!
STUPID! DON'T YOU KNOW YOU GOTTA MAKE TIME?
GOT IT?!
OKAY, I GOT IT!
MY BAD!
WA HA HA HA!
SO YOU ENDED UP IN A CLASS WITHOUT A SINGLE HOT GIRL!
ARE YOU KIDDING ME? AIN'T NO HOT REPEAT SCHOOL BABES, MAN!
Yuck!
What was that?!

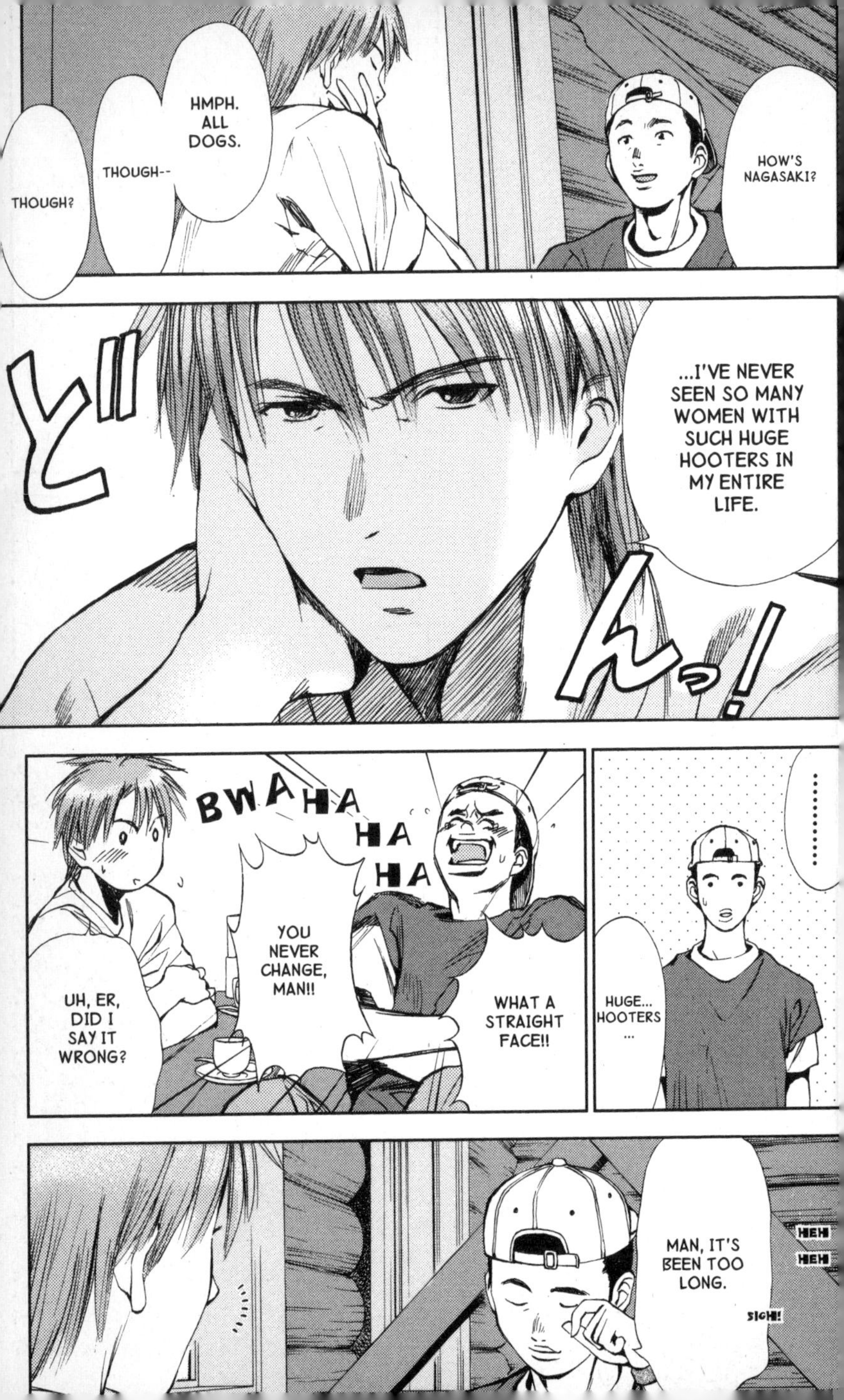
HOW'S NAGASAKI?
HMPH. ALL DOGS.
THOUGH--
THOUGH?
...I'VE NEVER SEEN SO MANY WOMEN WITH SUCH HUGE HOOTERS IN MY ENTIRE LIFE.
どんっ!
....
HUGE... HOOTERS ...
BWAHAHA HA HA
WHAT A STRAIGHT FACE!!
YOU NEVER CHANGE, MAN!!
UH, ER, DID I SAY IT WRONG?
HEH HEH
MAN, IT'S BEEN TOO LONG.
SIGH!

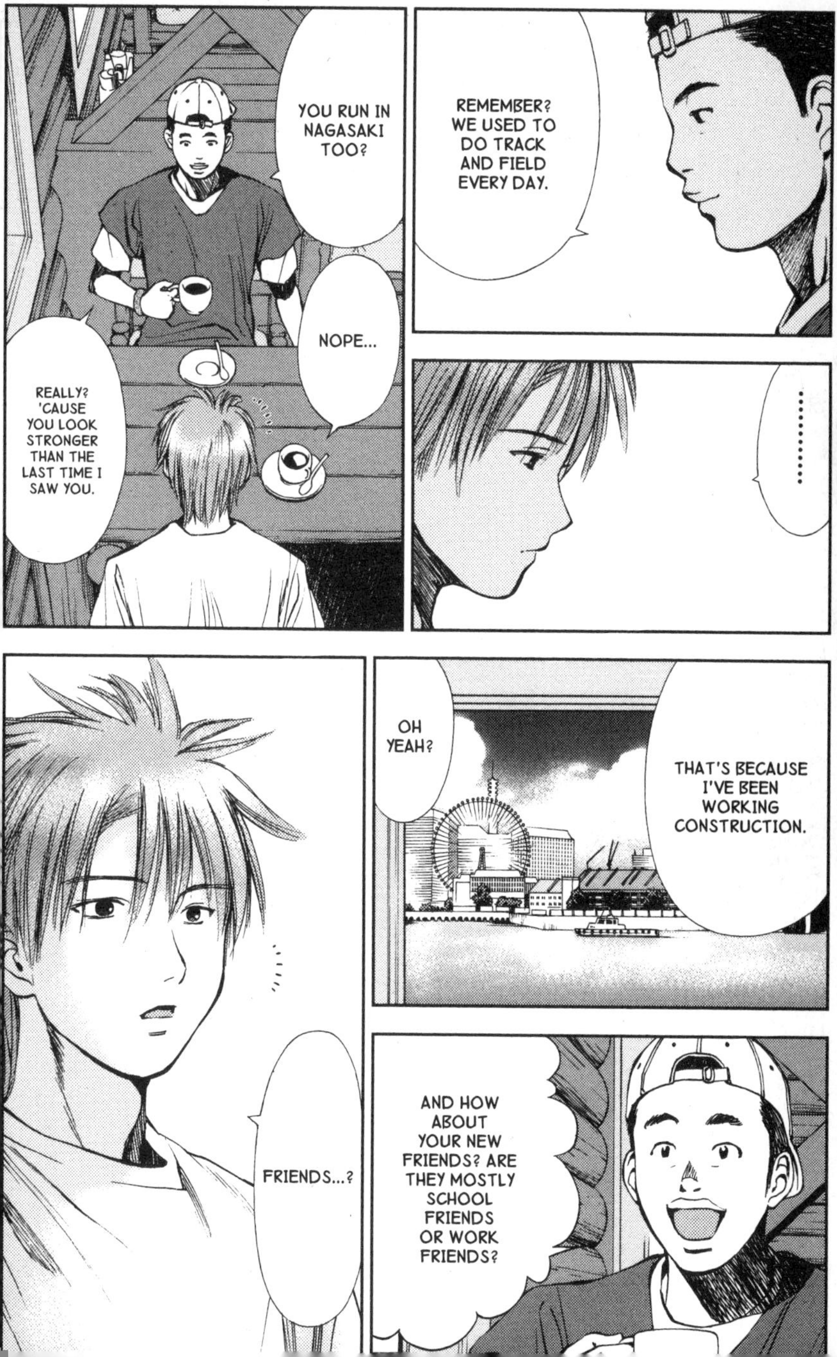
REMEMBER? WE USED TO DO TRACK AND FIELD EVERY DAY.
....
YOU RUN IN NAGASAKI TOO?
NOPE...
REALLY? 'CAUSE YOU LOOK STRONGER THAN THE LAST TIME I SAW YOU.
THAT'S BECAUSE I'VE BEEN WORKING CONSTRUCTION.
OH YEAH?
AND HOW ABOUT YOUR NEW FRIENDS? ARE THEY MOSTLY SCHOOL FRIENDS OR WORK FRIENDS?
FRIENDS...?

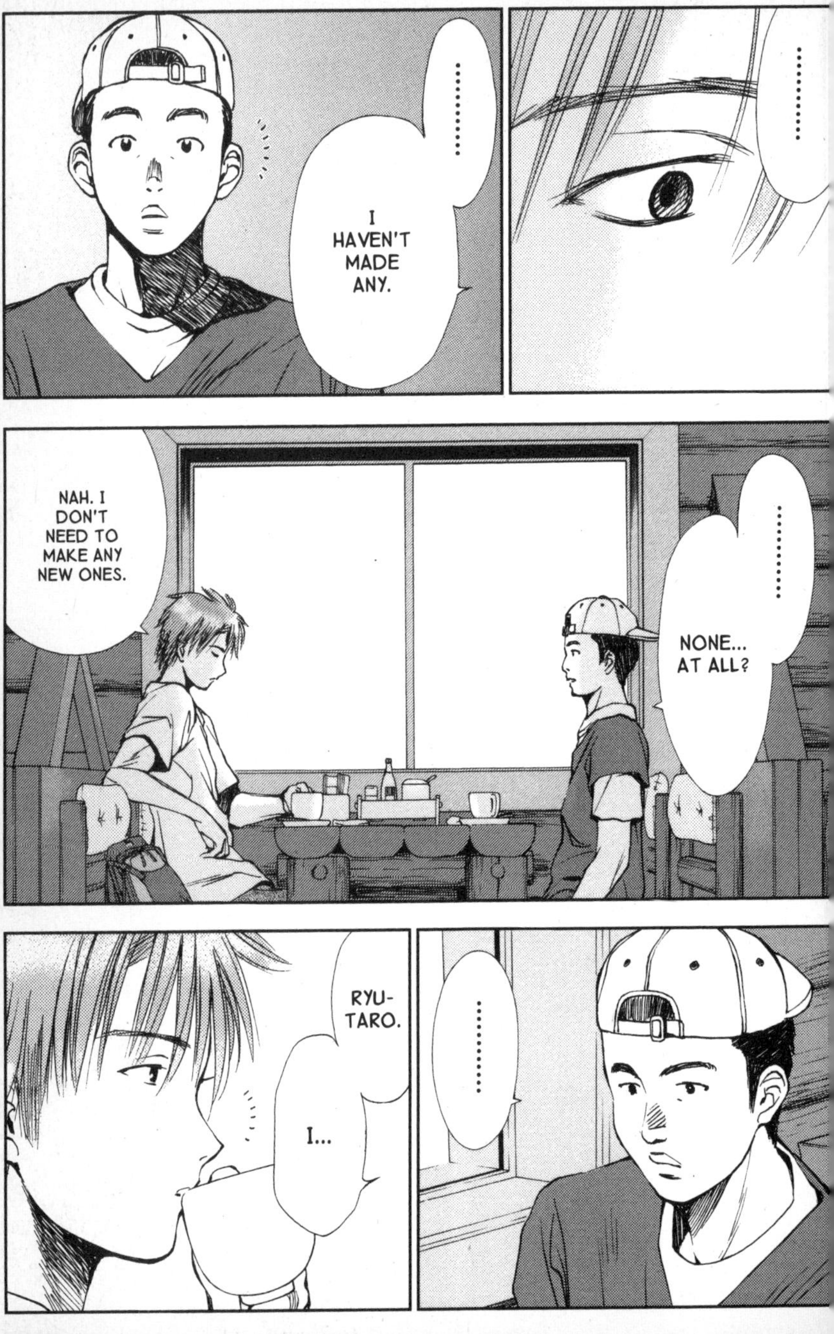
……
……
I HAVEN'T MADE ANY.
……
NONE... AT ALL?
NAH. I DON'T NEED TO MAKE ANY NEW ONES.
……
RYU-TARO.
I...

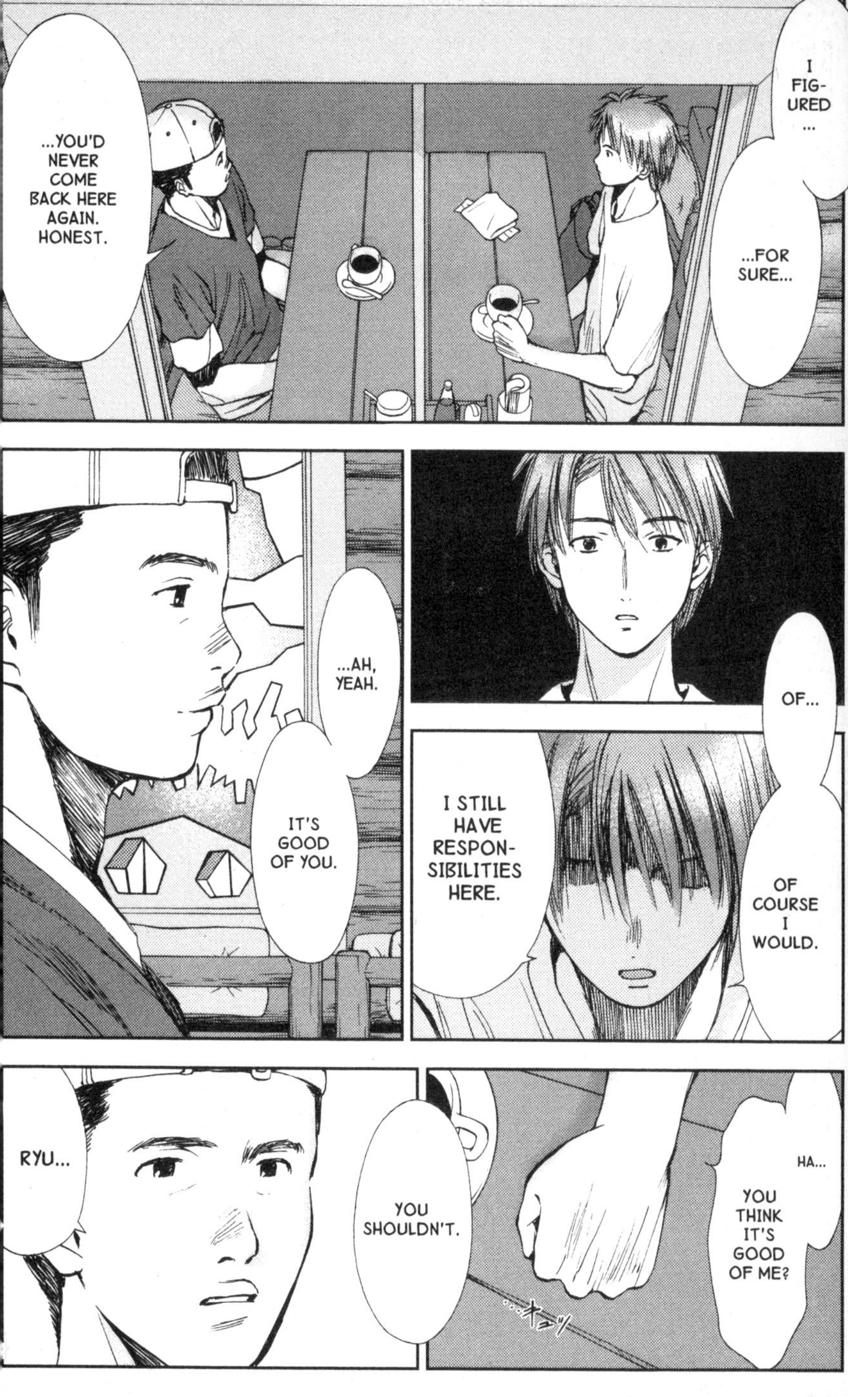
I FIG-URED...
...FOR SURE...
...YOU'D NEVER COME BACK HERE AGAIN. HONEST.
OF...
OF COURSE I WOULD.
I STILL HAVE RESPON-SIBILITIES HERE.
...AH, YEAH.
IT'S GOOD OF YOU.
HA...
YOU THINK IT'S GOOD OF ME?
YOU SHOULDN'T.
RYU...

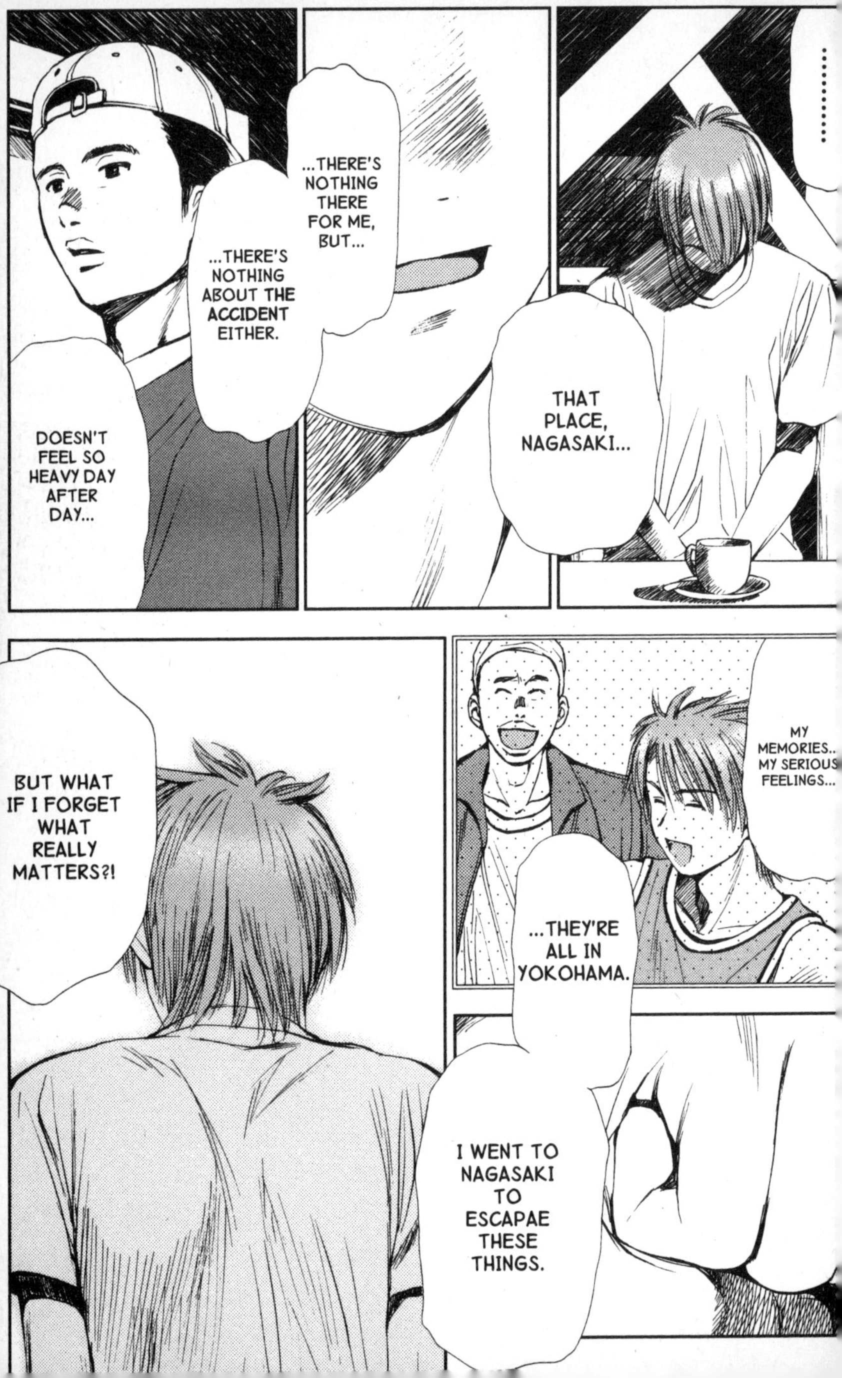

......
THAT PLACE, NAGASAKI...
...THERE'S NOTHING THERE FOR ME, BUT...
...THERE'S NOTHING ABOUT THE ACCIDENT EITHER.
DOESN'T FEEL SO HEAVY DAY AFTER DAY...
MY MEMORIES.. MY SERIOUS FEELINGS...
...THEY'RE ALL IN YOKOHAMA.
I WENT TO NAGASAKI TO ESCAPAE THESE THINGS.
BUT WHAT IF I FORGET WHAT REALLY MATTERS?!

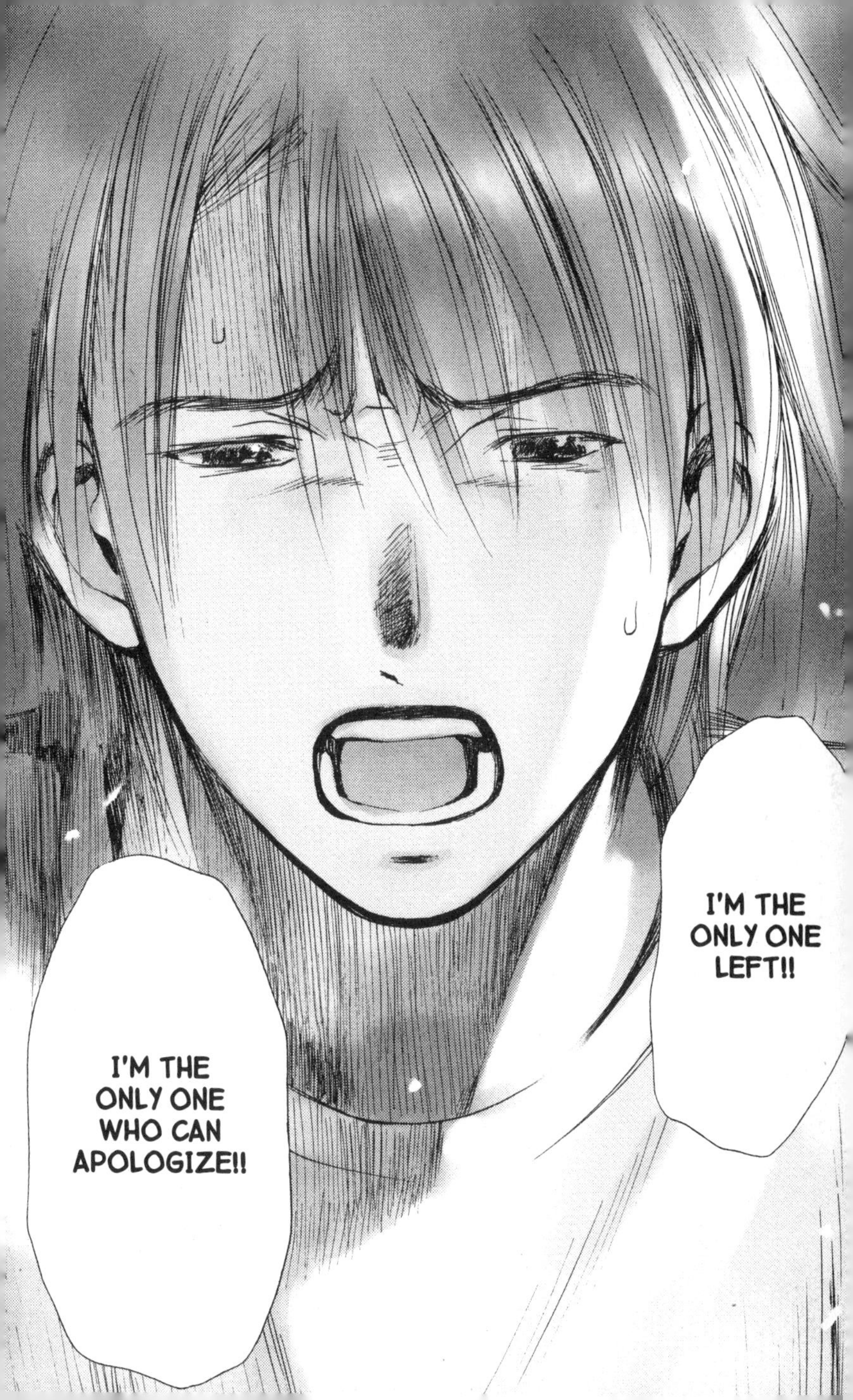
I'M THE ONLY ONE LEFT!!
I'M THE ONLY ONE WHO CAN APOLOGIZE!!

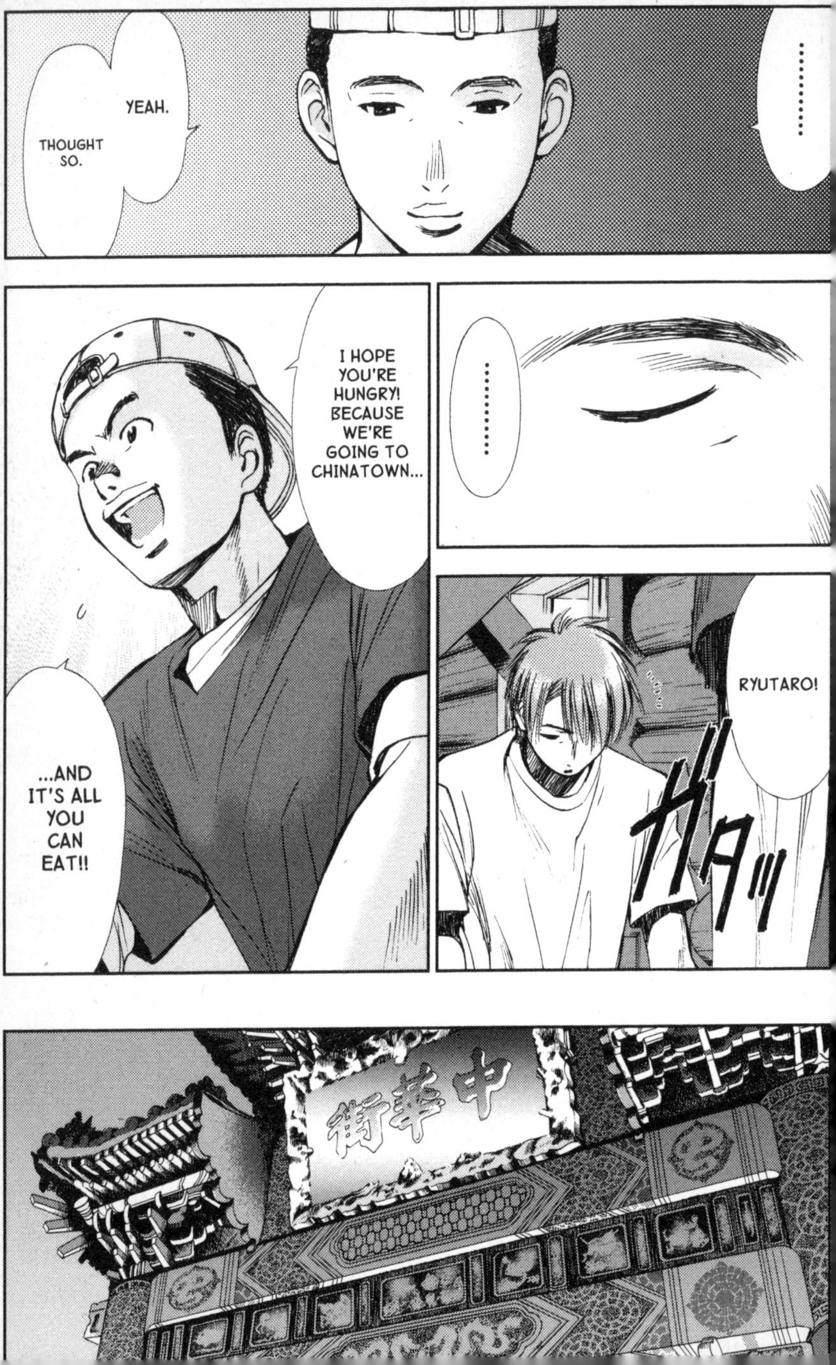
......
YEAH.
THOUGHT SO.
......
RYUTARO!
ガタッ
I HOPE YOU'RE HUNGRY! BECAUSE WE'RE GOING TO CHINATOWN...
...AND IT'S ALL YOU CAN EAT!!
中華街

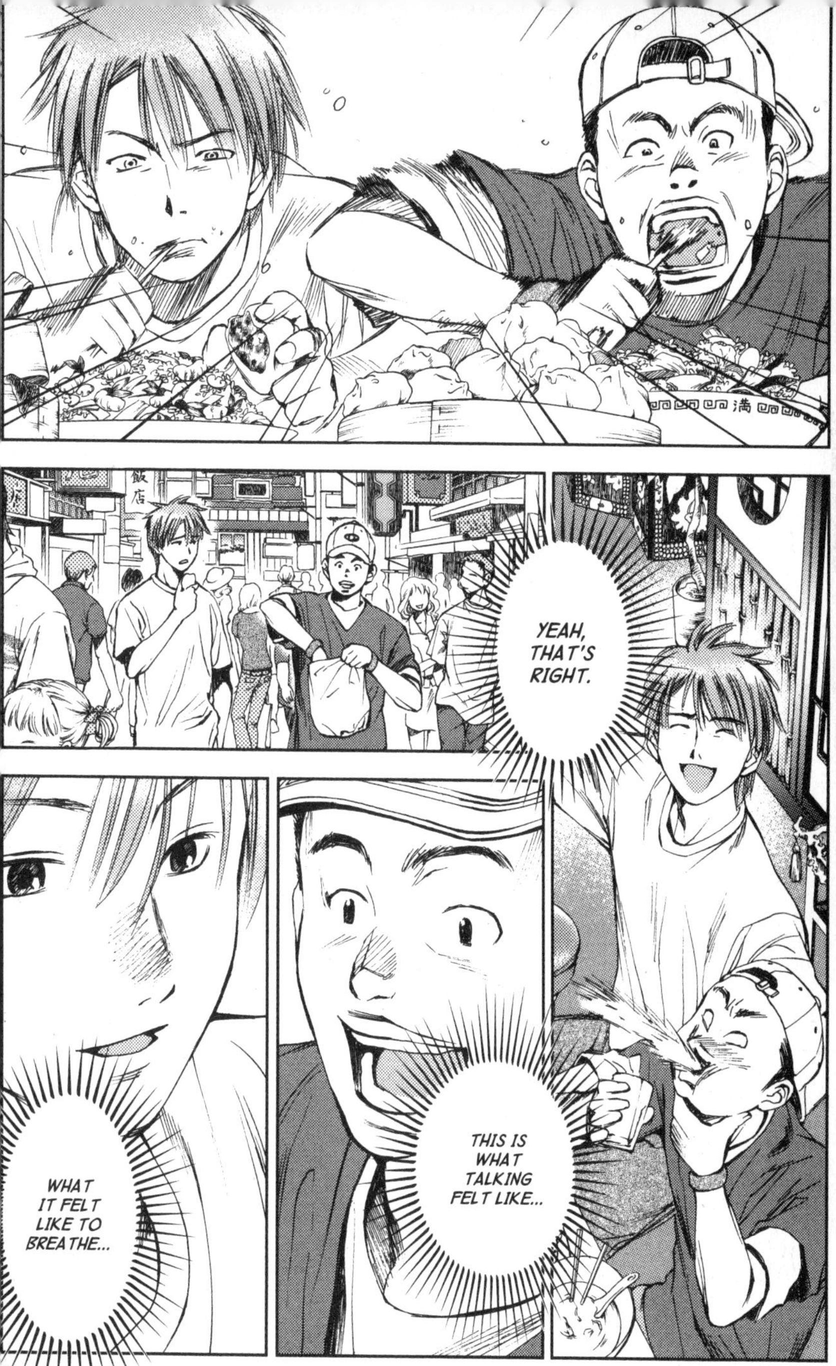
満
YEAH, THAT'S RIGHT.
飯店
THIS IS WHAT TALKING FELT LIKE...
WHAT IT FELT LIKE TO BREATHE...

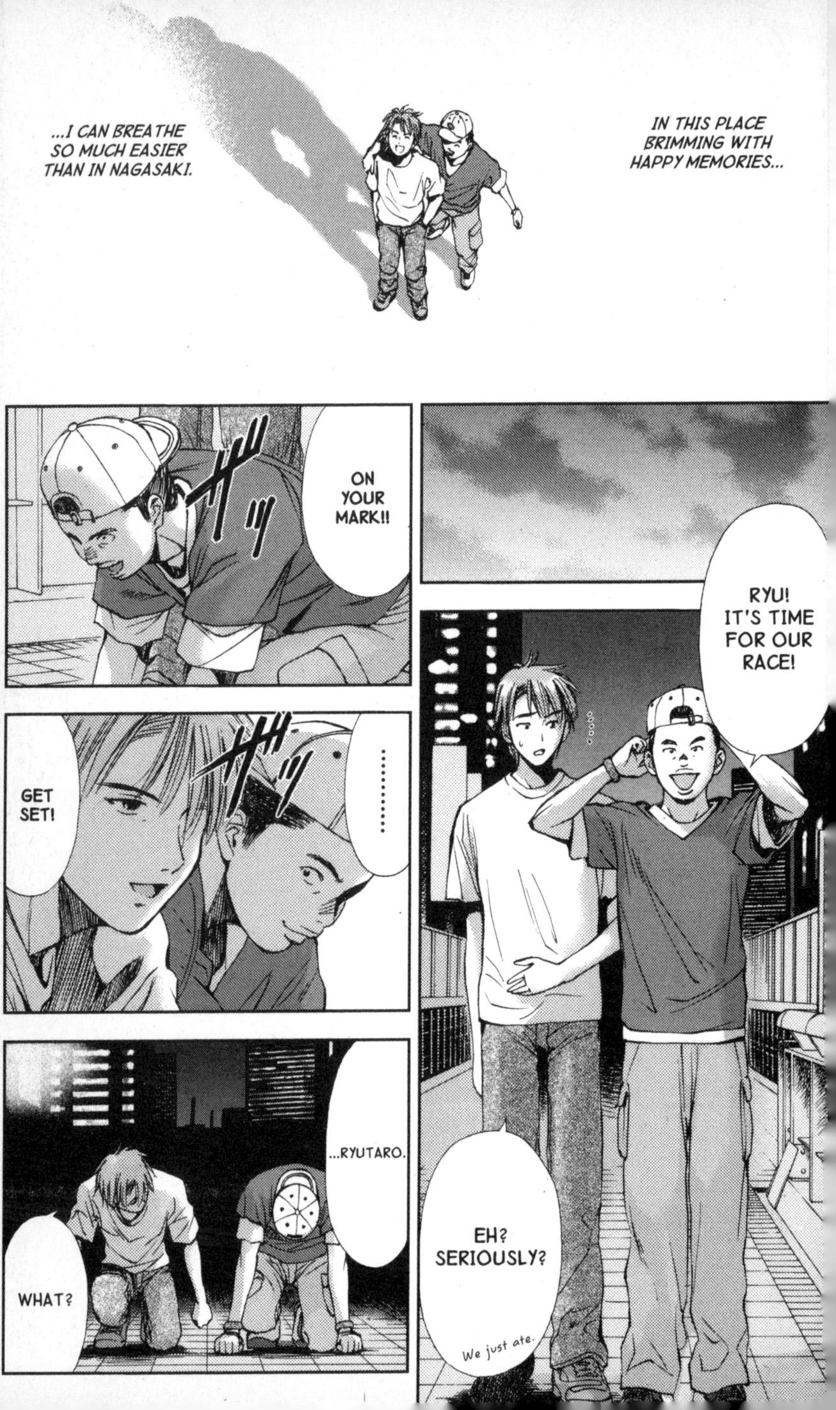
IN THIS PLACE BRIMMING WITH HAPPY MEMORIES...
...I CAN BREATHE SO MUCH EASIER THAN IN NAGASAKI.
RYU! IT'S TIME FOR OUR RACE!
EH? SERIOUSLY?
We just ate.
ON YOUR MARK!!
....
GET SET!
...RYUTARO.
WHAT?

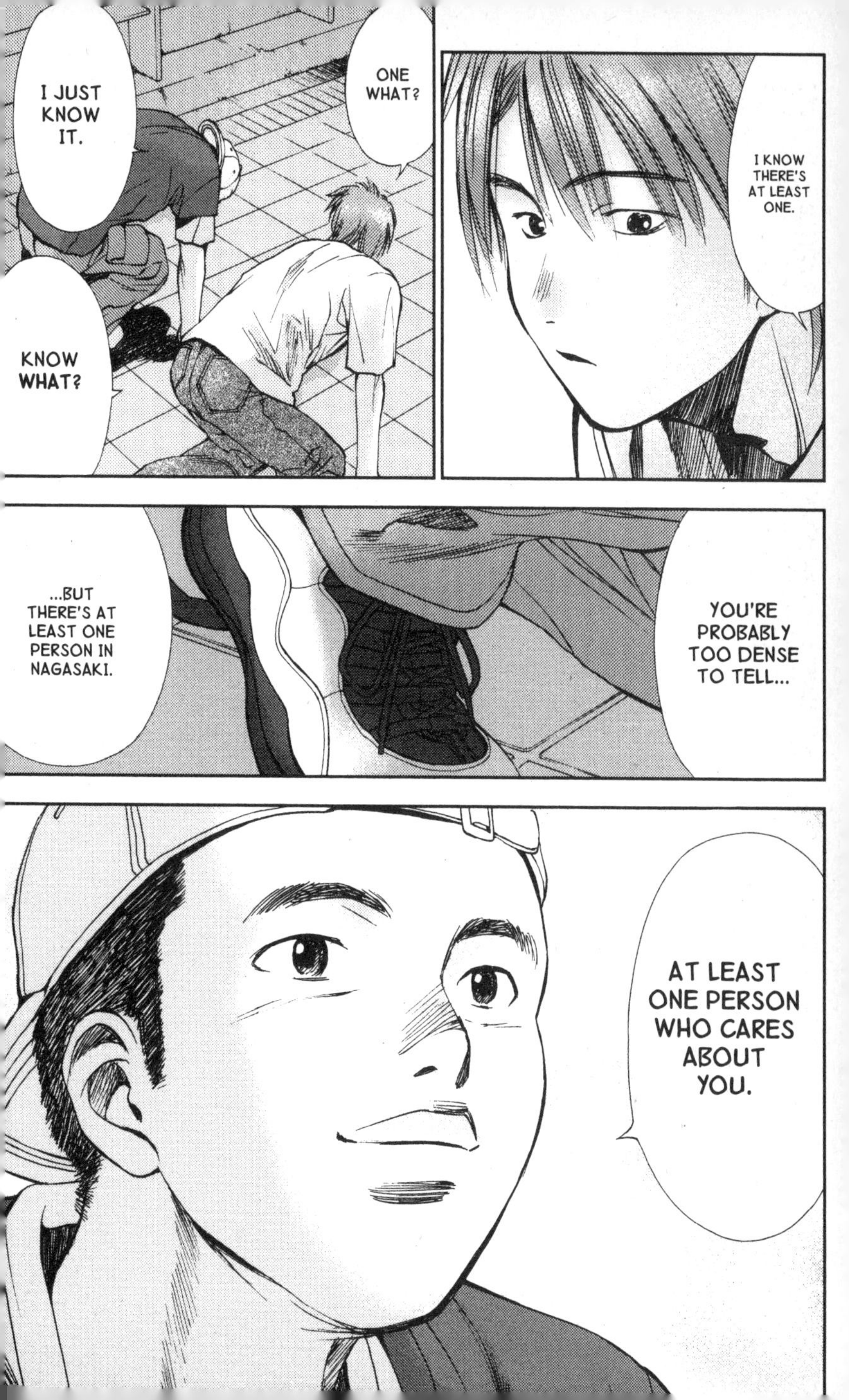
I KNOW THERE'S AT LEAST ONE.
ONE WHAT?
I JUST KNOW IT.
KNOW WHAT?
YOU'RE PROBABLY TOO DENSE TO TELL...
...BUT THERE'S AT LEAST ONE PERSON IN NAGASAKI.
AT LEAST ONE PERSON WHO CARES ABOUT YOU.

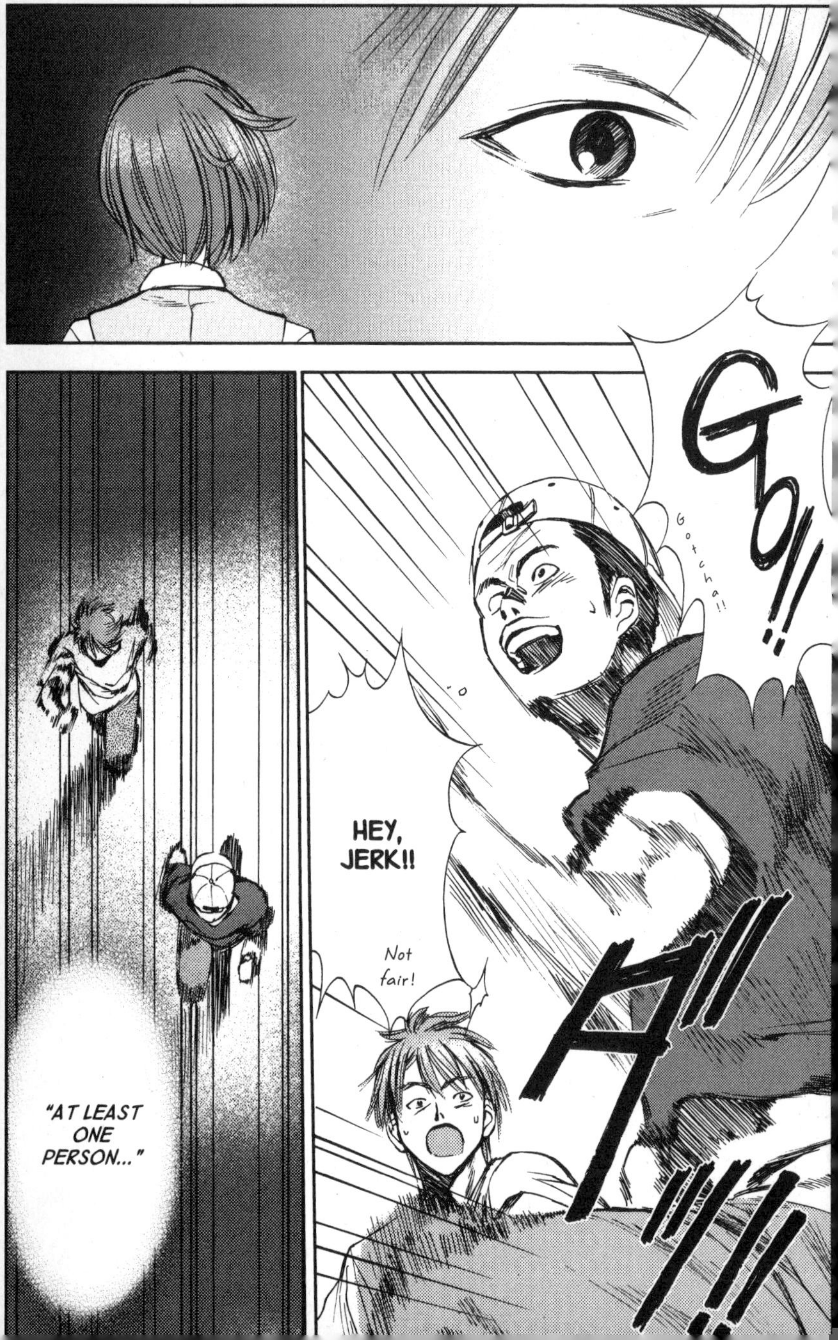
Gotcha!!
HEY, JERK!!
Not fair!
"AT LEAST ONE PERSON..."

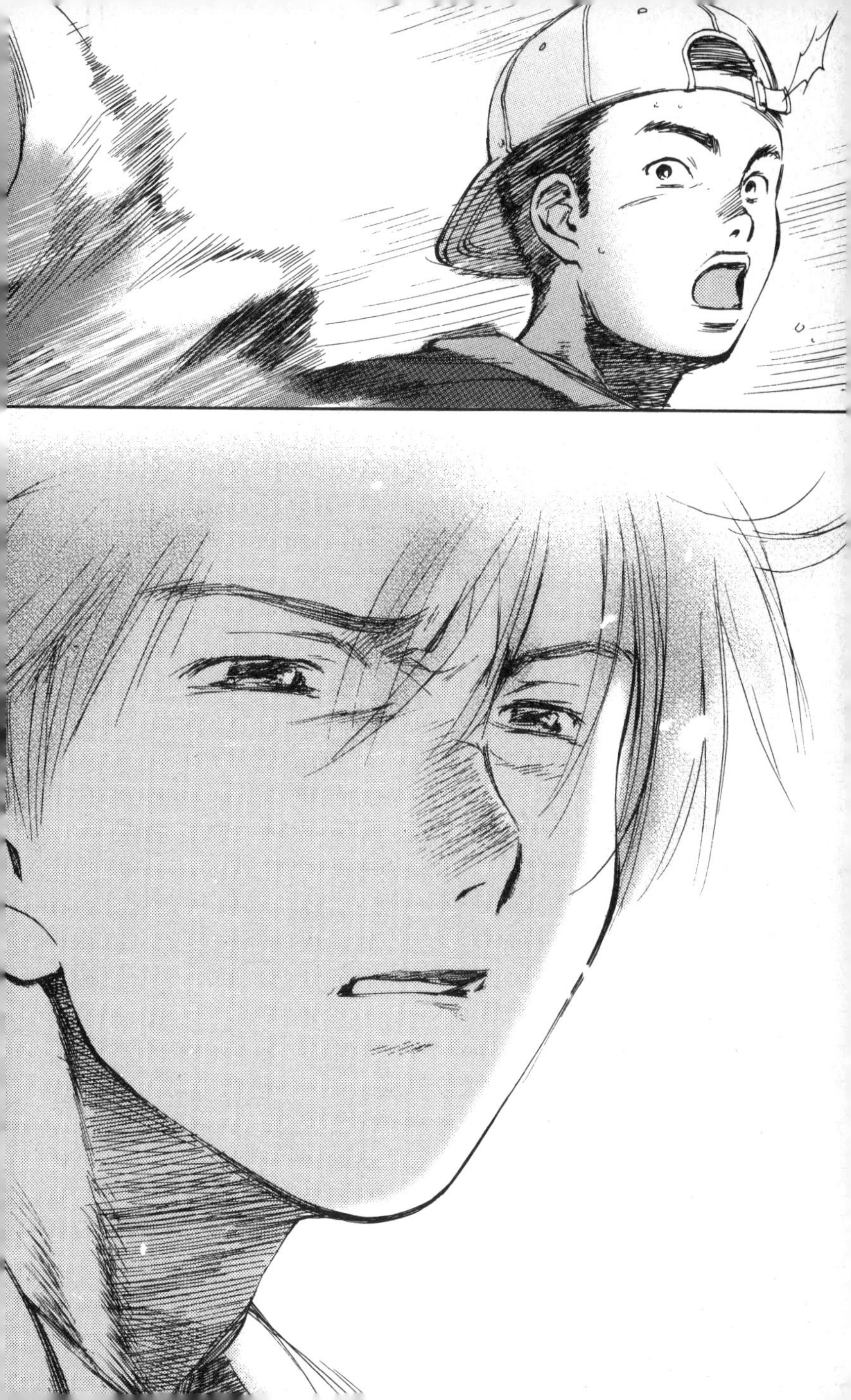

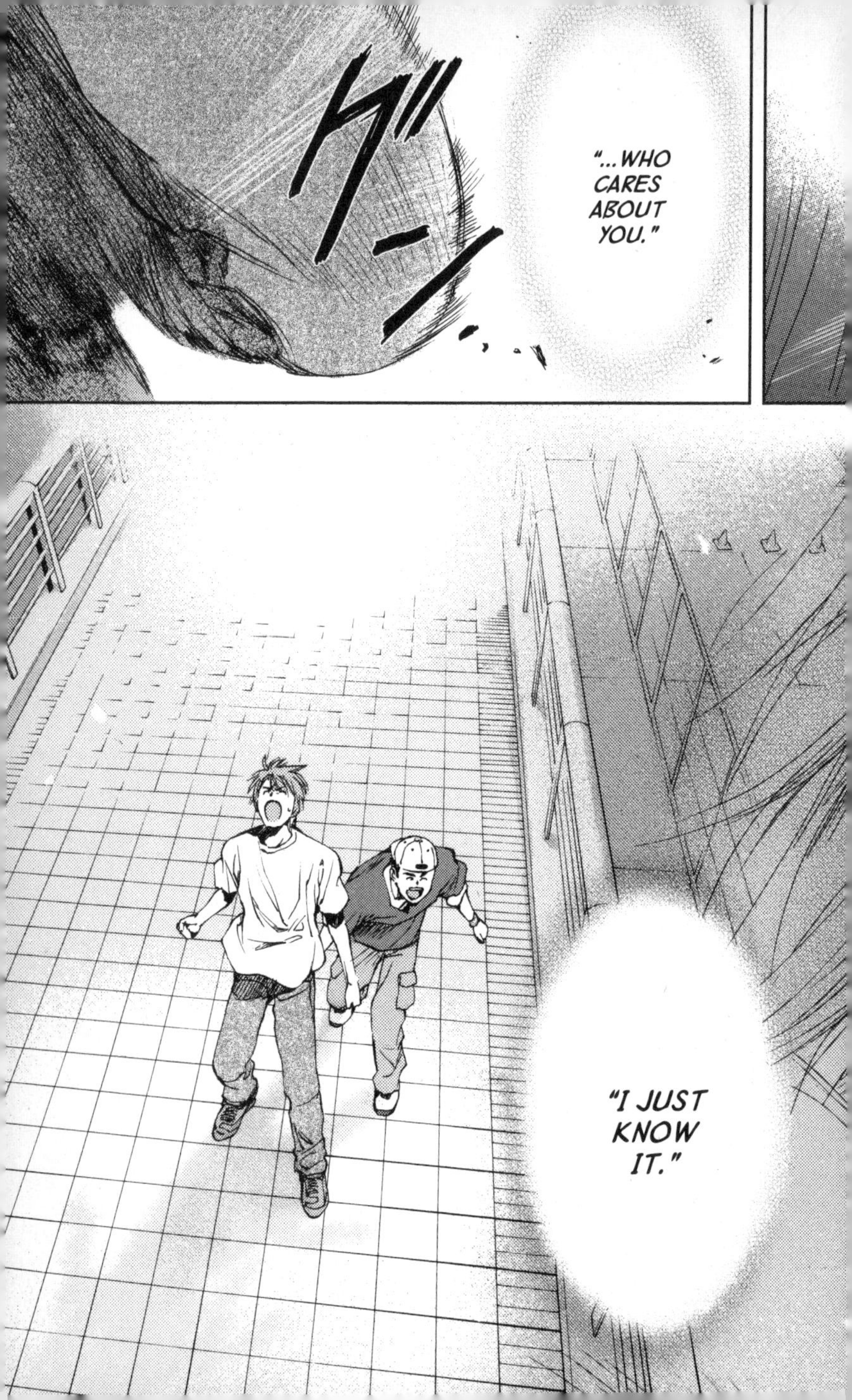
"...WHO CARES ABOUT YOU."
"I JUST KNOW IT."

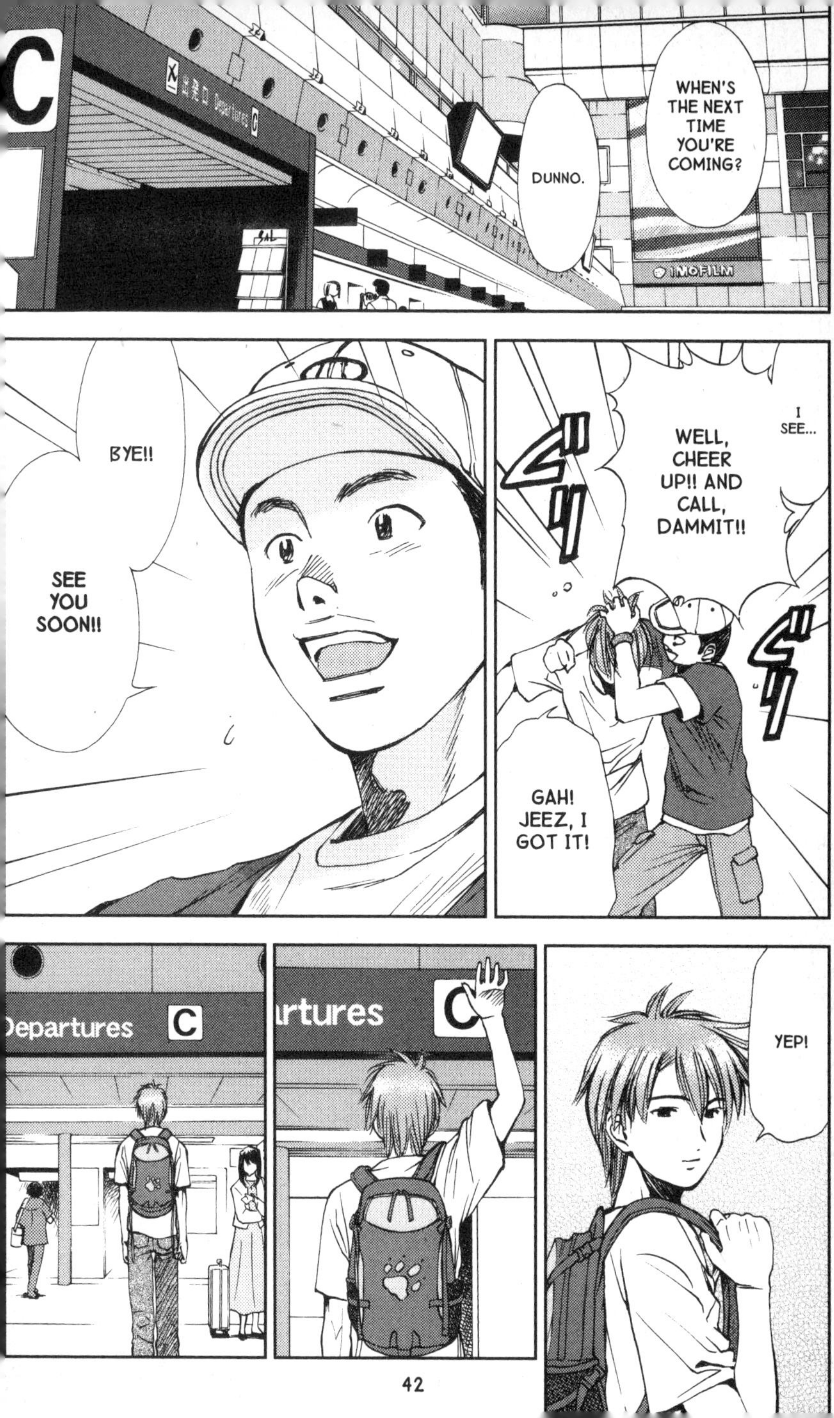
Departures C
WHEN'S THE NEXT TIME YOU'RE COMING?
DUNNO.
I SEE...
WELL, CHEER UP!! AND CALL, DAMMIT!!
GAH! JEEZ, I GOT IT!
BYE!!
SEE YOU SOON!!
YEP!

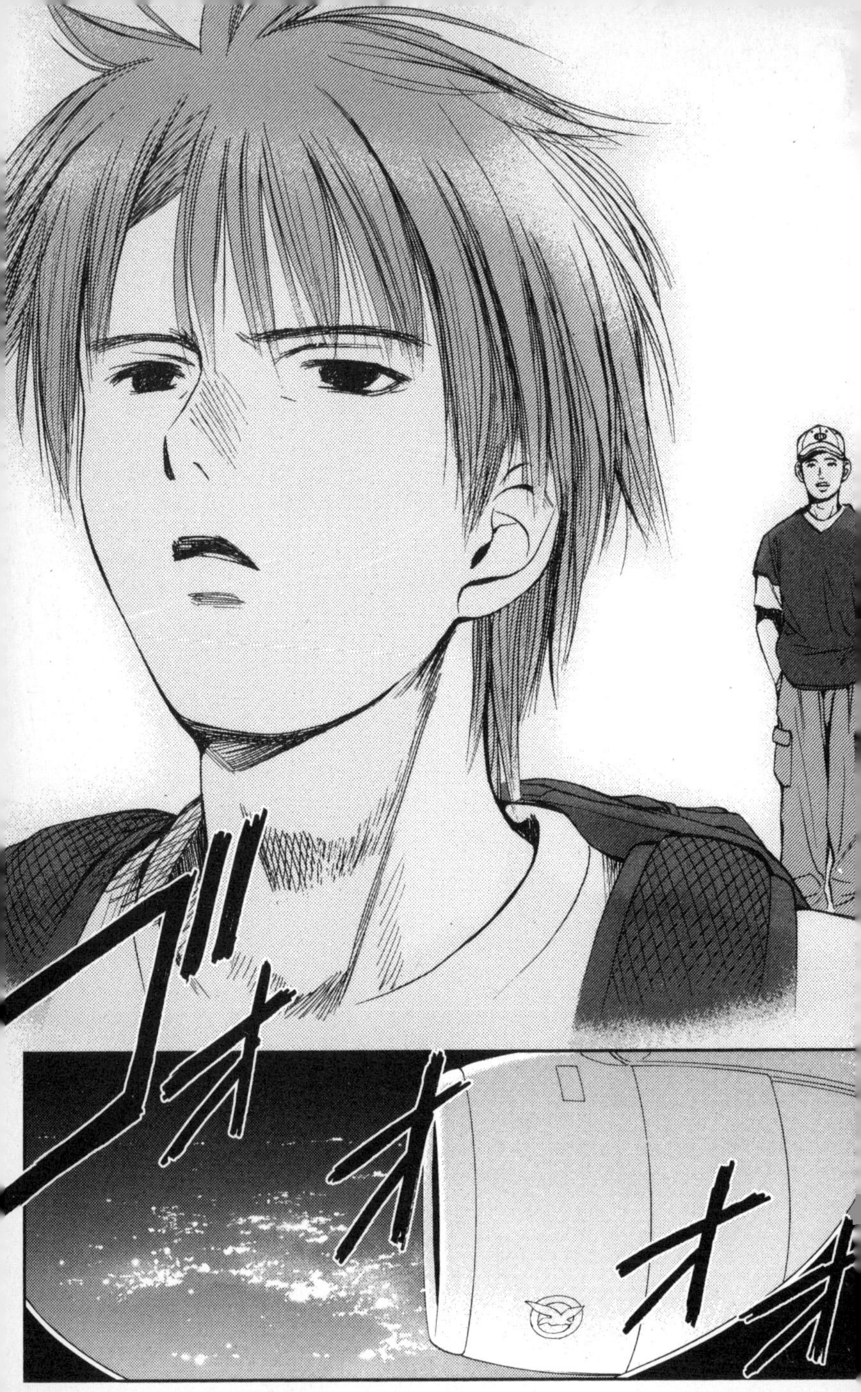
ゴオオオ

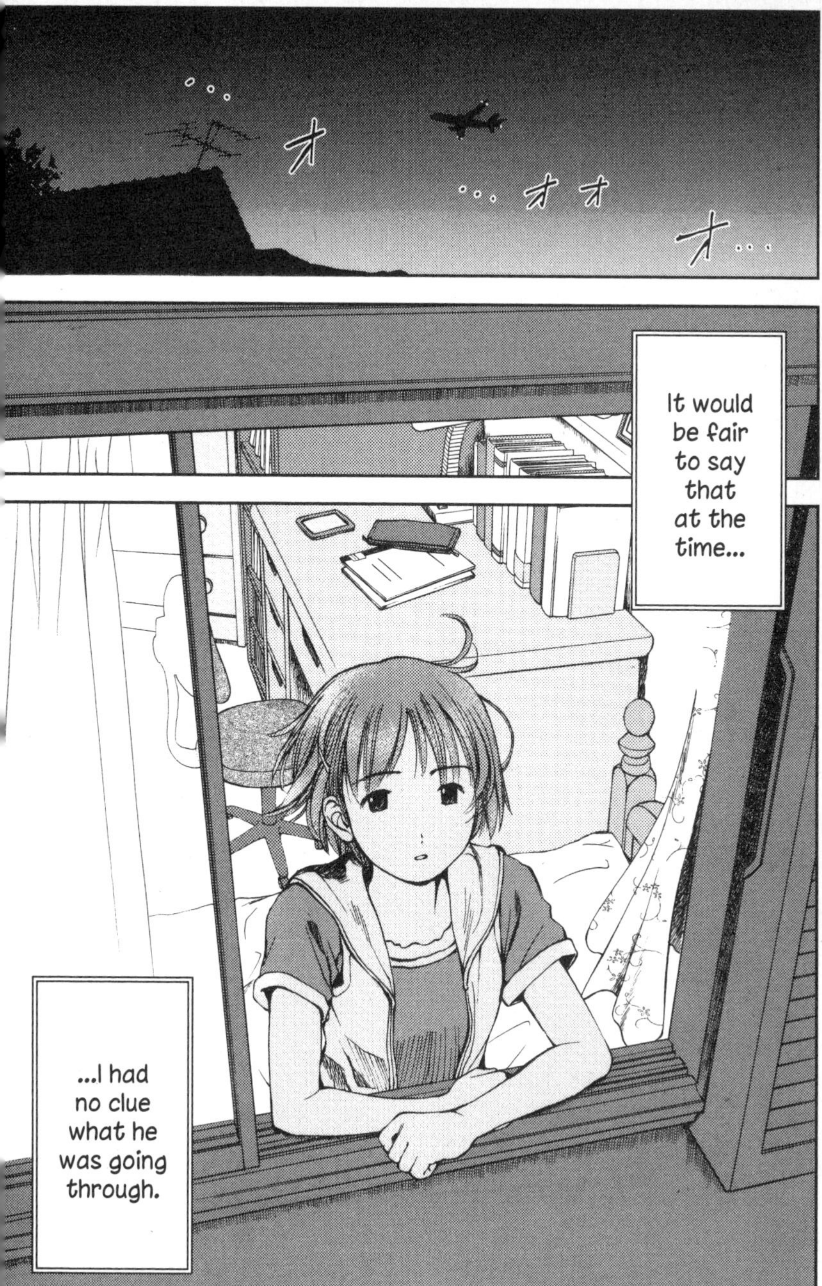
。。。オ
。。。オオ
オ。。。
It would be fair to say that at the time...
...I had no clue what he was going through.

Step.6:End

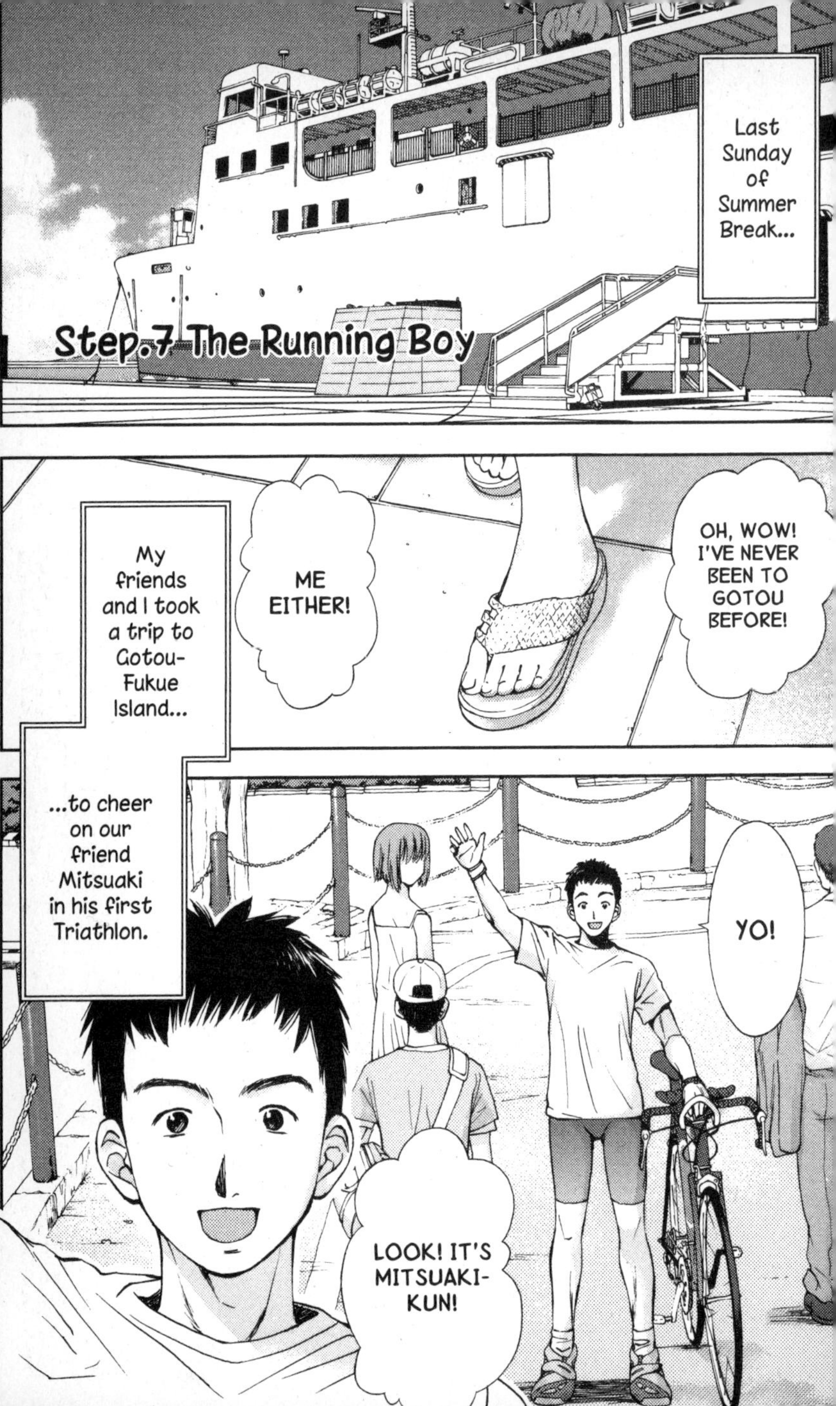
Last Sunday of Summer Break...
Step.7 The Running Boy
OH, WOW! I'VE NEVER BEEN TO GOTOU BEFORE!
ME EITHER!
My friends and I took a trip to Gotou-Fukue Island...
YO!
...to cheer on our friend Mitsuaki in his first Triathlon.
LOOK! IT'S MITSUAKI-KUN!

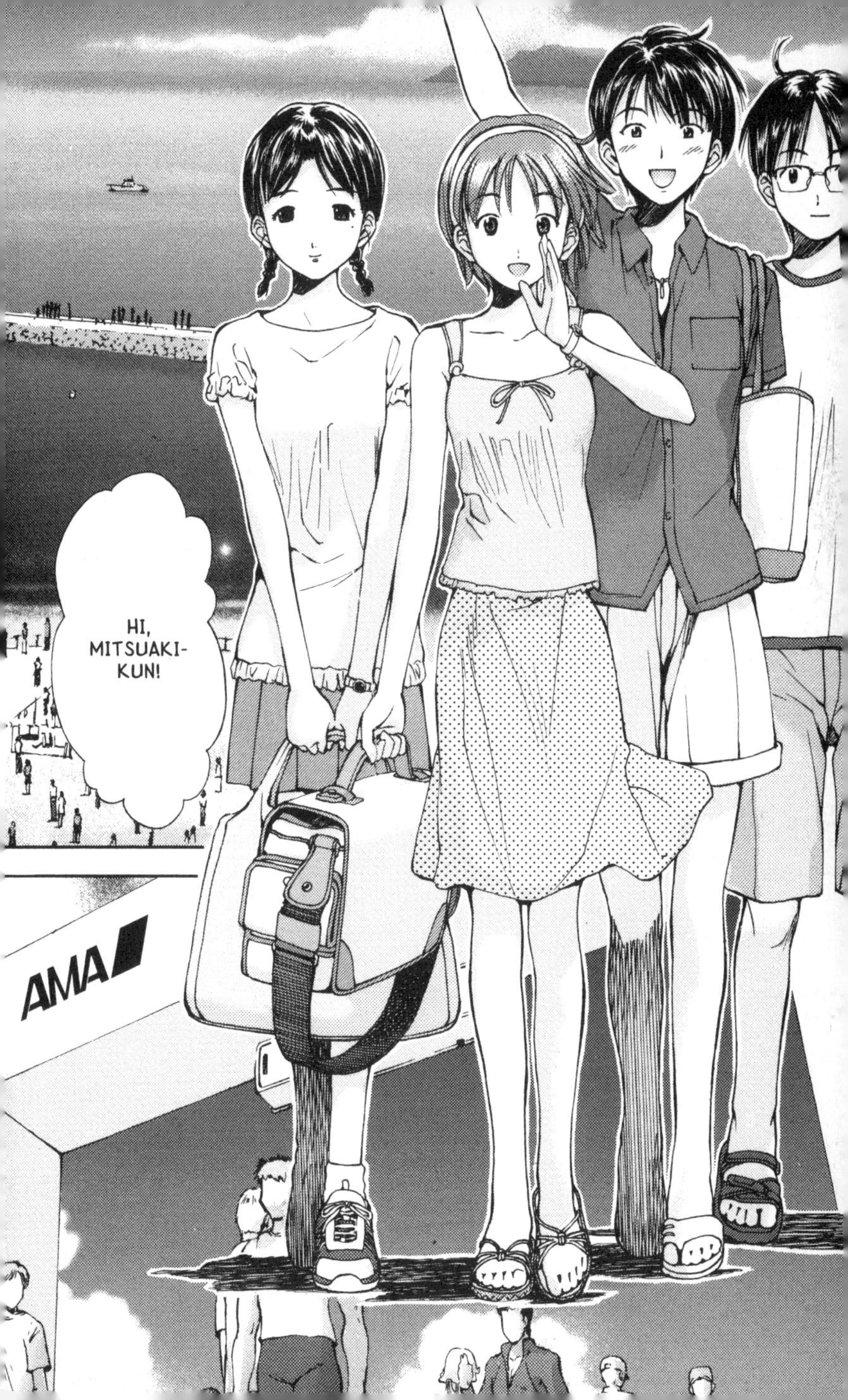
HI, MITSUAKI-KUN!
AMA

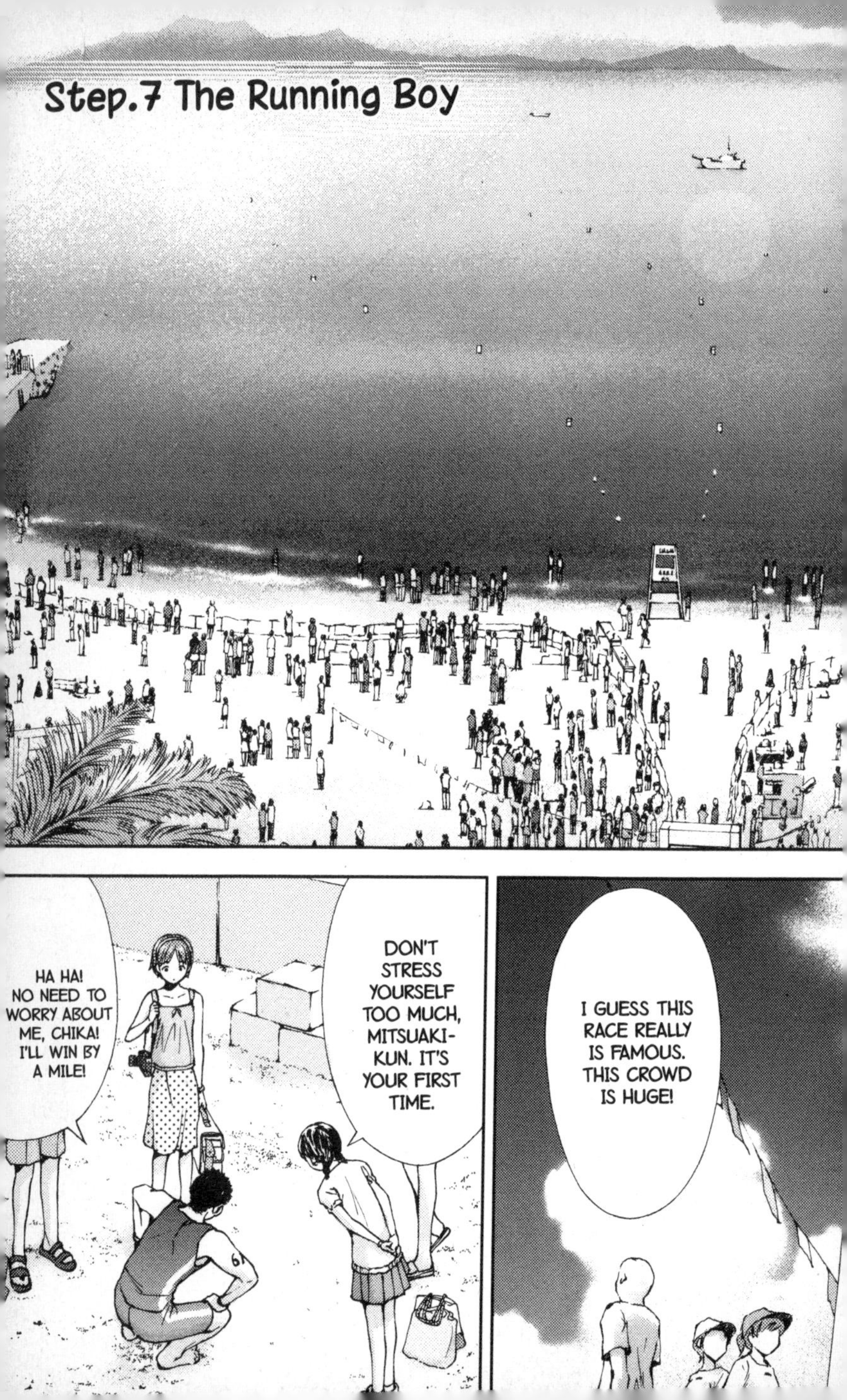
Step.7 The Running Boy
I GUESS THIS RACE REALLY IS FAMOUS. THIS CROWD IS HUGE!
DON'T STRESS YOURSELF TOO MUCH, MITSUAKI-KUN. IT'S YOUR FIRST TIME.
HA HA! NO NEED TO WORRY ABOUT ME, CHIKA! I'LL WIN BY A MILE!

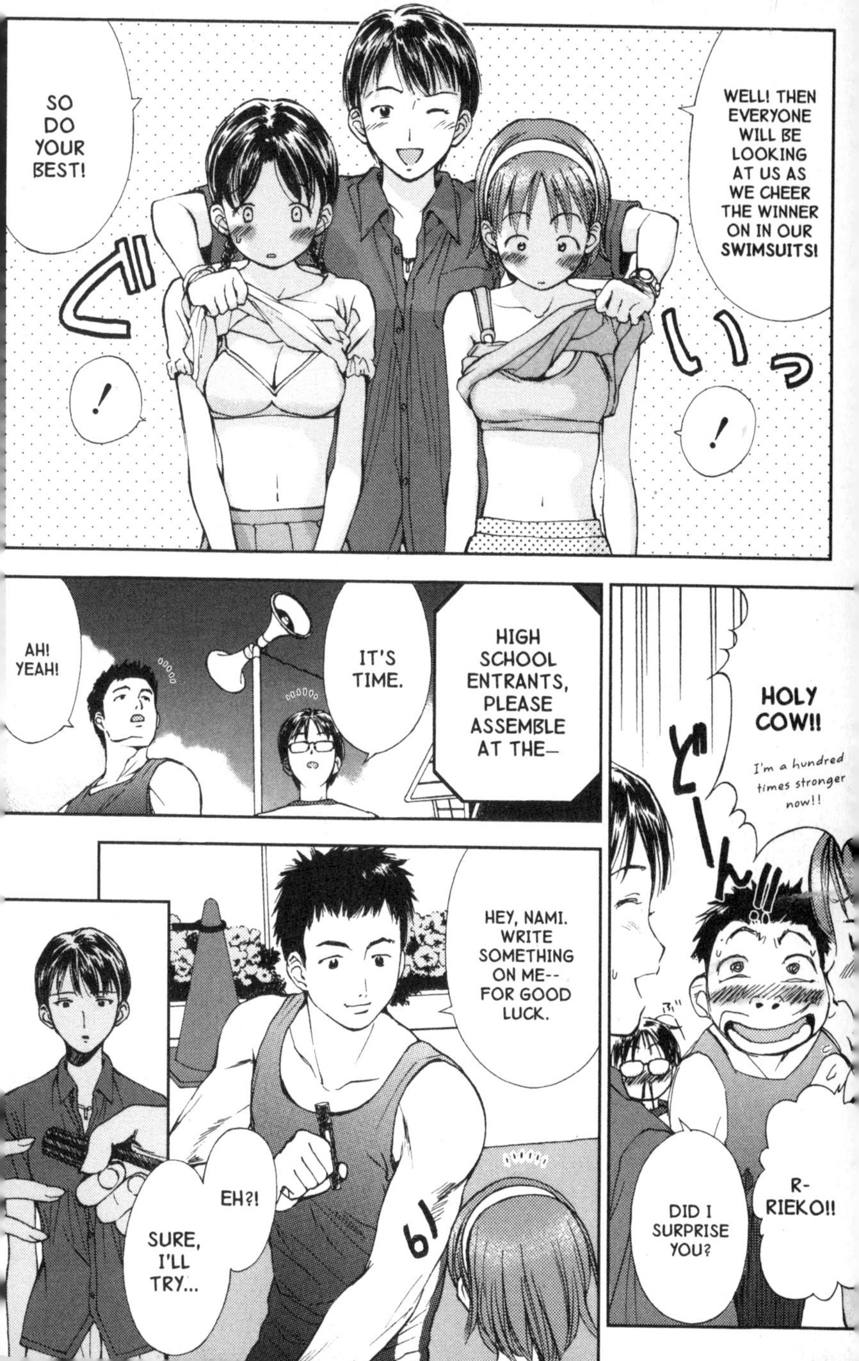
WELL! THEN EVERYONE WILL BE LOOKING AT US AS WE CHEER THE WINNER ON IN OUR SWIMSUITS!
!
SO DO YOUR BEST!
!
HOLY COW!!
I'm a hundred times stronger now!!
R-RIEKO!!
DID I SURPRISE YOU?
HIGH SCHOOL ENTRANTS, PLEASE ASSEMBLE AT THE–
IT'S TIME.
AH! YEAH!
HEY, NAMI. WRITE SOMETHING ON ME-- FOR GOOD LUCK.
EH?!
SURE, I'LL TRY...

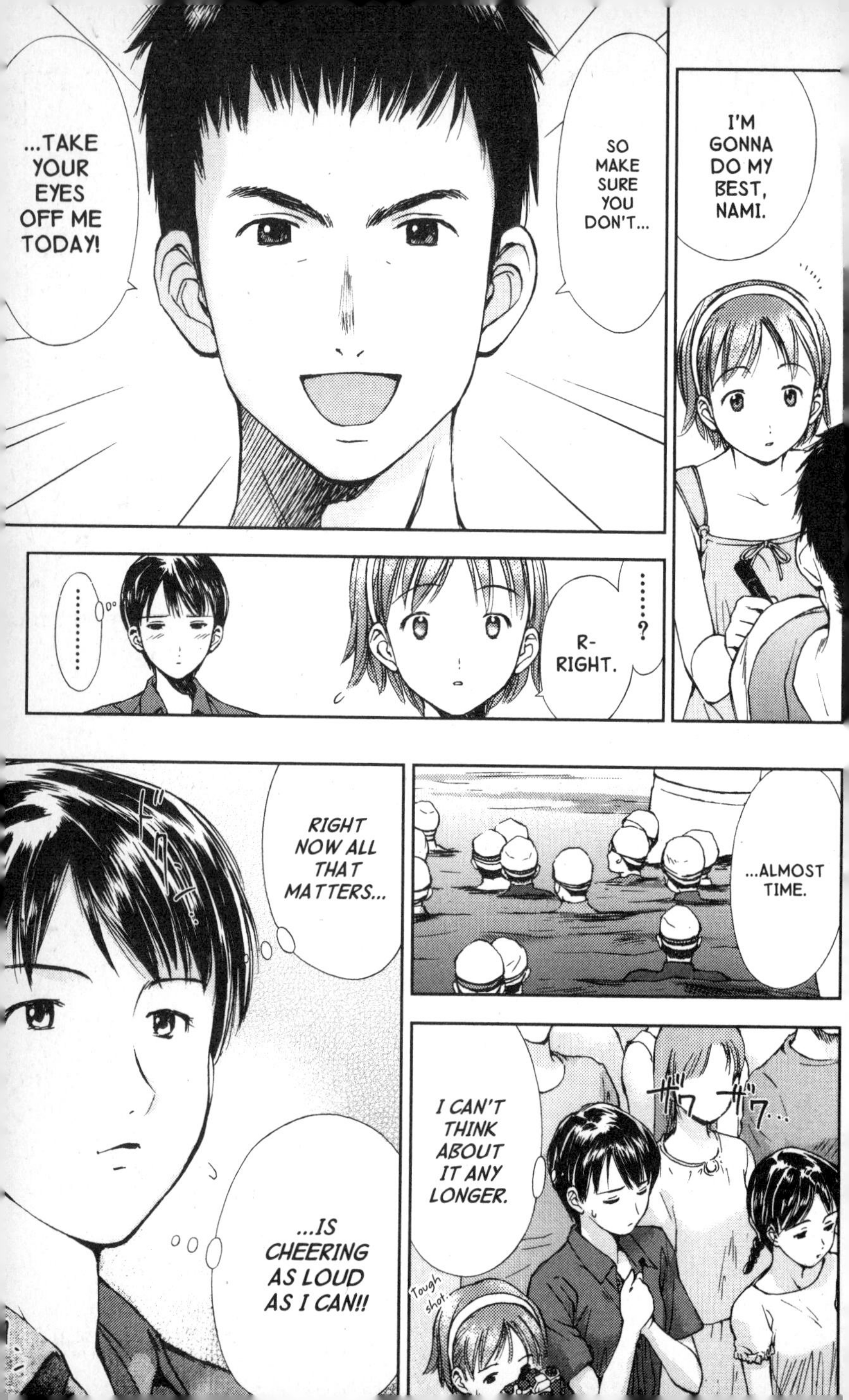
I'M GONNA DO MY BEST, NAMI.
SO MAKE SURE YOU DON'T...
...TAKE YOUR EYES OFF ME TODAY!
......?
R- RIGHT.
......
...ALMOST TIME.
ザワ ザワ...
I CAN'T THINK ABOUT IT ANY LONGER.
Tough shot.
RIGHT NOW ALL THAT MATTERS...
...IS CHEERING AS LOUD AS I CAN!!

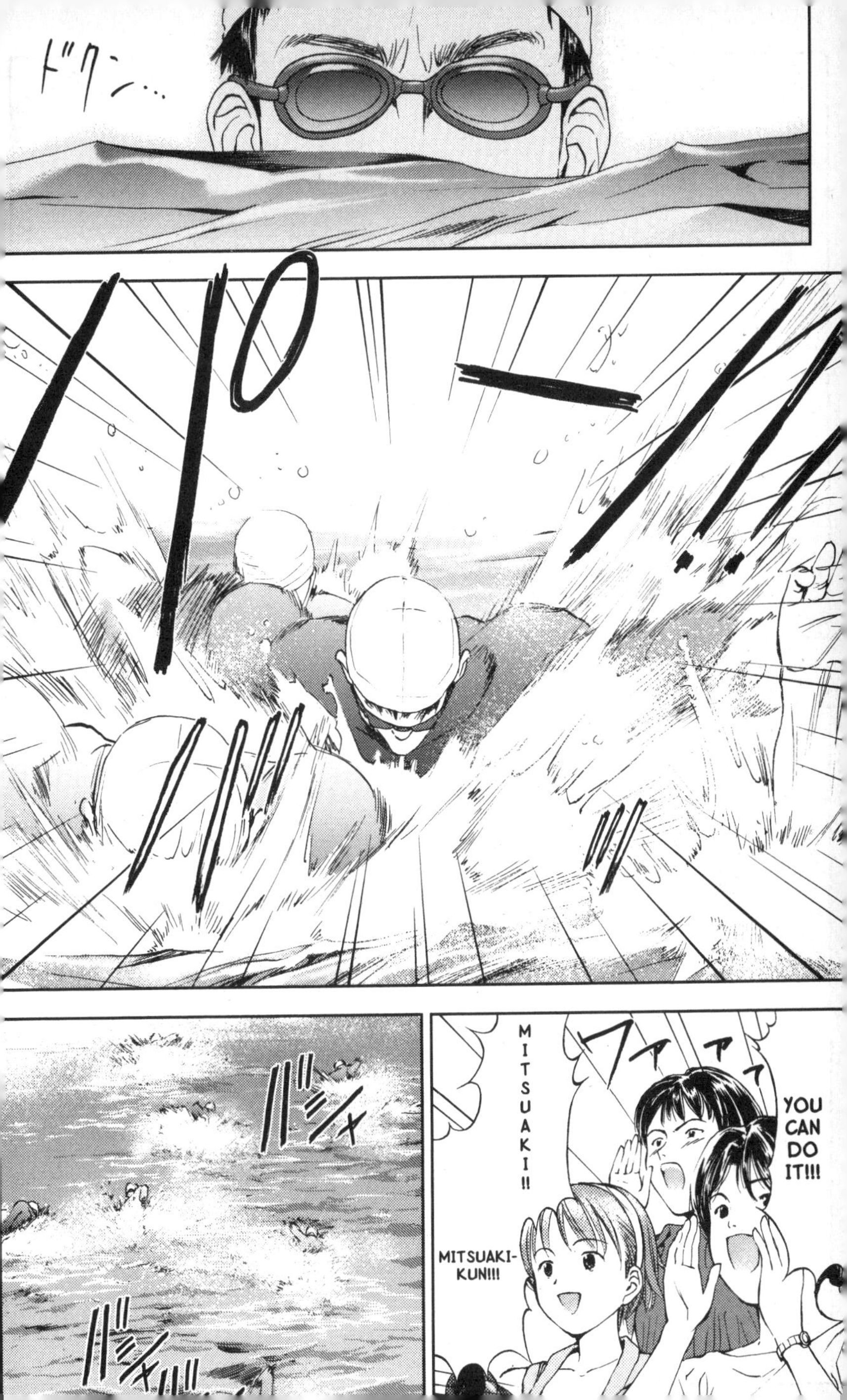
ドクン…
パーン!!
ワァァァ
MITSUAKI!!
YOU CAN DO IT!!!
MITSUAKI-KUN!!!
バシャ
バシャ!!!

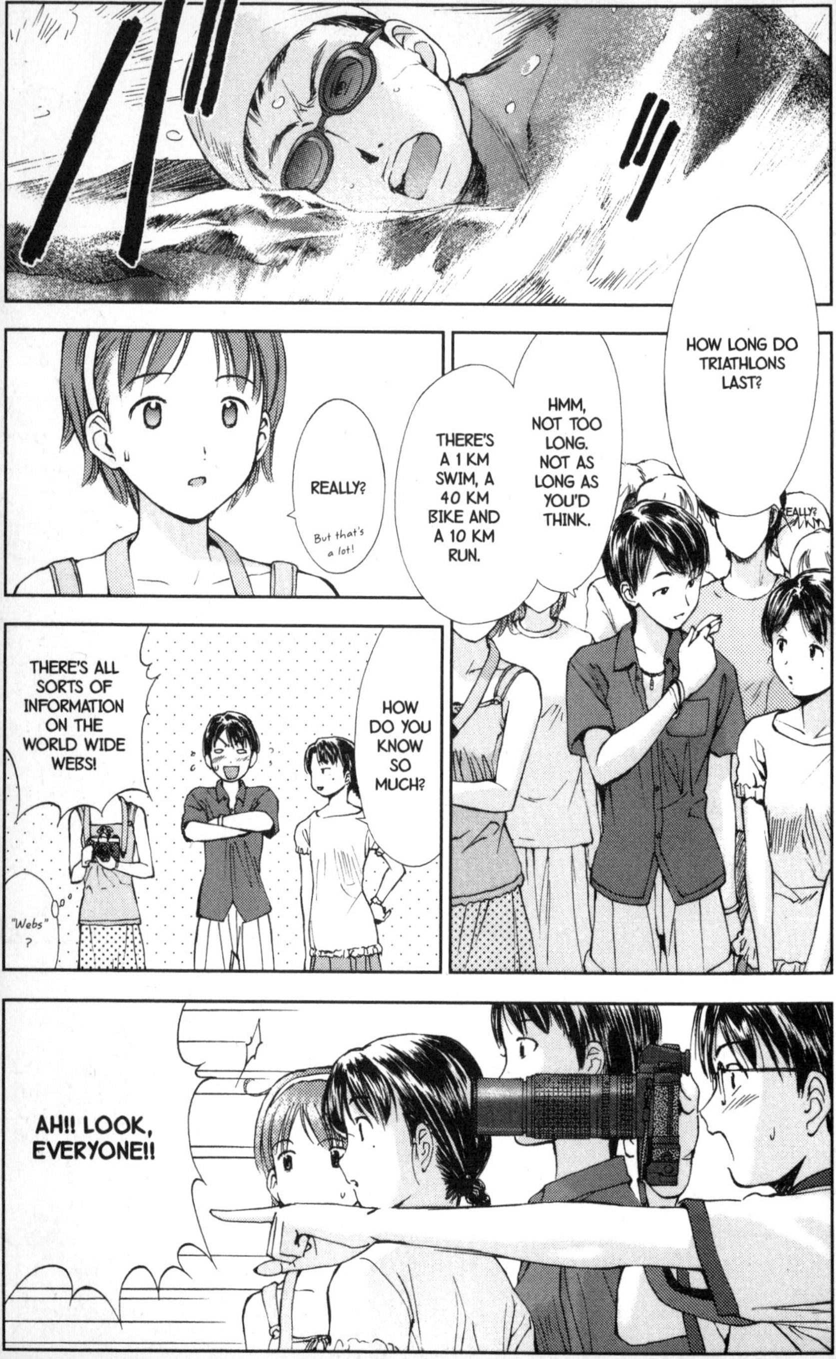
HOW LONG DO TRIATHLONS LAST?
REALLY?
HMM, NOT TOO LONG. NOT AS LONG AS YOU'D THINK.
THERE'S A 1 KM SWIM, A 40 KM BIKE AND A 10 KM RUN.
REALLY?
But that's a lot!
HOW DO YOU KNOW SO MUCH?
THERE'S ALL SORTS OF INFORMATION ON THE WORLD WIDE WEBS!
"Webs" ?
AH!! LOOK, EVERYONE!!

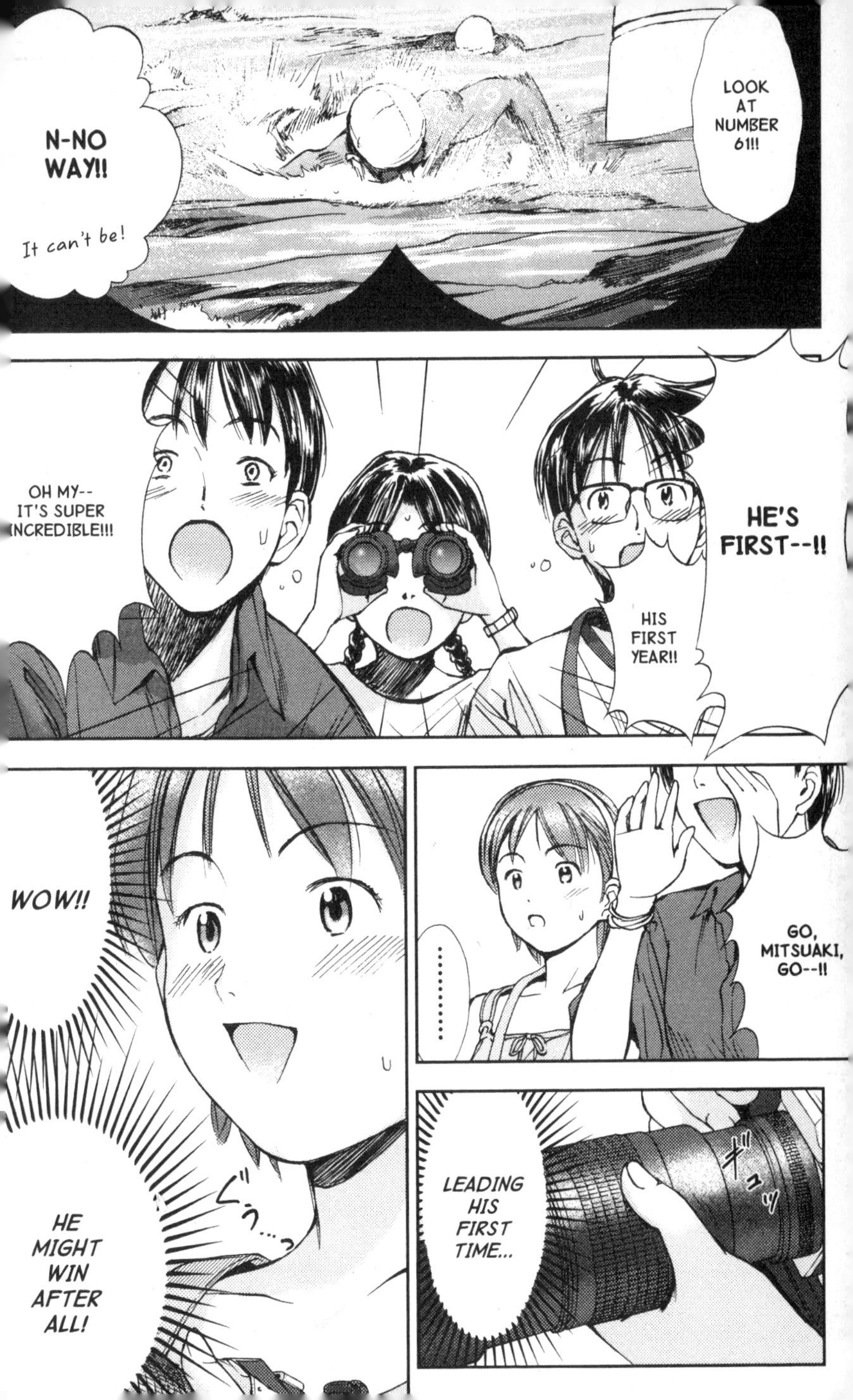
LOOK AT NUMBER 61!!
N-NO WAY!!
It can't be!
HE'S FIRST--!!
HIS FIRST YEAR!!
OH MY-- IT'S SUPER INCREDIBLE!!!
GO, MITSUAKI, GO--!!
......
ギュッ
LEADING HIS FIRST TIME...
WOW!!
HE MIGHT WIN AFTER ALL!

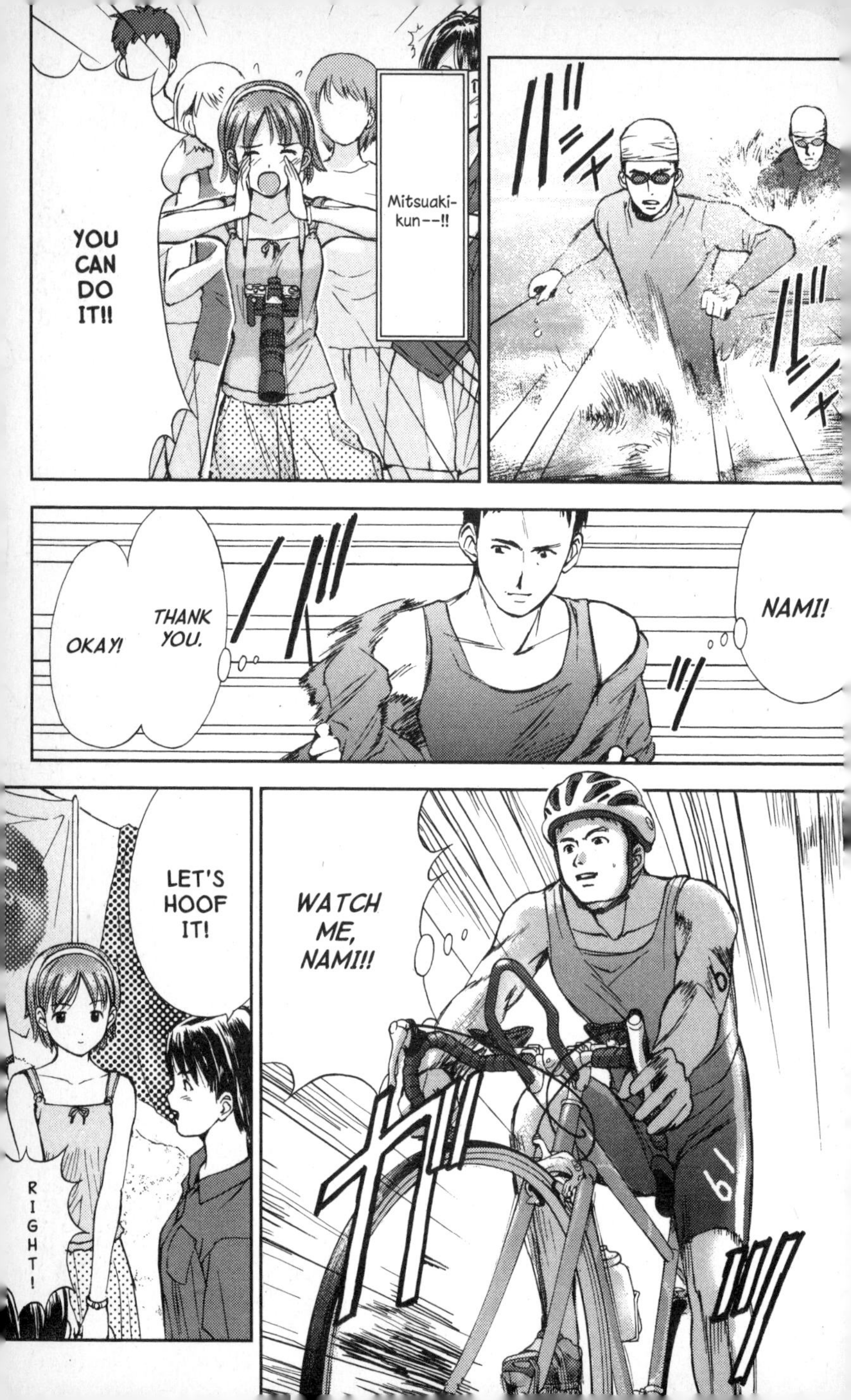
Mitsuaki-kun--!!
YOU CAN DO IT!!
NAMI!
THANK YOU.
OKAY!
WATCH ME, NAMI!!
LET'S HOOF IT!
RIGHT!

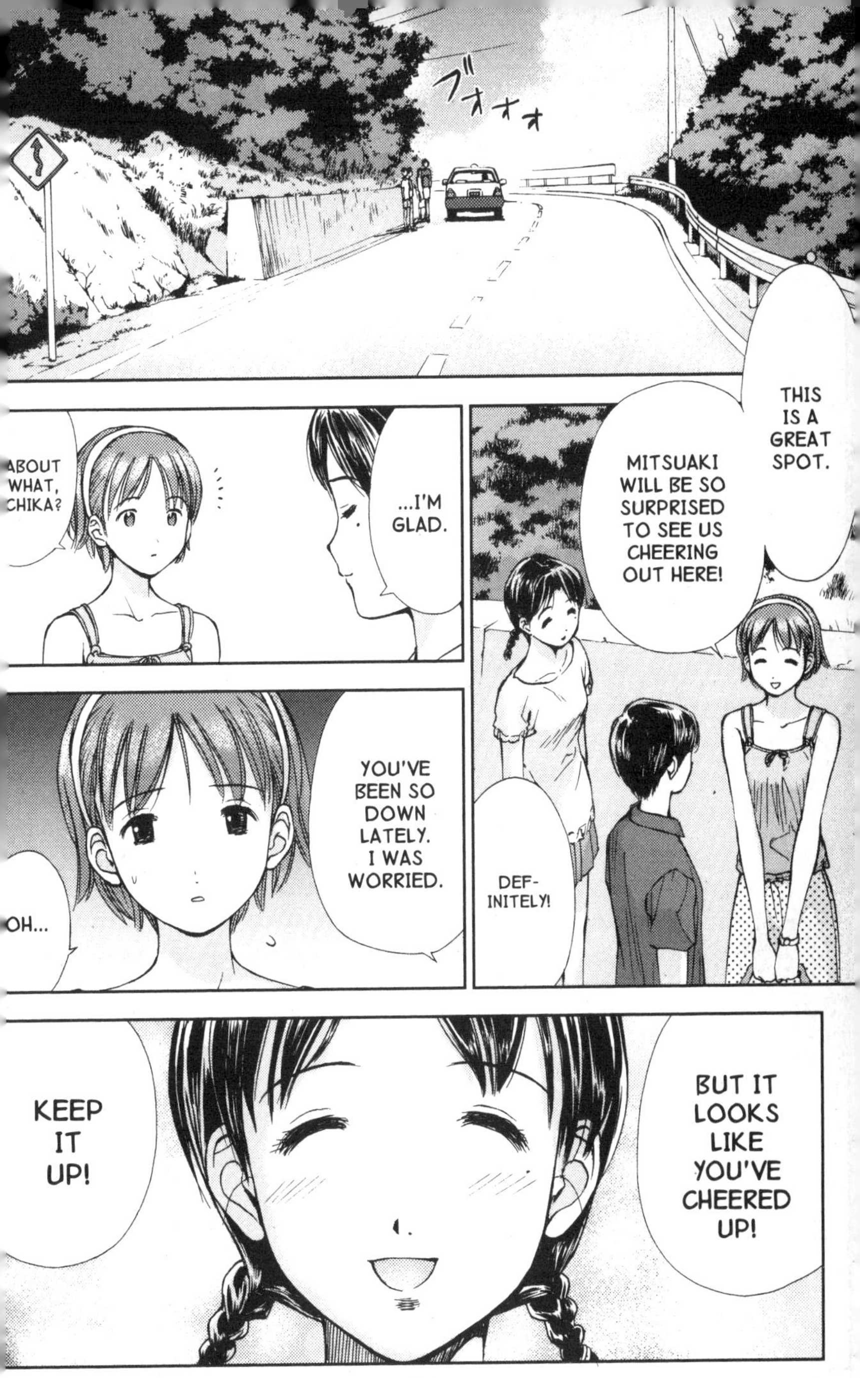
ブオォォ
THIS IS A GREAT SPOT.
MITSUAKI WILL BE SO SURPRISED TO SEE US CHEERING OUT HERE!
DEF-INITELY!
...I'M GLAD.
ABOUT WHAT, CHIKA?
YOU'VE BEEN SO DOWN LATELY. I WAS WORRIED.
OH...
BUT IT LOOKS LIKE YOU'VE CHEERED UP!
KEEP IT UP!

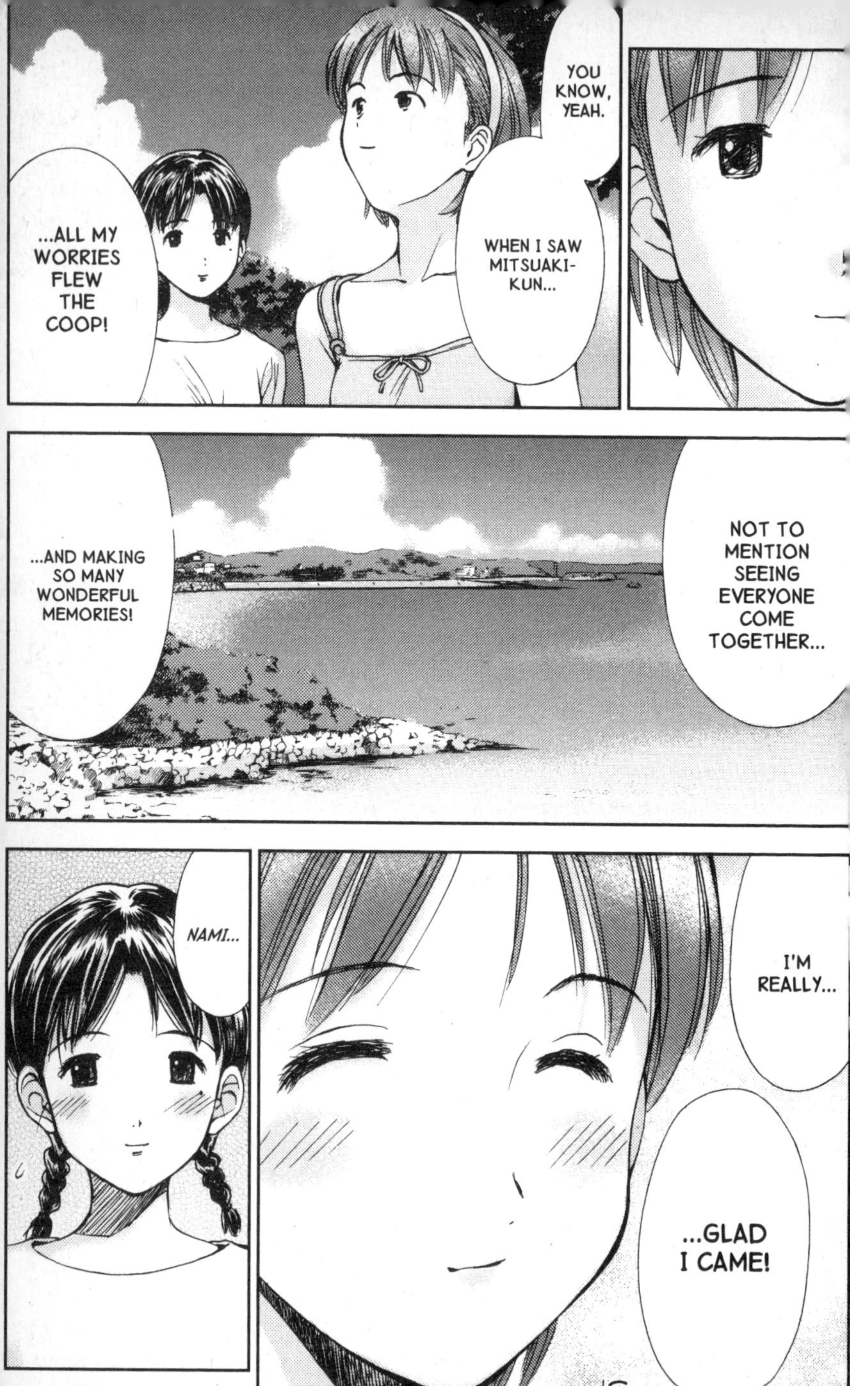
YOU KNOW, YEAH.
WHEN I SAW MITSUAKI-KUN...
...ALL MY WORRIES FLEW THE COOP!
NOT TO MENTION SEEING EVERYONE COME TOGETHER...
...AND MAKING SO MANY WONDERFUL MEMORIES!
I'M REALLY...
...GLAD I CAME!
NAMI...

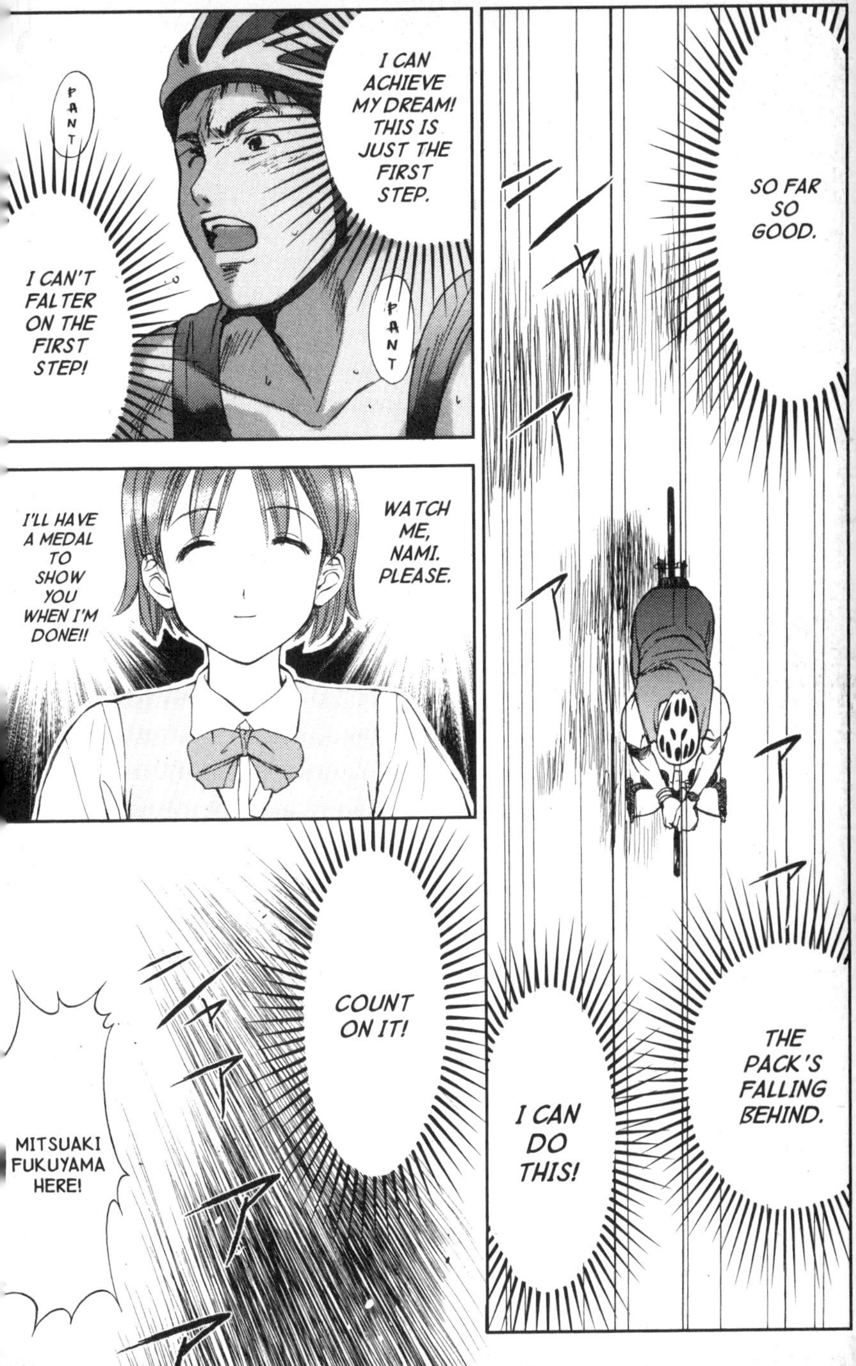
SO FAR SO GOOD.
THE PACK'S FALLING BEHIND.
I CAN DO THIS!
I CAN ACHIEVE MY DREAM! THIS IS JUST THE FIRST STEP.
PANT
PANT
I CAN'T FALTER ON THE FIRST STEP!
WATCH ME, NAMI. PLEASE.
I'LL HAVE A MEDAL TO SHOW YOU WHEN I'M DONE!!
COUNT ON IT!
MITSUAKI FUKUYAMA HERE!

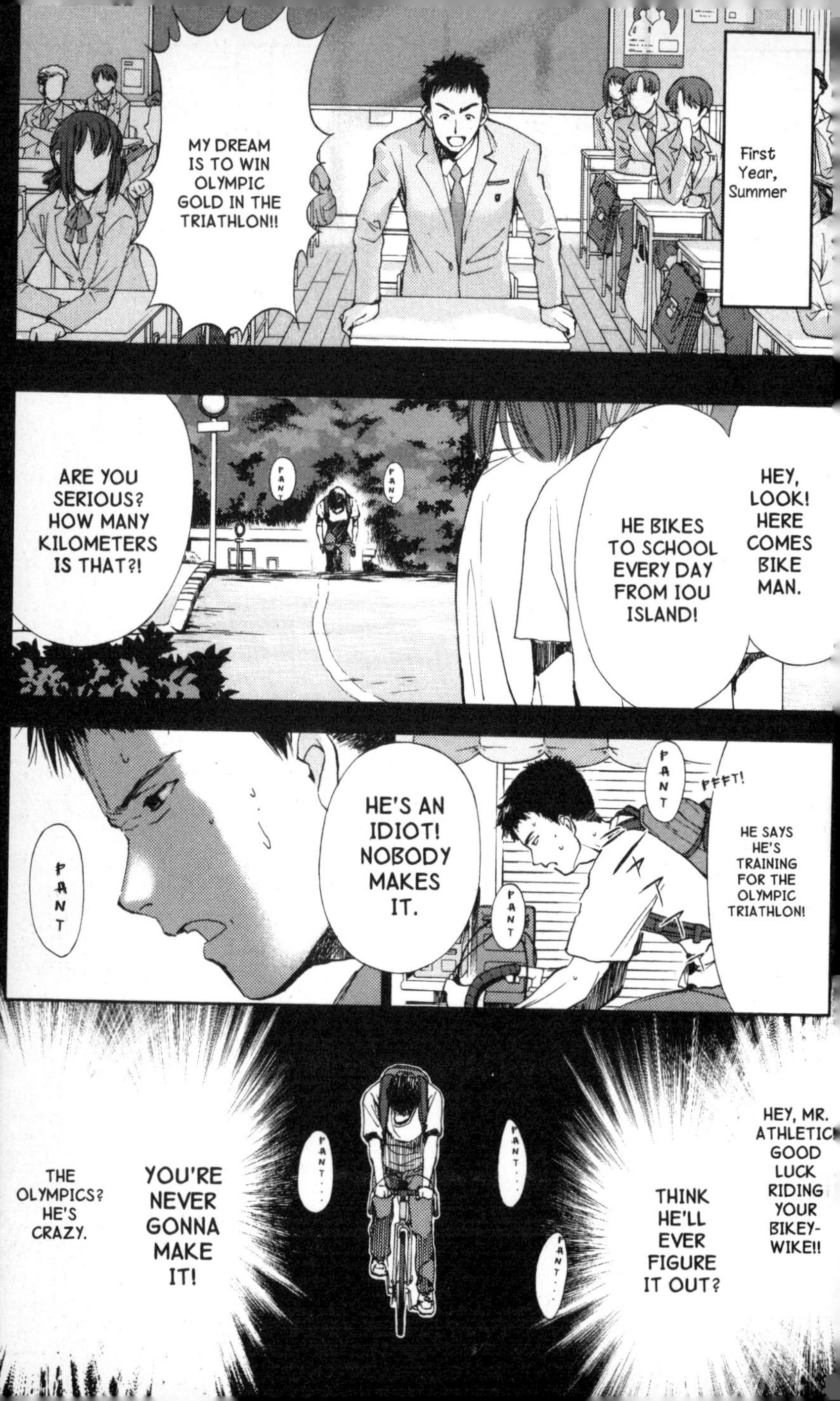
First Year, Summer
MY DREAM IS TO WIN OLYMPIC GOLD IN THE TRIATHLON!!
HEY, LOOK! HERE COMES BIKE MAN.
HE BIKES TO SCHOOL EVERY DAY FROM IOU ISLAND!
PANT
PANT
ARE YOU SERIOUS? HOW MANY KILOMETERS IS THAT?!
HE SAYS HE'S TRAINING FOR THE OLYMPIC TRIATHLON!
PFFT!
PANT
PANT
HE'S AN IDIOT! NOBODY MAKES IT.
PANT
HEY, MR. ATHLETIC GOOD LUCK RIDING YOUR BIKEY-WIKE!!
THINK HE'LL EVER FIGURE IT OUT?
PANT...
PANT...
PANT...
YOU'RE NEVER GONNA MAKE IT!
THE OLYMPICS? HE'S CRAZY.

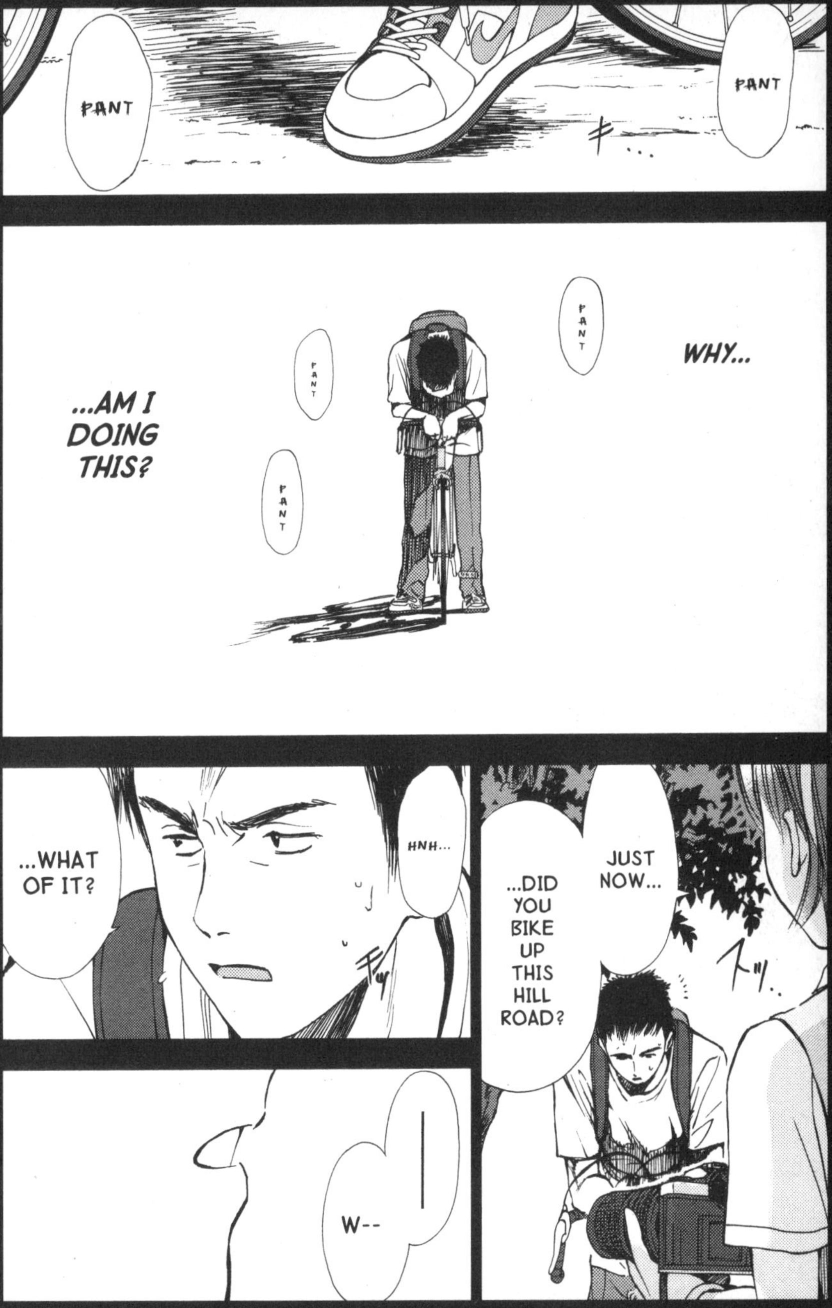
PANT
PANT
WHY...
PANT
PANT
PANT
...AM I DOING THIS?
JUST NOW...
...DID YOU BIKE UP THIS HILL ROAD?
HNH...
...WHAT OF IT?
W--

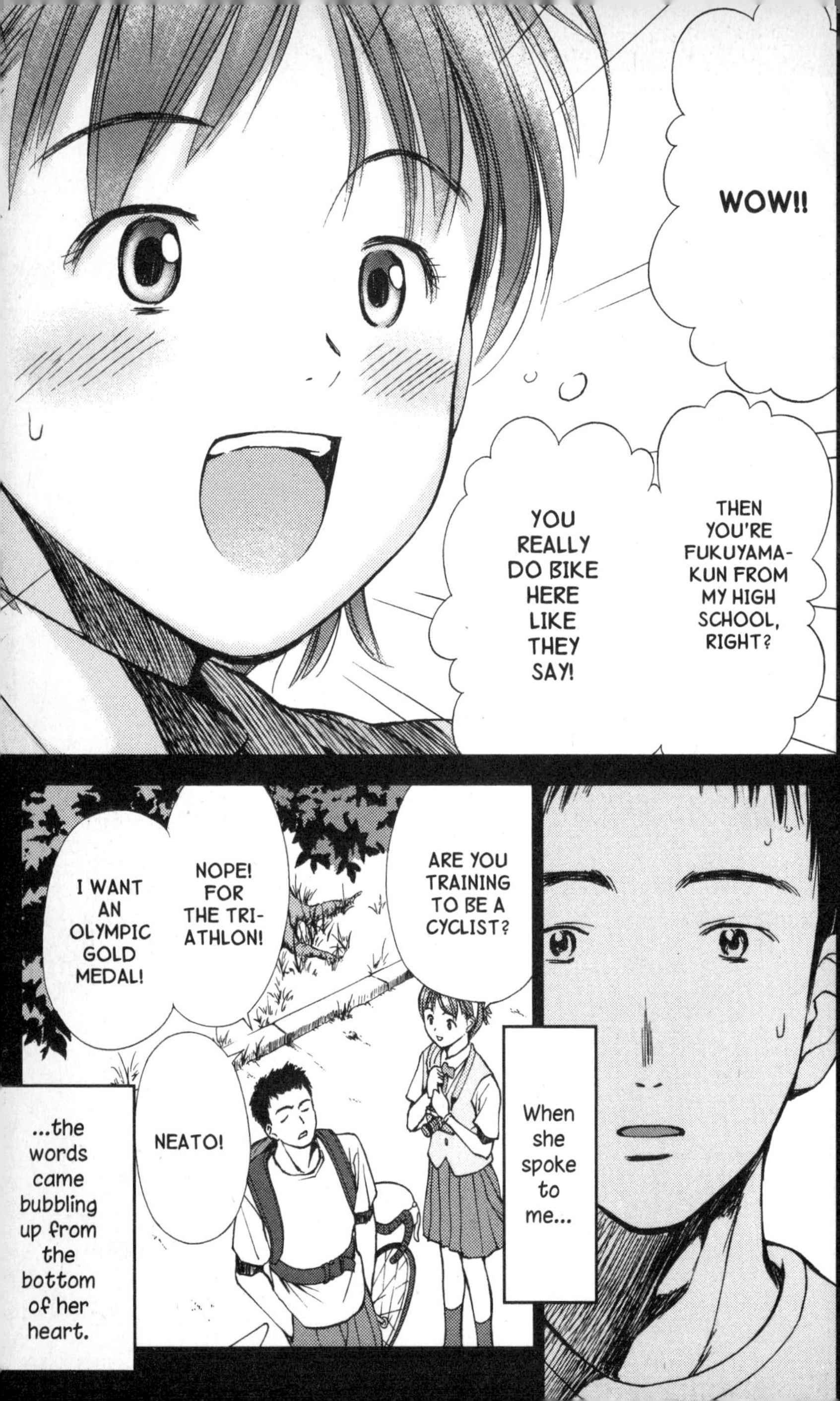
WOW!!
THEN YOU'RE FUKUYAMA-KUN FROM MY HIGH SCHOOL, RIGHT?
YOU REALLY DO BIKE HERE LIKE THEY SAY!
When she spoke to me...
ARE YOU TRAINING TO BE A CYCLIST?
NOPE! FOR THE TRI-ATHLON!
I WANT AN OLYMPIC GOLD MEDAL!
NEATO!
...the words came bubbling up from the bottom of her heart.

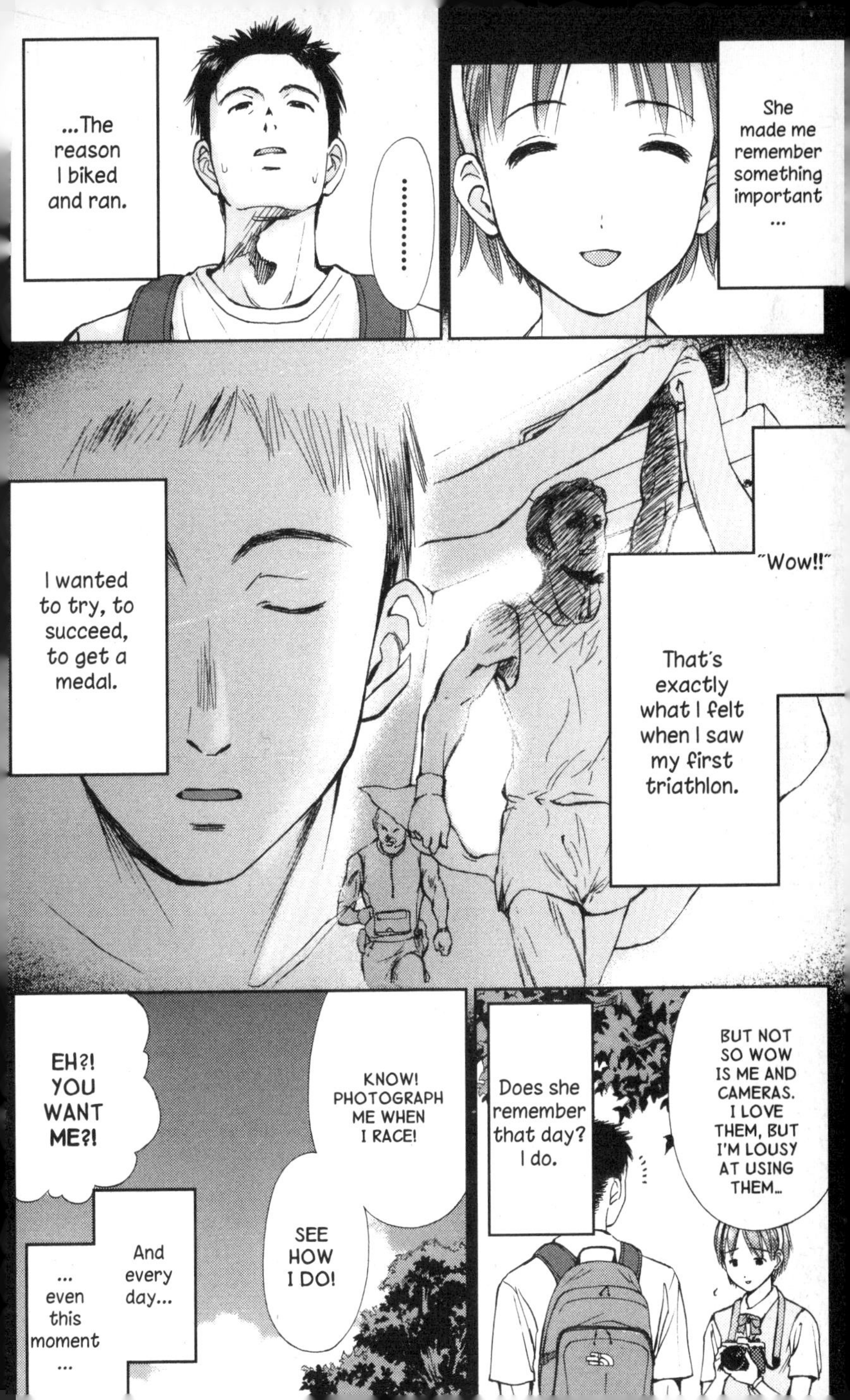
She made me remember something important ...
......
...The reason I biked and ran.
"Wow!!"
That's exactly what I felt when I saw my first triathlon.
I wanted to try, to succeed, to get a medal.
BUT NOT SO WOW IS ME AND CAMERAS. I LOVE THEM, BUT I'M LOUSY AT USING THEM...
Does she remember that day? I do.
KNOW! PHOTOGRAPH ME WHEN I RACE!
SEE HOW I DO!
EH?! YOU WANT ME?!
And every day...
... even this moment ...

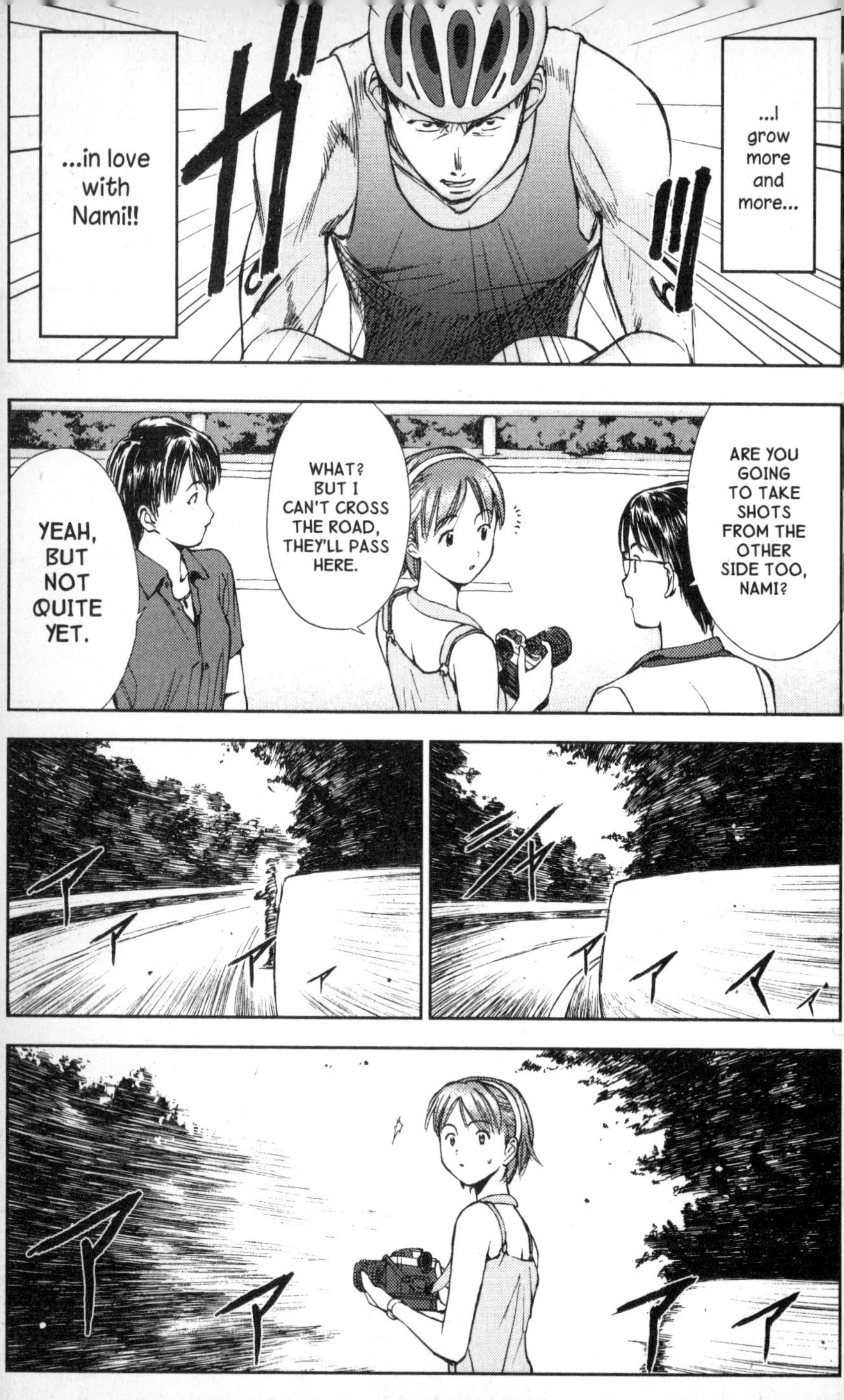
...I grow more and more...
...in love with Nami!!
ARE YOU GOING TO TAKE SHOTS FROM THE OTHER SIDE TOO, NAMI?
WHAT? BUT I CAN'T CROSS THE ROAD, THEY'LL PASS HERE.
YEAH, BUT NOT QUITE YET.

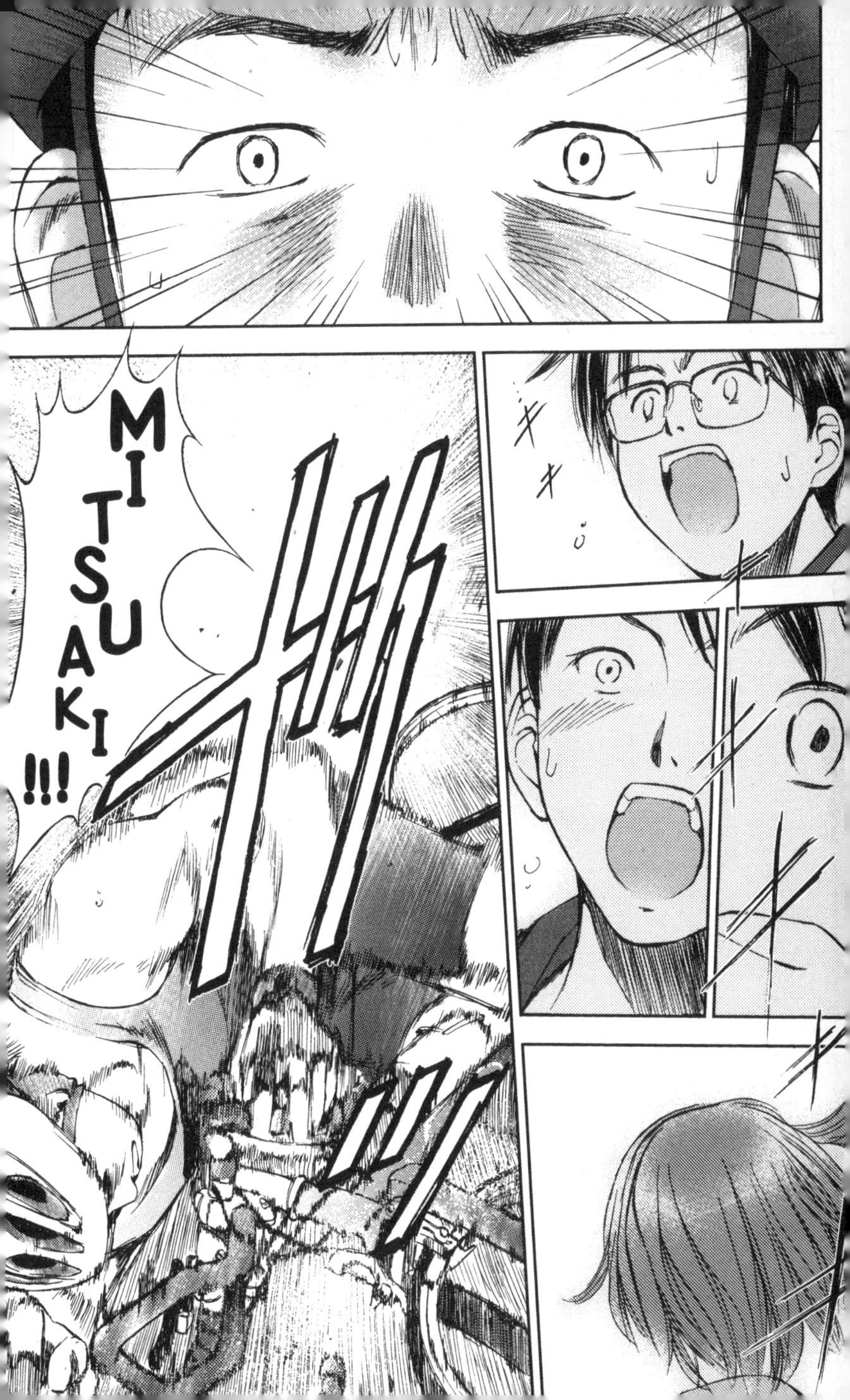
MITSUAKI!!!

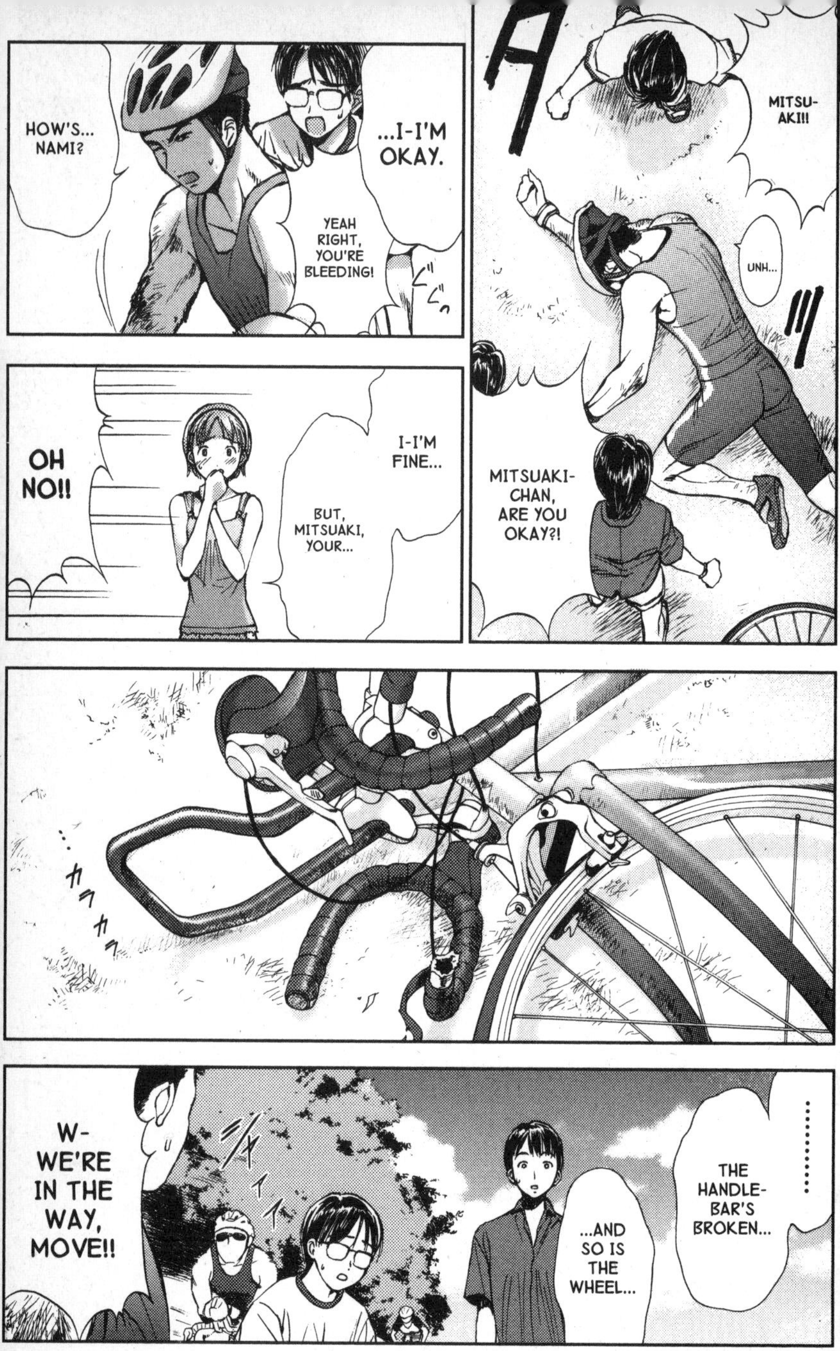
MITSU-AKI!!
UNH...
MITSUAKI-CHAN, ARE YOU OKAY?!
...I-I'M OKAY.
YEAH RIGHT, YOU'RE BLEEDING!
HOW'S... NAMI?
I-I'M FINE...
BUT, MITSUAKI, YOUR...
OH NO!!
......
THE HANDLE-BAR'S BROKEN...
...AND SO IS THE WHEEL...
W- WE'RE IN THE WAY, MOVE!!

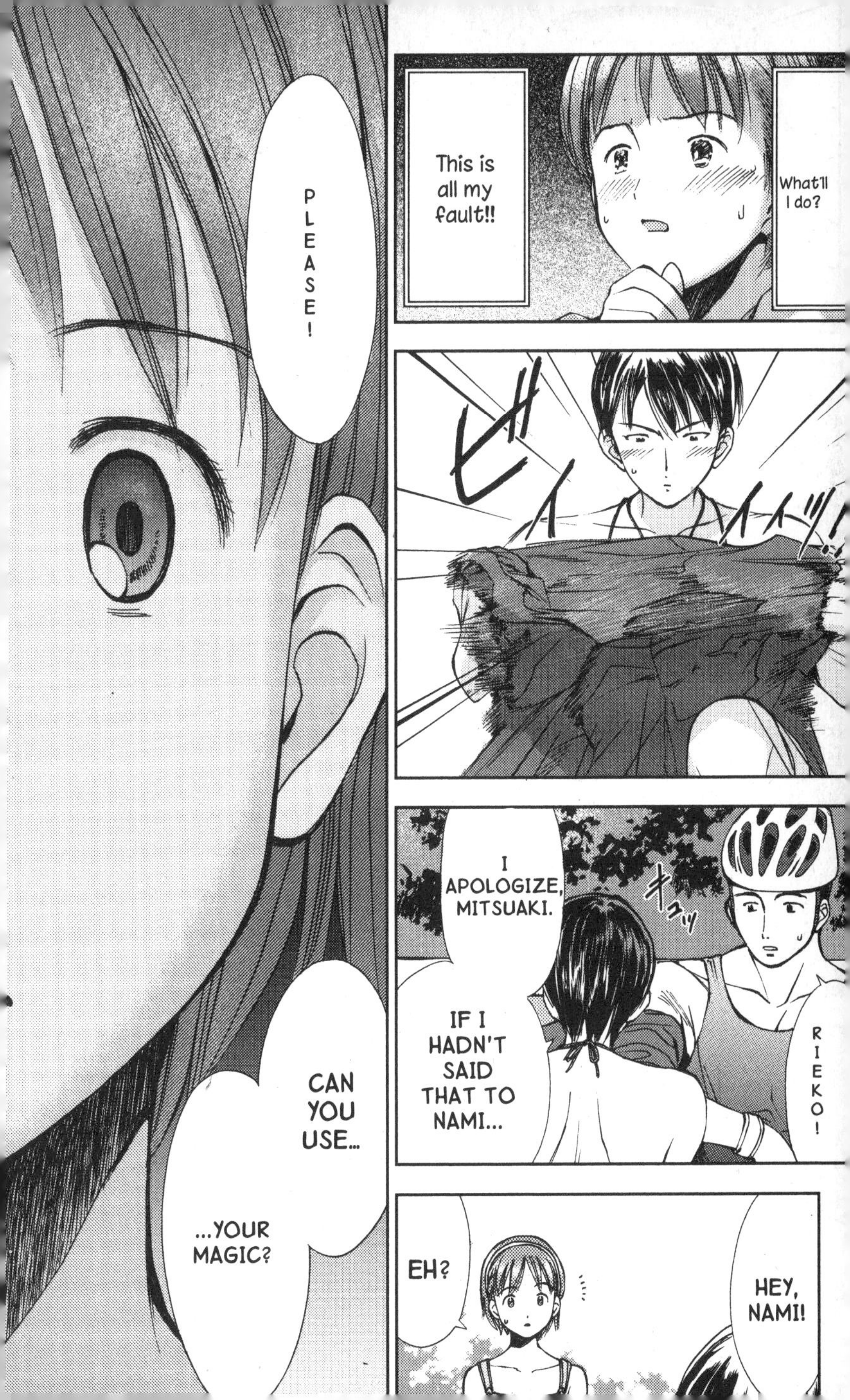
What'll I do?
This is all my fault!!
ビイイイッ!
RIEKO!
キュッ
I APOLOGIZE, MITSUAKI.
IF I HADN'T SAID THAT TO NAMI...
HEY, NAMI!
EH?
PLEASE!
CAN YOU USE...
...YOUR MAGIC?

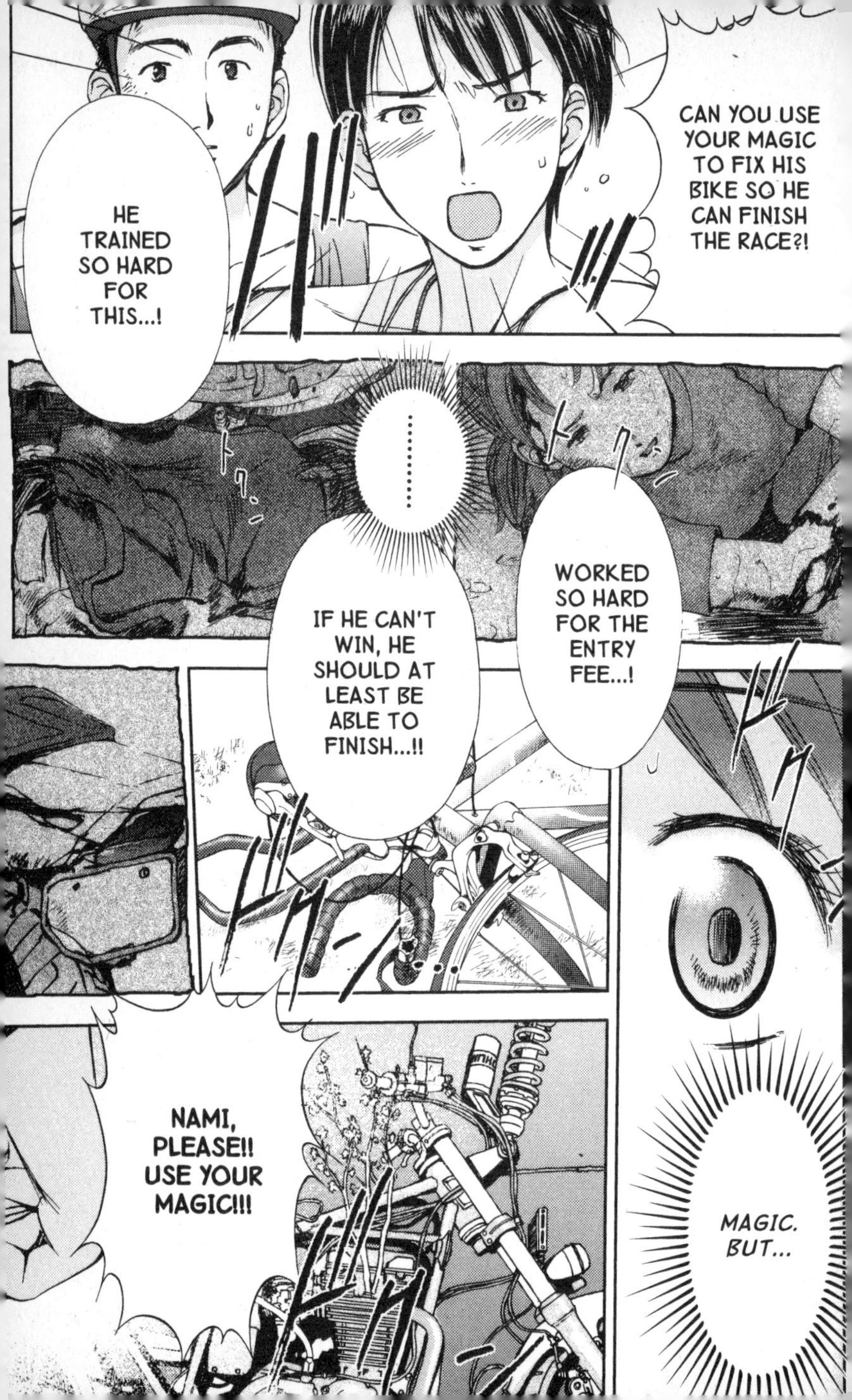
CAN YOU USE YOUR MAGIC TO FIX HIS BIKE SO HE CAN FINISH THE RACE?!
HE TRAINED SO HARD FOR THIS...!
WORKED SO HARD FOR THE ENTRY FEE...!
......
IF HE CAN'T WIN, HE SHOULD AT LEAST BE ABLE TO FINISH...!!
MAGIC. BUT...
NAMI, PLEASE!! USE YOUR MAGIC!!!

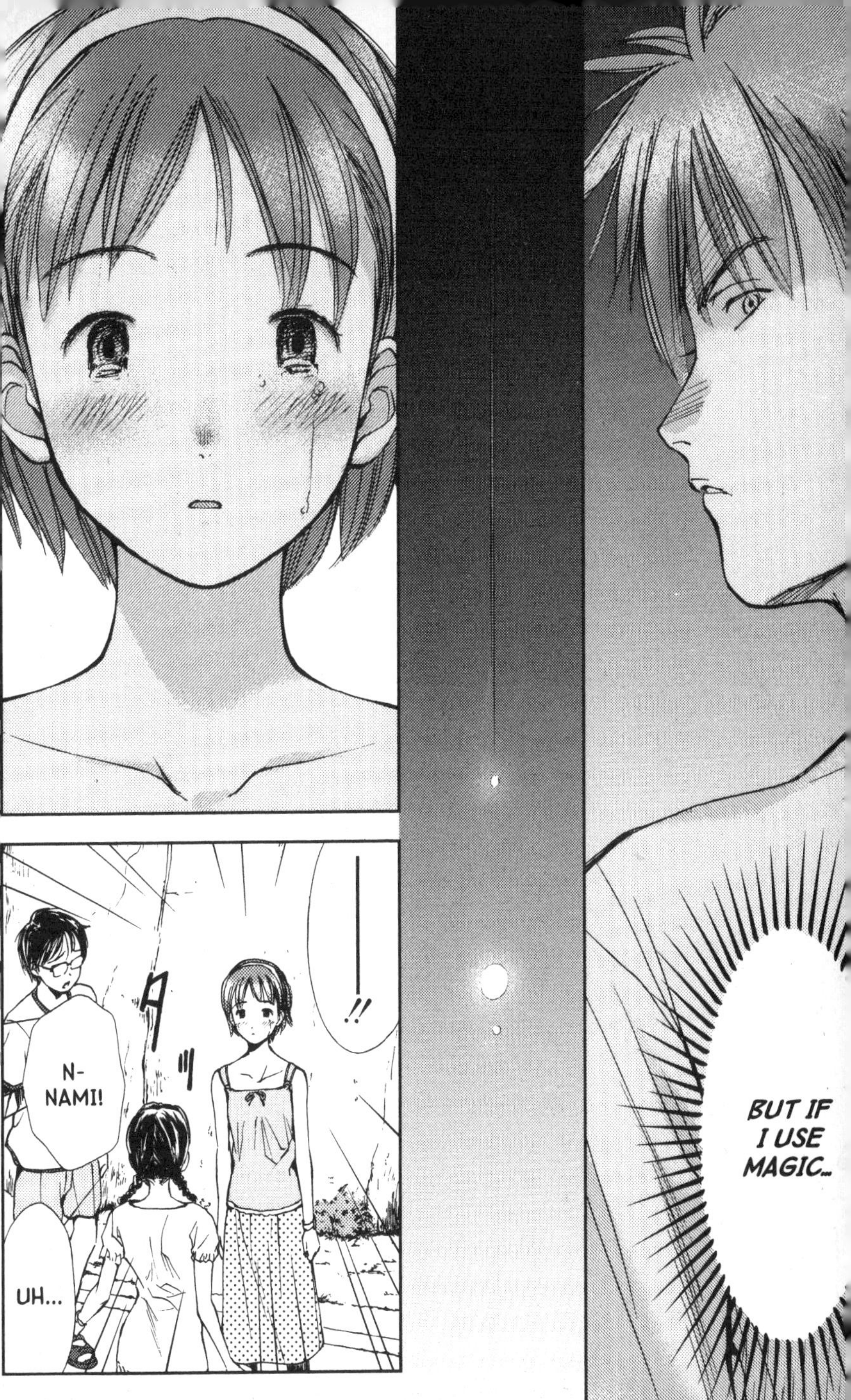
BUT IF I USE MAGIC...
――!!
N-NAMI!
UH...

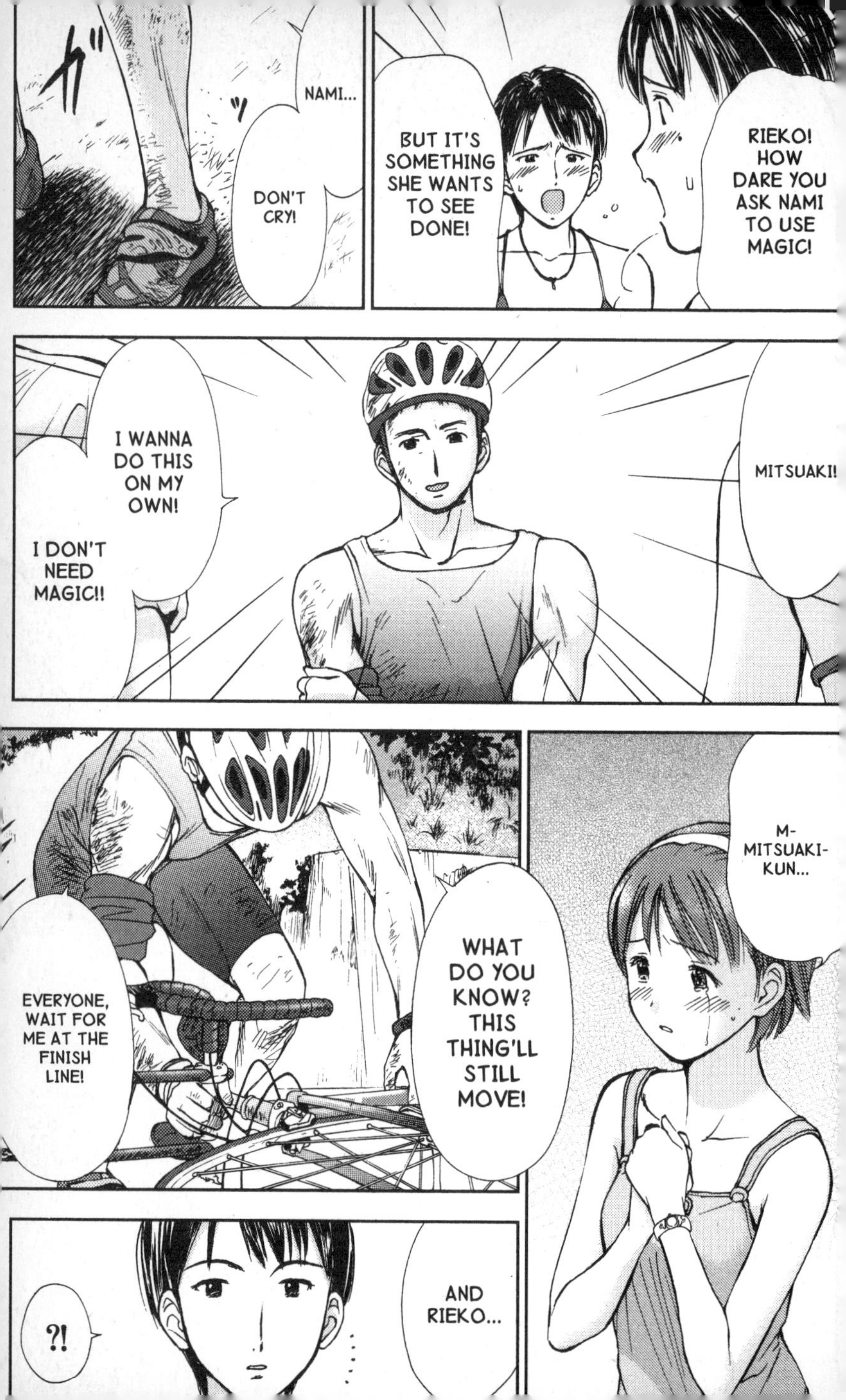
RIEKO! HOW DARE YOU ASK NAMI TO USE MAGIC!
BUT IT'S SOMETHING SHE WANTS TO SEE DONE!
NAMI...
DON'T CRY!
ガッ
MITSUAKI!
I WANNA DO THIS ON MY OWN!
I DON'T NEED MAGIC!!
M-MITSUAKI-KUN...
WHAT DO YOU KNOW? THIS THING'LL STILL MOVE!
EVERYONE, WAIT FOR ME AT THE FINISH LINE!
AND RIEKO...
?!

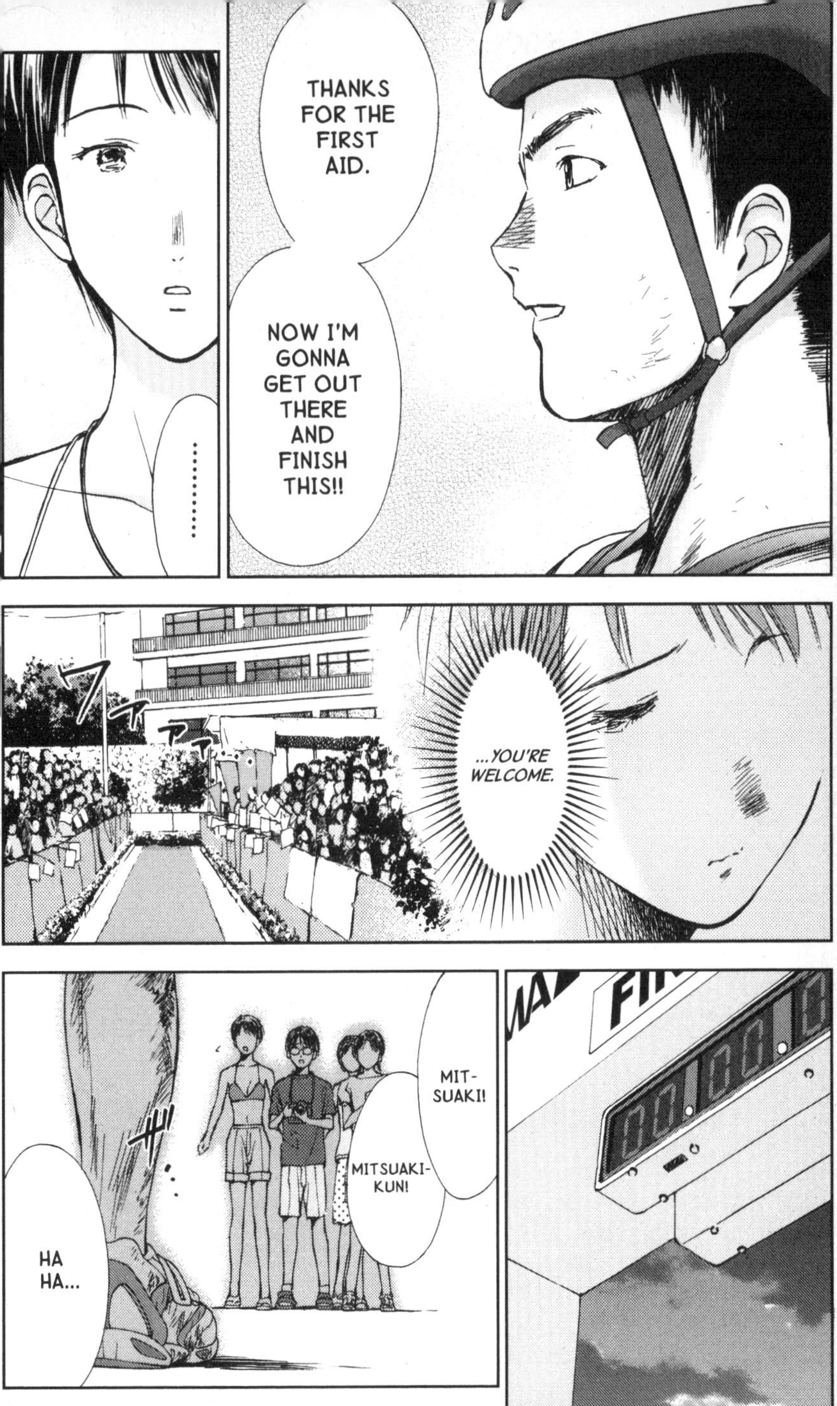
THANKS FOR THE FIRST AID.
NOW I'M GONNA GET OUT THERE AND FINISH THIS!!
......
...YOU'RE WELCOME.
MIT-SUAKI!
MITSUAKI-KUN!
HA HA...

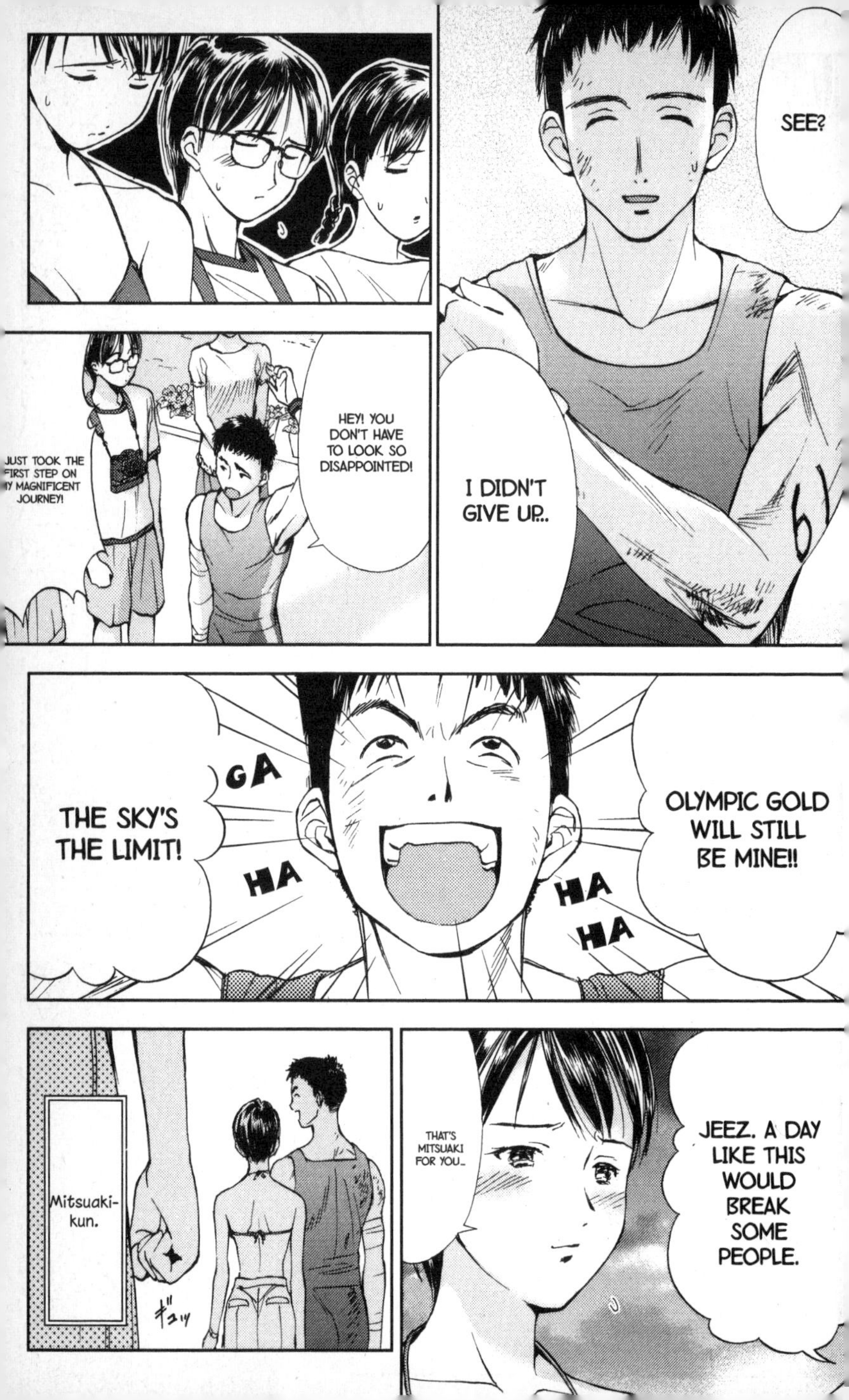
SEE?
I DIDN'T GIVE UP...
HEY! YOU DON'T HAVE TO LOOK SO DISAPPOINTED!
JUST TOOK THE FIRST STEP ON IY MAGNIFICENT JOURNEY!
OLYMPIC GOLD WILL STILL BE MINE!!
GA
HA
HA
HA
THE SKY'S THE LIMIT!
JEEZ. A DAY LIKE THIS WOULD BREAK SOME PEOPLE.
THAT'S MITSUAKI FOR YOU...
Mitsuaki-kun.
ギュッ

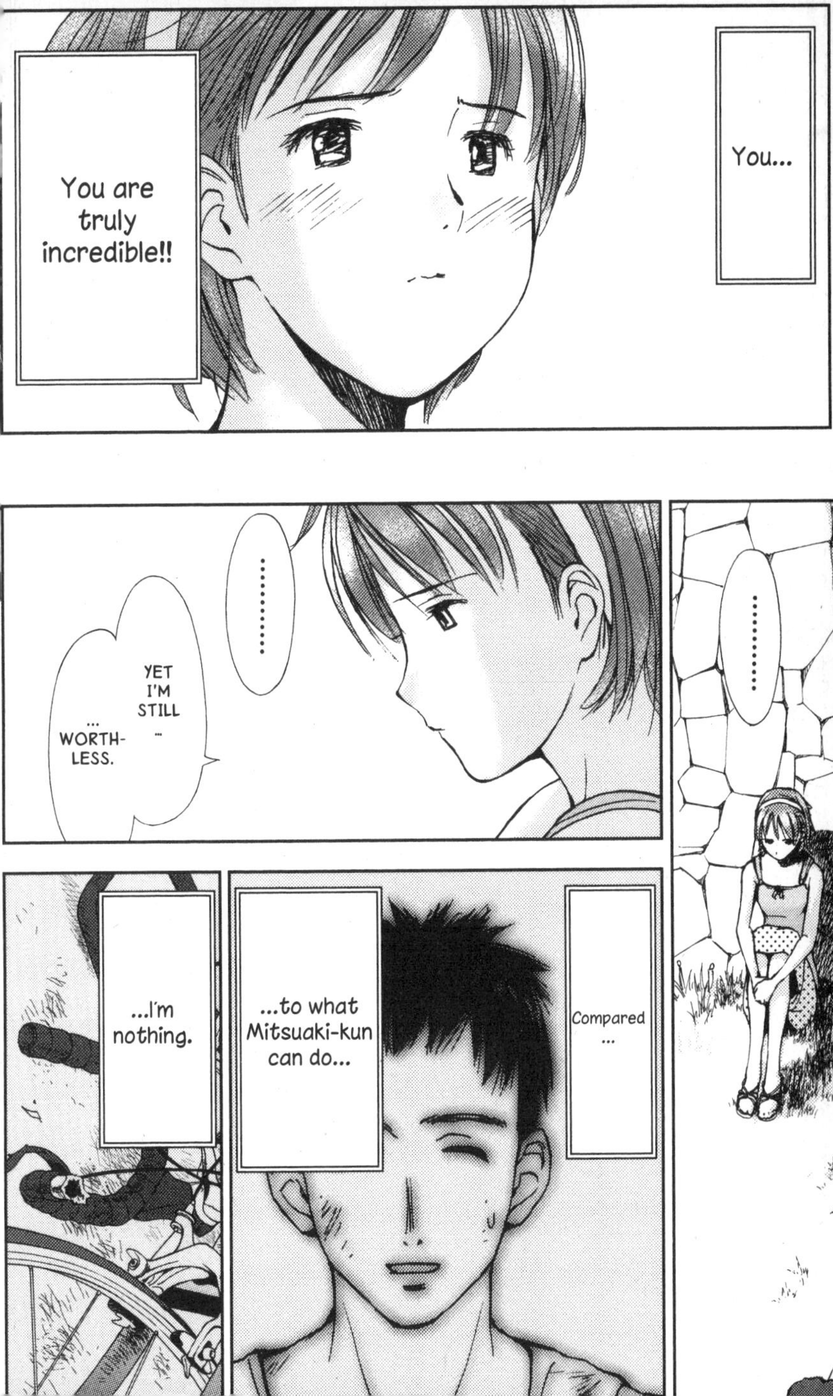
You...
You are truly incredible!!
....
....
YET I'M STILL ... ... WORTH-LESS.
Compared ...
...to what Mitsuaki-kun can do...
...I'm nothing.

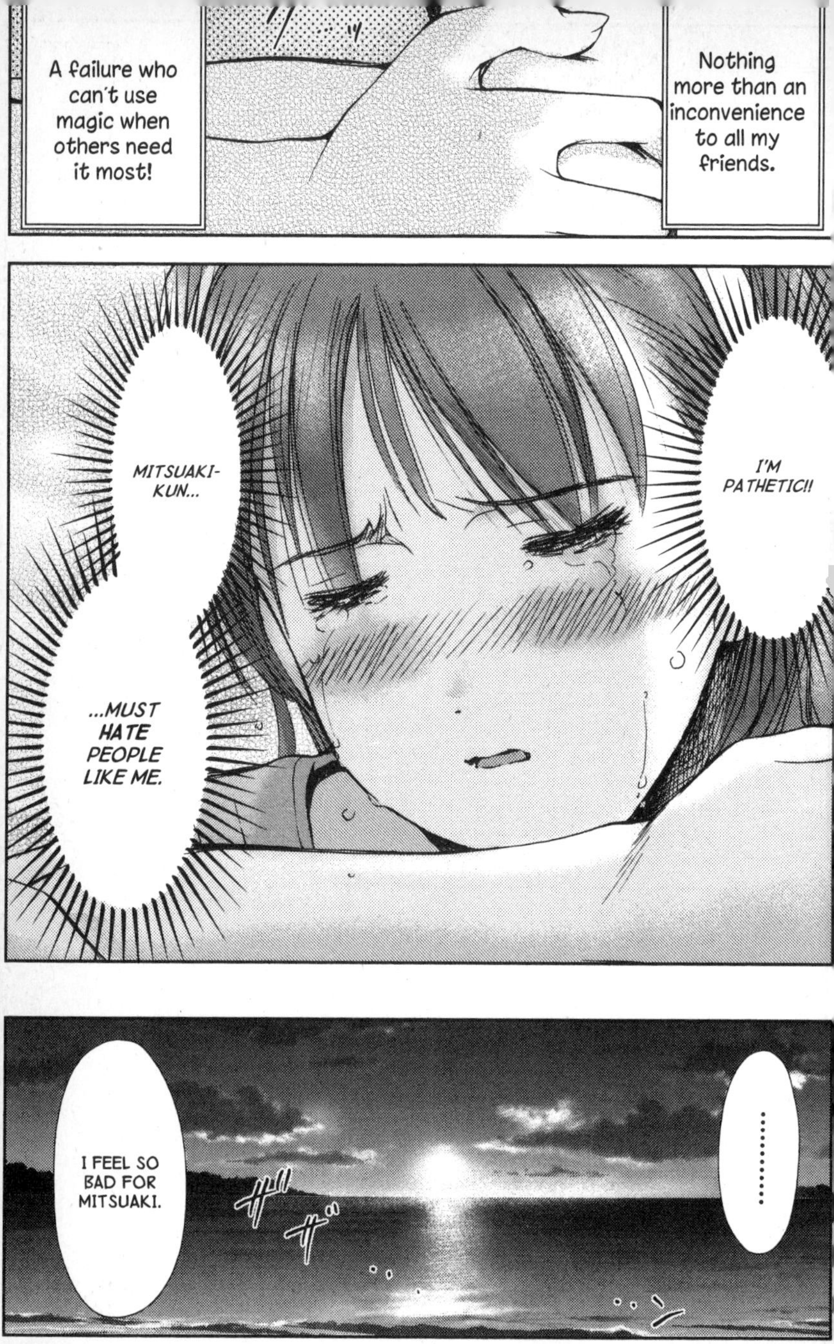
Nothing more than an inconvenience to all my friends.
A failure who can't use magic when others need it most!
I'M PATHETIC!!
MITSUAKI-KUN...
...MUST HATE PEOPLE LIKE ME.
....
I FEEL SO BAD FOR MITSUAKI.

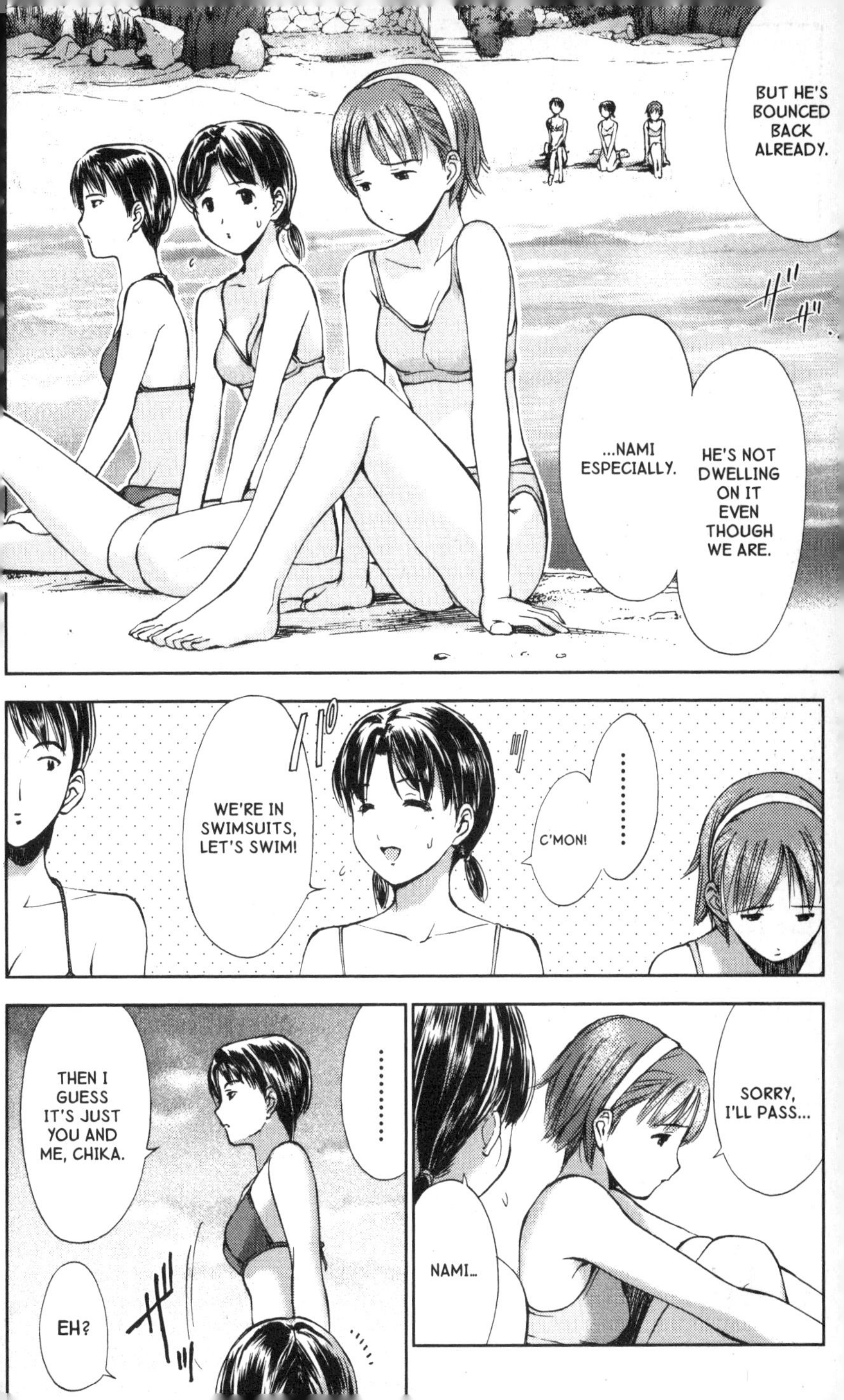
BUT HE'S BOUNCED BACK ALREADY.
HE'S NOT DWELLING ON IT EVEN THOUGH WE ARE.
...NAMI ESPECIALLY.
....
C'MON!
WE'RE IN SWIMSUITS, LET'S SWIM!
SORRY, I'LL PASS...
NAMI...
....
THEN I GUESS IT'S JUST YOU AND ME, CHIKA.
EH?

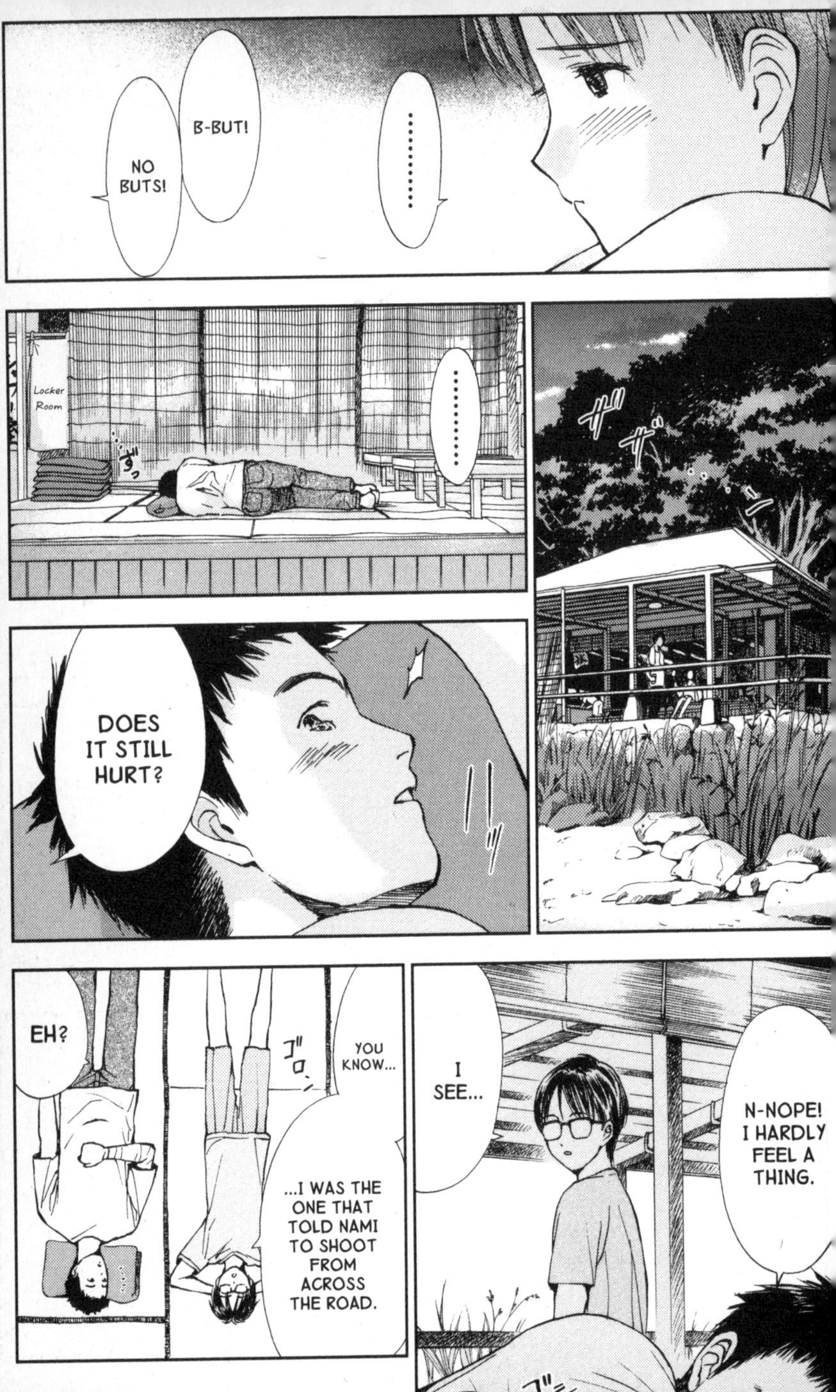
......
B-BUT!
NO BUTS!
Locker Room
......
DOES IT STILL HURT?
N-NOPE! I HARDLY FEEL A THING.
I SEE...
YOU KNOW...
...I WAS THE ONE THAT TOLD NAMI TO SHOOT FROM ACROSS THE ROAD.
EH?

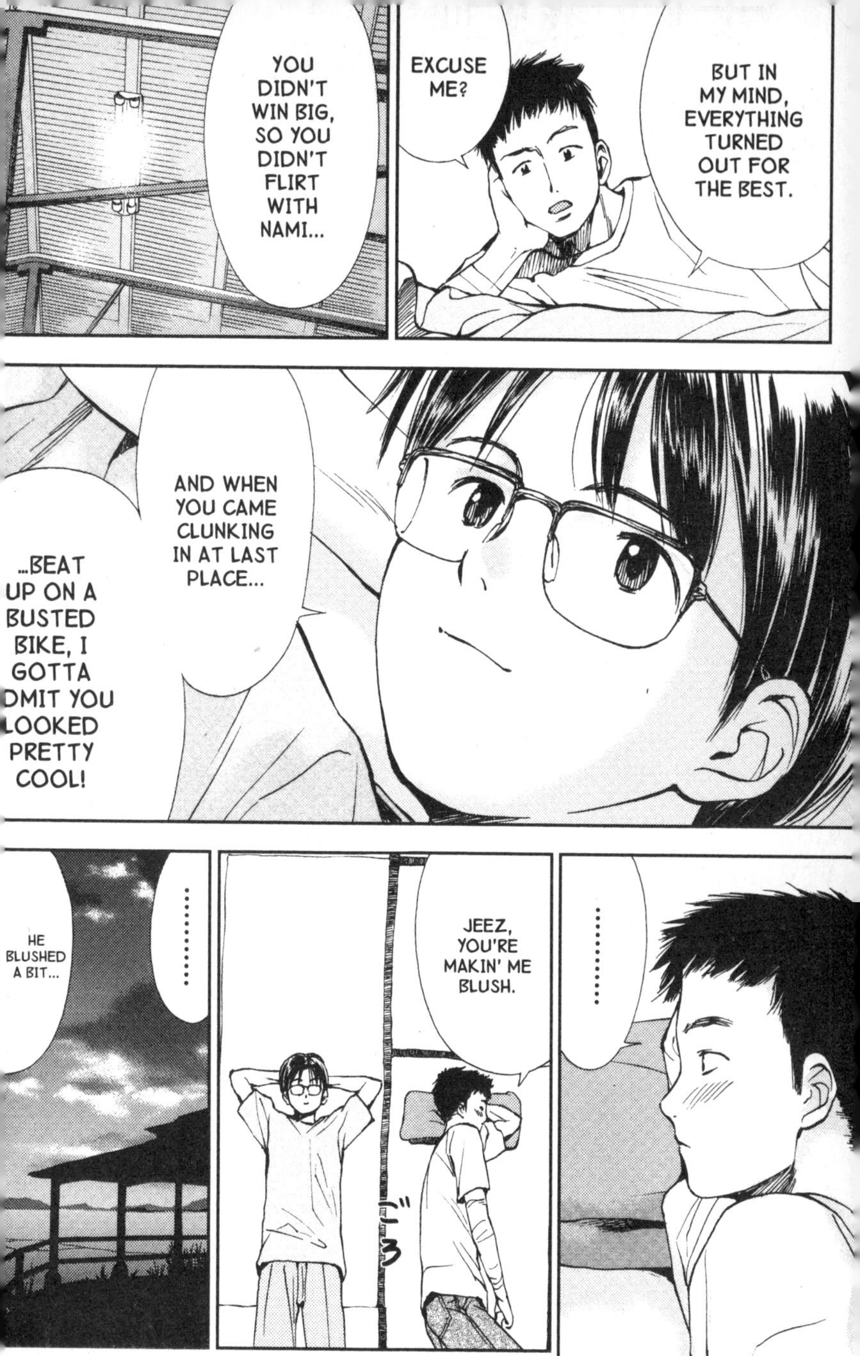
BUT IN MY MIND, EVERYTHING TURNED OUT FOR THE BEST.
EXCUSE ME?
YOU DIDN'T WIN BIG, SO YOU DIDN'T FLIRT WITH NAMI...
AND WHEN YOU CAME CLUNKING IN AT LAST PLACE...
...BEAT UP ON A BUSTED BIKE, I GOTTA DMIT YOU LOOKED PRETTY COOL!
....
JEEZ, YOU'RE MAKIN' ME BLUSH.
ごろ
....
HE BLUSHED A BIT...

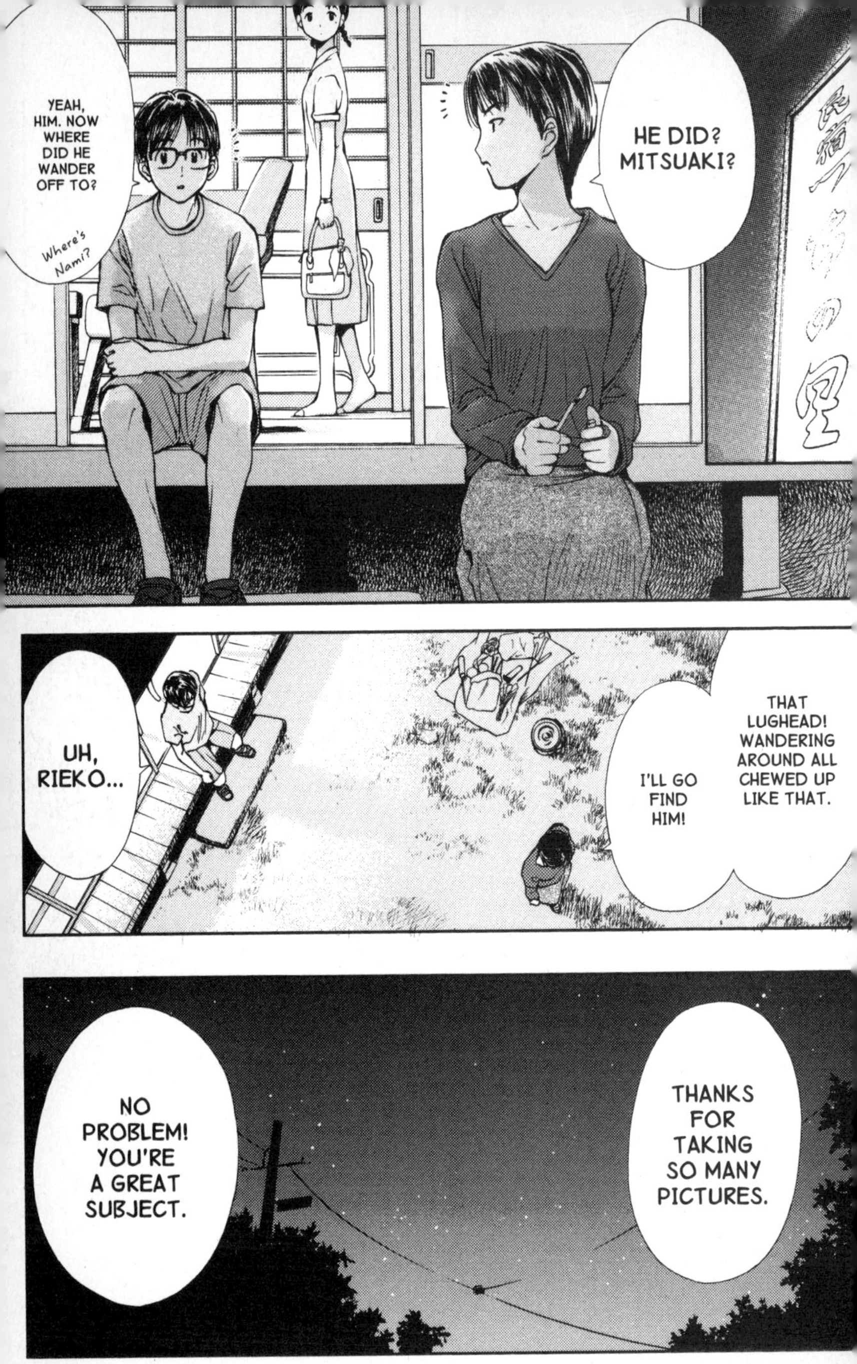
HE DID? MITSUAKI?
YEAH, HIM. NOW WHERE DID HE WANDER OFF TO?
Where's Nami?
THAT LUGHEAD! WANDERING AROUND ALL CHEWED UP LIKE THAT.
I'LL GO FIND HIM!
UH, RIEKO...
THANKS FOR TAKING SO MANY PICTURES.
NO PROBLEM! YOU'RE A GREAT SUBJECT.

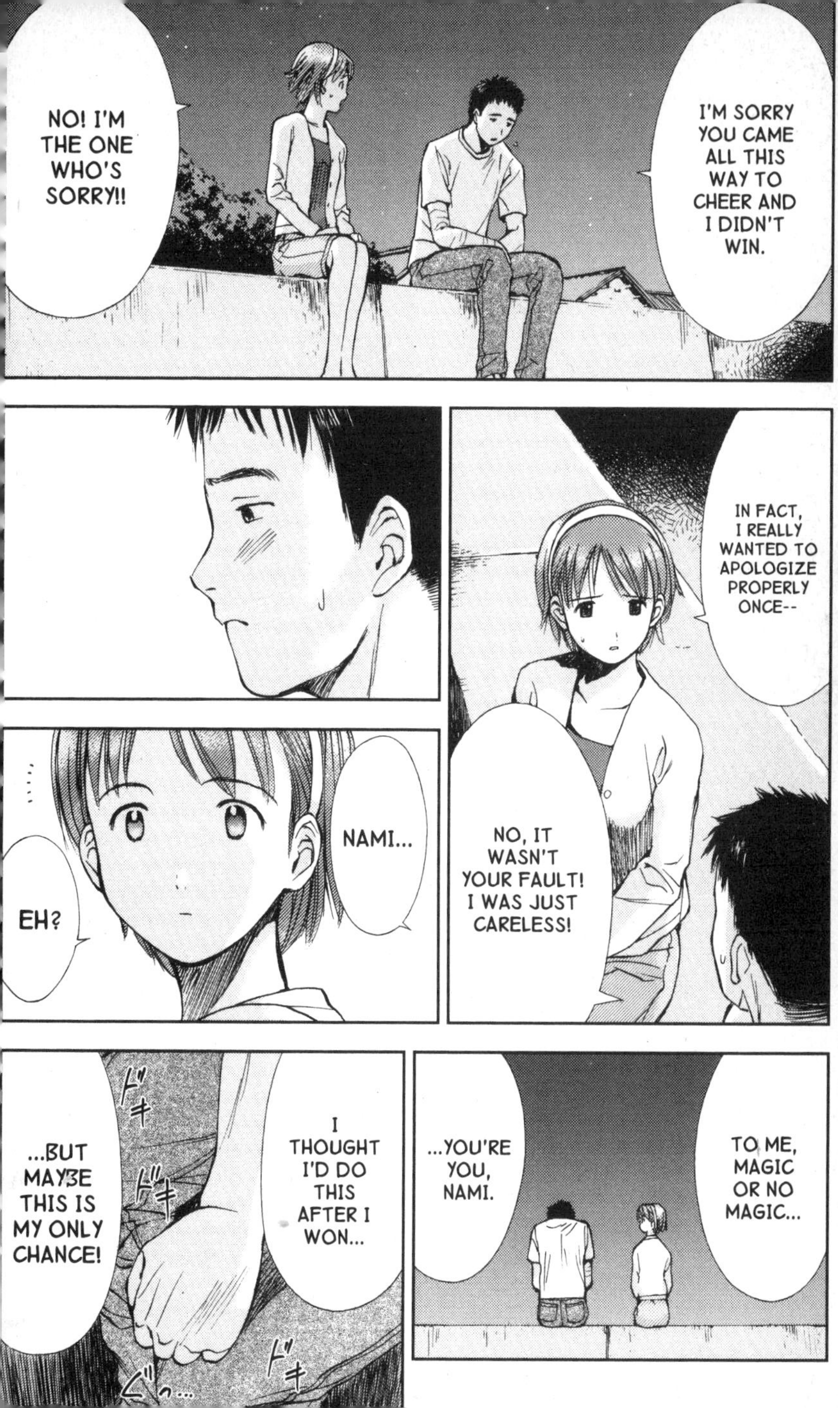
I'M SORRY YOU CAME ALL THIS WAY TO CHEER AND I DIDN'T WIN.
NO! I'M THE ONE WHO'S SORRY!!
IN FACT, I REALLY WANTED TO APOLOGIZE PROPERLY ONCE--
NO, IT WASN'T YOUR FAULT! I WAS JUST CARELESS!
NAMI...
.....
EH?
TO ME, MAGIC OR NO MAGIC...
...YOU'RE YOU, NAMI.
I THOUGHT I'D DO THIS AFTER I WON...
...BUT MAYBE THIS IS MY ONLY CHANCE!
ドキ
ドキ
ドキ
ぐっ...

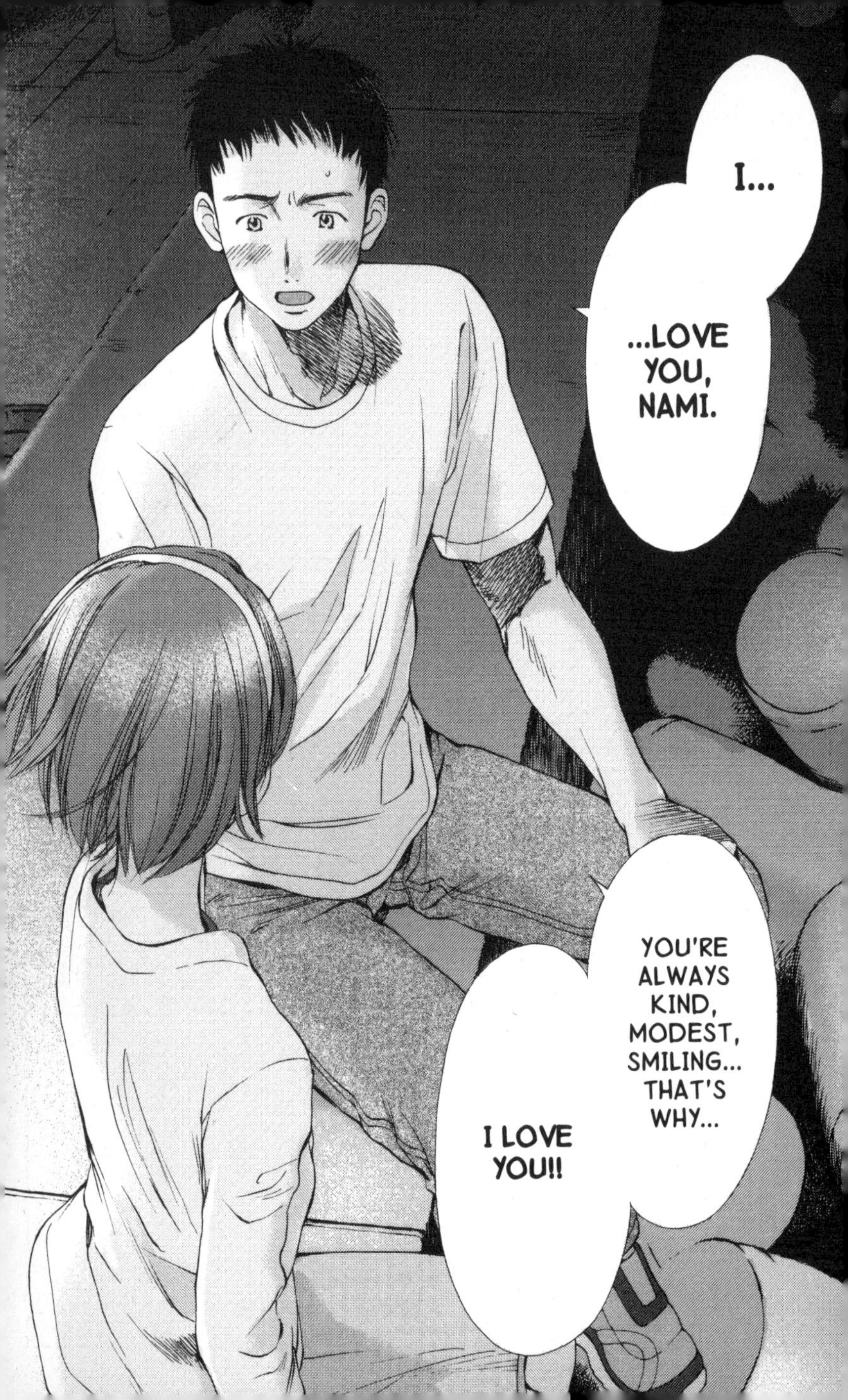
I...
...LOVE YOU, NAMI.
YOU'RE ALWAYS KIND, MODEST, SMILING... THAT'S WHY...
I LOVE YOU!!

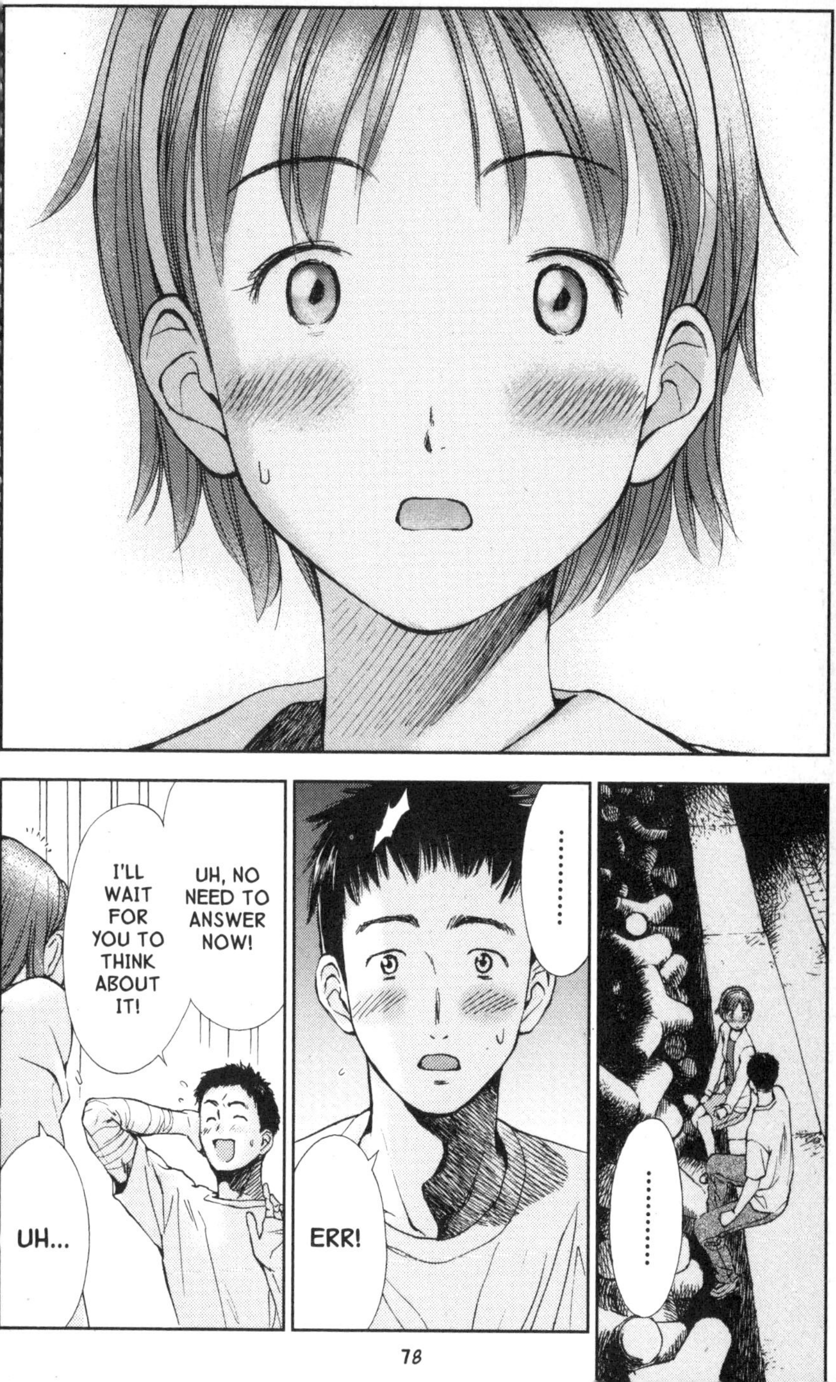
....
....
ERR!
UH, NO NEED TO ANSWER NOW!
I'LL WAIT FOR YOU TO THINK ABOUT IT!
UH...

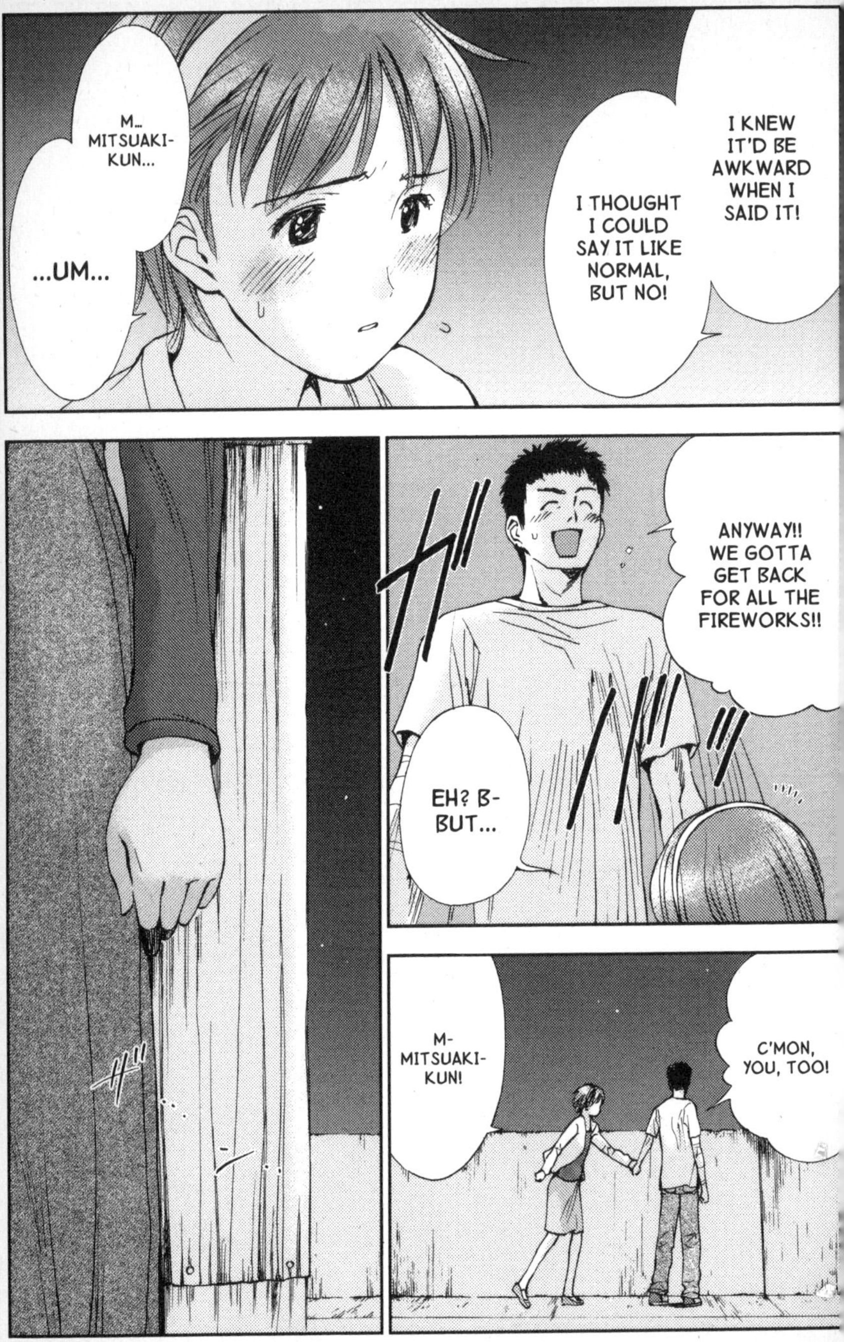
I KNEW IT'D BE AWKWARD WHEN I SAID IT!
I THOUGHT I COULD SAY IT LIKE NORMAL, BUT NO!
M... MITSUAKI-KUN...
...UM...
ANYWAY!! WE GOTTA GET BACK FOR ALL THE FIREWORKS!!
EH? B-BUT...
C'MON, YOU, TOO!
M-MITSUAKI-KUN!

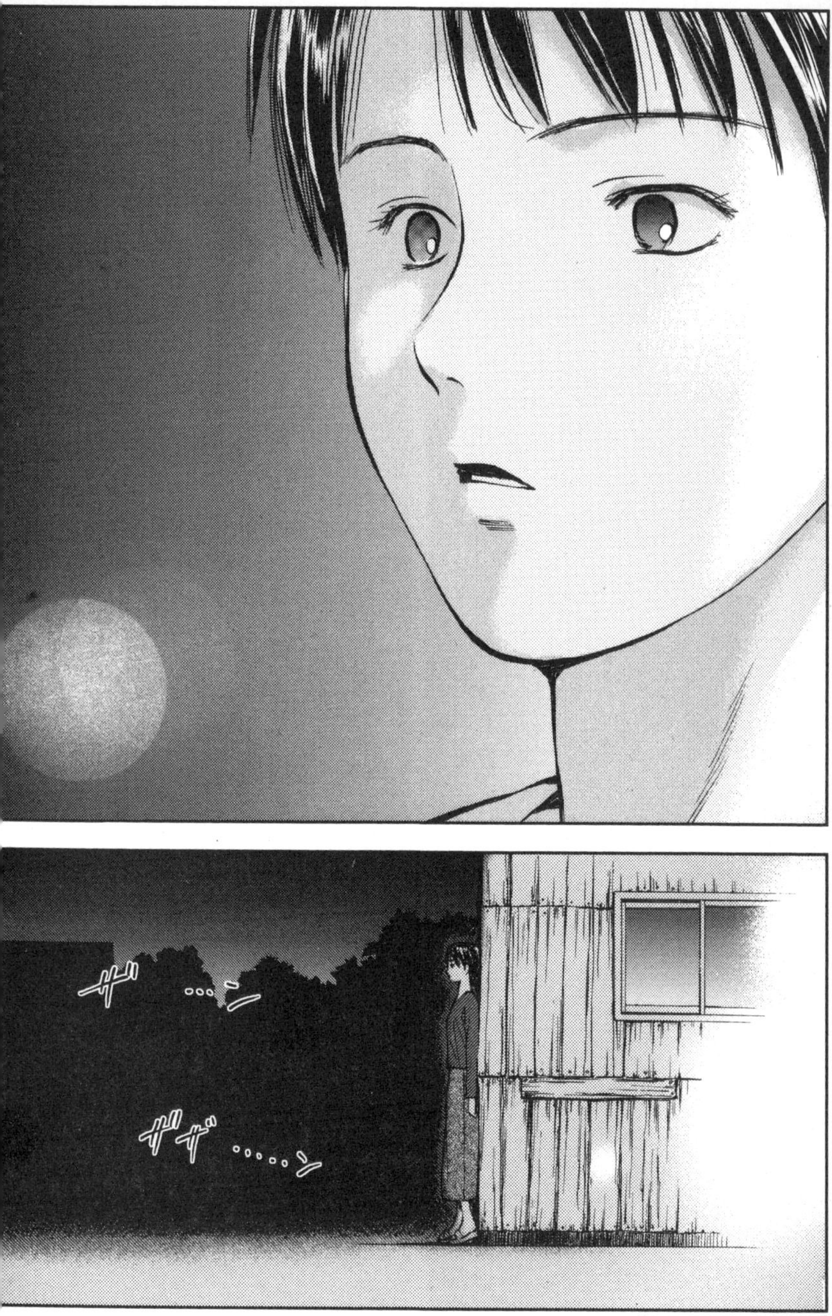
ザ…ン
ザザ……ン

Step.7:End

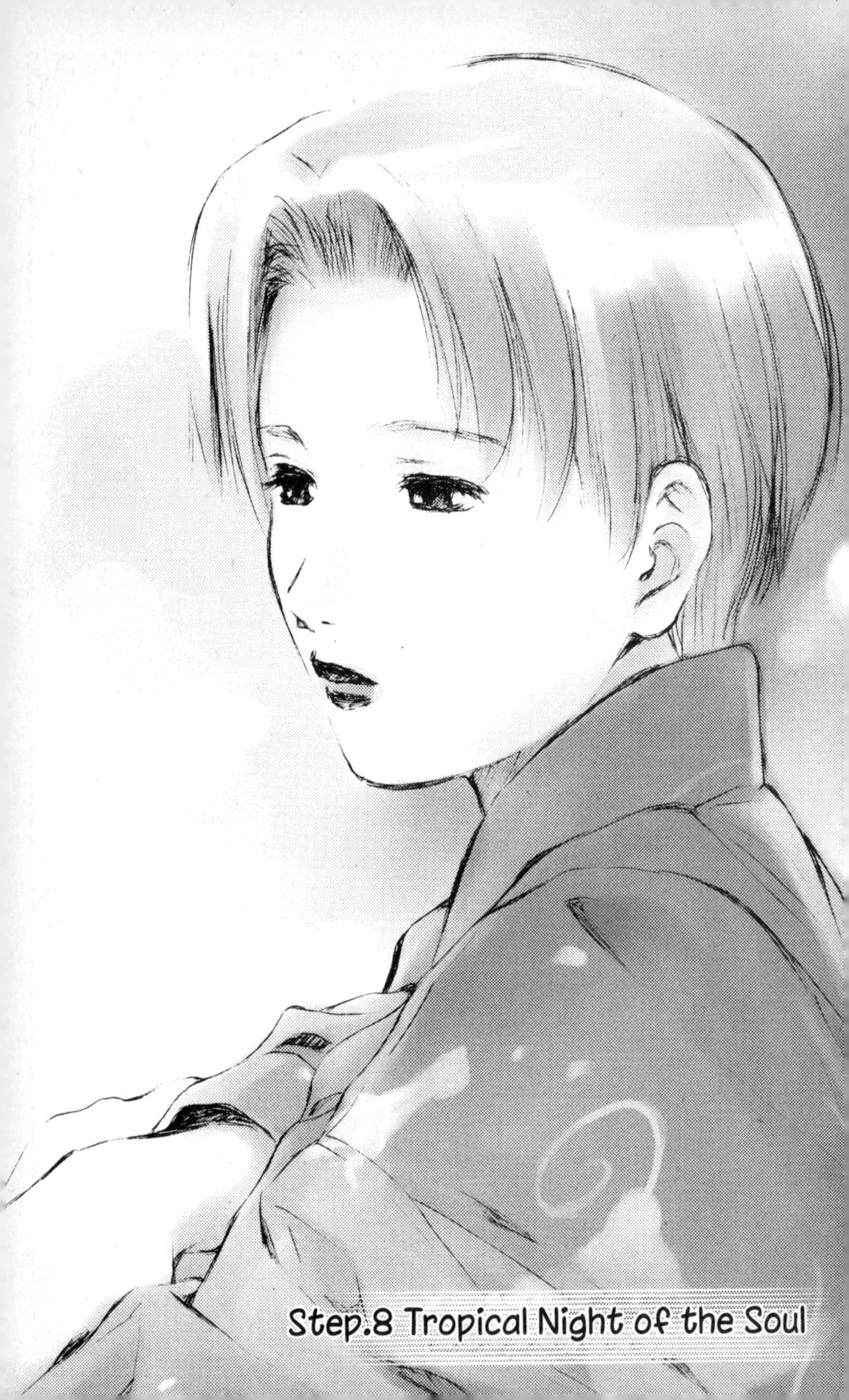

Step.8 Tropical Night of the Soul

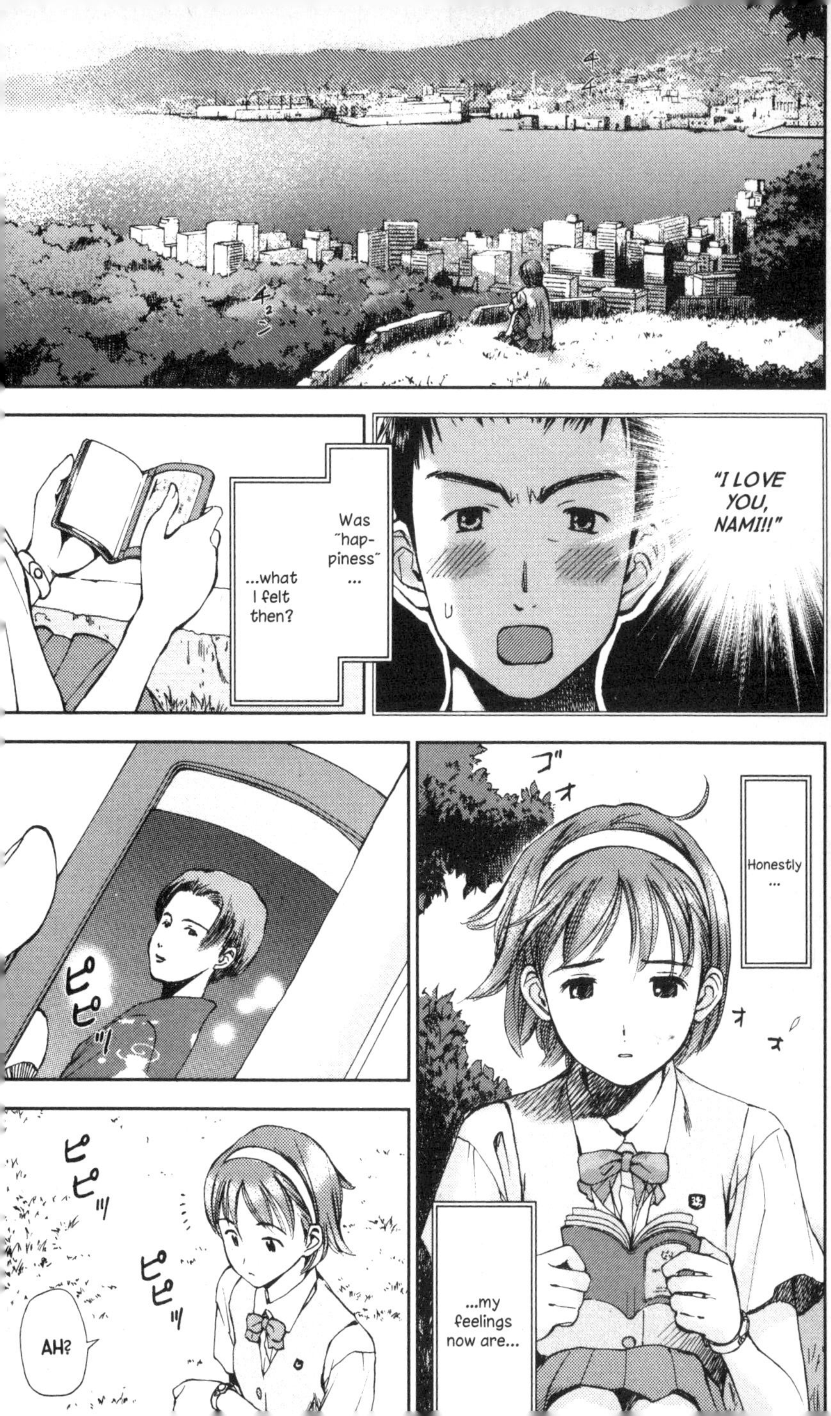
"I LOVE YOU, NAMI!!"
Was "happiness"...
...what I felt then?
ゴオ
Honestly...
オオ
...my feelings now are...
ピピッ
ピピッ
ピピッ
AH?

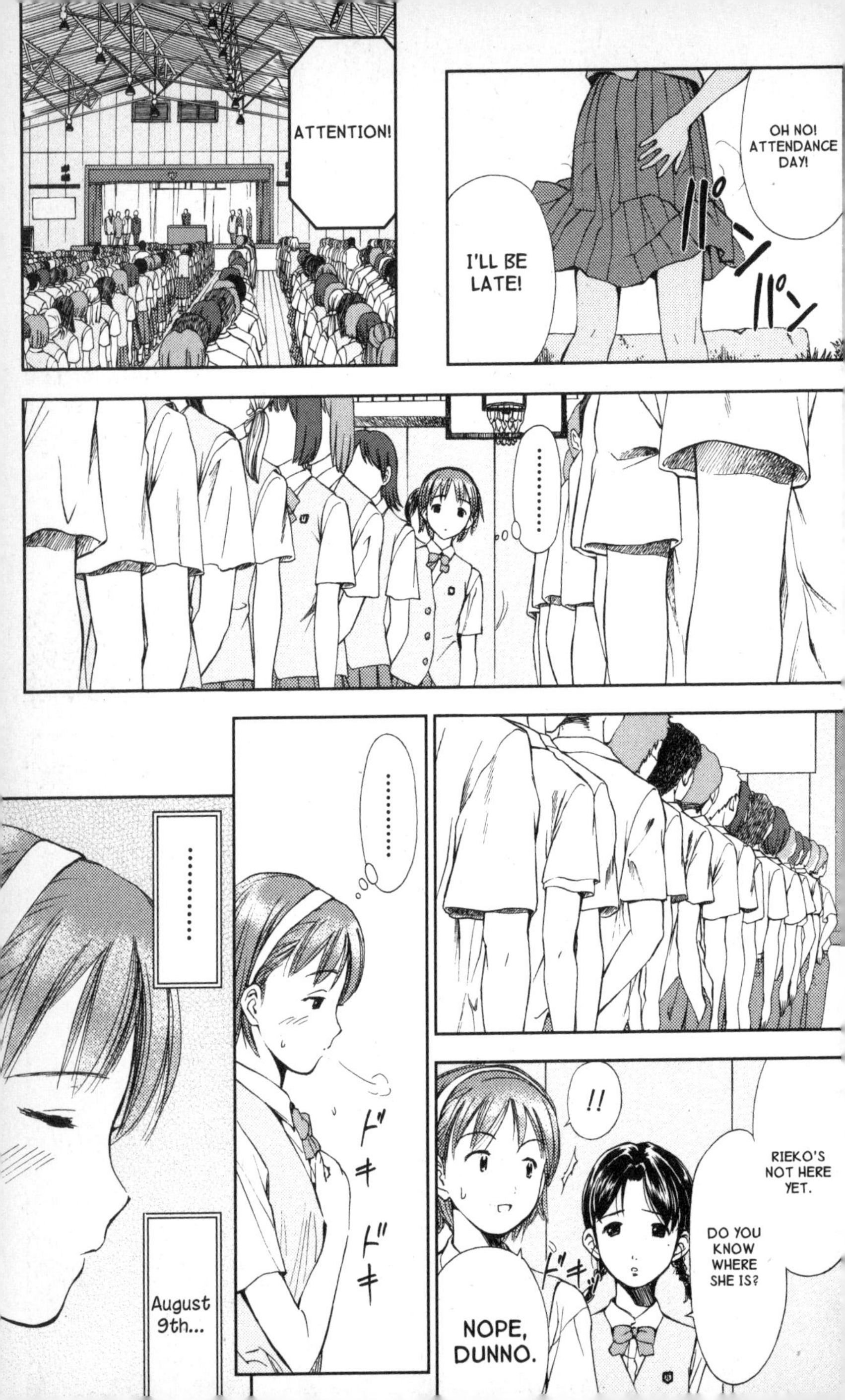
OH NO! ATTENDANCE DAY!
I'LL BE LATE!
パン
パン
ATTENTION!
....
RIEKO'S NOT HERE YET.
DO YOU KNOW WHERE SHE IS?
!!
ドキ
NOPE, DUNNO.
....
ドキ
ドキ
....
August 9th...

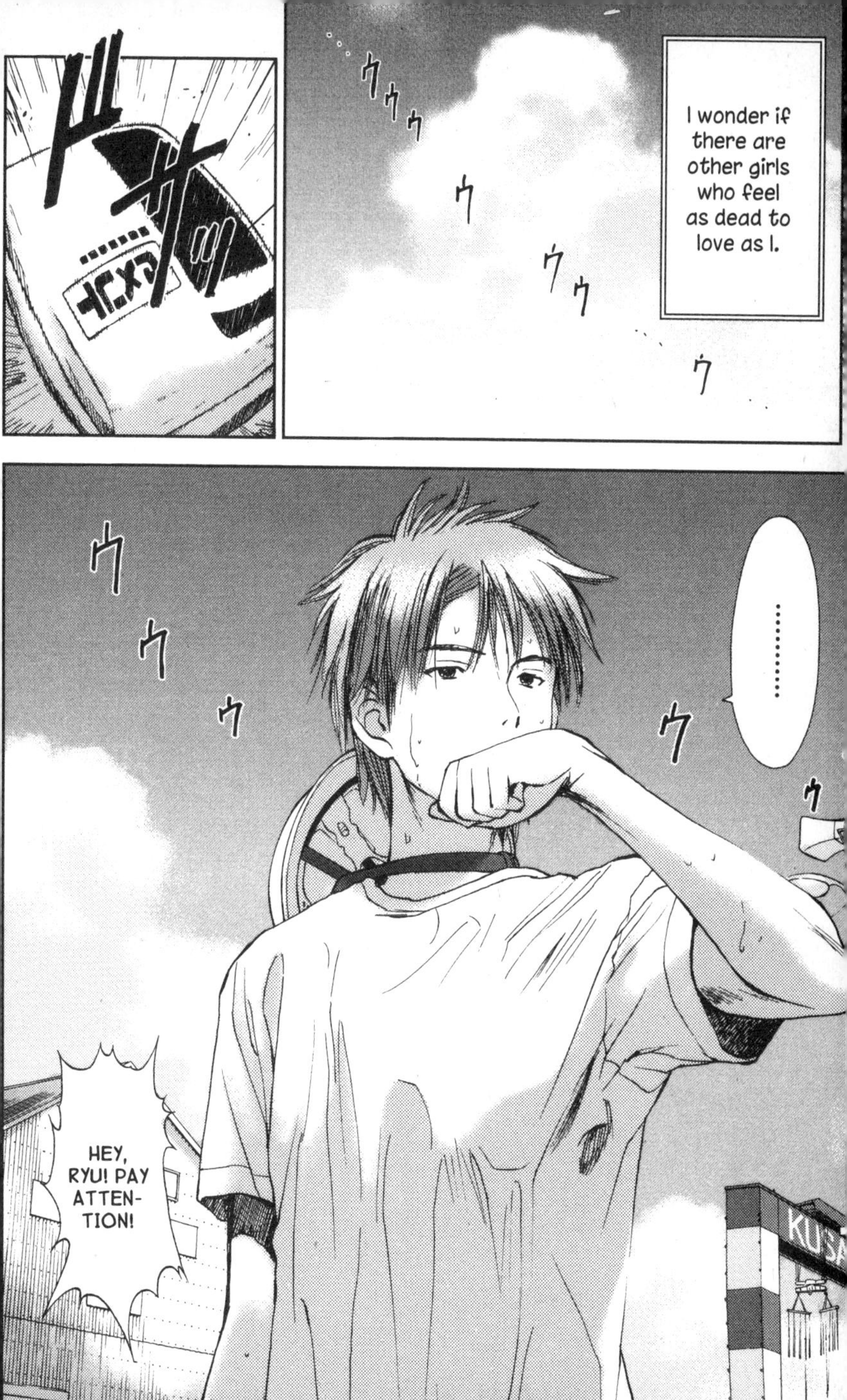
I wonder if there are other girls who feel as dead to love as I.
ウウウ
ウ
ウウ
ウ
ドサッ
……
ウ
ウ
ウ
ウ
ウ
HEY, RYU! PAY ATTEN- TION!

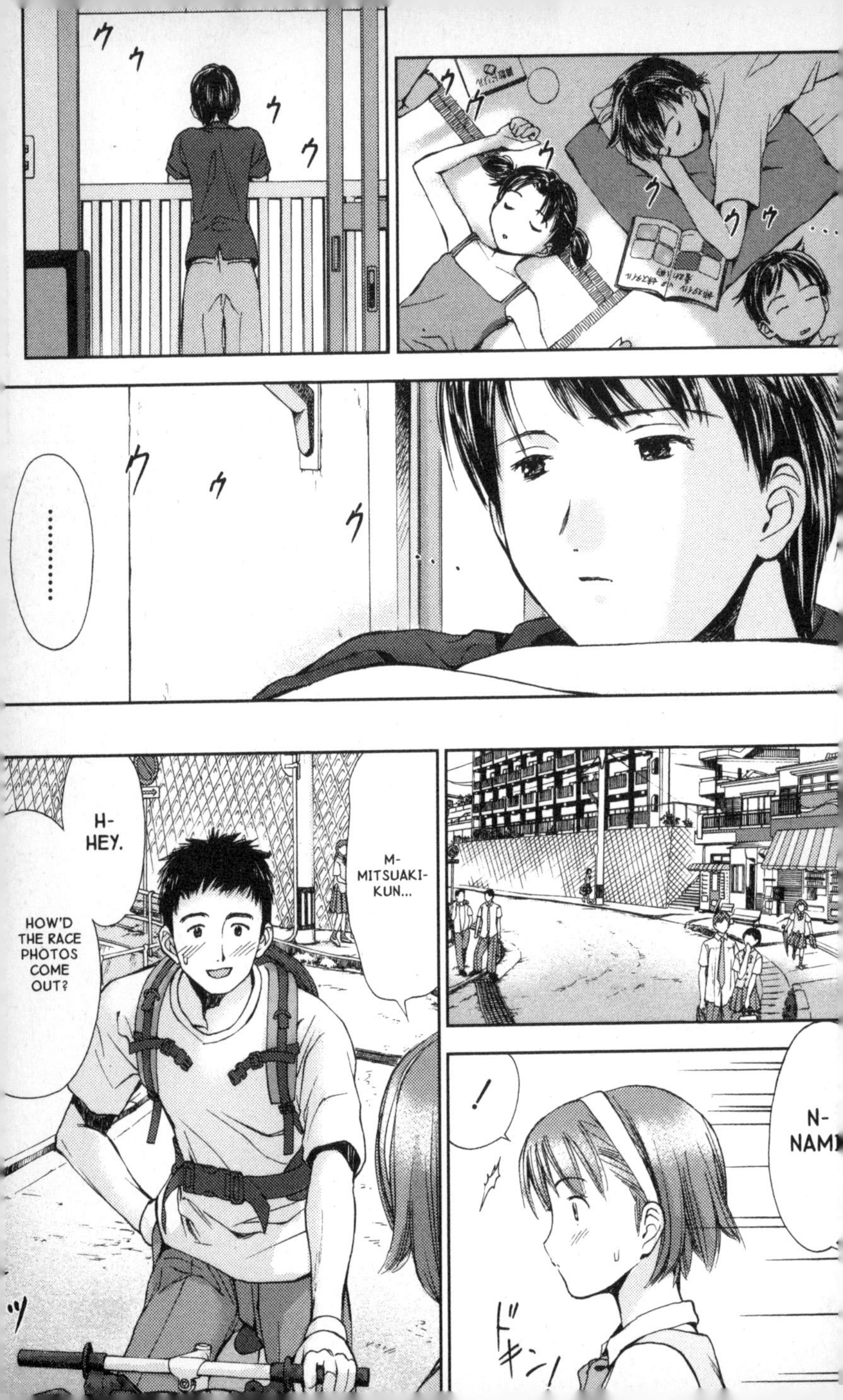
……
N- NAMI
!
ドキン!
M- MITSUAKI-KUN...
H- HEY.
HOW'D THE RACE PHOTOS COME OUT?

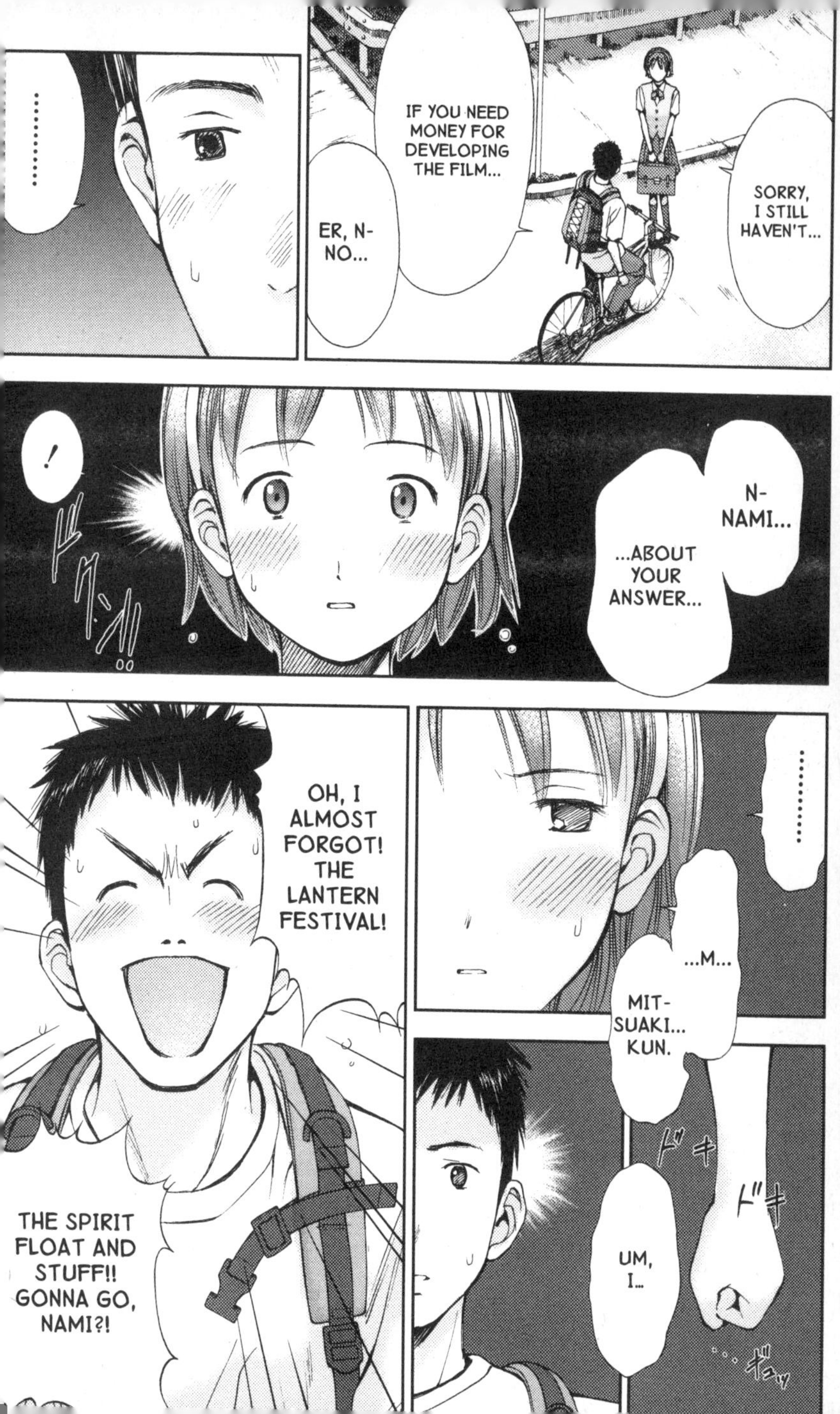
SORRY, I STILL HAVEN'T...
IF YOU NEED MONEY FOR DEVELOPING THE FILM...
ER, N-NO...
....
N-NAMI...
...ABOUT YOUR ANSWER...
!
ドクン!!
....
...M...
MIT-SUAKI... KUN.
ドキ
ドキ
UM, I...
ギュッ
OH, I ALMOST FORGOT! THE LANTERN FESTIVAL!
THE SPIRIT FLOAT AND STUFF!! GONNA GO, NAMI?!

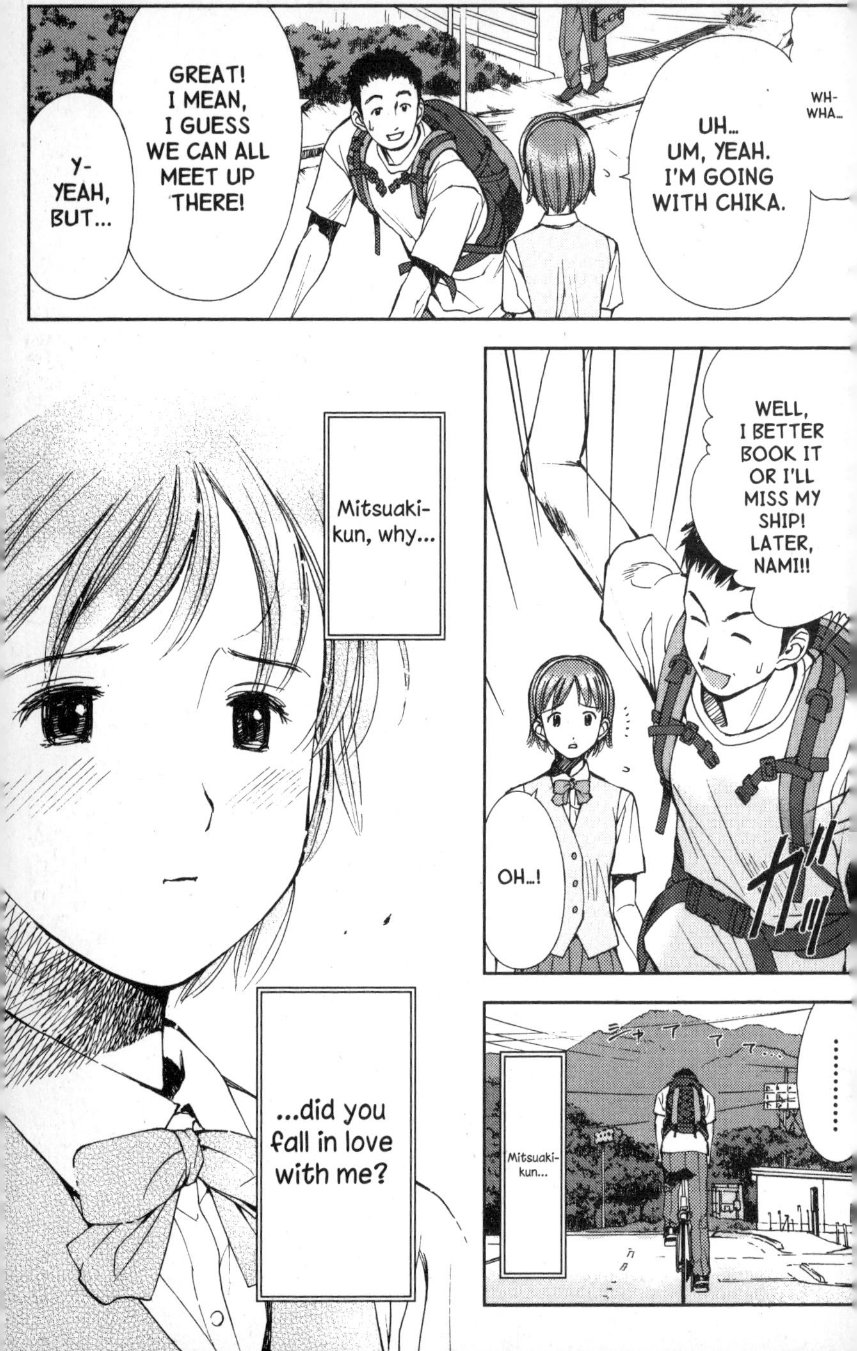
WH- WHA...
UH... UM, YEAH. I'M GOING WITH CHIKA.
GREAT! I MEAN, I GUESS WE CAN ALL MEET UP THERE!
Y- YEAH, BUT...
WELL, I BETTER BOOK IT OR I'LL MISS MY SHIP! LATER, NAMI!!
OH...!
....
Mitsuaki-kun...
Mitsuaki-kun, why...
...did you fall in love with me?

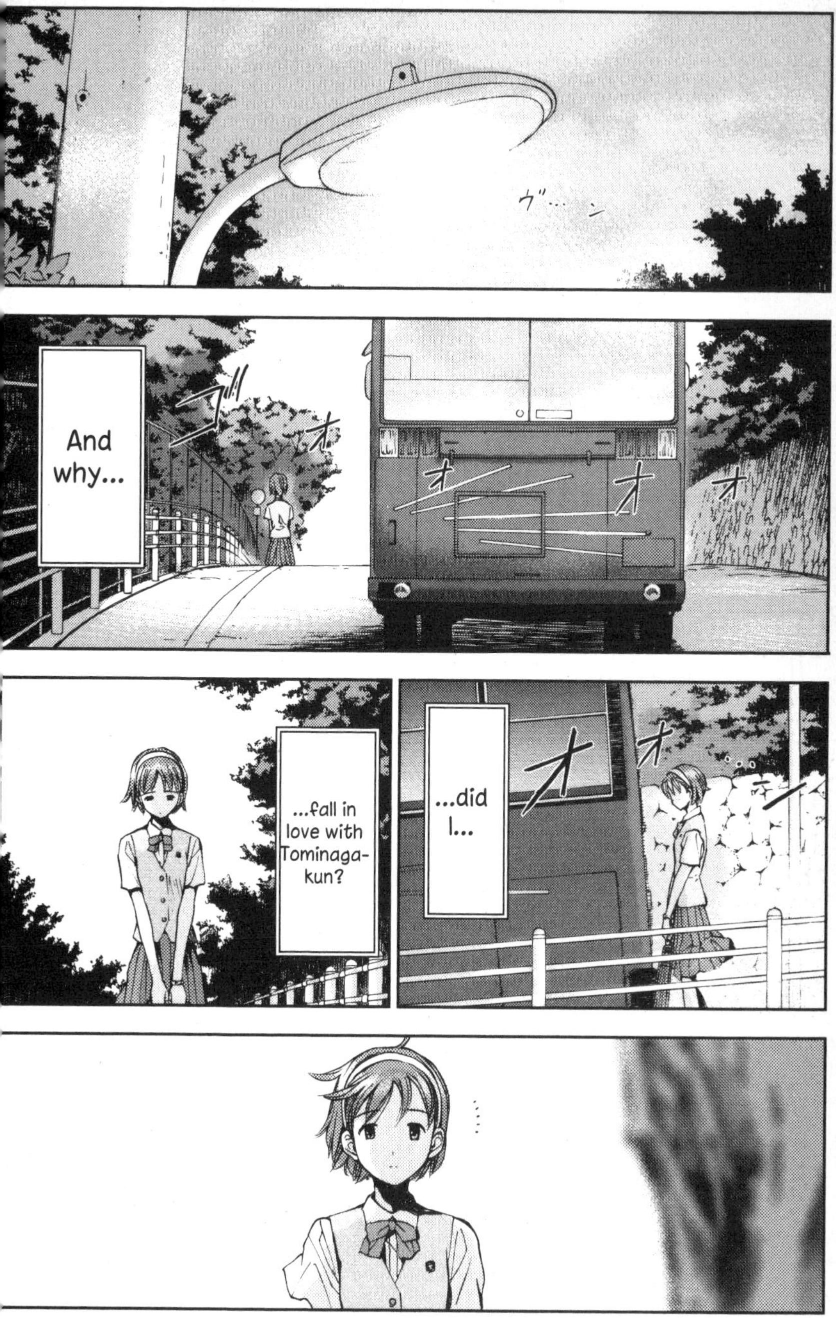
ヴ…ン
ゴォ
オ
オ
オ
オ
And why...
...did I...
オオ…ン
...fall in love with Tominaga-kun?
......

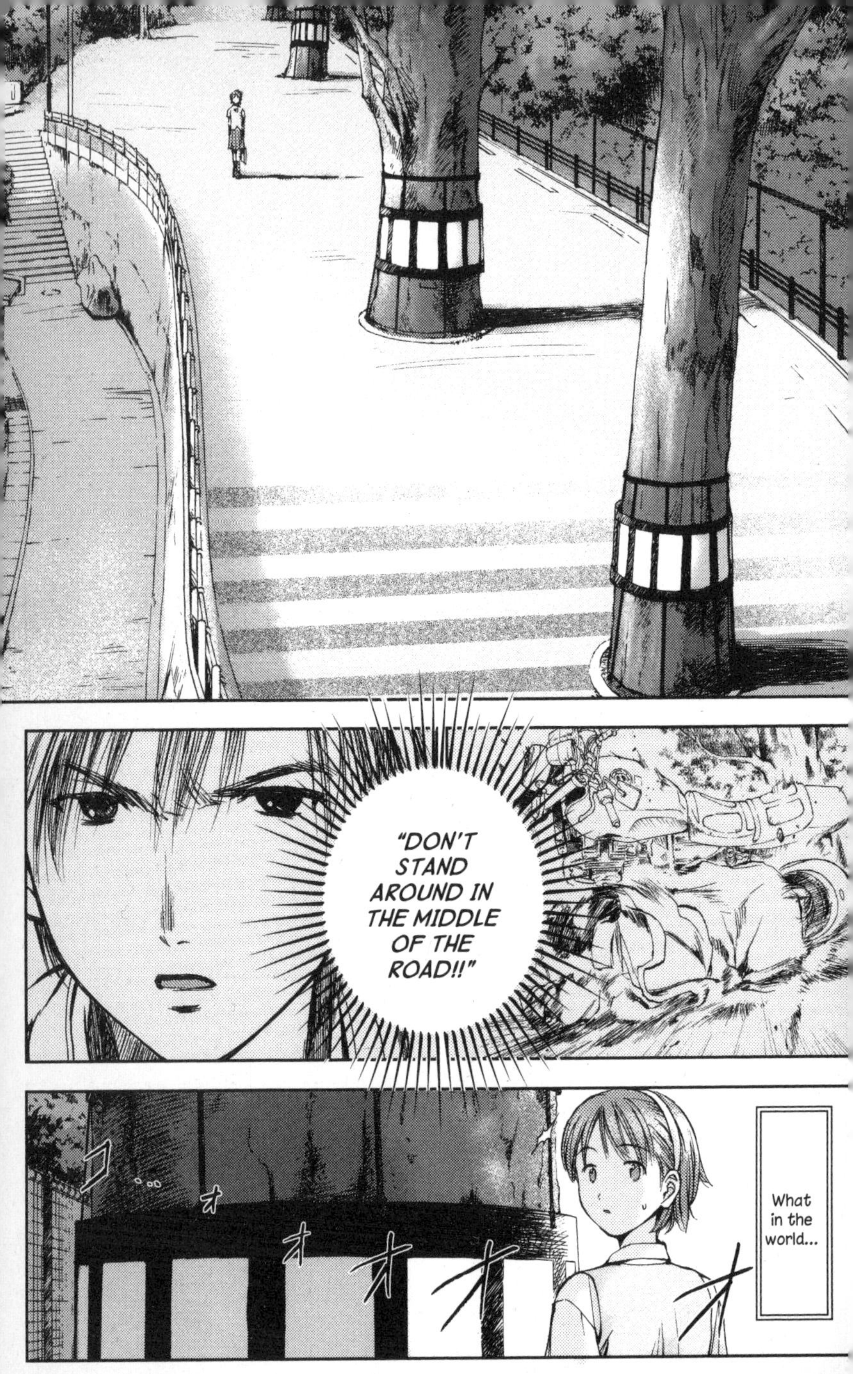
"DON'T STAND AROUND IN THE MIDDLE OF THE ROAD!!"
What in the world...

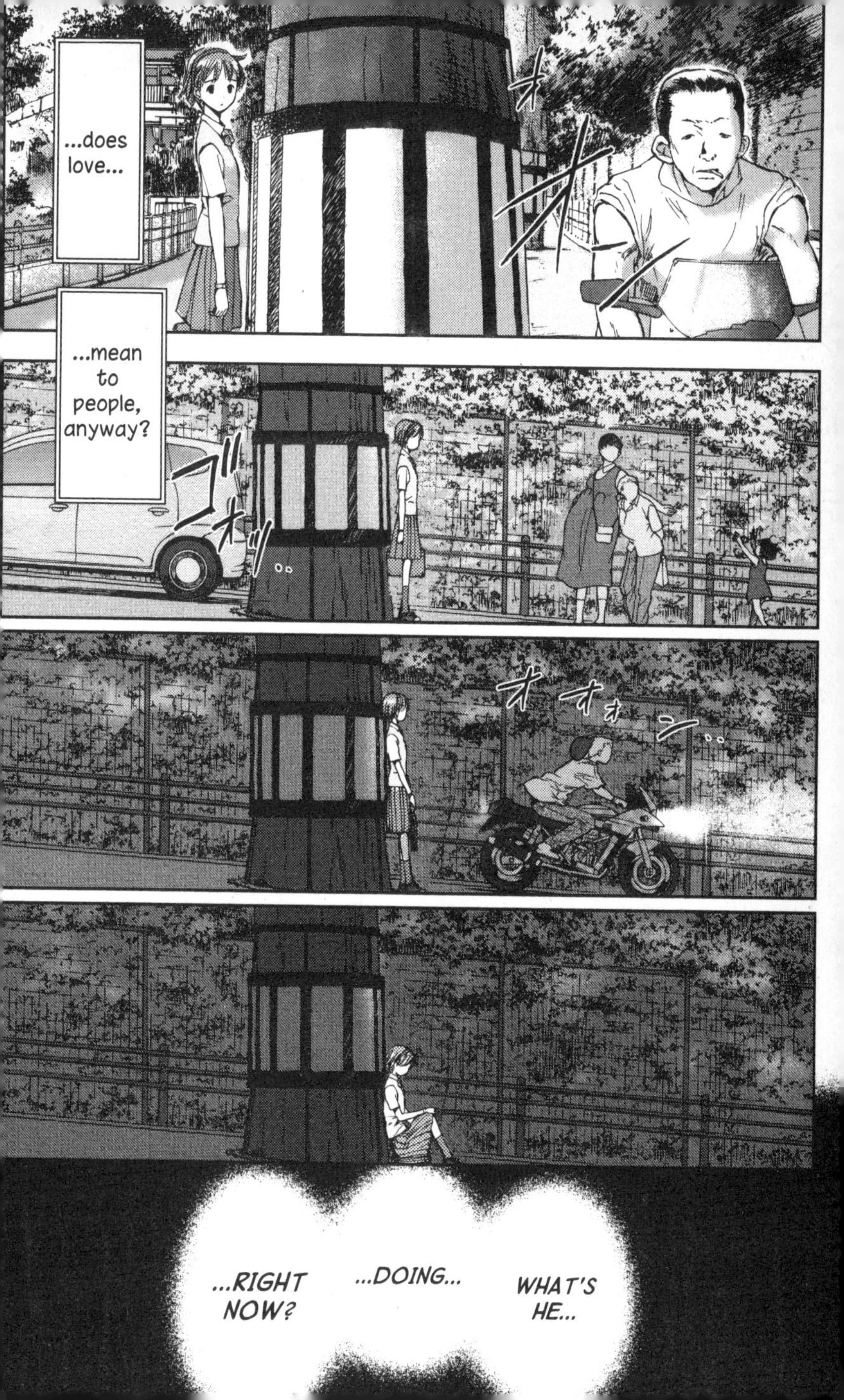
オォォ
...does love...
...mean to people, anyway?
ゴォッ
オォォン
WHAT'S HE...
...DOING...
...RIGHT NOW?

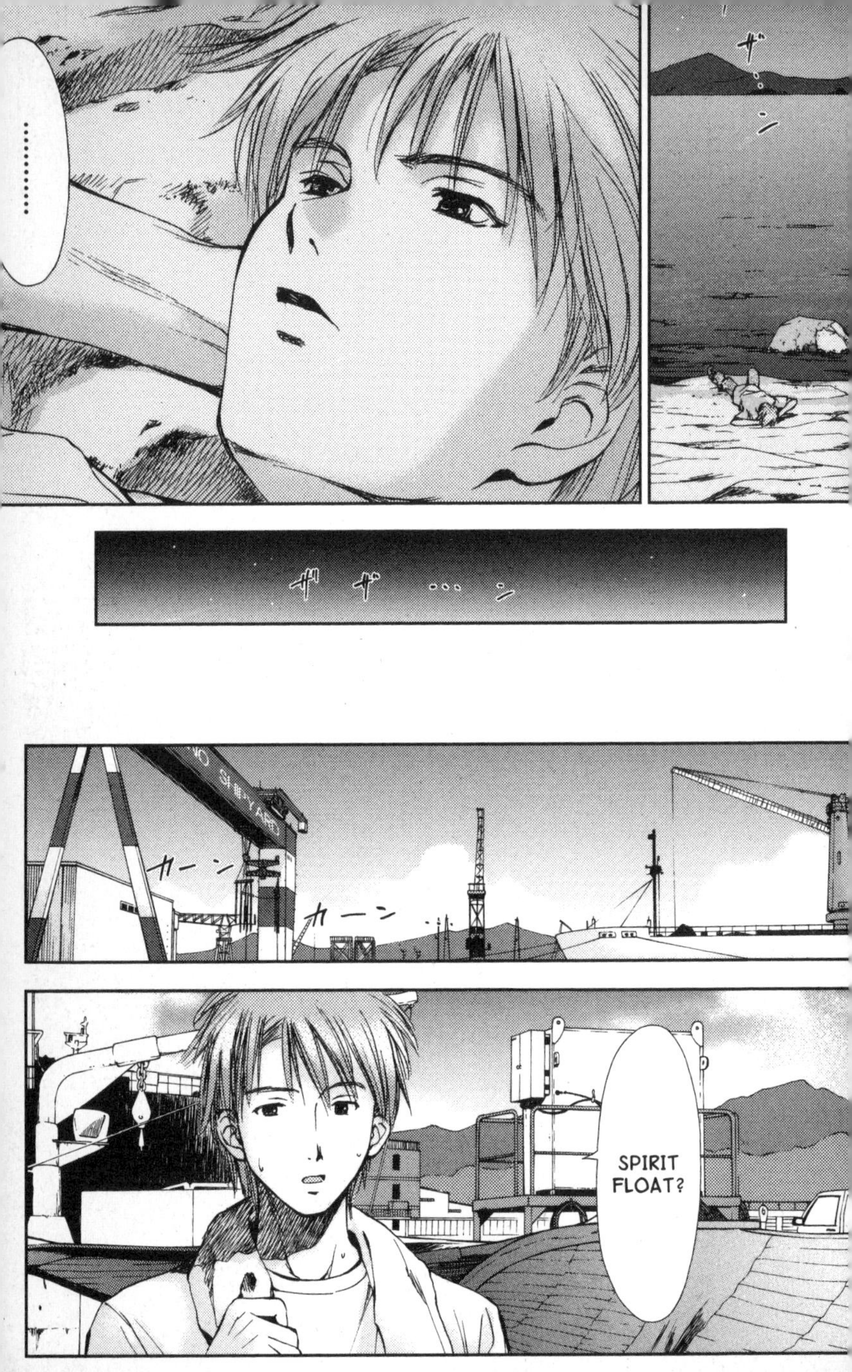
ザ…ン
……
ザザ…ン
カーン
カーン
SPIRIT FLOAT?

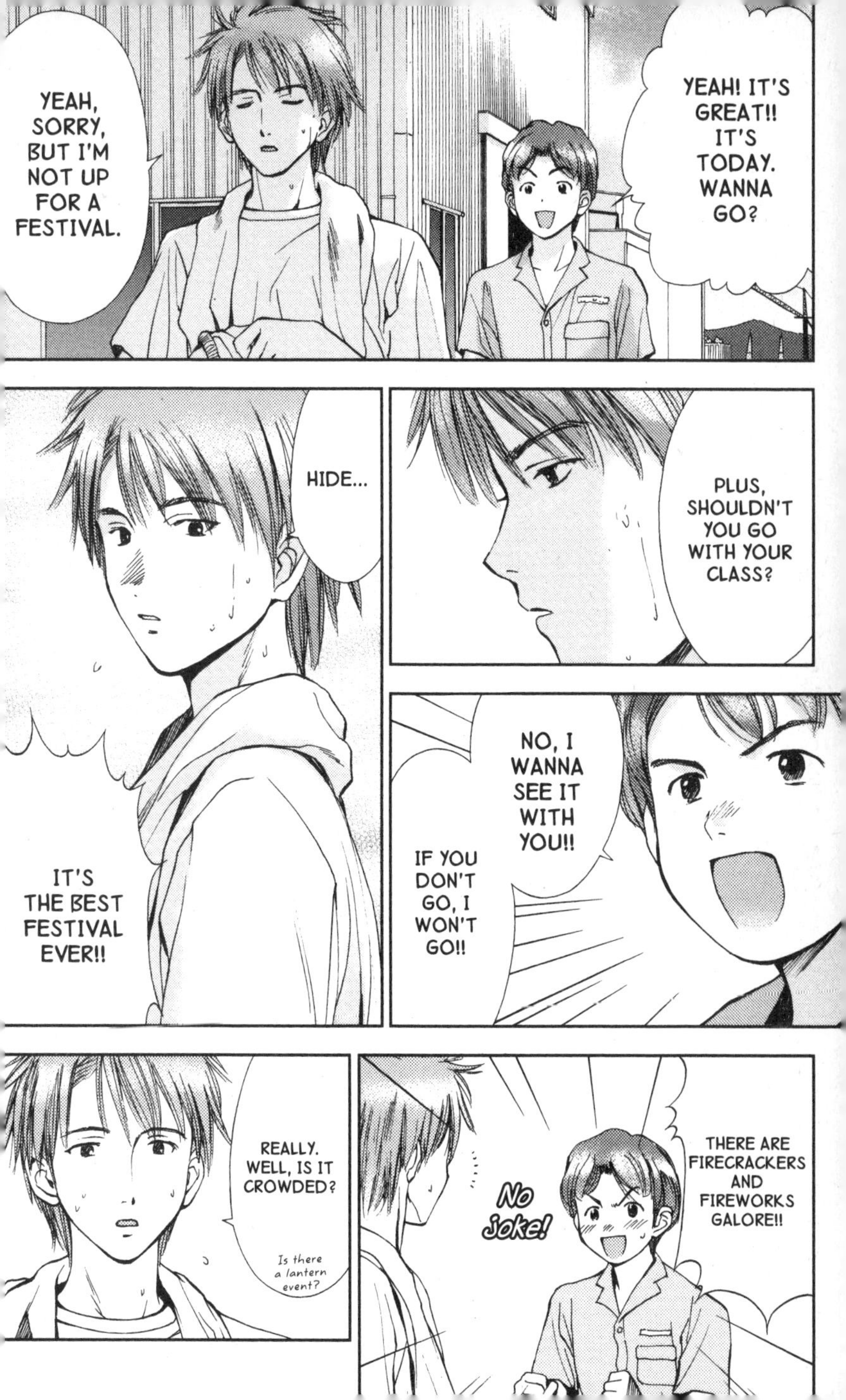
YEAH! IT'S GREAT!! IT'S TODAY. WANNA GO?
YEAH, SORRY, BUT I'M NOT UP FOR A FESTIVAL.
PLUS, SHOULDN'T YOU GO WITH YOUR CLASS?
NO, I WANNA SEE IT WITH YOU!!
IF YOU DON'T GO, I WON'T GO!!
HIDE...
IT'S THE BEST FESTIVAL EVER!!
THERE ARE FIRECRACKERS AND FIREWORKS GALORE!!
No joke!
REALLY. WELL, IS IT CROWDED?
Is there a lantern event?

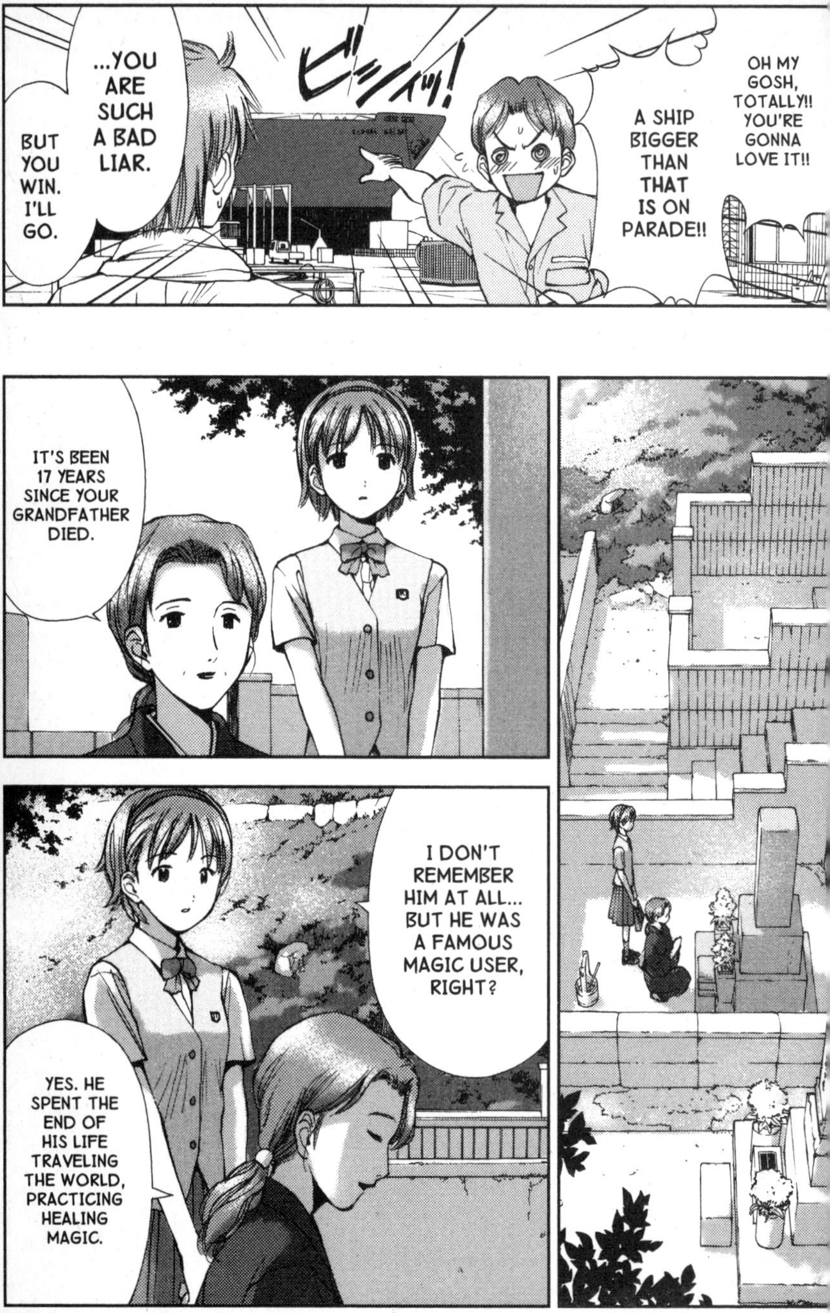
OH MY GOSH, TOTALLY!! YOU'RE GONNA LOVE IT!!
A SHIP BIGGER THAN THAT IS ON PARADE!!
ビシィッ!
...YOU ARE SUCH A BAD LIAR.
BUT YOU WIN. I'LL GO.
IT'S BEEN 17 YEARS SINCE YOUR GRANDFATHER DIED.
I DON'T REMEMBER HIM AT ALL... BUT HE WAS A FAMOUS MAGIC USER, RIGHT?
YES. HE SPENT THE END OF HIS LIFE TRAVELING THE WORLD, PRACTICING HEALING MAGIC.

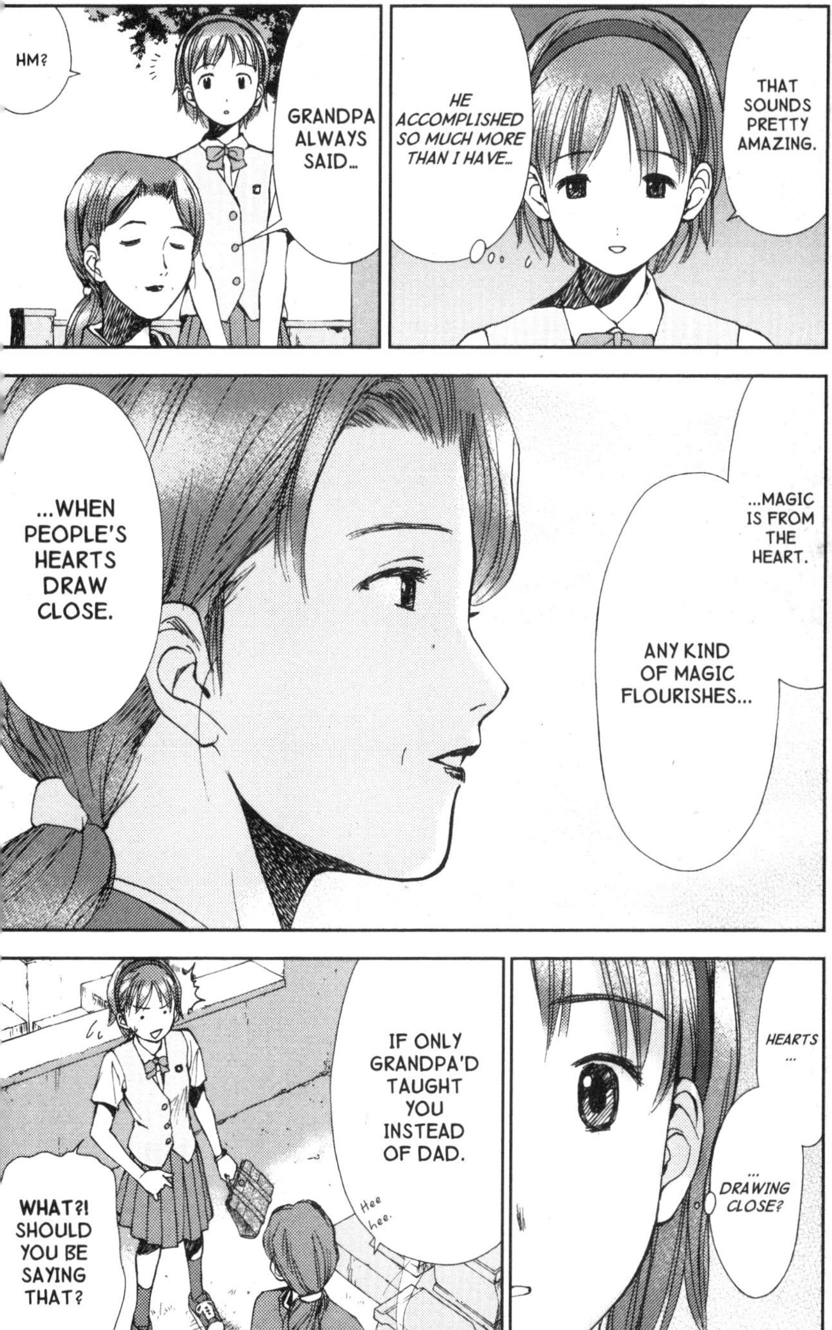
THAT SOUNDS PRETTY AMAZING.
HE ACCOMPLISHED SO MUCH MORE THAN I HAVE...
GRANDPA ALWAYS SAID...
HM?
...MAGIC IS FROM THE HEART.
ANY KIND OF MAGIC FLOURISHES...
...WHEN PEOPLE'S HEARTS DRAW CLOSE.
HEARTS ...
... DRAWING CLOSE?
IF ONLY GRANDPA'D TAUGHT YOU INSTEAD OF DAD.
Hee hee.
WHAT?! SHOULD YOU BE SAYING THAT?

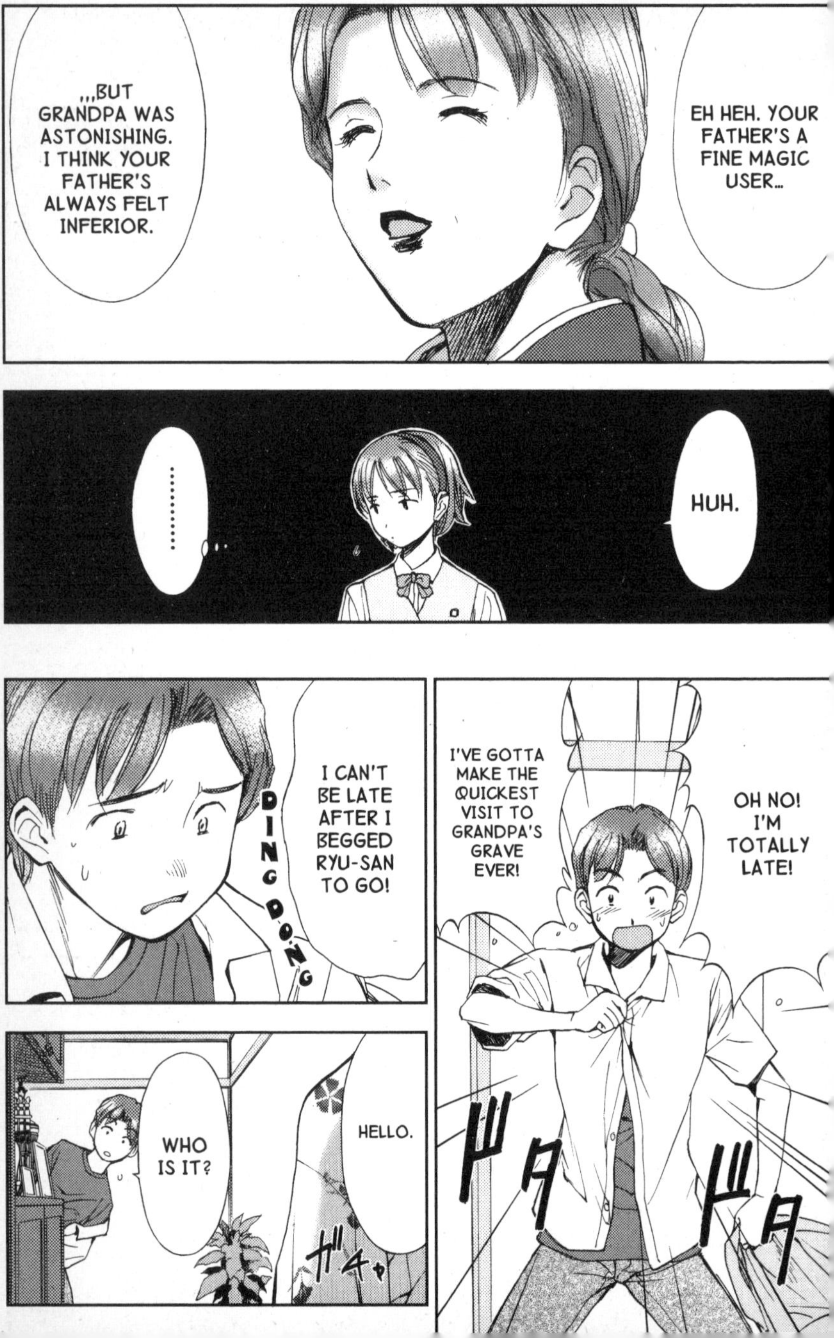
EH HEH. YOUR FATHER'S A FINE MAGIC USER...
...BUT GRANDPA WAS ASTONISHING. I THINK YOUR FATHER'S ALWAYS FELT INFERIOR.
HUH.
....
OH NO! I'M TOTALLY LATE!
I'VE GOTTA MAKE THE QUICKEST VISIT TO GRANDPA'S GRAVE EVER!
ドタ
ドタ
I CAN'T BE LATE AFTER I BEGGED RYU-SAN TO GO!
DING DONG
HELLO.
WHO IS IT?
ガチャ

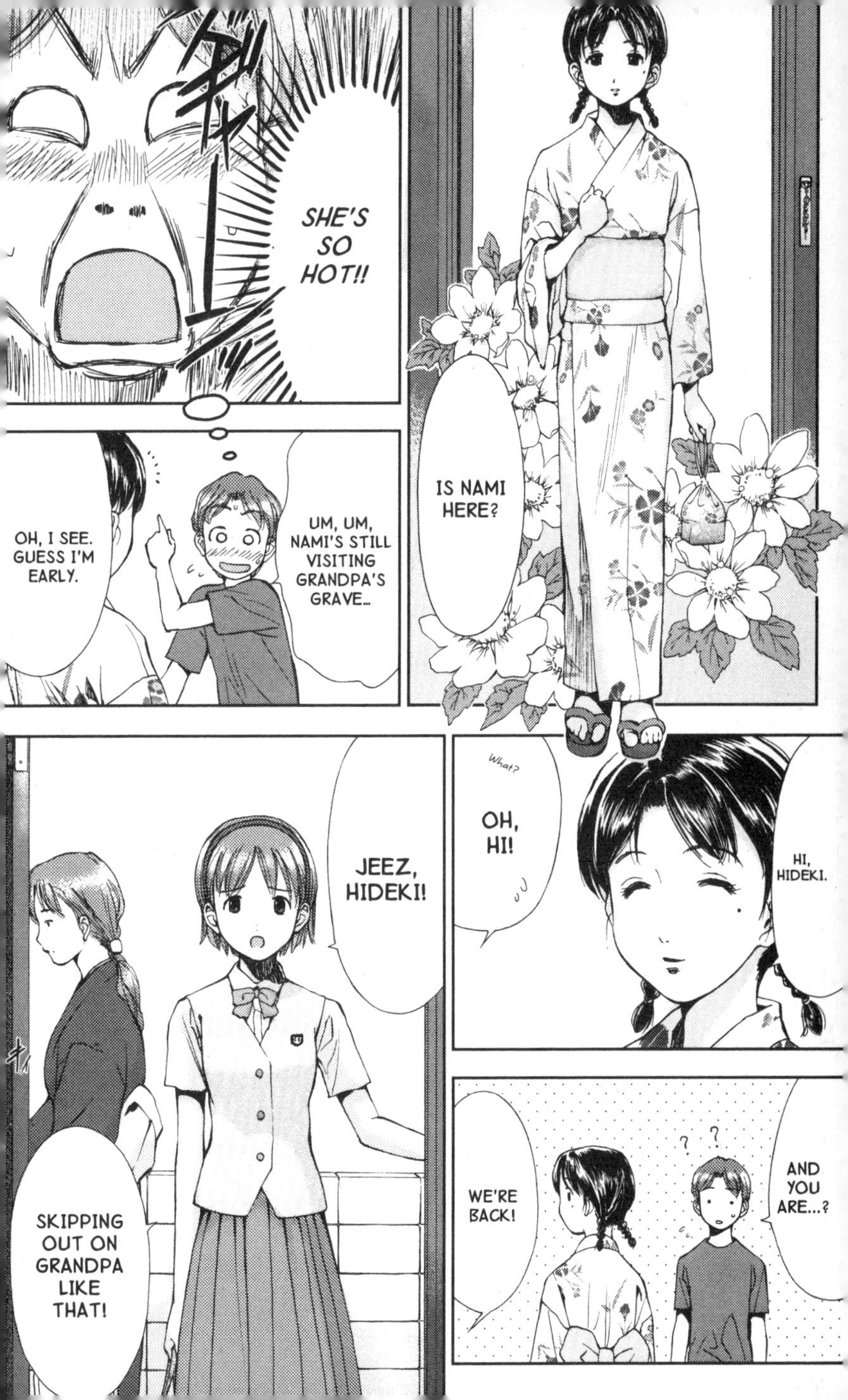
IS NAMI HERE?
SHE'S SO HOT!!
UM, UM, NAMI'S STILL VISITING GRANDPA'S GRAVE...
OH, I SEE. GUESS I'M EARLY.
HI, HIDEKI.
What?
OH, HI!
AND YOU ARE...?
WE'RE BACK!
JEEZ, HIDEKI!
SKIPPING OUT ON GRANDPA LIKE THAT!

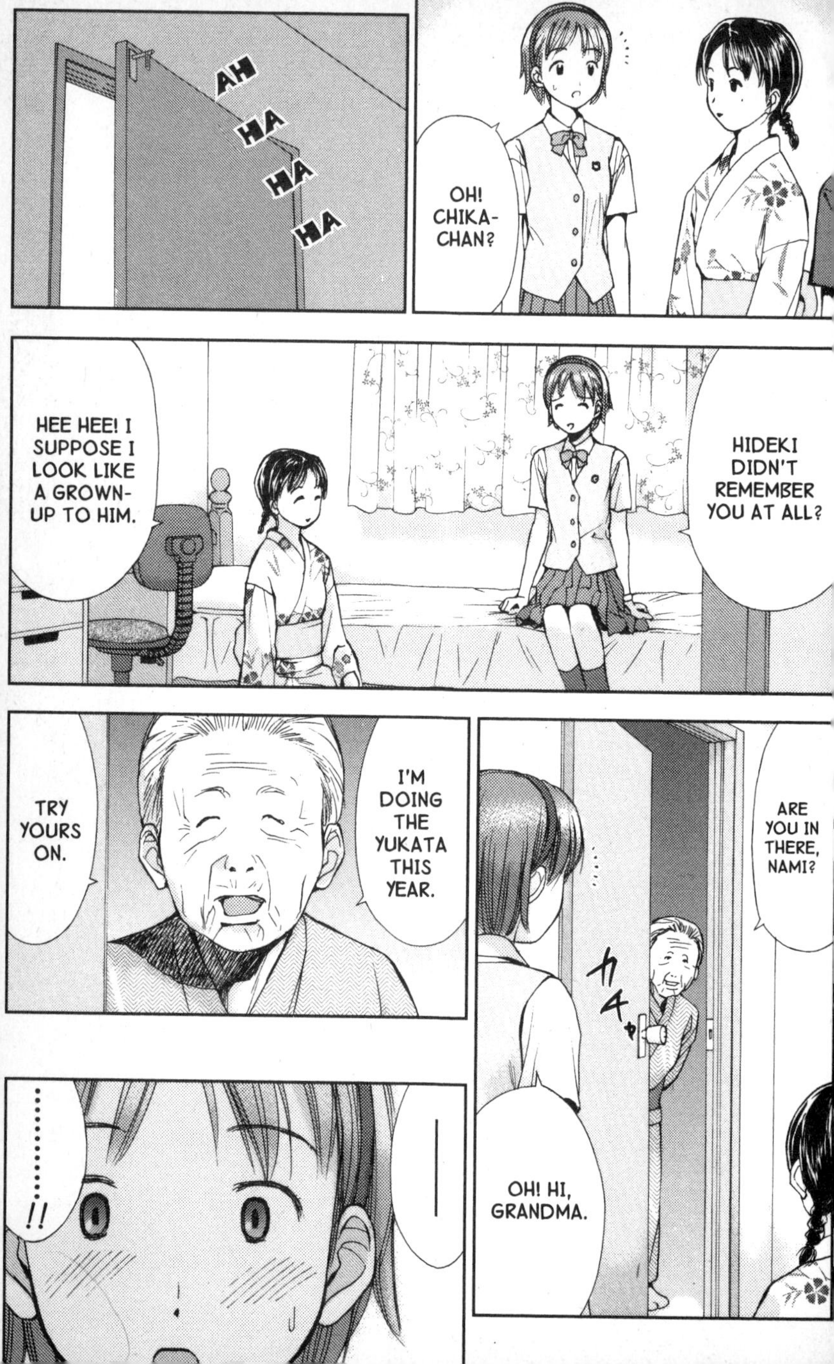
OH! CHIKA-CHAN?
AH HA HA HA
HIDEKI DIDN'T REMEMBER YOU AT ALL?
HEE HEE! I SUPPOSE I LOOK LIKE A GROWN-UP TO HIM.
ARE YOU IN THERE, NAMI?
カチャ
OH! HI, GRANDMA.
I'M DOING THE YUKATA THIS YEAR.
TRY YOURS ON.
—
......!!

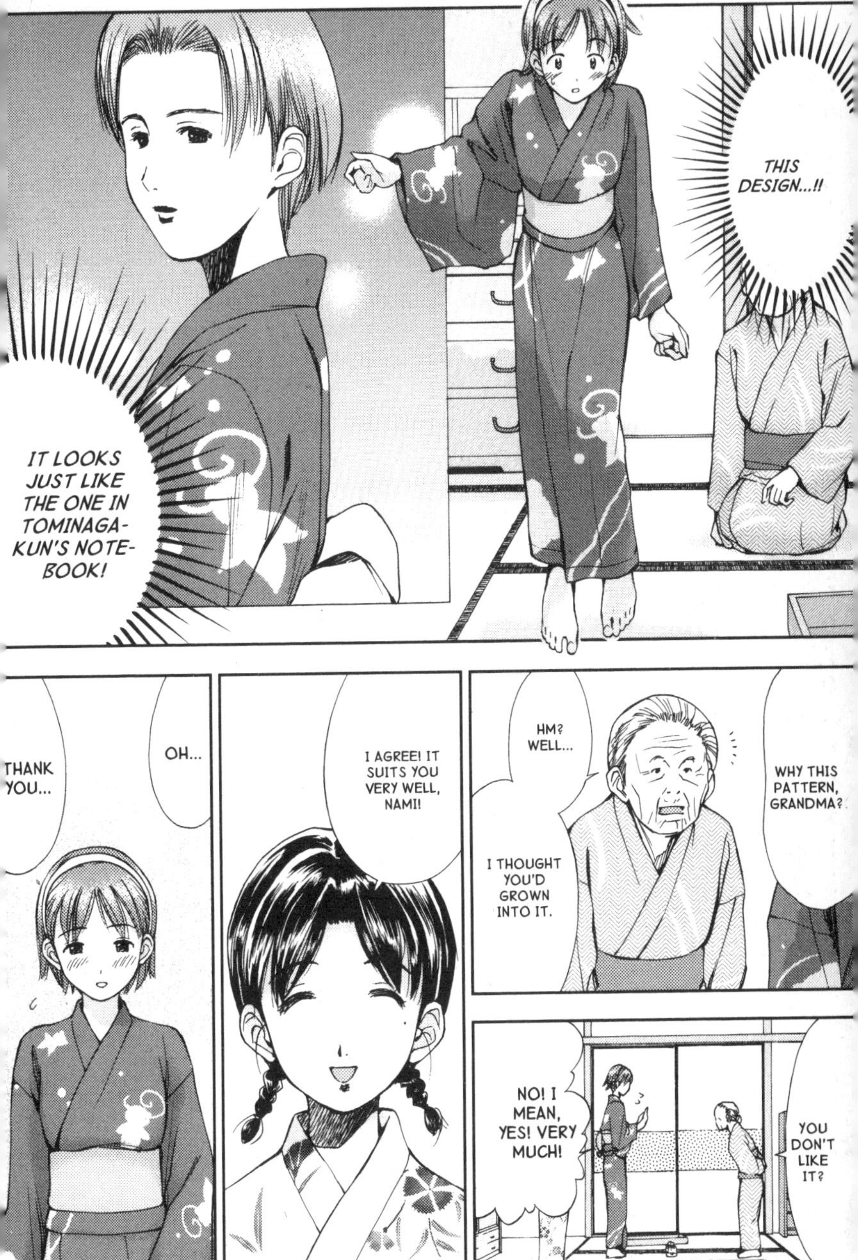
THIS DESIGN...!!
IT LOOKS JUST LIKE THE ONE IN TOMINAGA-KUN'S NOTE-BOOK!
WHY THIS PATTERN, GRANDMA?
HM? WELL...
I THOUGHT YOU'D GROWN INTO IT.
YOU DON'T LIKE IT?
NO! I MEAN, YES! VERY MUCH!
I AGREE! IT SUITS YOU VERY WELL, NAMI!
OH...
THANK YOU...

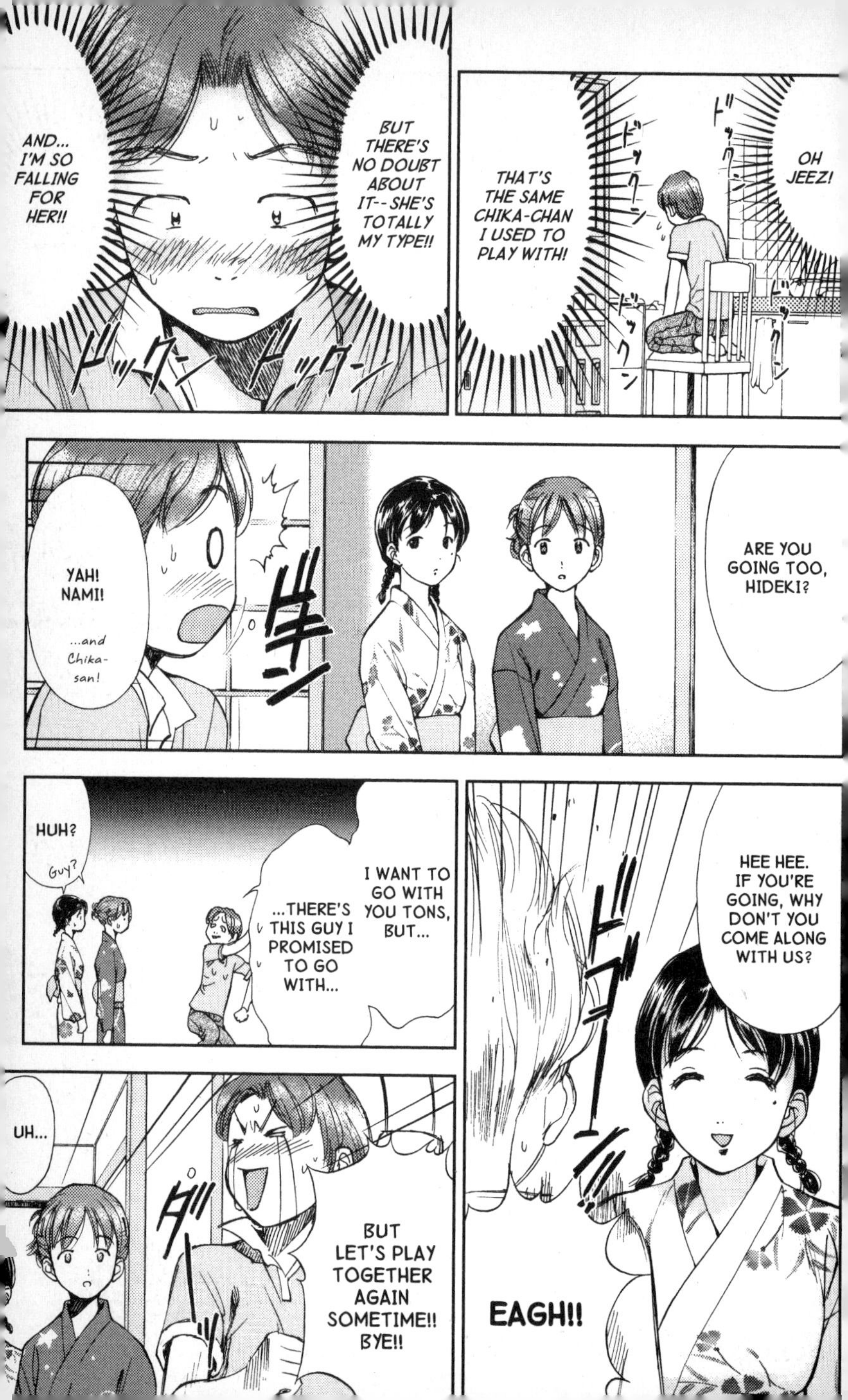
OH JEEZ!
THAT'S THE SAME CHIKA-CHAN I USED TO PLAY WITH!
BUT THERE'S NO DOUBT ABOUT IT-- SHE'S TOTALLY MY TYPE!!
AND... I'M SO FALLING FOR HER!!
ARE YOU GOING TOO, HIDEKI?
YAH! NAMI!
...and Chika-san!
HEE HEE. IF YOU'RE GOING, WHY DON'T YOU COME ALONG WITH US?
EAGH!!
I WANT TO GO WITH YOU TONS, BUT...
...THERE'S THIS GUY I PROMISED TO GO WITH...
HUH?
Guy?
BUT LET'S PLAY TOGETHER AGAIN SOMETIME!! BYE!!
UH...

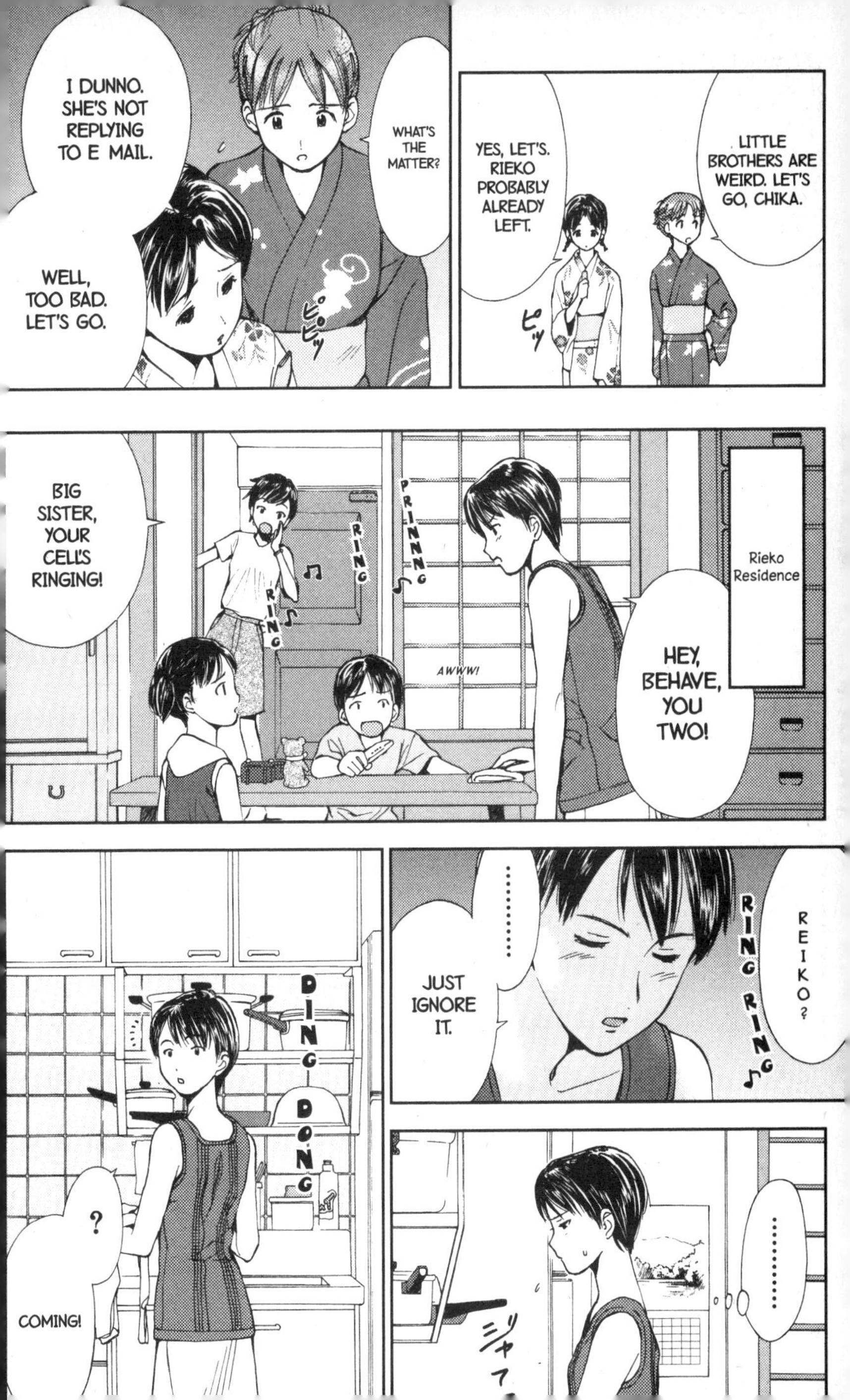

LITTLE BROTHERS ARE WEIRD. LET'S GO, CHIKA.
YES, LET'S. RIEKO PROBABLY ALREADY LEFT.
ピッ
WHAT'S THE MATTER?
ピッピッ
I DUNNO. SHE'S NOT REPLYING TO E MAIL.
WELL, TOO BAD. LET'S GO.
Rieko Residence
HEY, BEHAVE, YOU TWO!
PRINNNG
RING
AWWW!
RING
BIG SISTER, YOUR CELL'S RINGING!
REIKO?
RING RING
......
JUST IGNORE IT.
......
シャア
DING DONG
?
COMING!

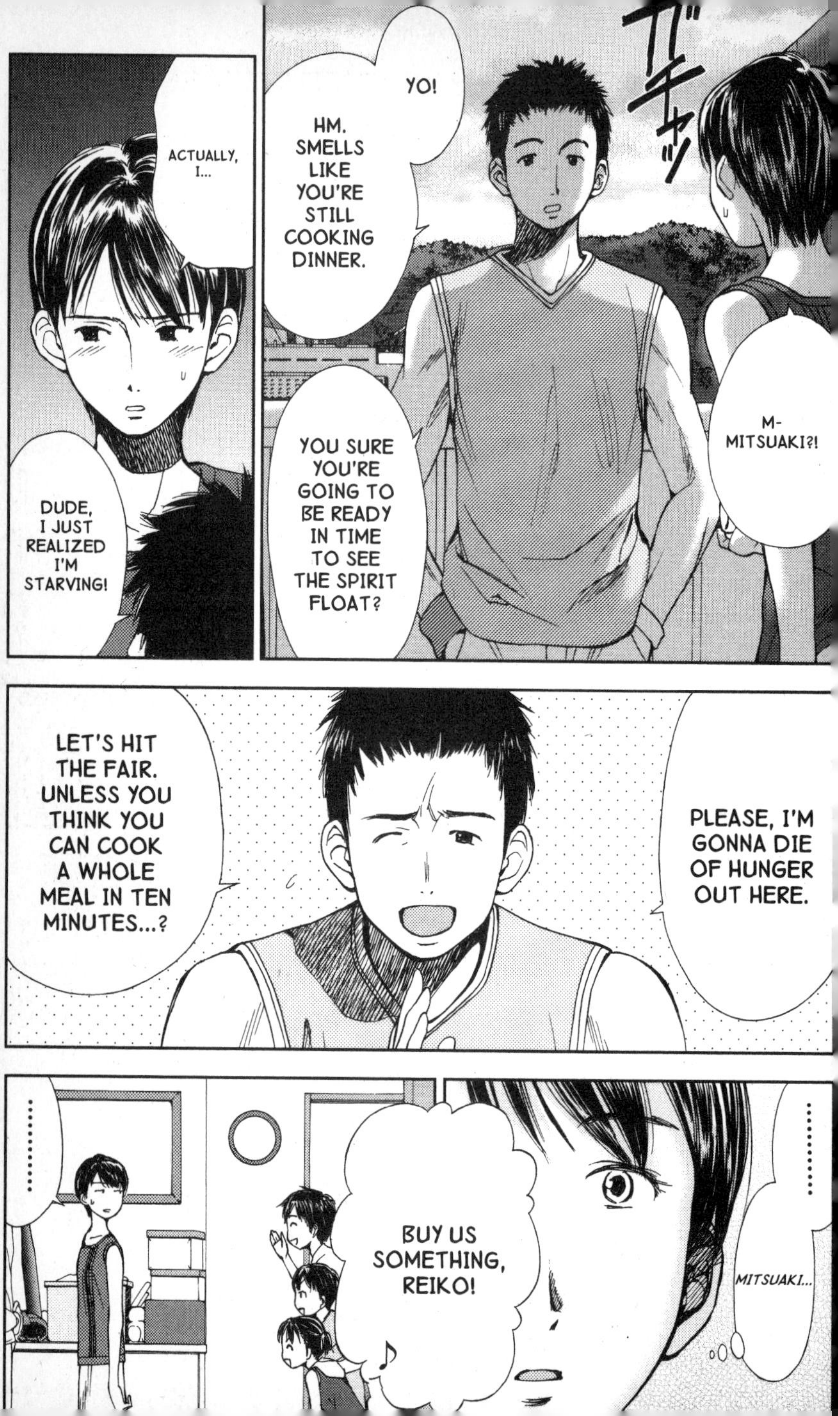
ガチャッ
M-MITSUAKI?!
YO!
HM. SMELLS LIKE YOU'RE STILL COOKING DINNER.
YOU SURE YOU'RE GOING TO BE READY IN TIME TO SEE THE SPIRIT FLOAT?
ACTUALLY, I...
DUDE, I JUST REALIZED I'M STARVING!
PLEASE, I'M GONNA DIE OF HUNGER OUT HERE.
LET'S HIT THE FAIR. UNLESS YOU THINK YOU CAN COOK A WHOLE MEAL IN TEN MINUTES...?
....
MITSUAKI...
BUY US SOMETHING, REIKO! ♪
....

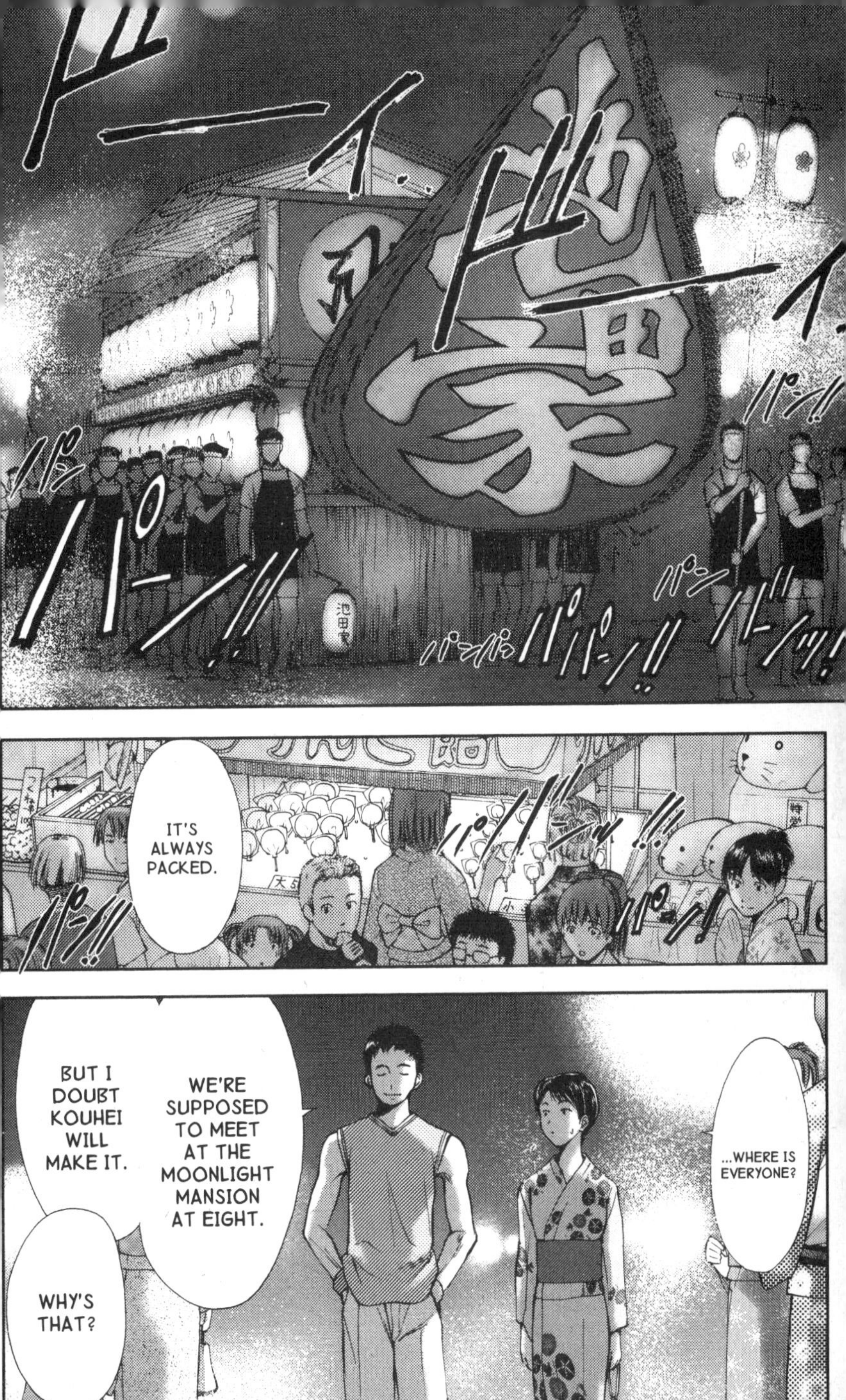
IT'S ALWAYS PACKED.
...WHERE IS EVERYONE?
WE'RE SUPPOSED TO MEET AT THE MOONLIGHT MANSION AT EIGHT.
BUT I DOUBT KOUHEI WILL MAKE IT.
WHY'S THAT?

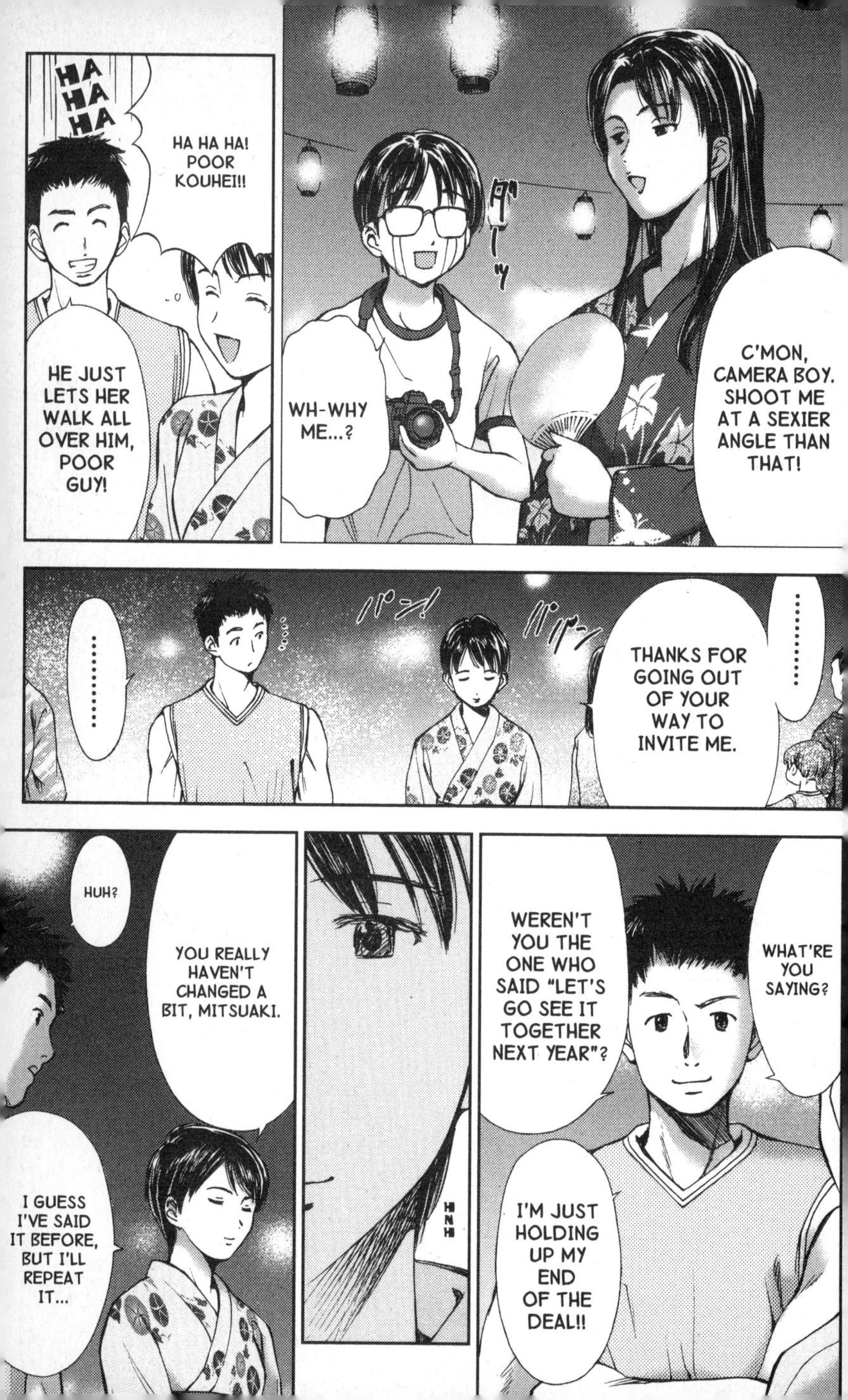
C'MON, CAMERA BOY. SHOOT ME AT A SEXIER ANGLE THAN THAT!
WH-WHY ME...?
HA HA HA
HA HA HA! POOR KOUHEI!!
HE JUST LETS HER WALK ALL OVER HIM, POOR GUY!
......
THANKS FOR GOING OUT OF YOUR WAY TO INVITE ME.
......
WHAT'RE YOU SAYING?
WEREN'T YOU THE ONE WHO SAID "LET'S GO SEE IT TOGETHER NEXT YEAR"?
I'M JUST HOLDING UP MY END OF THE DEAL!!
HNH
HUH?
YOU REALLY HAVEN'T CHANGED A BIT, MITSUAKI.
I GUESS I'VE SAID IT BEFORE, BUT I'LL REPEAT IT...

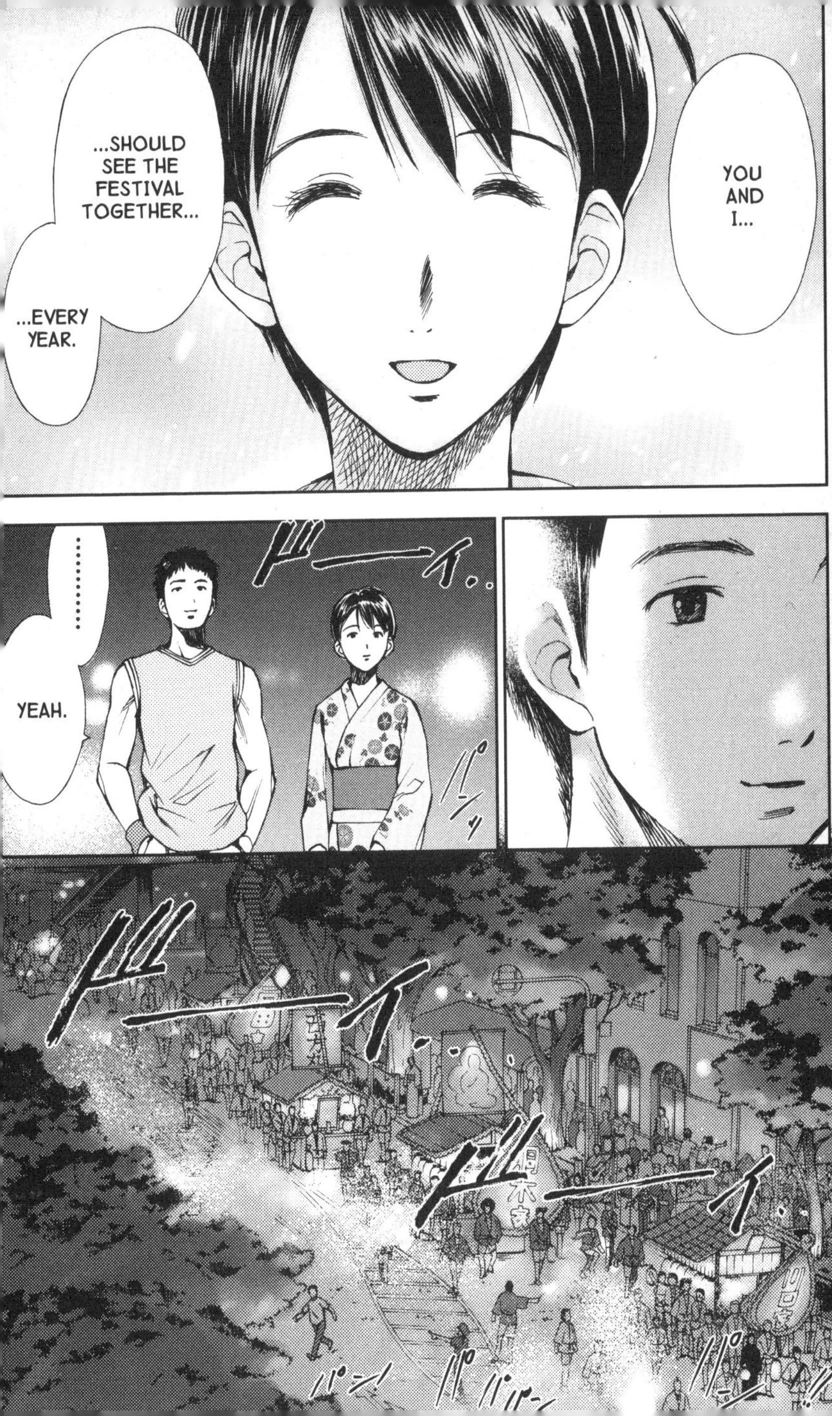
YOU AND I...
...SHOULD SEE THE FESTIVAL TOGETHER...
...EVERY YEAR.
....
YEAH.

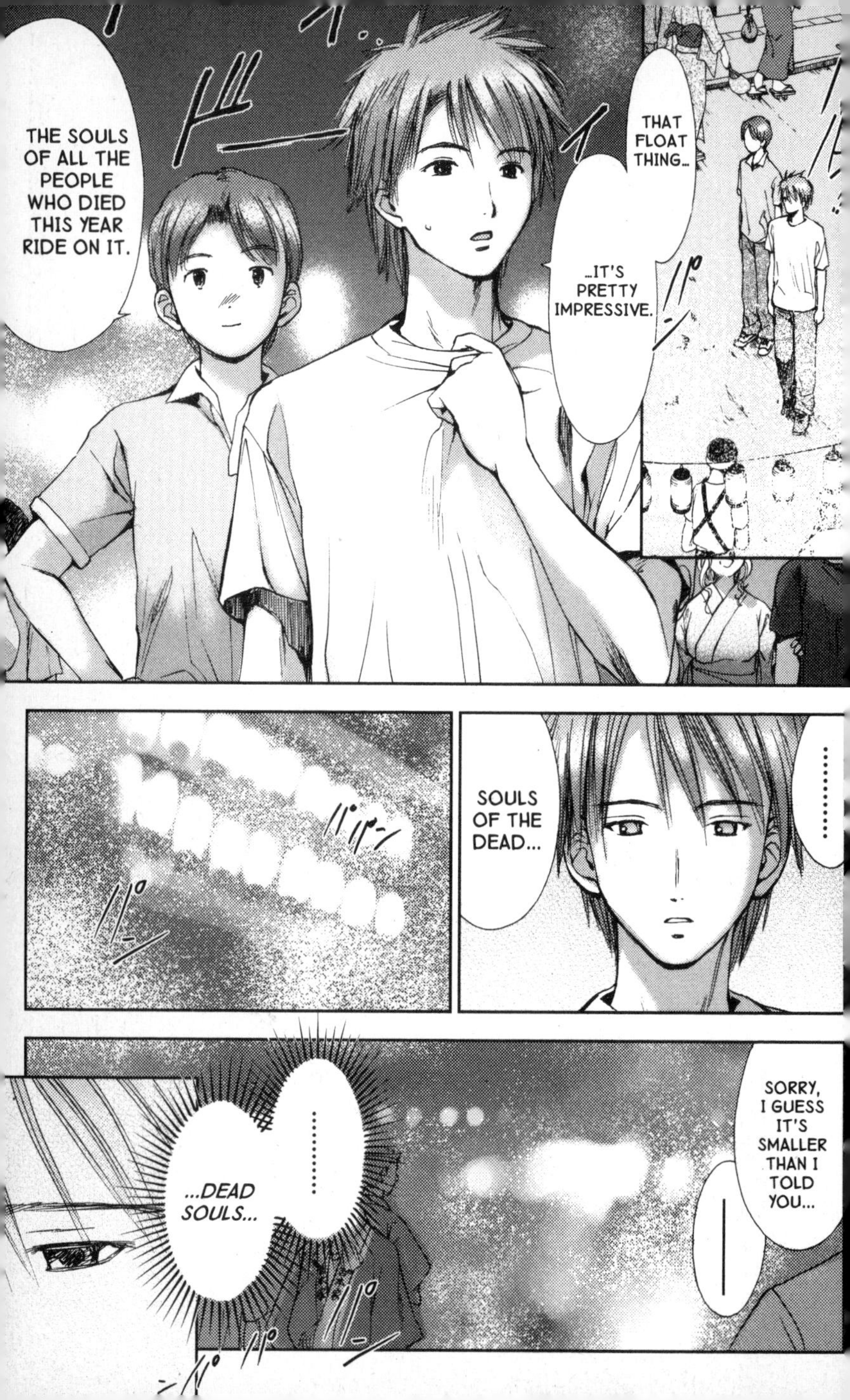
THAT FLOAT THING...
...IT'S PRETTY IMPRESSIVE.
THE SOULS OF ALL THE PEOPLE WHO DIED THIS YEAR RIDE ON IT.
......
SOULS OF THE DEAD...
SORRY, I GUESS IT'S SMALLER THAN I TOLD YOU...
—
......
...DEAD SOULS...

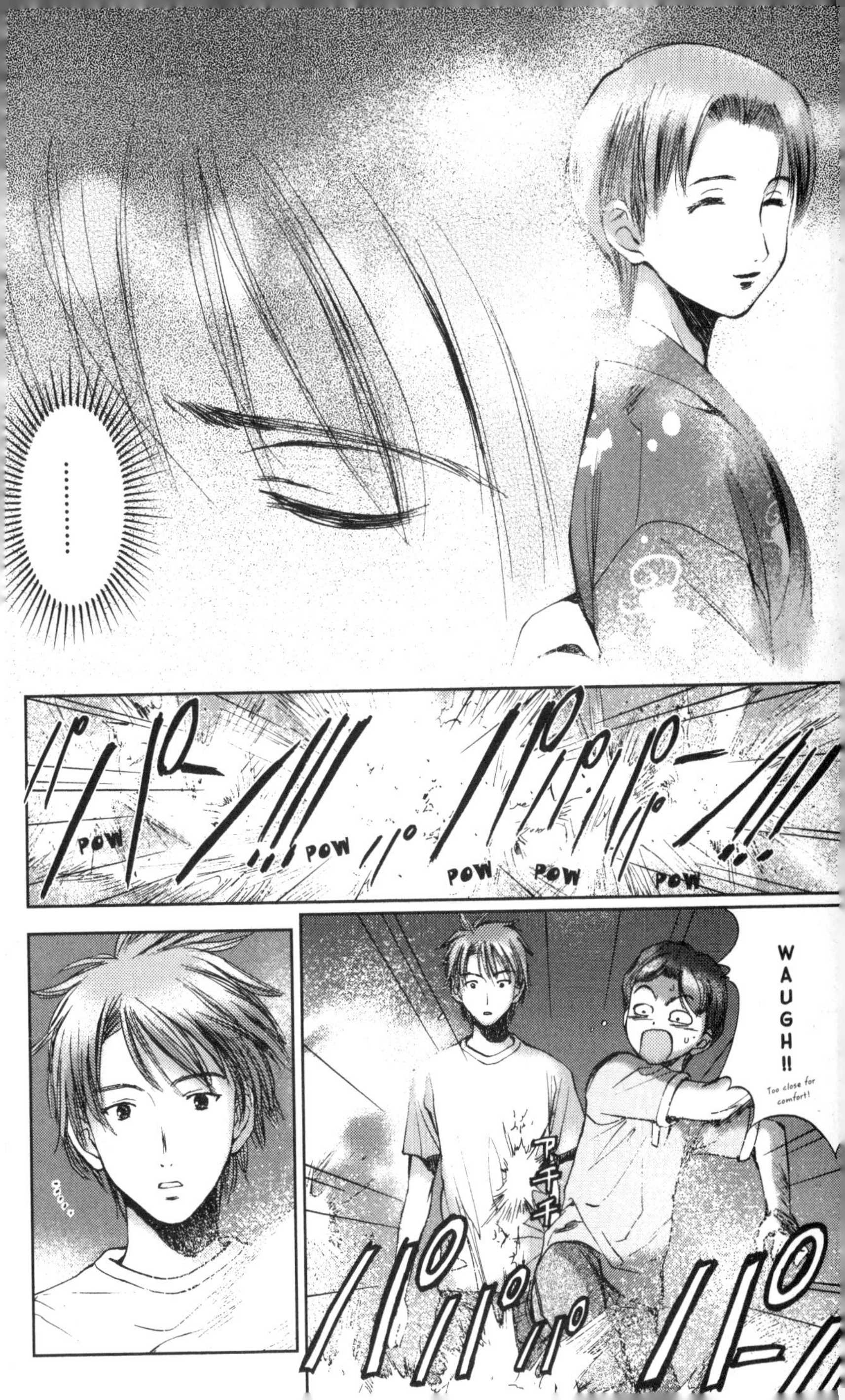
......
パン!!
パパパーン!!
POW
POW
POW
POW
POW
WAUGH!!
Too close for comfort!
アチチ
パパパ
パパ

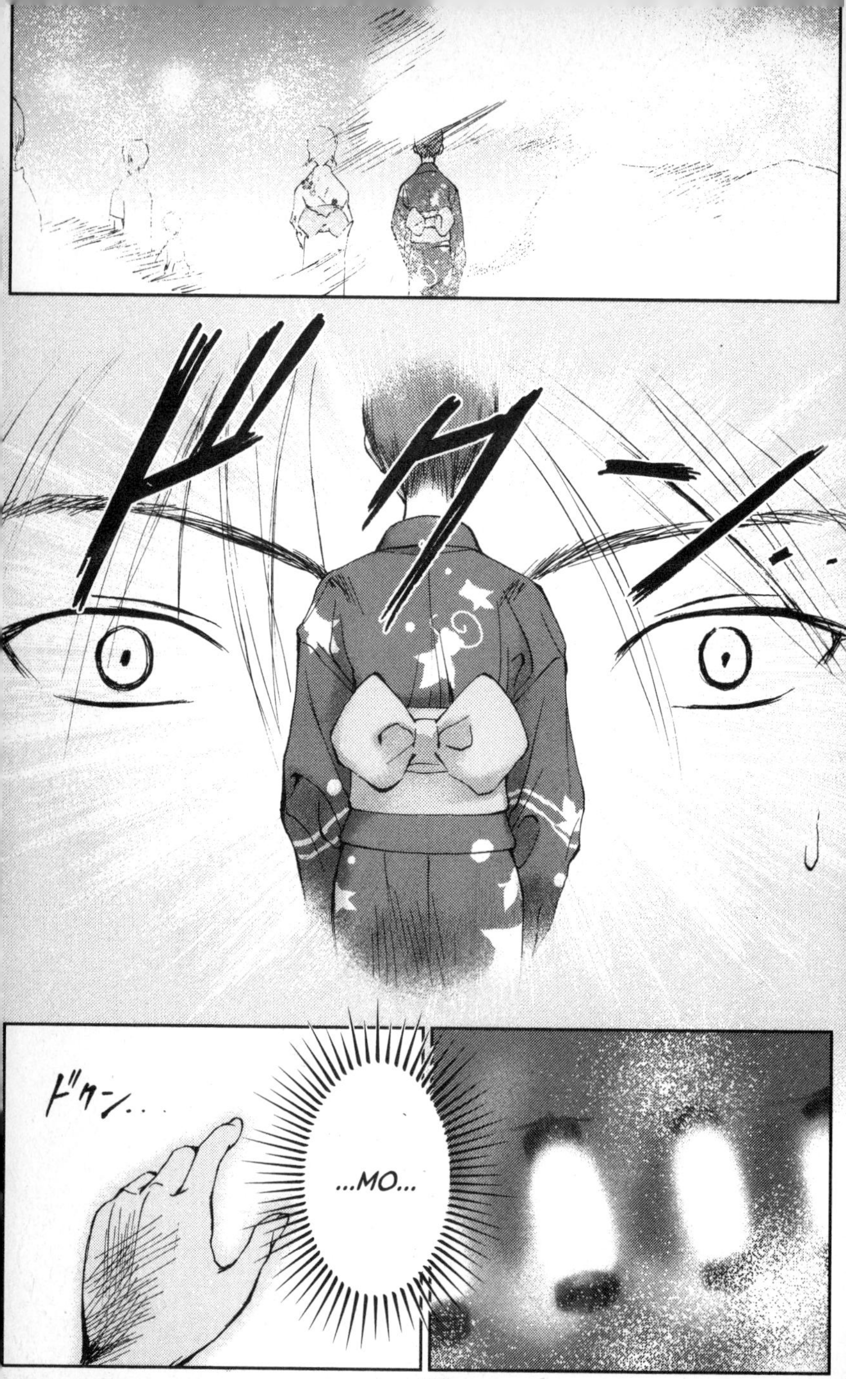
ドクーン…
...MO...
ドクン…

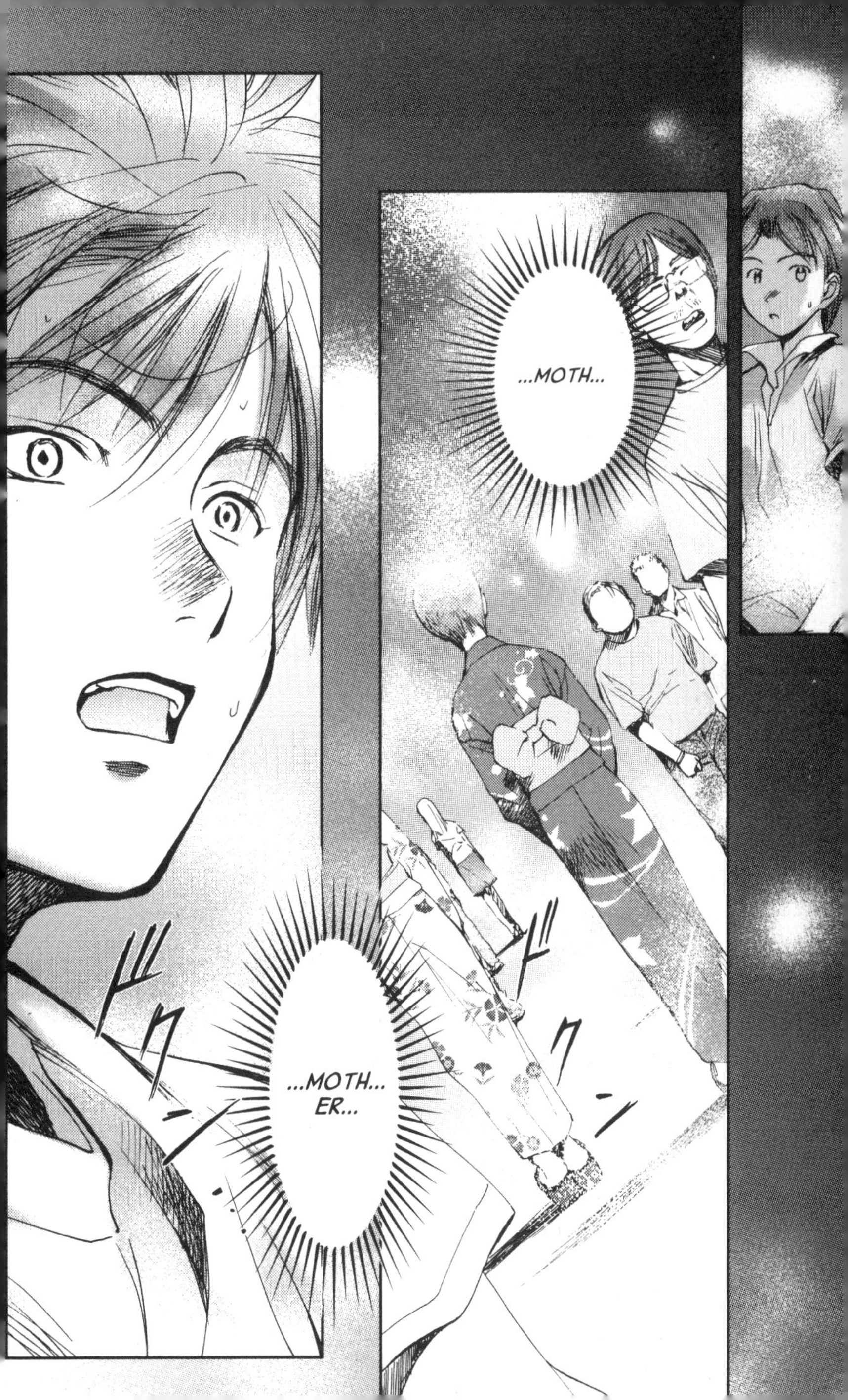
...MOTH...
...MOTH... ER...

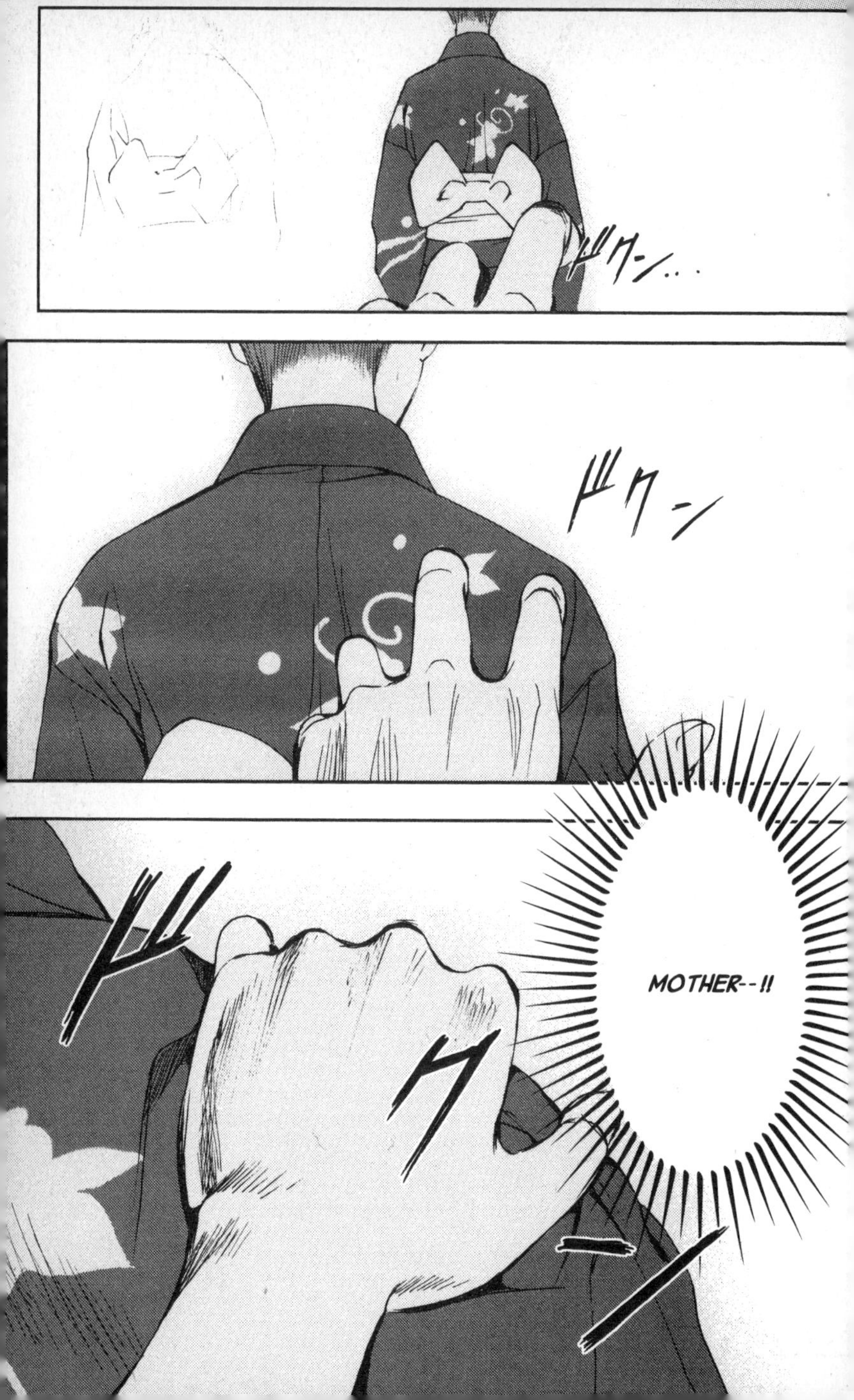
ドクン…
ドクン
MOTHER--!!

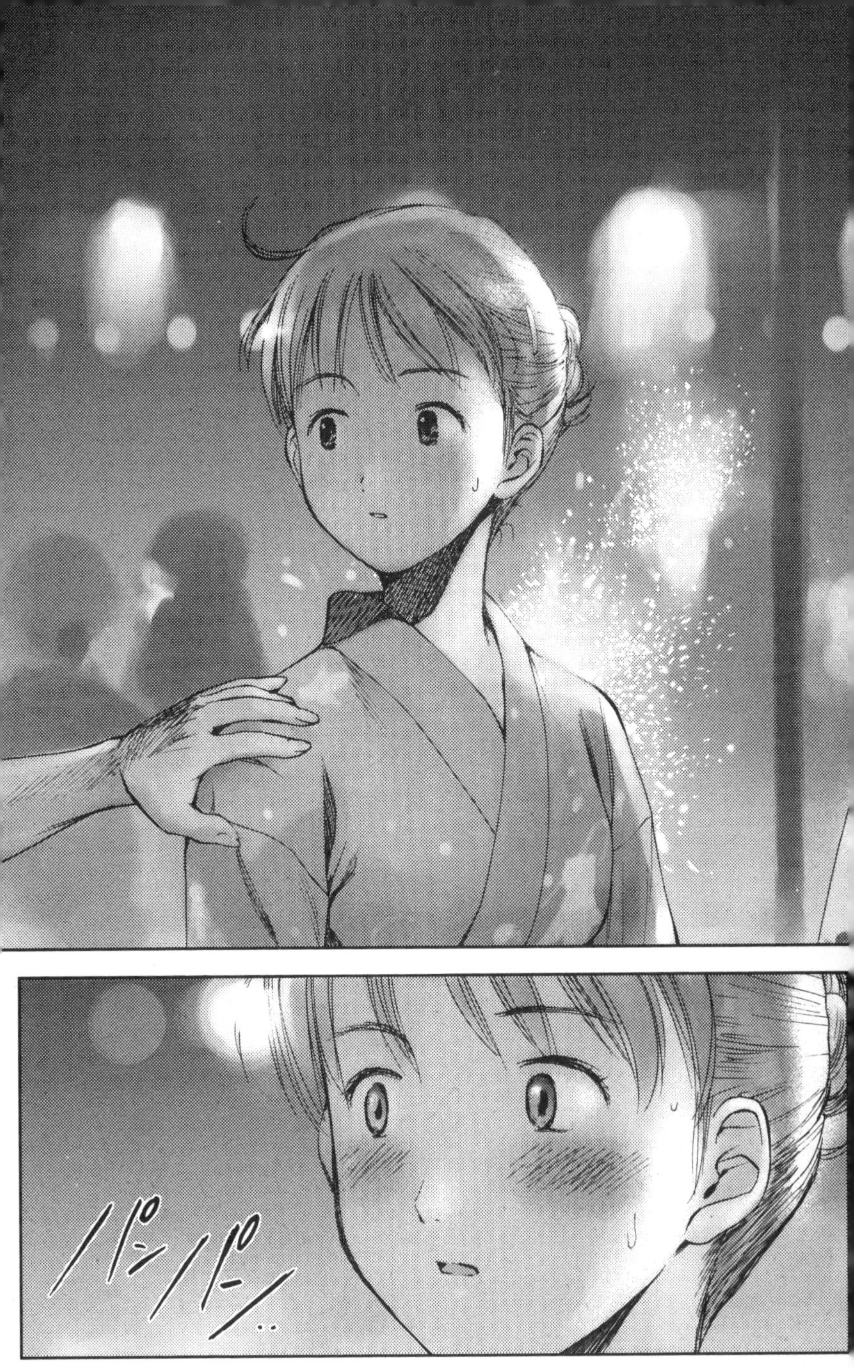
パンパン‥

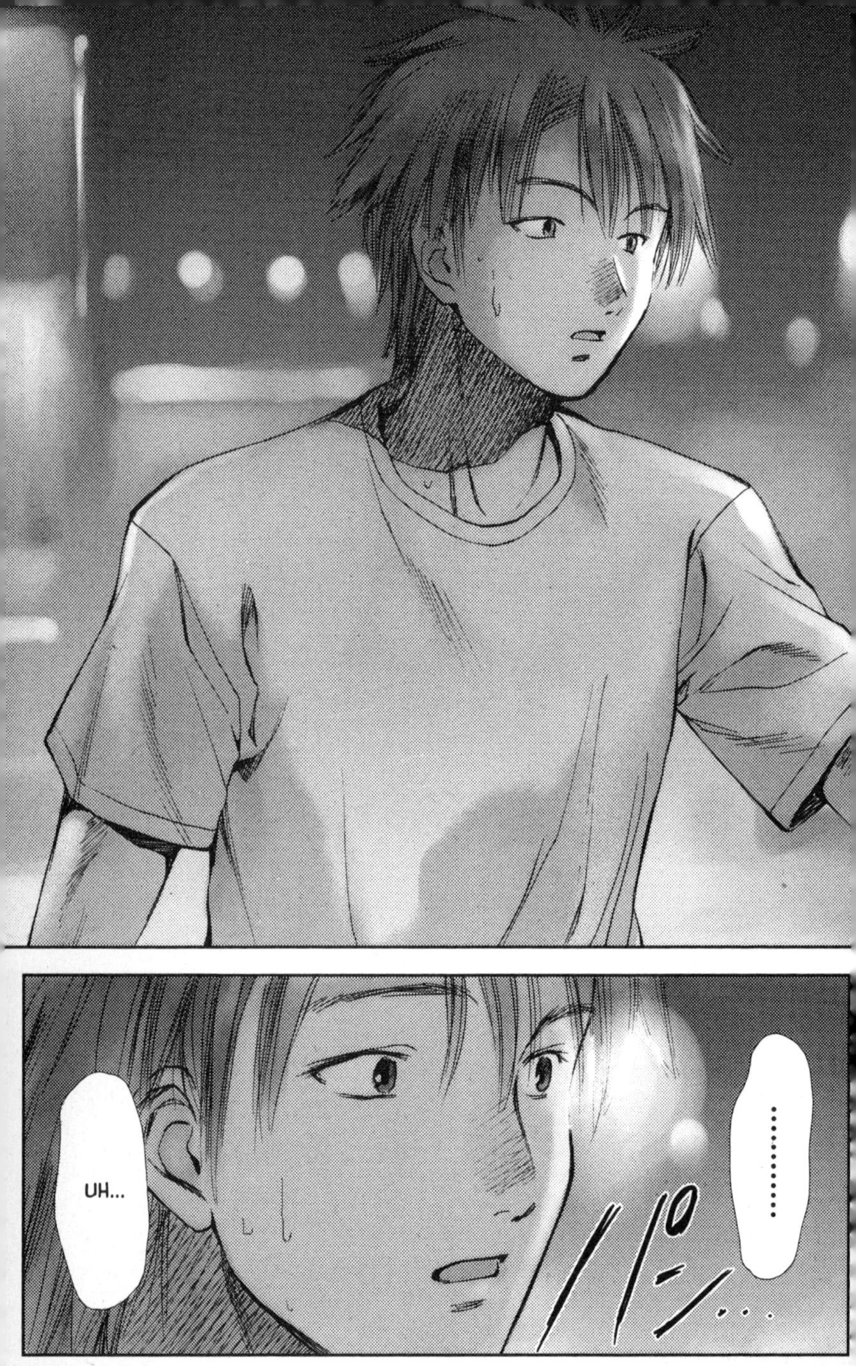
…………
パン…
UH...

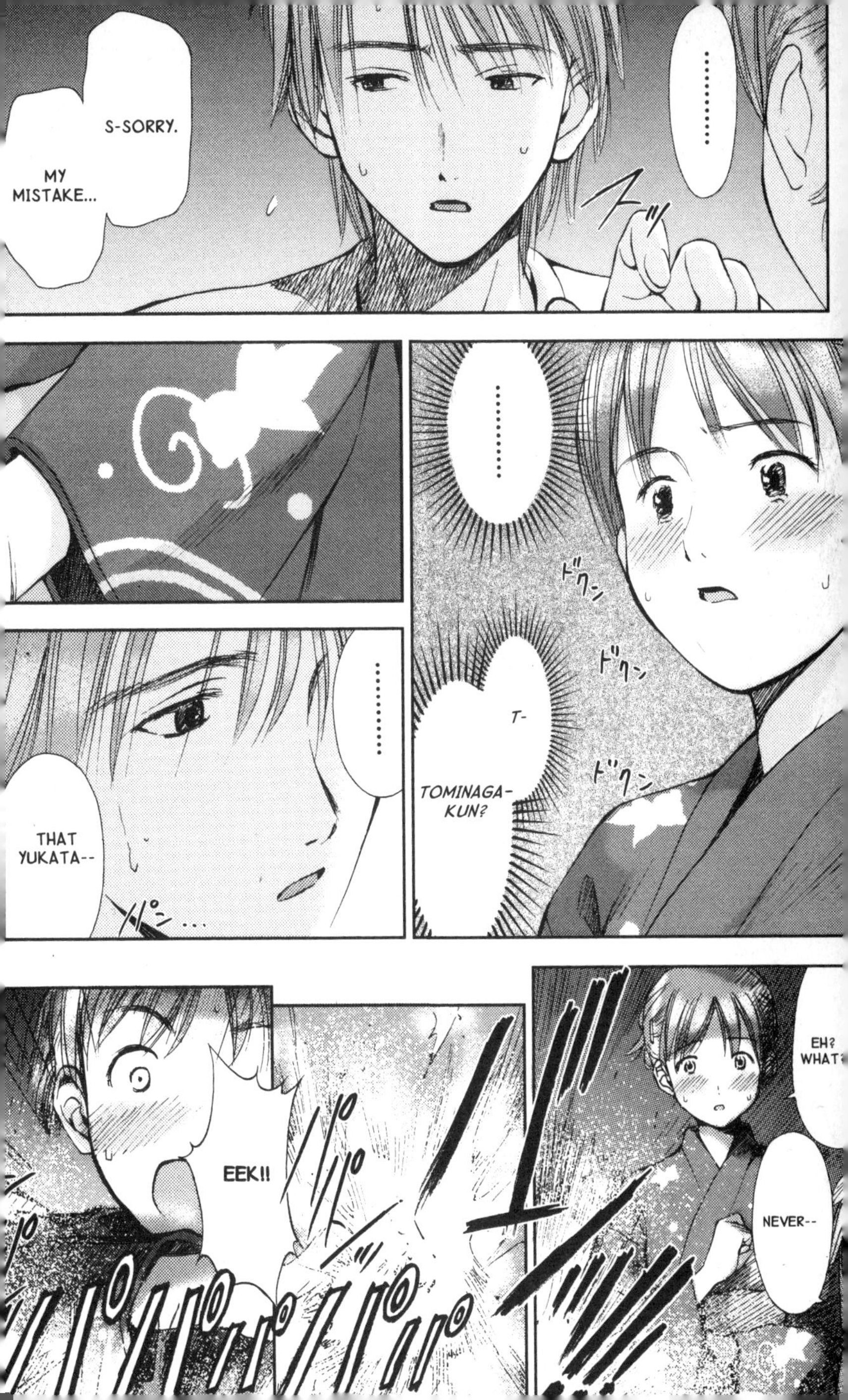
......
S-SORRY.
MY MISTAKE...
......
T-
TOMINAGA-KUN?
......
THAT YUKATA--
EH? WHAT?
NEVER--
EEK!!

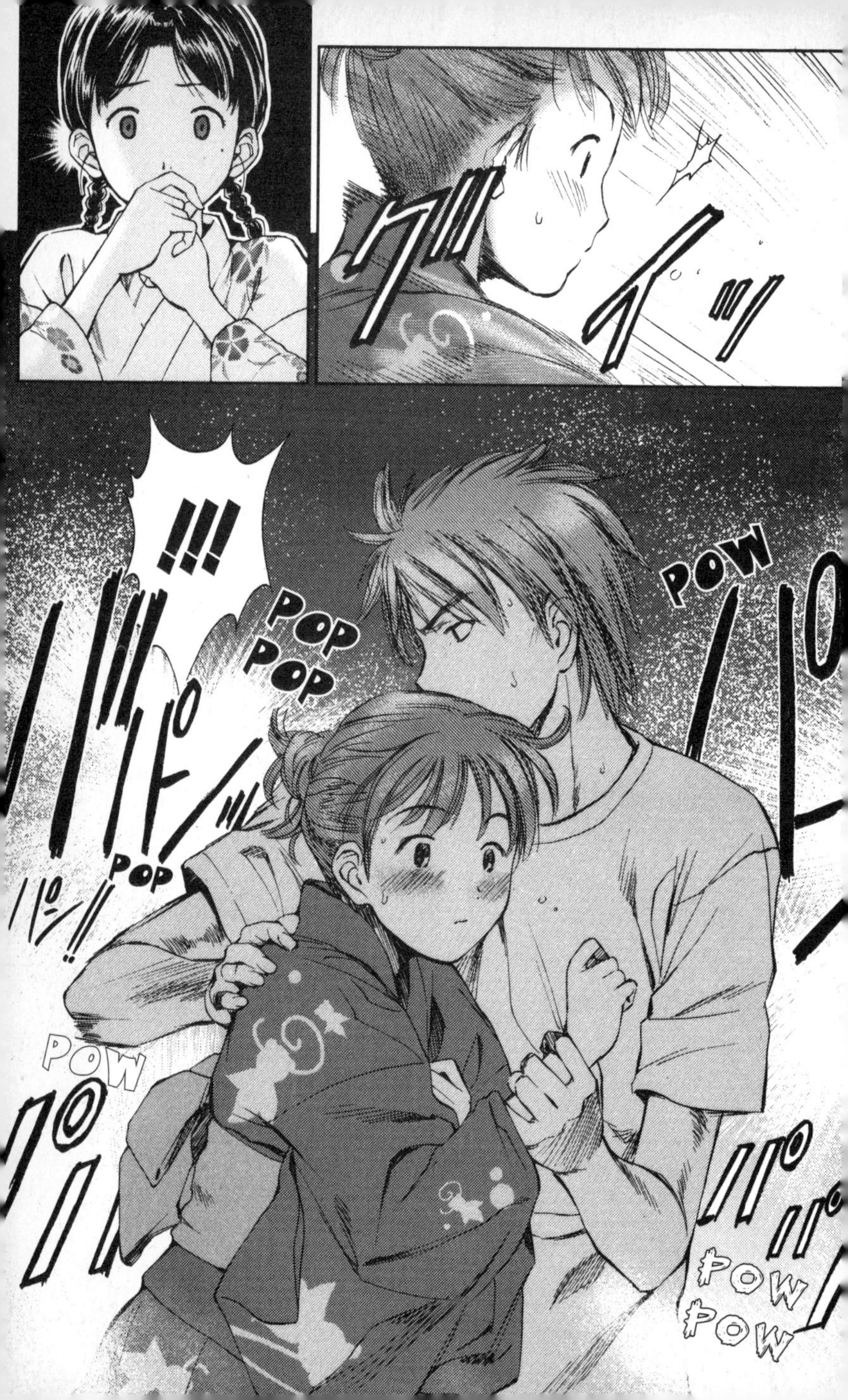
グイッ
POW
!!!
POP
POP
POP
POW
POW
POW

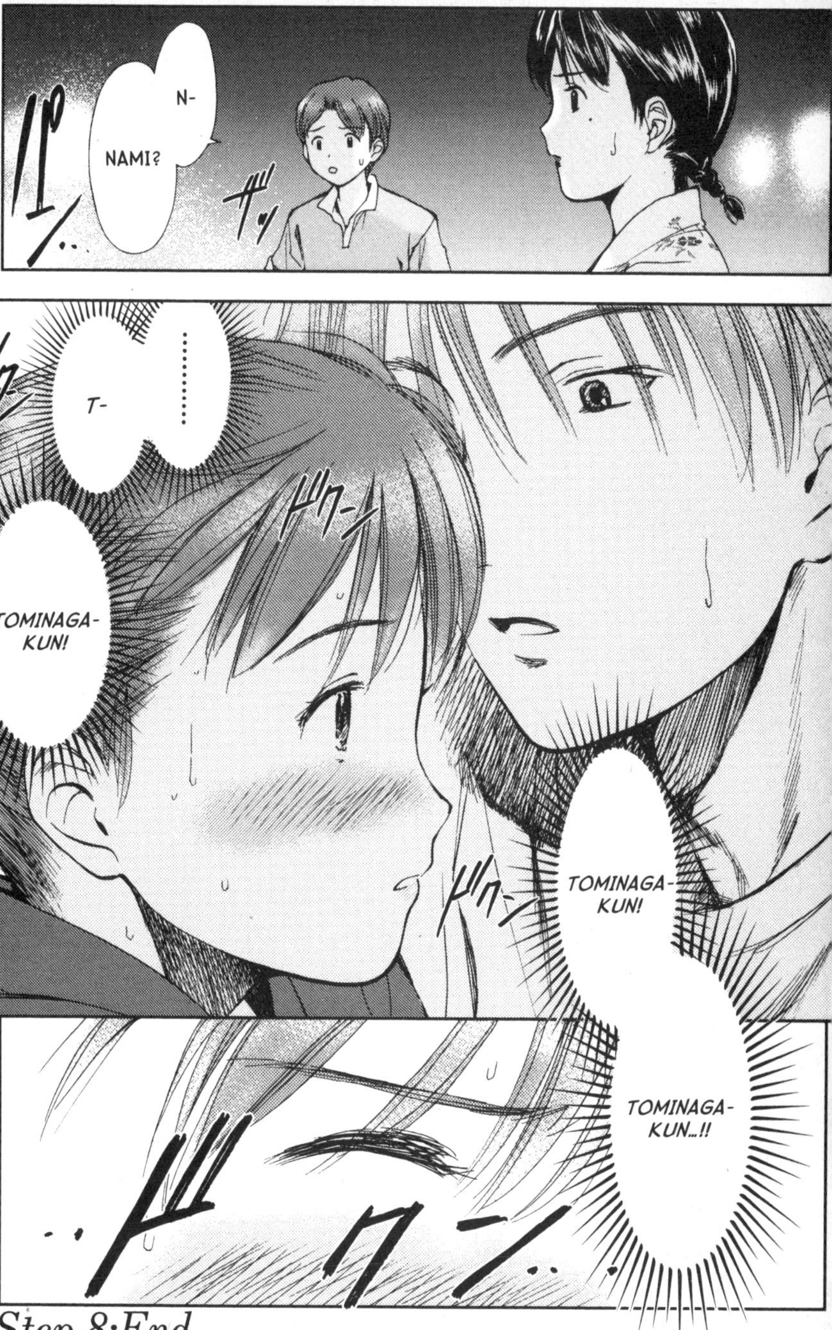
N-
NAMI?
......
T-
TOMINAGA-KUN!
TOMINAGA-KUN!
TOMINAGA-KUN...!!

Step.8:End

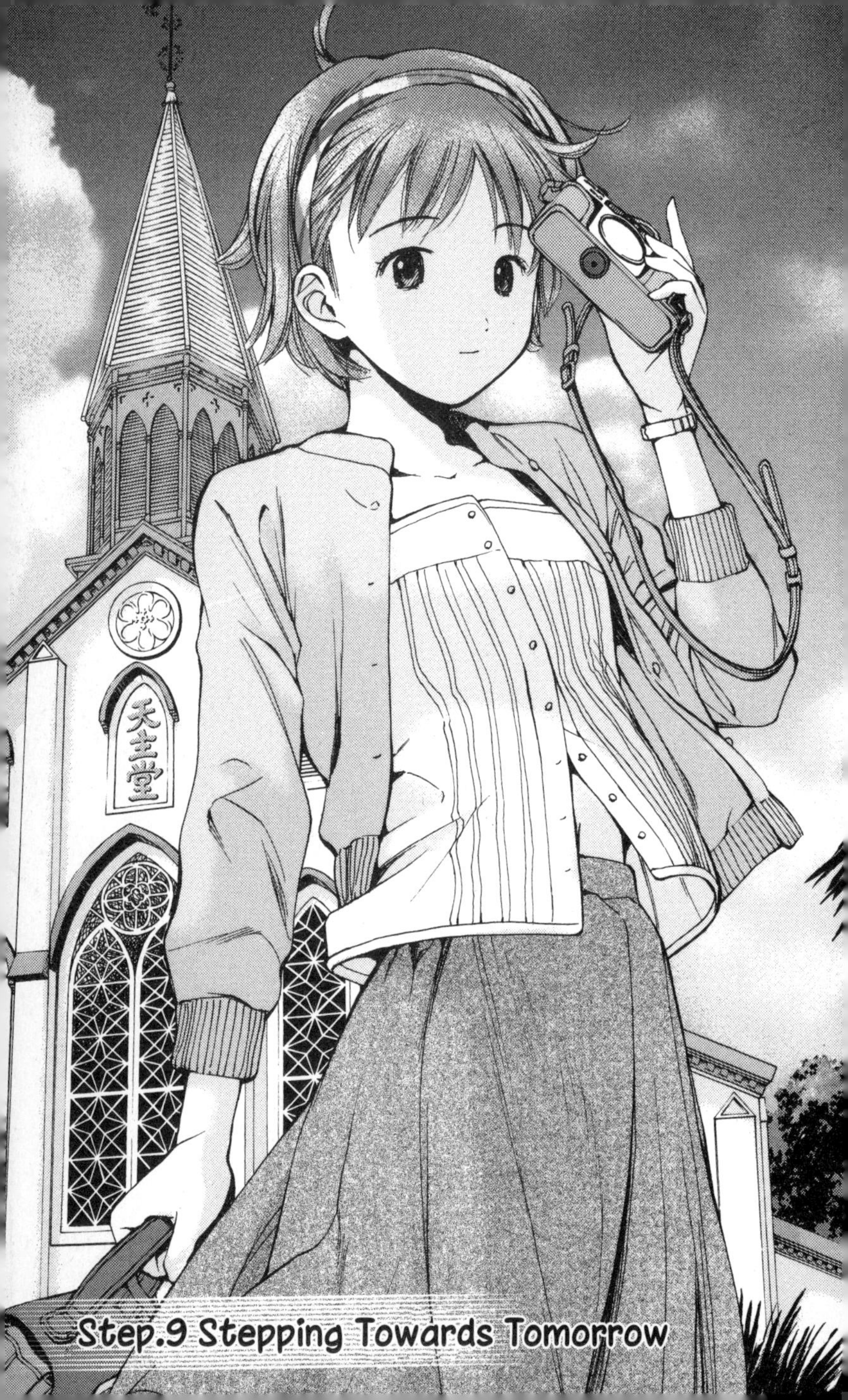
天主堂

Step.9 Stepping Towards Tomorrow

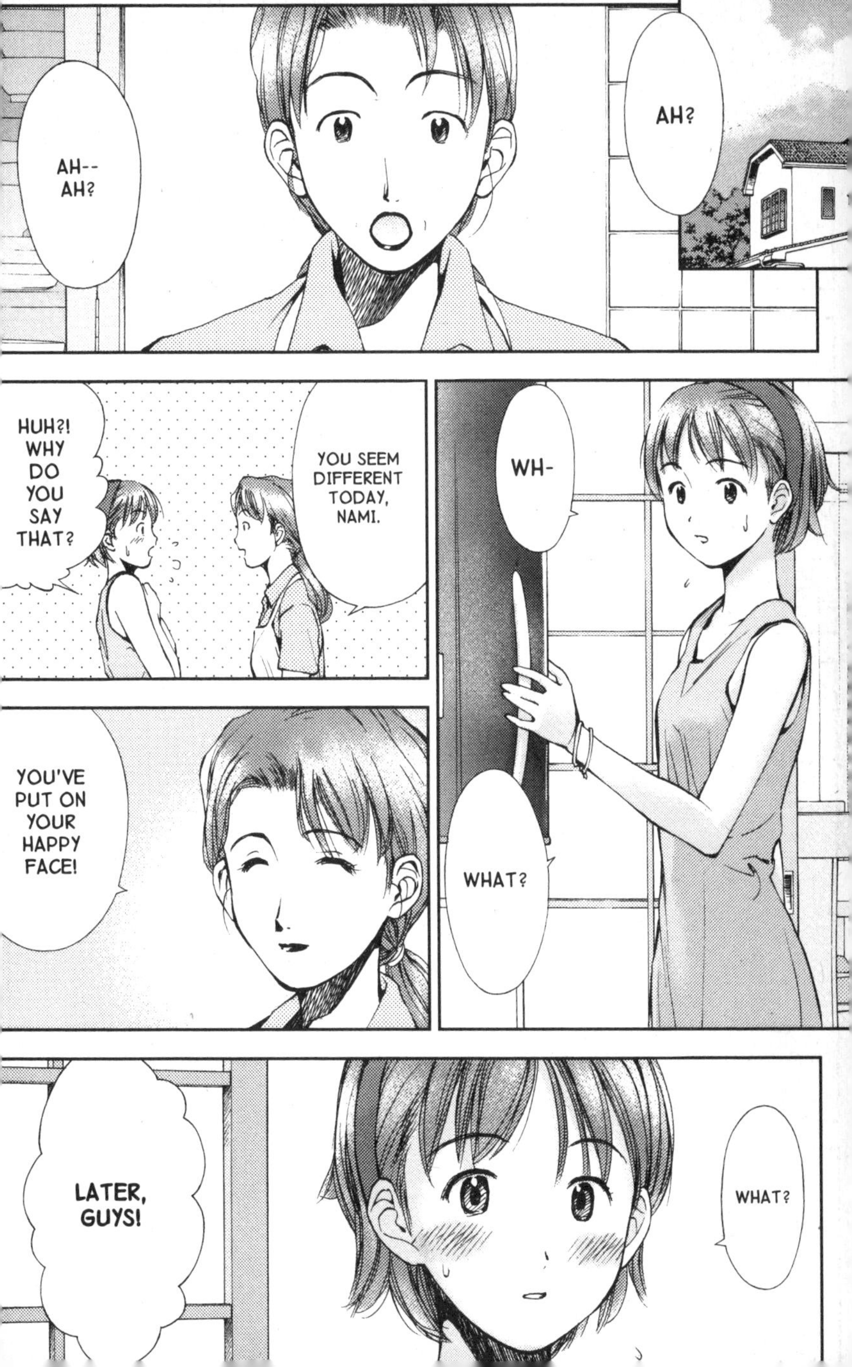
AH?
AH-- AH?
WH-
WHAT?
YOU SEEM DIFFERENT TODAY, NAMI.
HUH?! WHY DO YOU SAY THAT?
YOU'VE PUT ON YOUR HAPPY FACE!
WHAT?
LATER, GUYS!

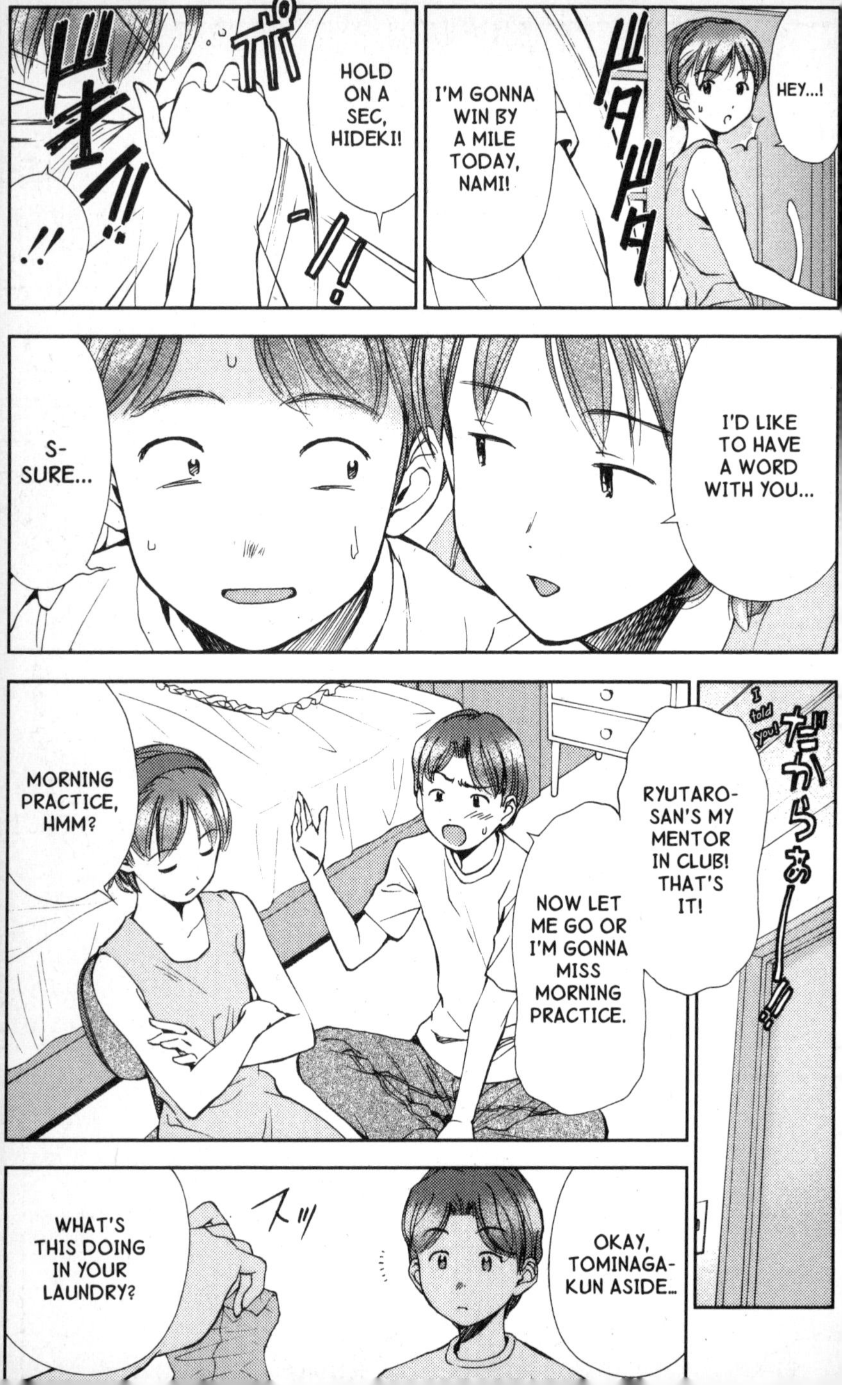
HEY...!
ドタドタ
I'M GONNA WIN BY A MILE TODAY, NAMI!
HOLD ON A SEC, HIDEKI!
ポ
!!
I'D LIKE TO HAVE A WORD WITH YOU...
S- SURE...
I told you!
だからぁー!!
RYUTARO-SAN'S MY MENTOR IN CLUB! THAT'S IT!
NOW LET ME GO OR I'M GONNA MISS MORNING PRACTICE.
MORNING PRACTICE, HMM?
OKAY, TOMINAGA-KUN ASIDE...
スッ
WHAT'S THIS DOING IN YOUR LAUNDRY?

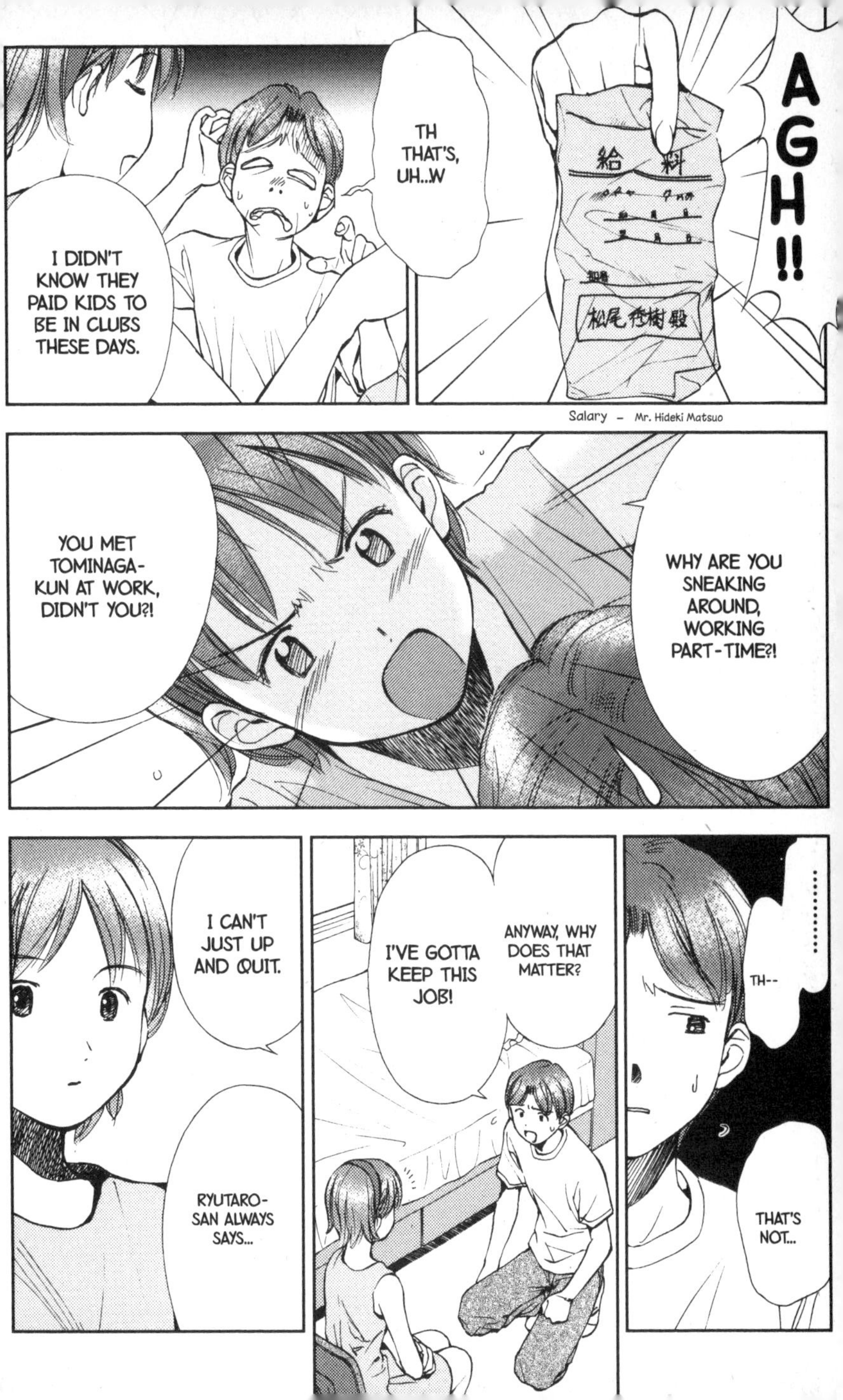
AGH!!
給料
松尾秀樹殿
Salary – Mr. Hideki Matsuo
TH THAT'S, UH...W
I DIDN'T KNOW THEY PAID KIDS TO BE IN CLUBS THESE DAYS.
WHY ARE YOU SNEAKING AROUND, WORKING PART-TIME?!
YOU MET TOMINAGA-KUN AT WORK, DIDN'T YOU?!
....
TH--
THAT'S NOT...
ANYWAY, WHY DOES THAT MATTER?
I'VE GOTTA KEEP THIS JOB!
I CAN'T JUST UP AND QUIT.
RYUTARO-SAN ALWAYS SAYS...

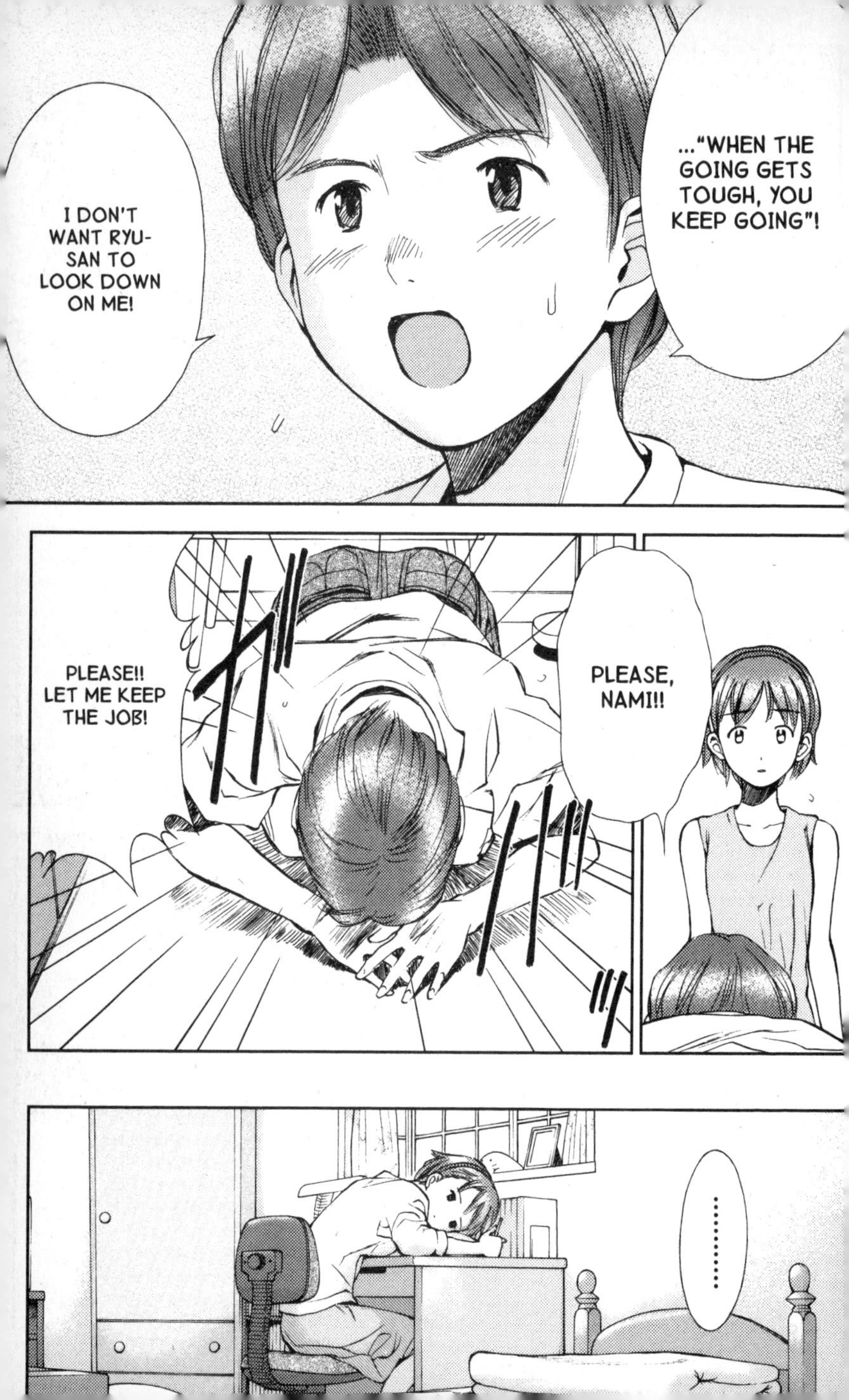
..."WHEN THE GOING GETS TOUGH, YOU KEEP GOING"!
I DON'T WANT RYU-SAN TO LOOK DOWN ON ME!
PLEASE, NAMI!!
PLEASE!! LET ME KEEP THE JOB!
....

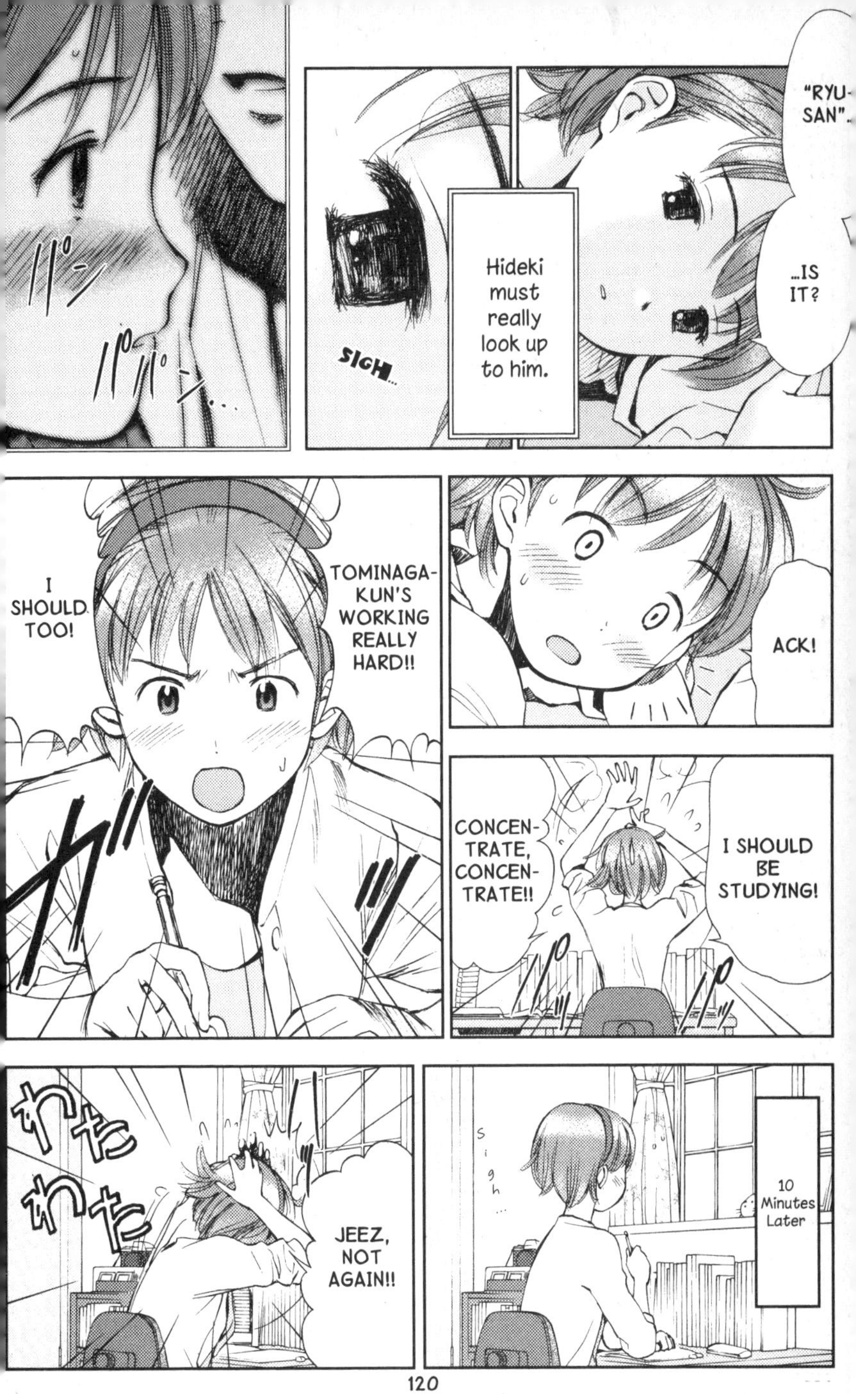
"RYU-SAN"...
...IS IT?
Hideki must really look up to him.
SIGH...
ACK!
I SHOULD BE STUDYING!
CONCEN-TRATE, CONCEN-TRATE!!
TOMINAGA-KUN'S WORKING REALLY HARD!!
I SHOULD TOO!
10 Minutes Later
sigh...
JEEZ, NOT AGAIN!!
わたわた

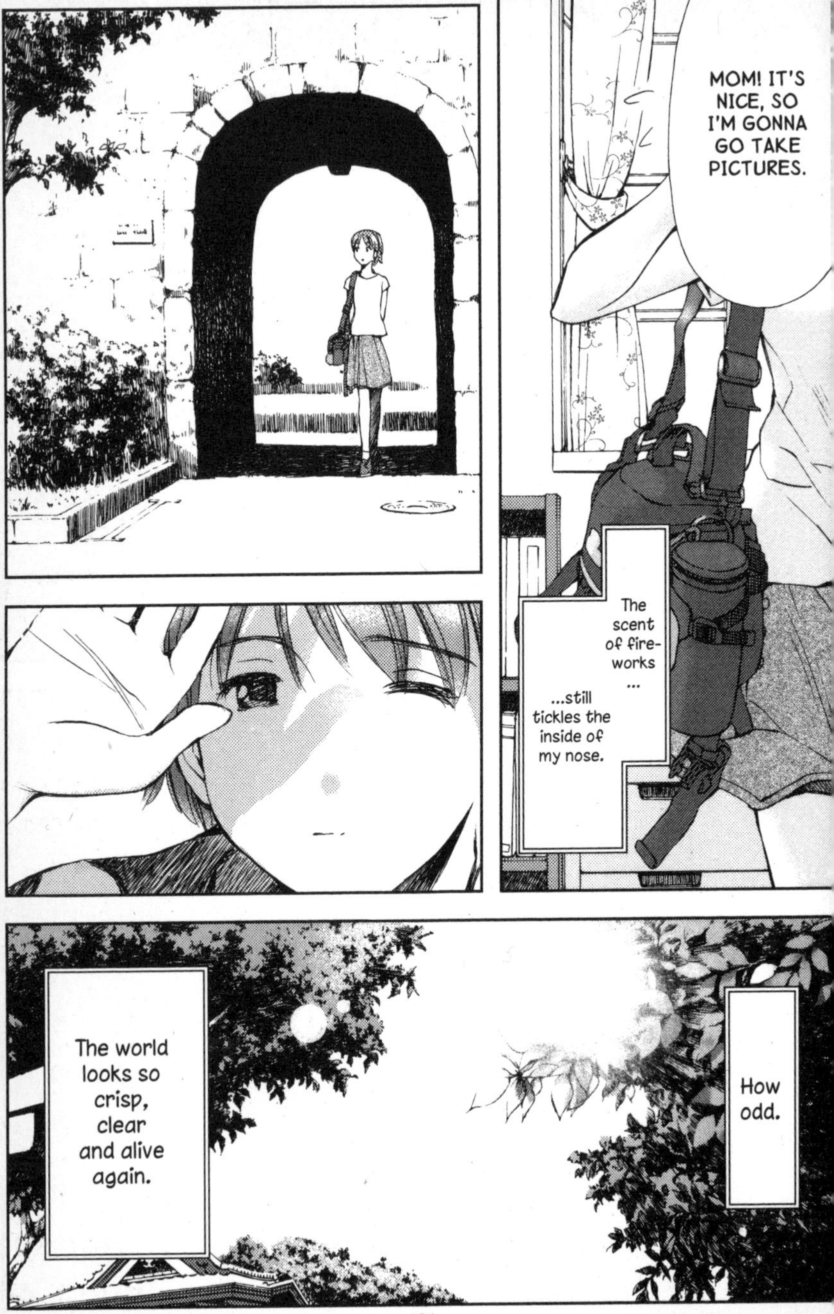
MOM! IT'S NICE, SO I'M GONNA GO TAKE PICTURES.
The scent of fire-works ...
...still tickles the inside of my nose.
How odd.
The world looks so crisp, clear and alive again.

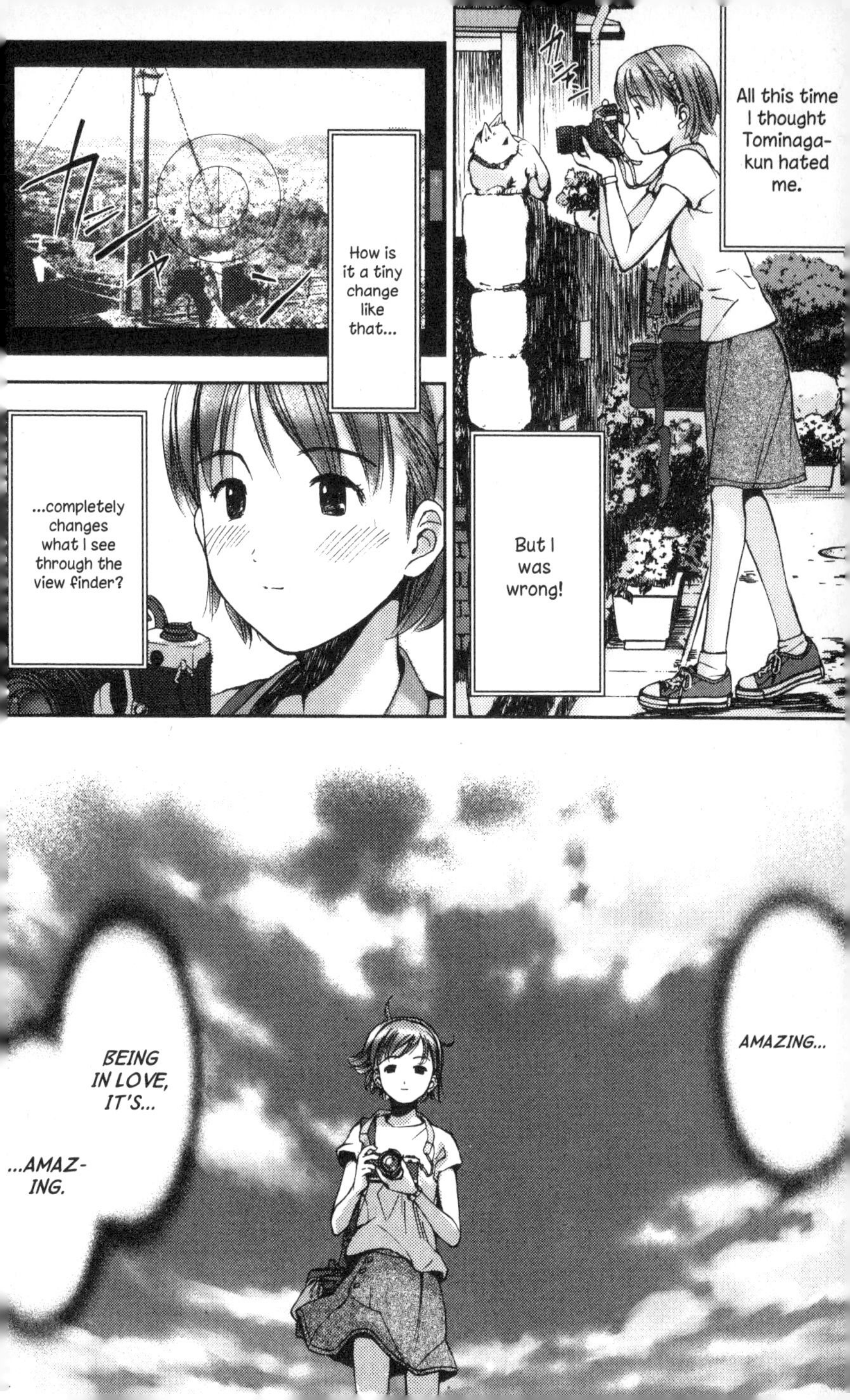
All this time I thought Tominaga-kun hated me.
But I was wrong!
How is it a tiny change like that...
...completely changes what I see through the view finder?
AMAZING...
BEING IN LOVE, IT'S...
...AMAZ-ING.

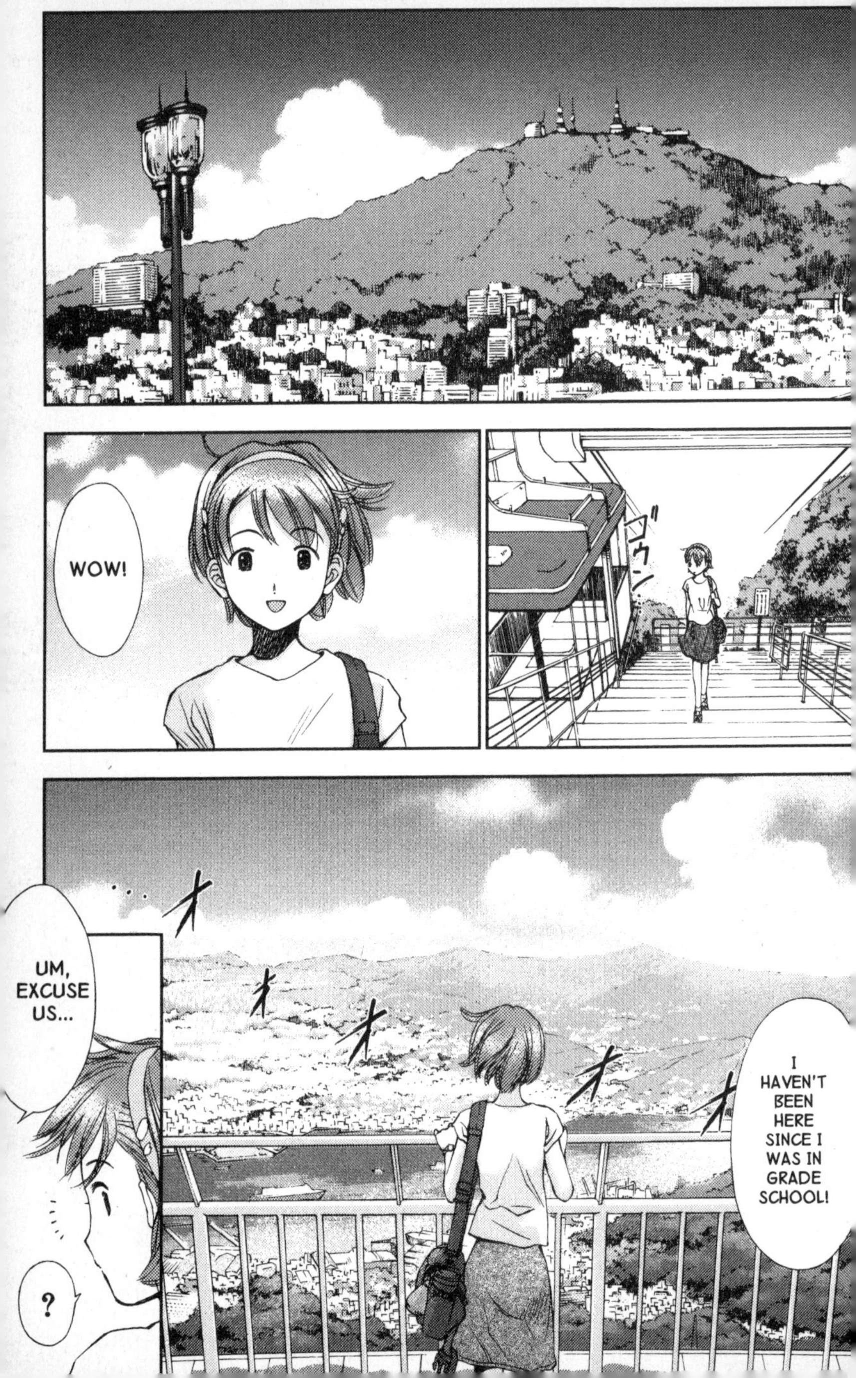
ゴウン
WOW!
I HAVEN'T BEEN HERE SINCE I WAS IN GRADE SCHOOL!
...
UM, EXCUSE US...
?

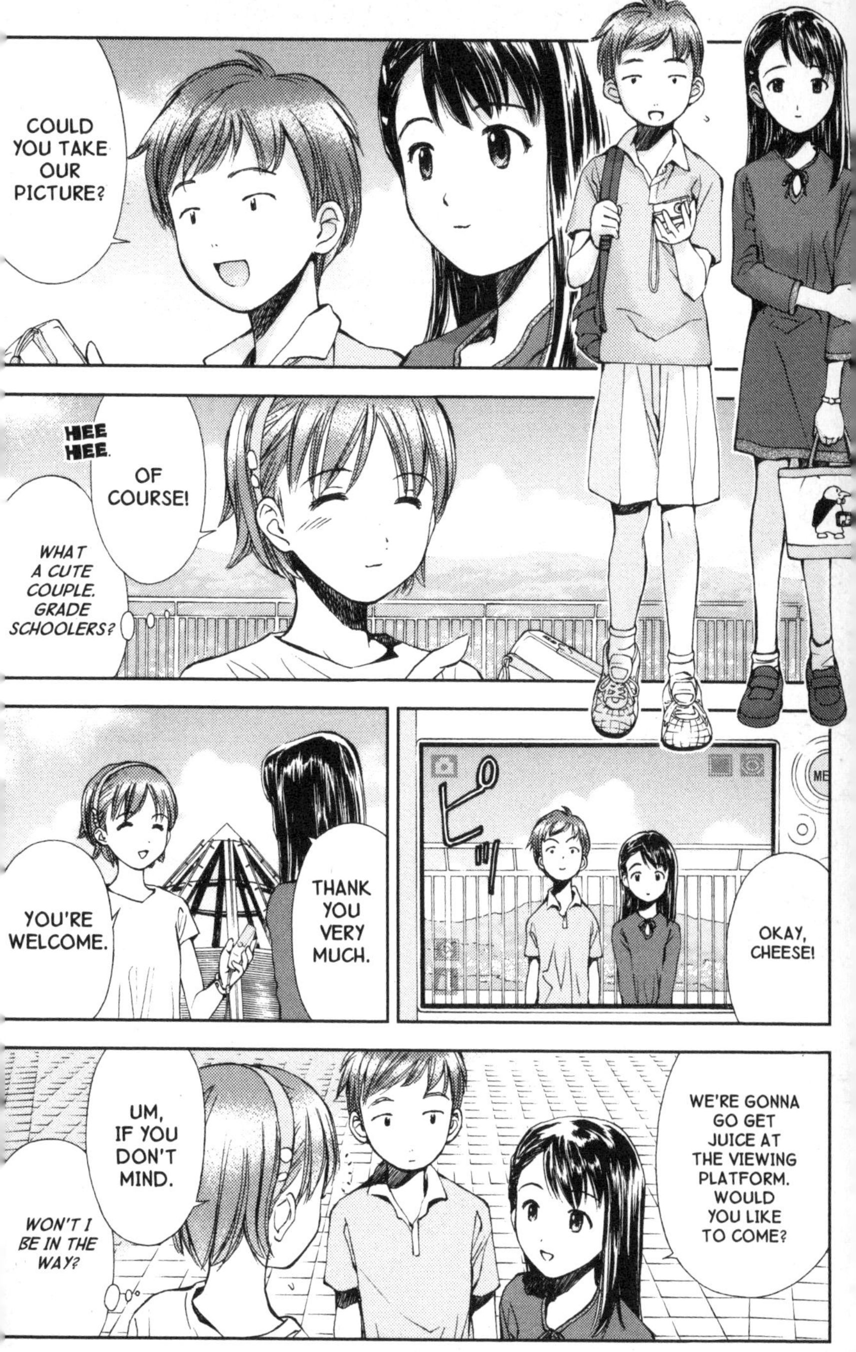
COULD YOU TAKE OUR PICTURE?
HEE HEE.
OF COURSE!
WHAT A CUTE COUPLE. GRADE SCHOOLERS?
ピッ
OKAY, CHEESE!
THANK YOU VERY MUCH.
YOU'RE WELCOME.
WE'RE GONNA GO GET JUICE AT THE VIEWING PLATFORM. WOULD YOU LIKE TO COME?
UM, IF YOU DON'T MIND.
WON'T I BE IN THE WAY?

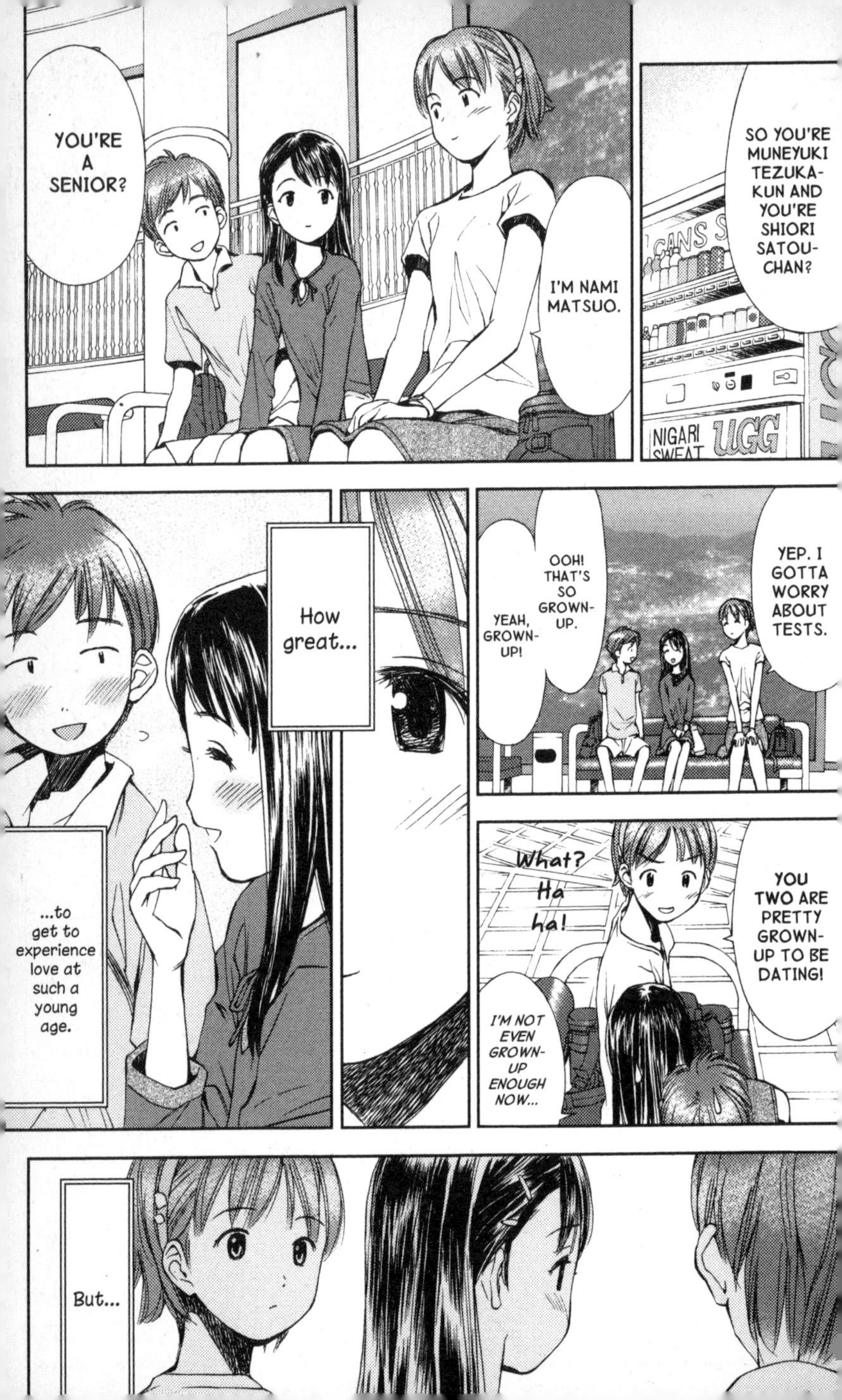

SO YOU'RE MUNEYUKI TEZUKA-KUN AND YOU'RE SHIORI SATOU-CHAN?
NIGARI
UGG
I'M NAMI MATSUO.
YOU'RE A SENIOR?
YEP. I GOTTA WORRY ABOUT TESTS.
OOH! THAT'S SO GROWN-UP.
YEAH, GROWN-UP!
YOU TWO ARE PRETTY GROWN-UP TO BE DATING!
What? Ha ha!
I'M NOT EVEN GROWN-UP ENOUGH NOW...
How great...
...to get to experience love at such a young age.
But...

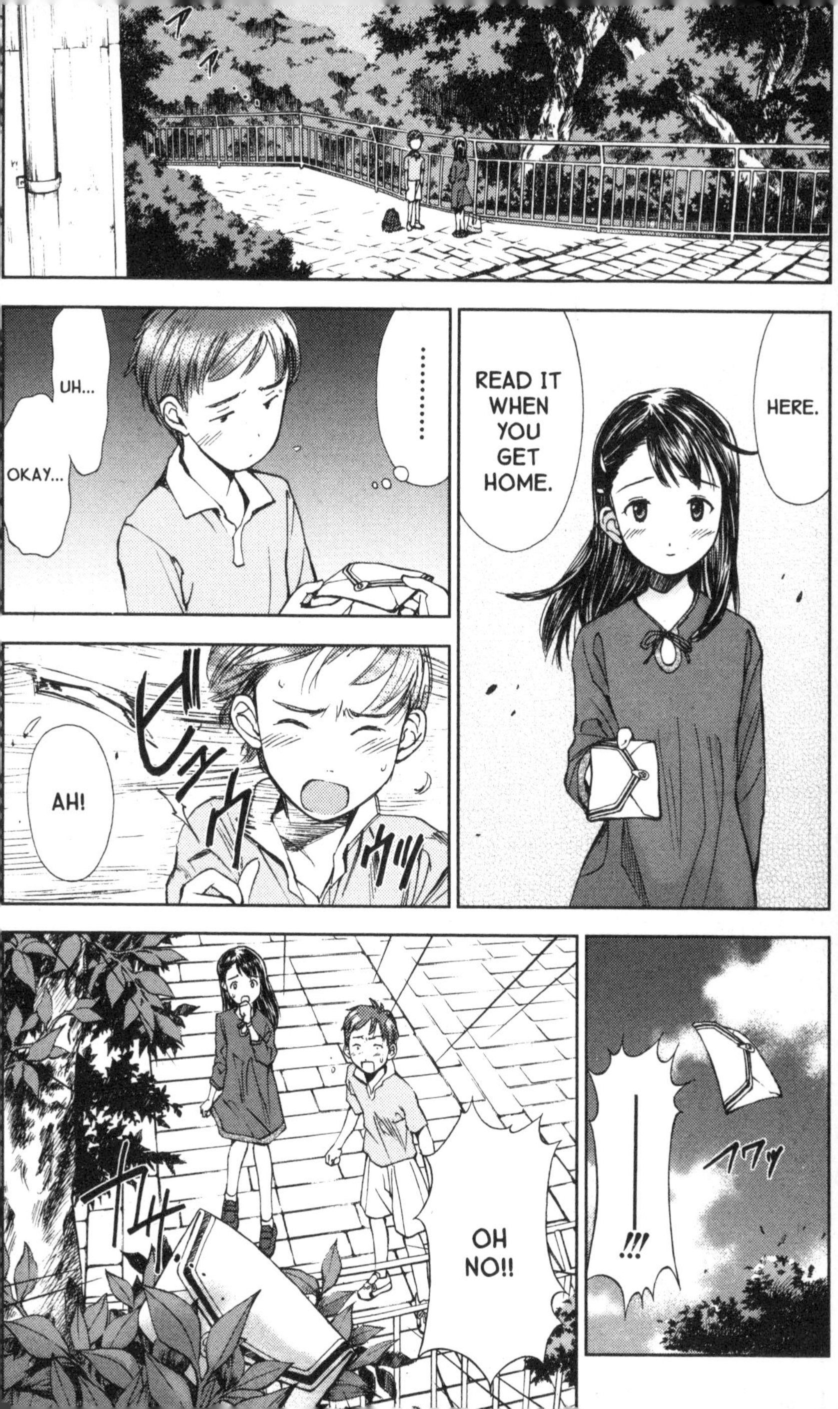
HERE.
READ IT WHEN YOU GET HOME.
....
UH... OKAY...
AH!
!!!
OH NO!!

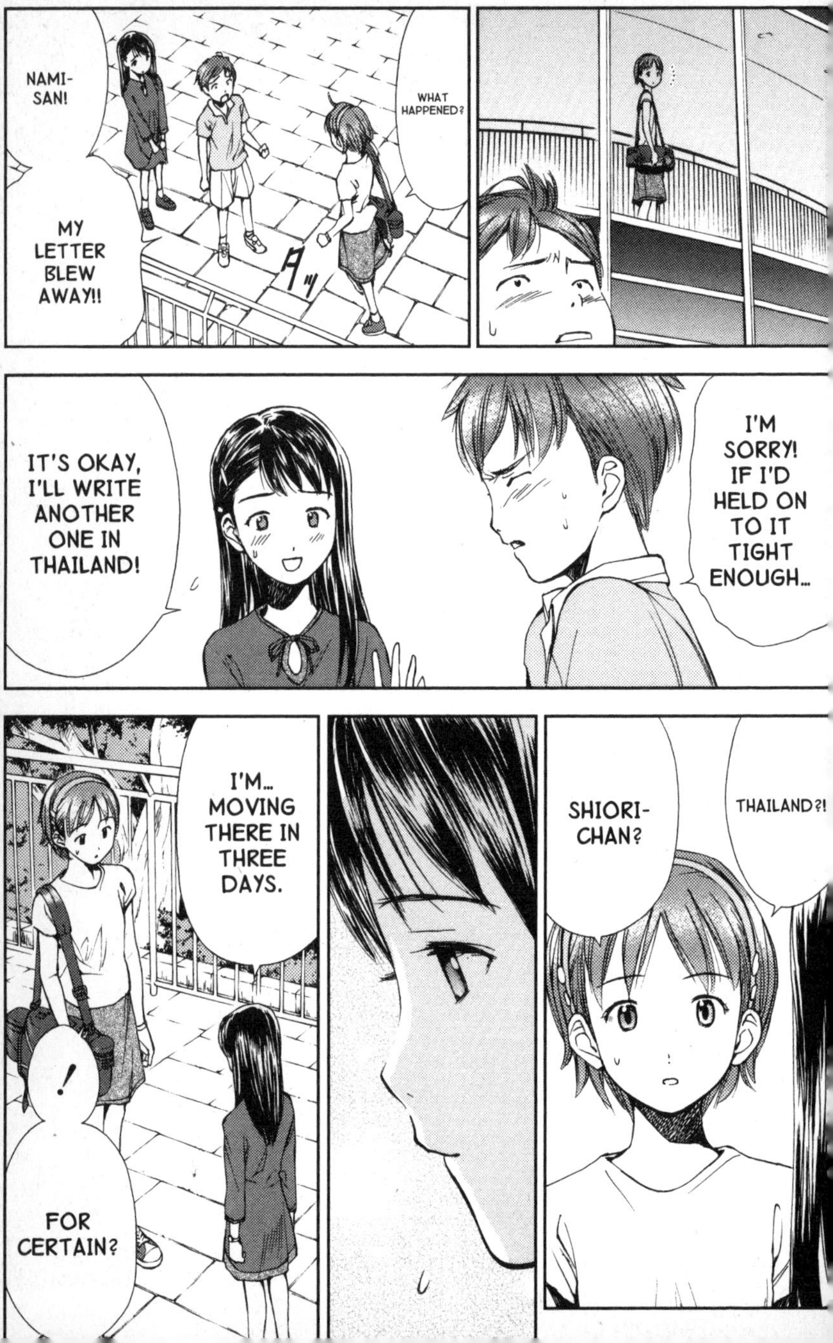
WHAT HAPPENED?
NAMI-SAN!
MY LETTER BLEW AWAY!!
タッ
I'M SORRY! IF I'D HELD ON TO IT TIGHT ENOUGH...
IT'S OKAY, I'LL WRITE ANOTHER ONE IN THAILAND!
THAILAND?!
SHIORI-CHAN?
I'M... MOVING THERE IN THREE DAYS.
!
FOR CERTAIN?

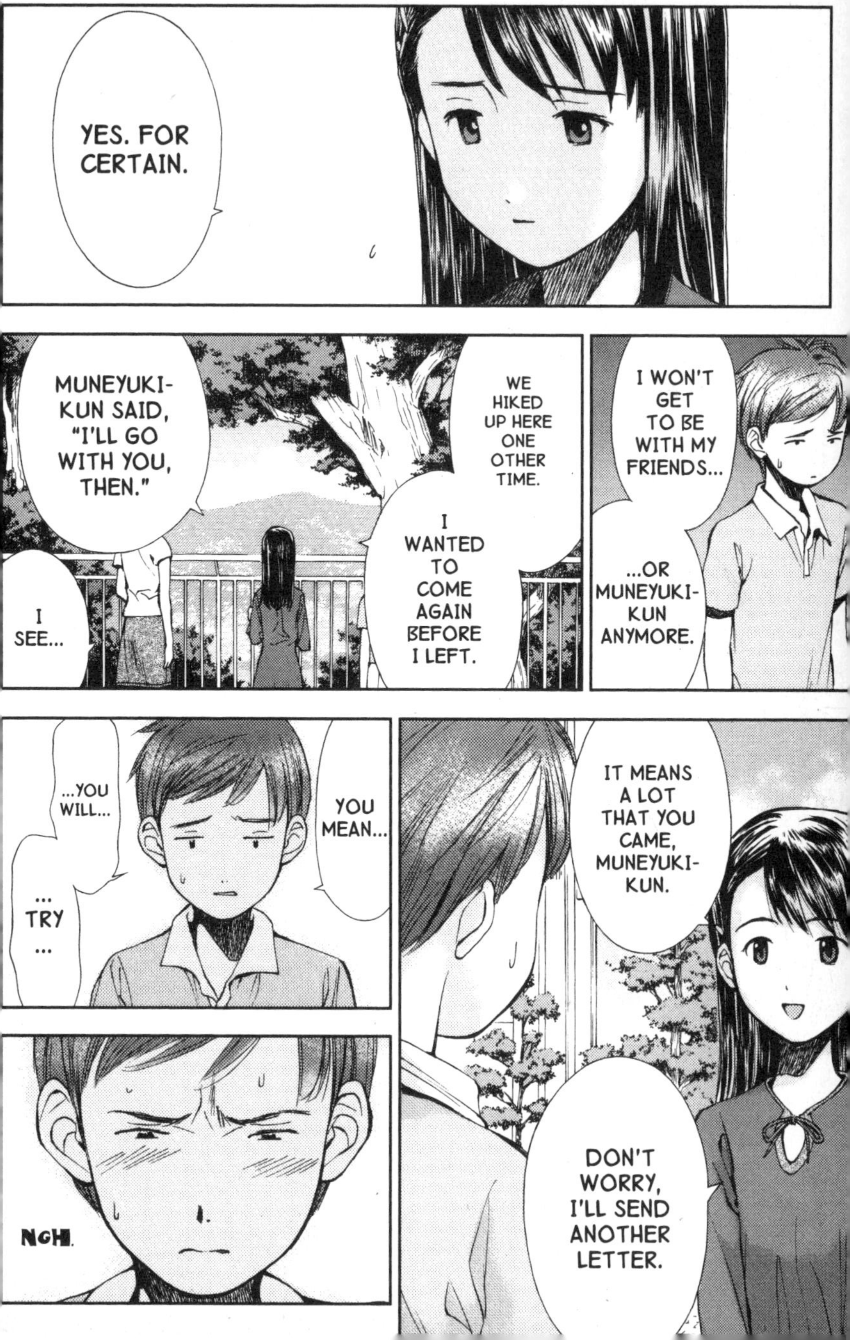
YES. FOR CERTAIN.
I WON'T GET TO BE WITH MY FRIENDS...
...OR MUNEYUKI-KUN ANYMORE.
WE HIKED UP HERE ONE OTHER TIME.
I WANTED TO COME AGAIN BEFORE I LEFT.
MUNEYUKI-KUN SAID, "I'LL GO WITH YOU, THEN."
I SEE...
IT MEANS A LOT THAT YOU CAME, MUNEYUKI-KUN.
DON'T WORRY, I'LL SEND ANOTHER LETTER.
YOU MEAN...
...YOU WILL...
... TRY ...
NGH.

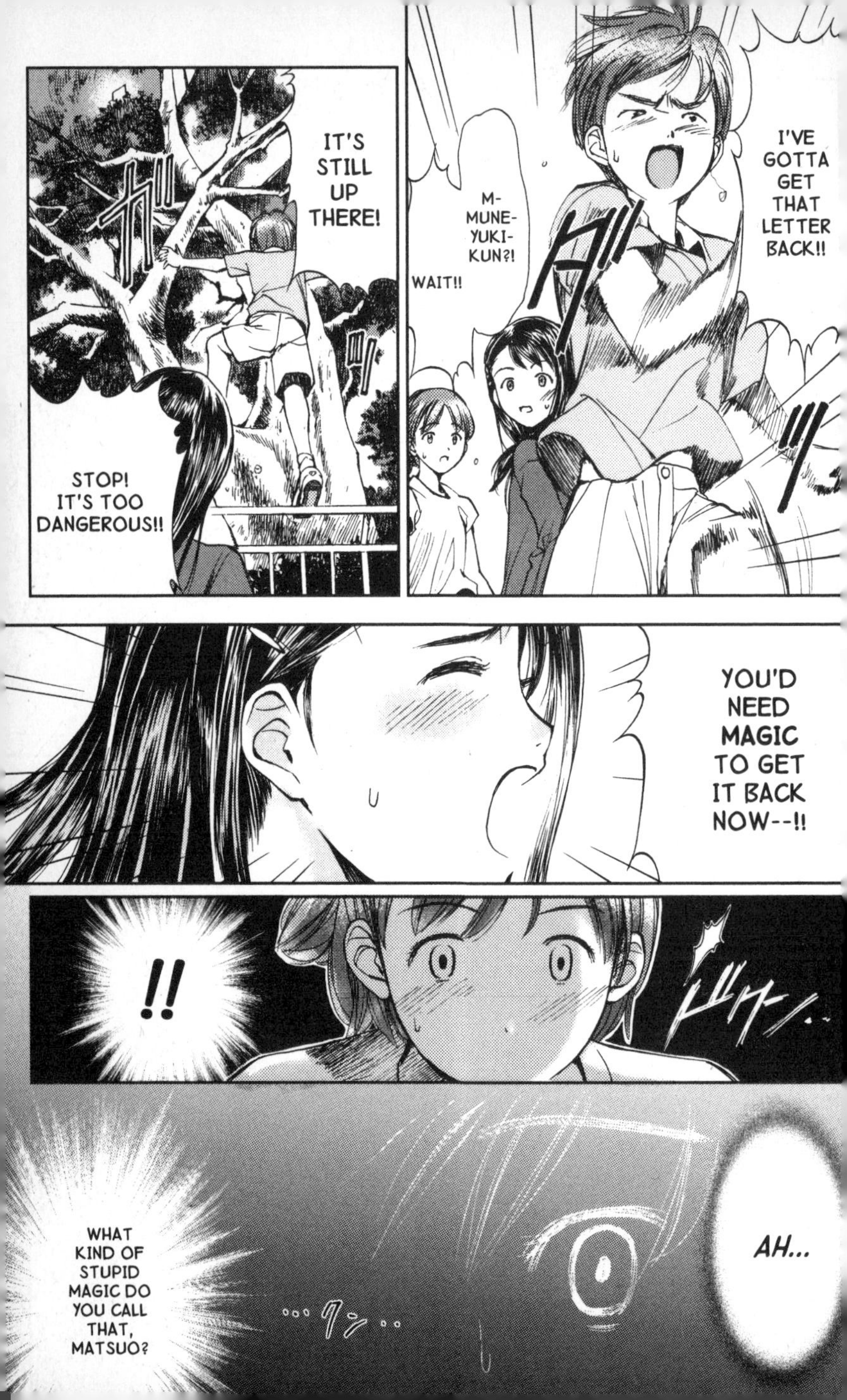
I'VE GOTTA GET THAT LETTER BACK!!
M-MUNE-YUKI-KUN?!
WAIT!!
IT'S STILL UP THERE!
STOP! IT'S TOO DANGEROUS!!
YOU'D NEED MAGIC TO GET IT BACK NOW--!!
!!
AH...
WHAT KIND OF STUPID MAGIC DO YOU CALL THAT, MATSUO?

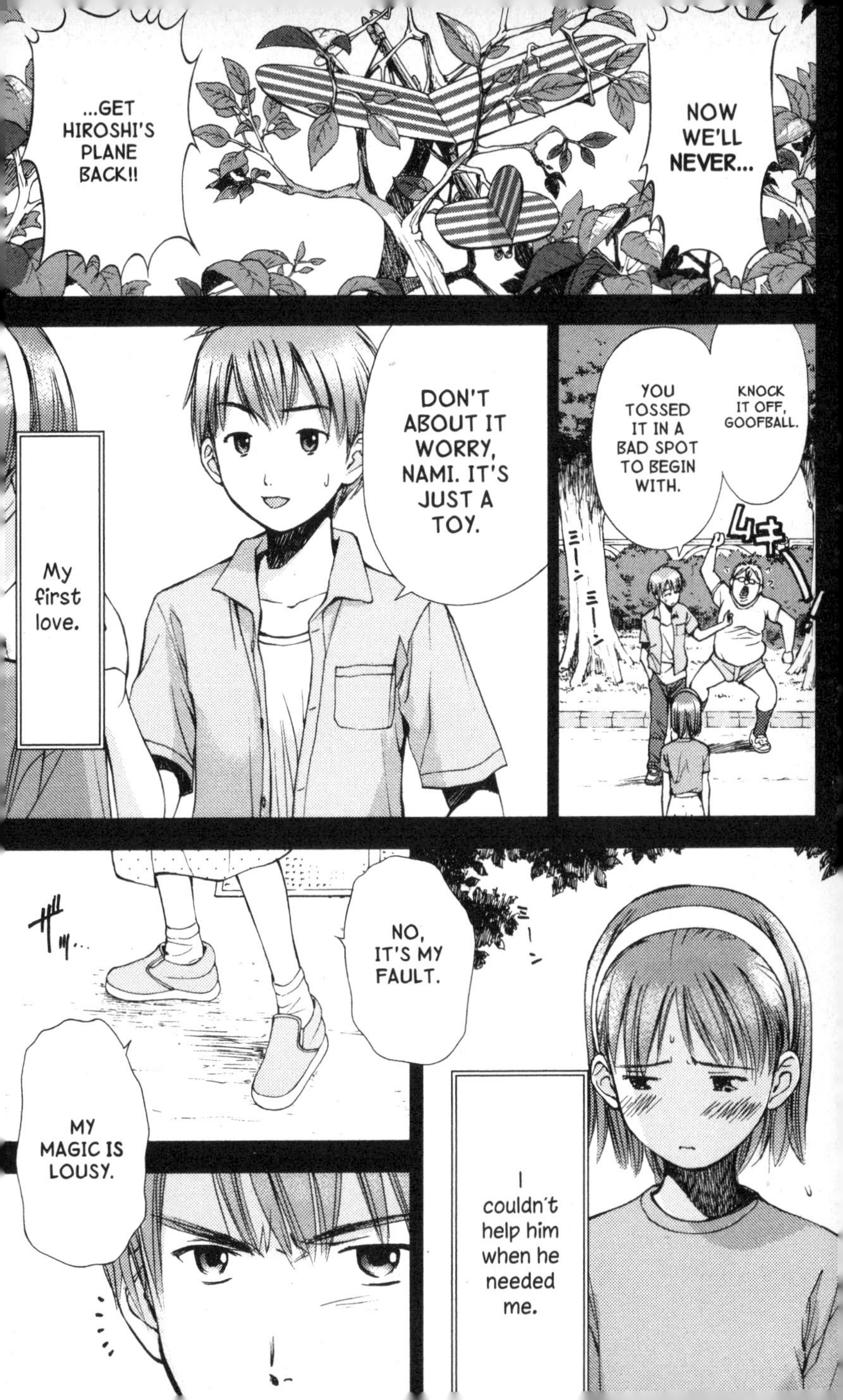
NOW WE'LL NEVER...
...GET HIROSHI'S PLANE BACK!!
KNOCK IT OFF, GOOFBALL.
YOU TOSSED IT IN A BAD SPOT TO BEGIN WITH.
ムキ
DON'T ABOUT IT WORRY, NAMI. IT'S JUST A TOY.
My first love.
I couldn't help him when he needed me.
NO, IT'S MY FAULT.
MY MAGIC IS LOUSY.

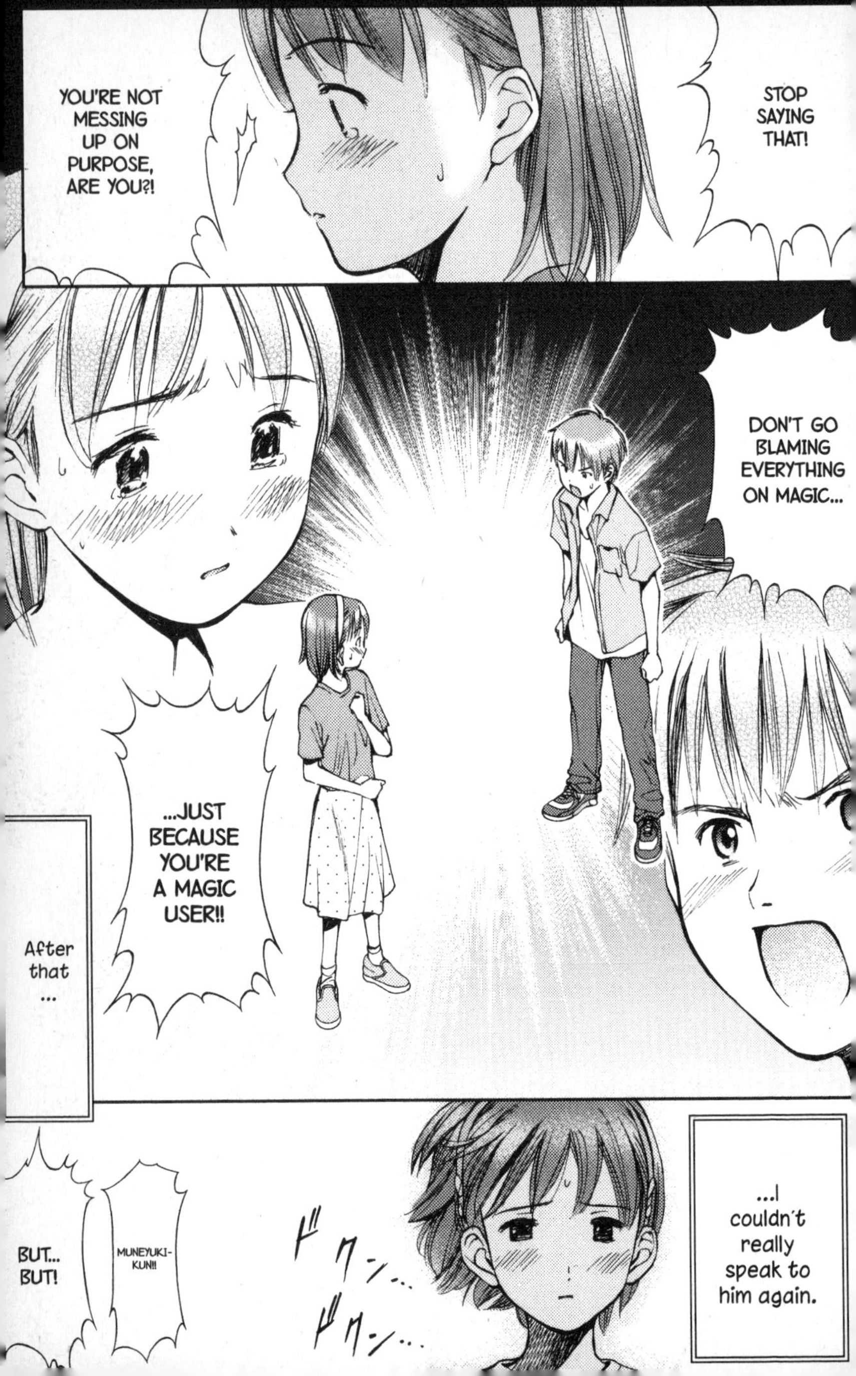
STOP SAYING THAT!
YOU'RE NOT MESSING UP ON PURPOSE, ARE YOU?!
DON'T GO BLAMING EVERYTHING ON MAGIC...
...JUST BECAUSE YOU'RE A MAGIC USER!!
After that ...
...I couldn't really speak to him again.
ドクン…
ドクン…
MUNEYUKI-KUN!!
BUT... BUT!

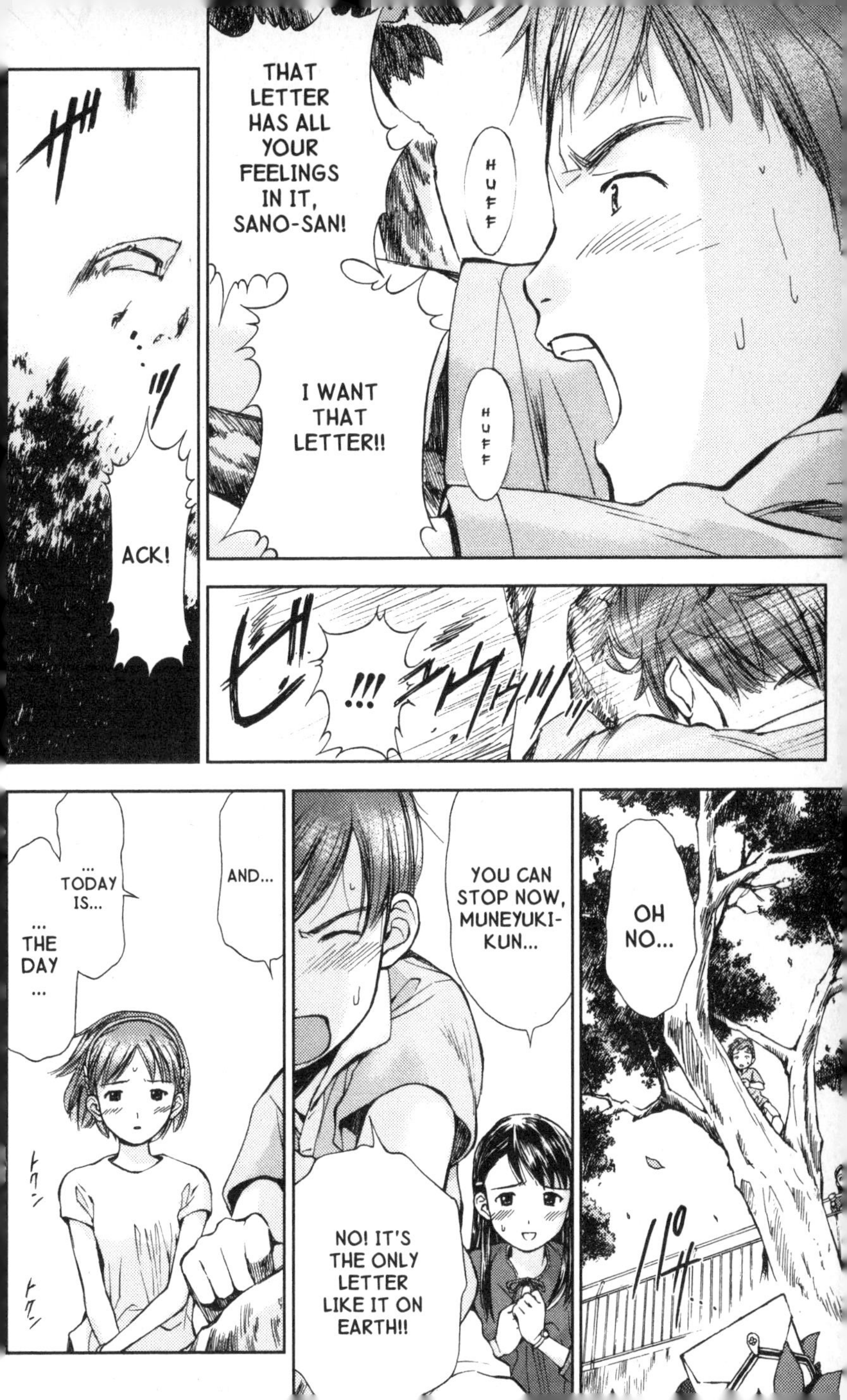
HUFF
THAT LETTER HAS ALL YOUR FEELINGS IN IT, SANO-SAN!
HUFF
I WANT THAT LETTER!!
!!!
ACK!
OH NO...
YOU CAN STOP NOW, MUNEYUKI-KUN...
NO! IT'S THE ONLY LETTER LIKE IT ON EARTH!!
AND...
... TODAY IS...
... THE DAY ...

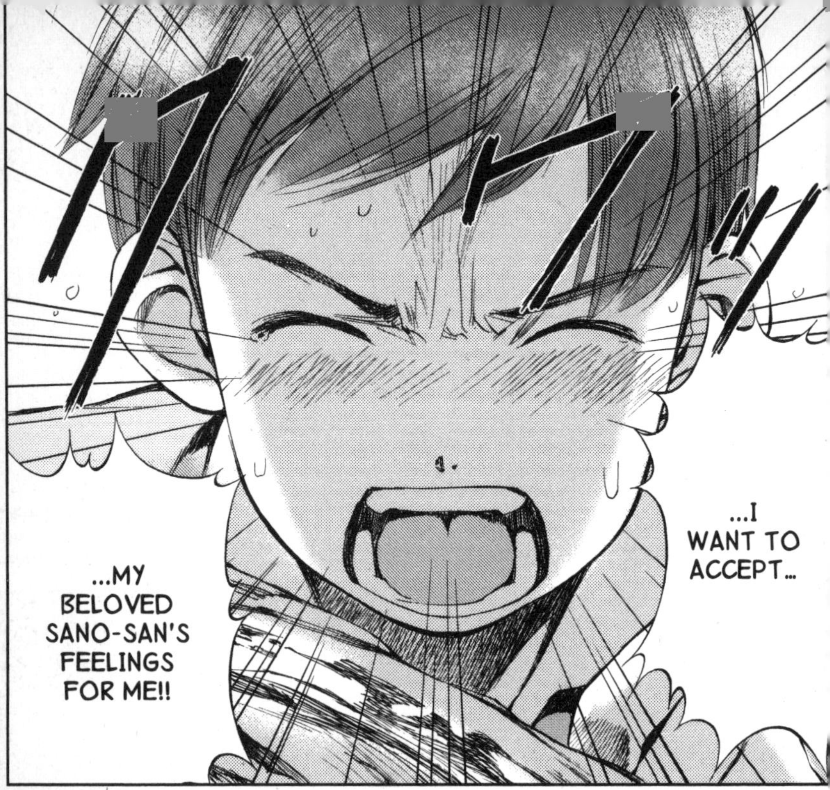
...I WANT TO ACCEPT...
...MY BELOVED SANO-SAN'S FEELINGS FOR ME!!

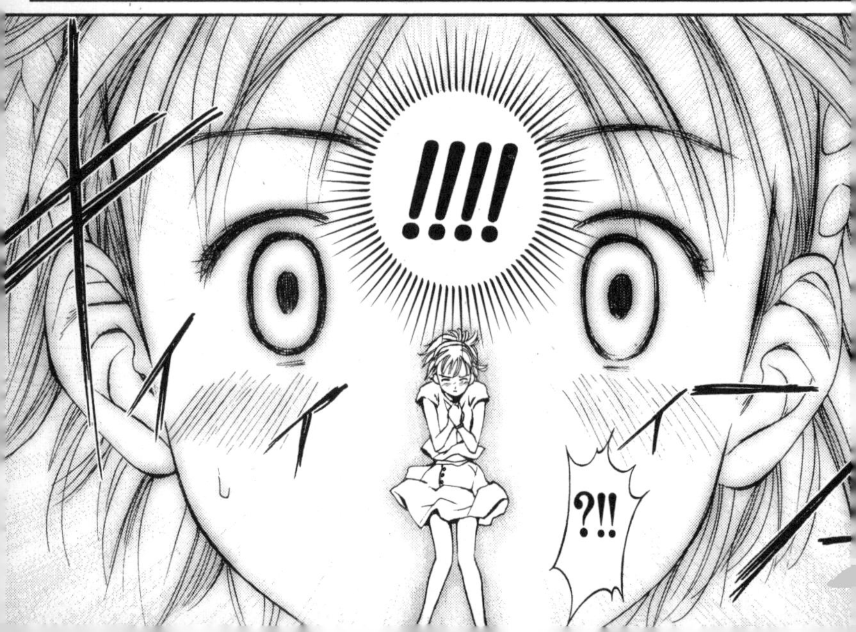
!!!!
?!!

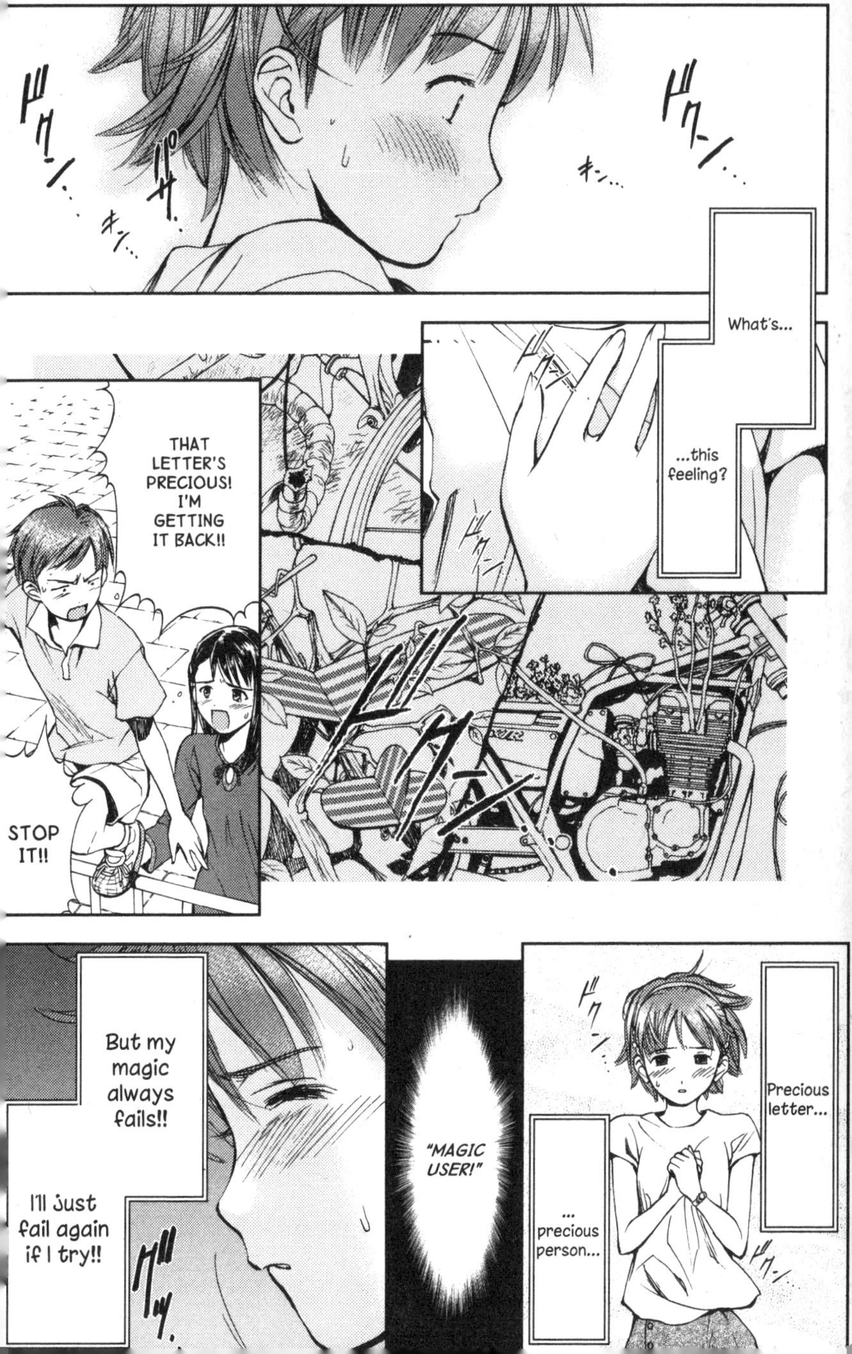
What's...
...this feeling?
THAT LETTER'S PRECIOUS! I'M GETTING IT BACK!!
STOP IT!!
Precious letter...
...precious person...
"MAGIC USER!"
But my magic always fails!!
I'll just fail again if I try!!

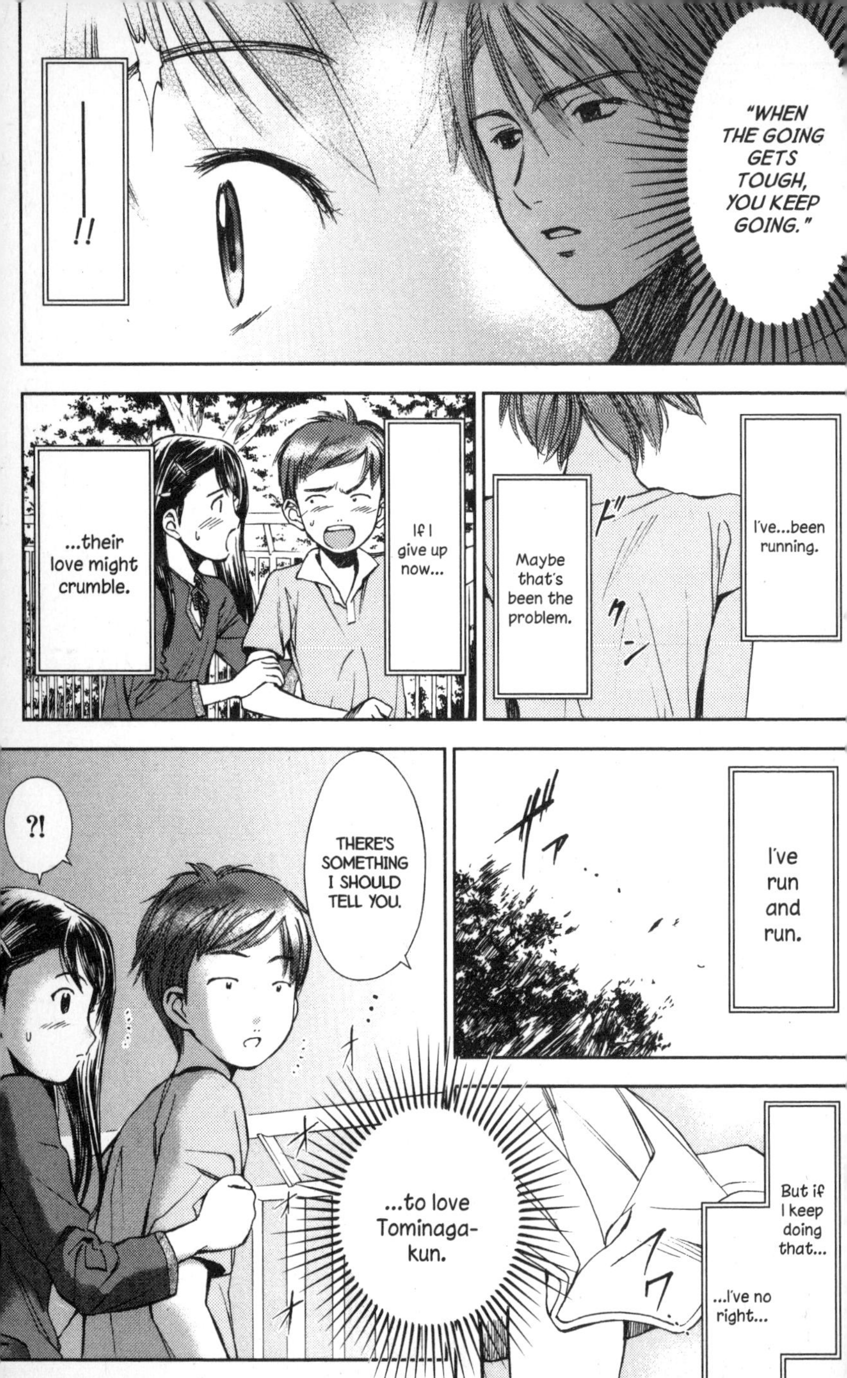
"WHEN THE GOING GETS TOUGH, YOU KEEP GOING."
—!!
I've...been running.
Maybe that's been the problem.
If I give up now...
...their love might crumble.
I've run and run.
But if I keep doing that...
...I've no right...
THERE'S SOMETHING I SHOULD TELL YOU.
?!
...to love Tominaga-kun.

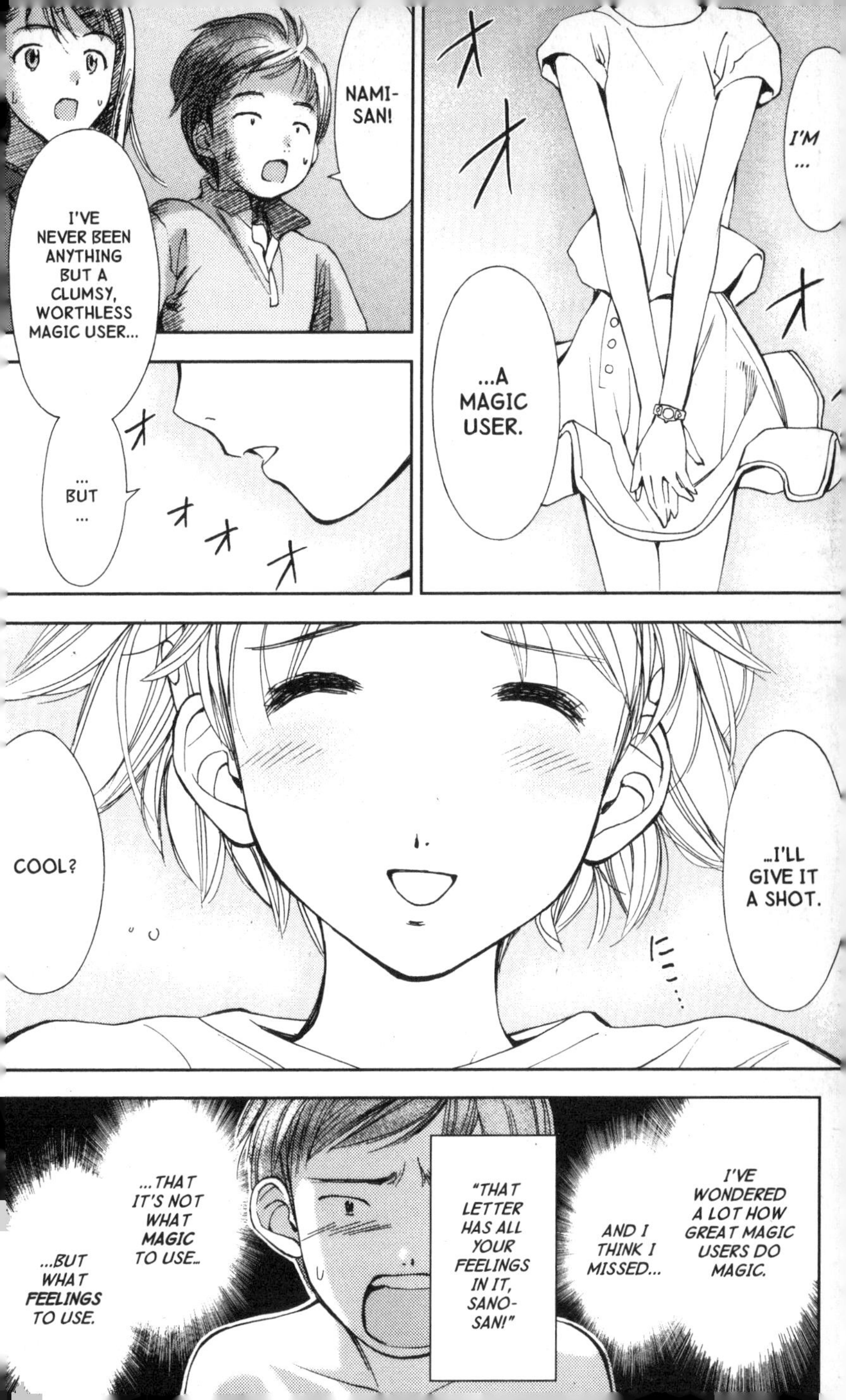
I'M ...
...A MAGIC USER.
NAMI-SAN!
I'VE NEVER BEEN ANYTHING BUT A CLUMSY, WORTHLESS MAGIC USER...
... BUT ...
...I'LL GIVE IT A SHOT.
COOL?
I'VE WONDERED A LOT HOW GREAT MAGIC USERS DO MAGIC.
AND I THINK I MISSED...
"THAT LETTER HAS ALL YOUR FEELINGS IN IT, SANO-SAN!"
...THAT IT'S NOT WHAT MAGIC TO USE..
...BUT WHAT FEELINGS TO USE.

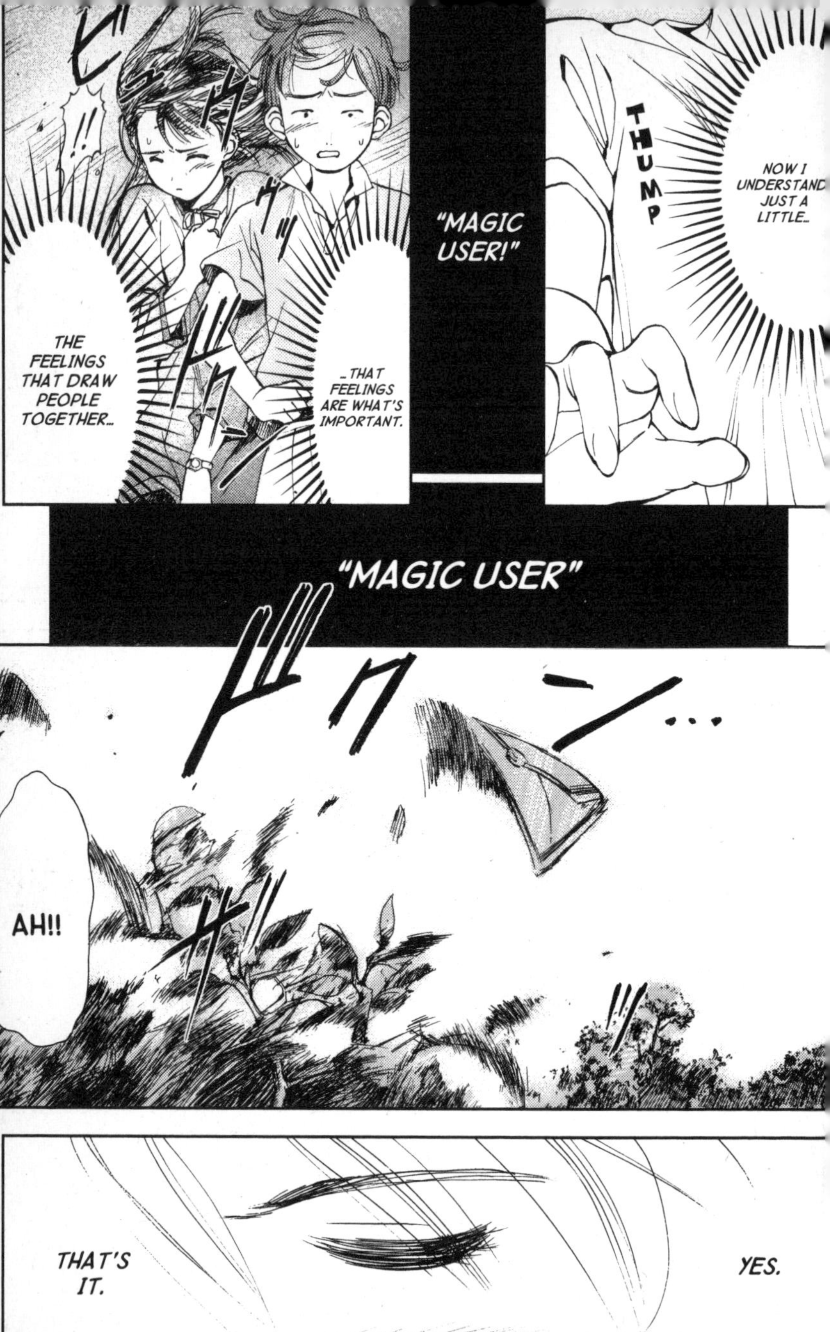
NOW I UNDERSTAND JUST A LITTLE..
THUMP
"MAGIC USER!"
...THAT FEELINGS ARE WHAT'S IMPORTANT.
THE FEELINGS THAT DRAW PEOPLE TOGETHER...
"MAGIC USER"
AH!!
YES.
THAT'S IT.

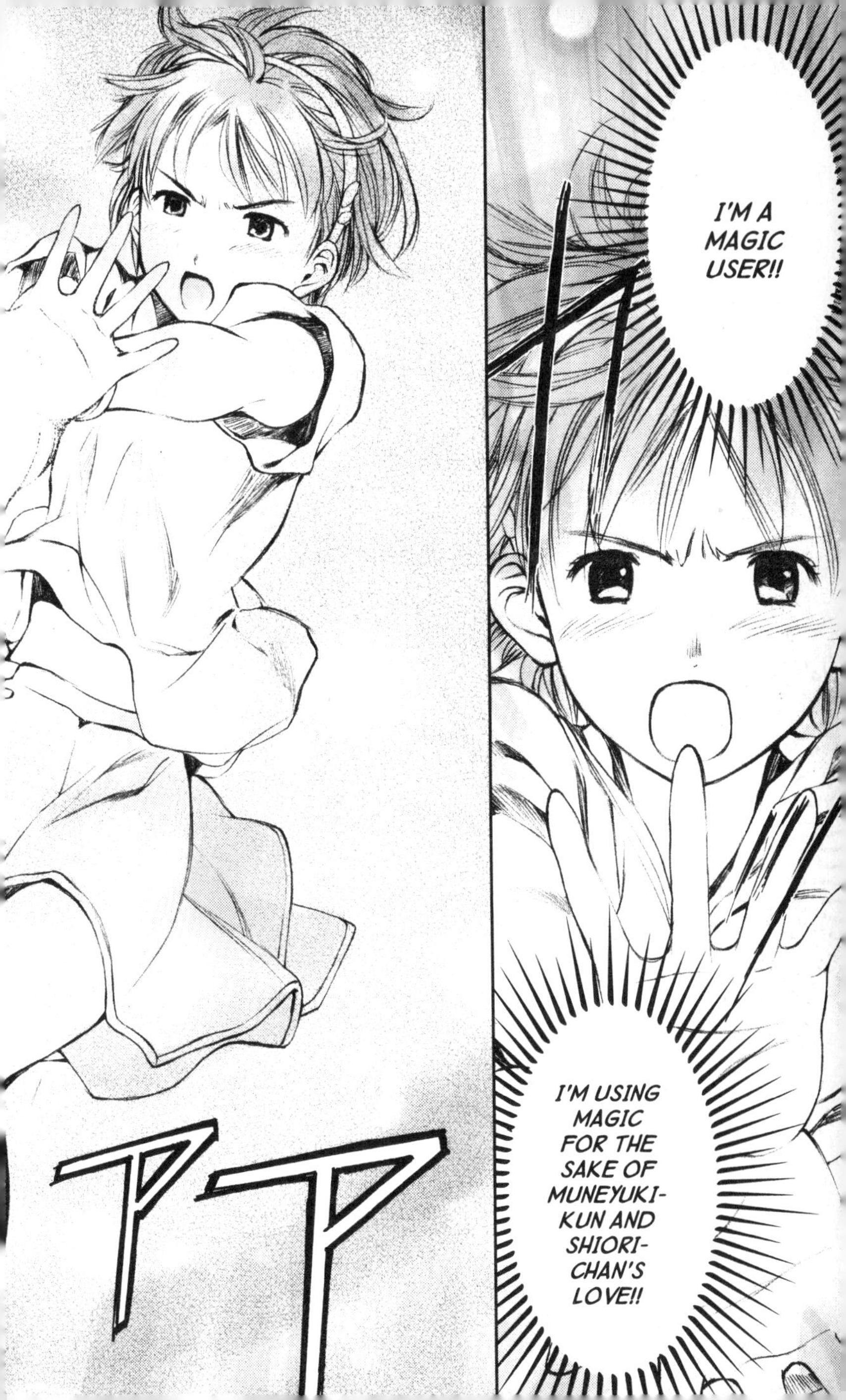
I'M A MAGIC USER!!
I'M USING MAGIC FOR THE SAKE OF MUNEYUKI-KUN AND SHIORI-CHAN'S LOVE!!

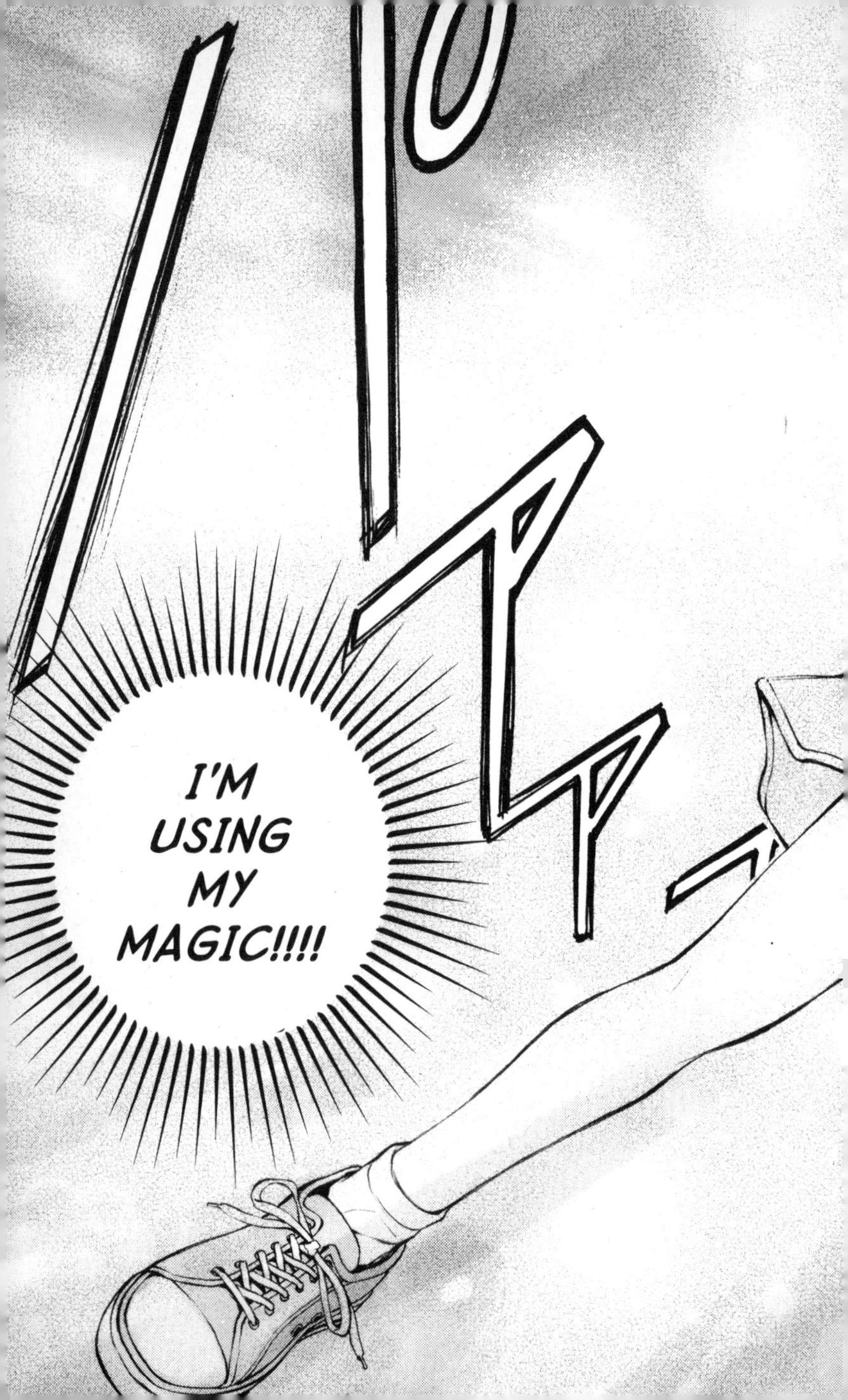
I'M USING MY MAGIC!!!!

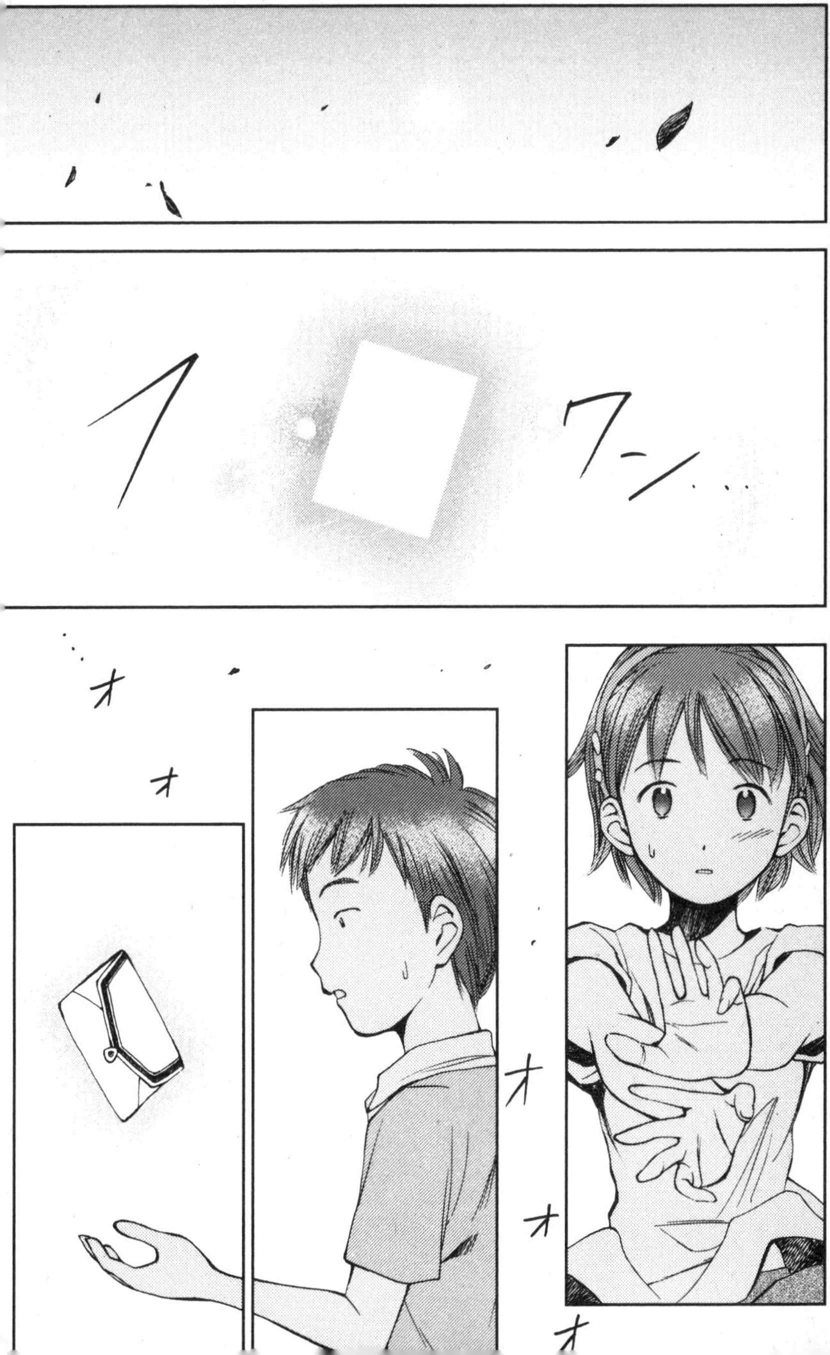
フワン……
…オ
オ
オ
オ
オ

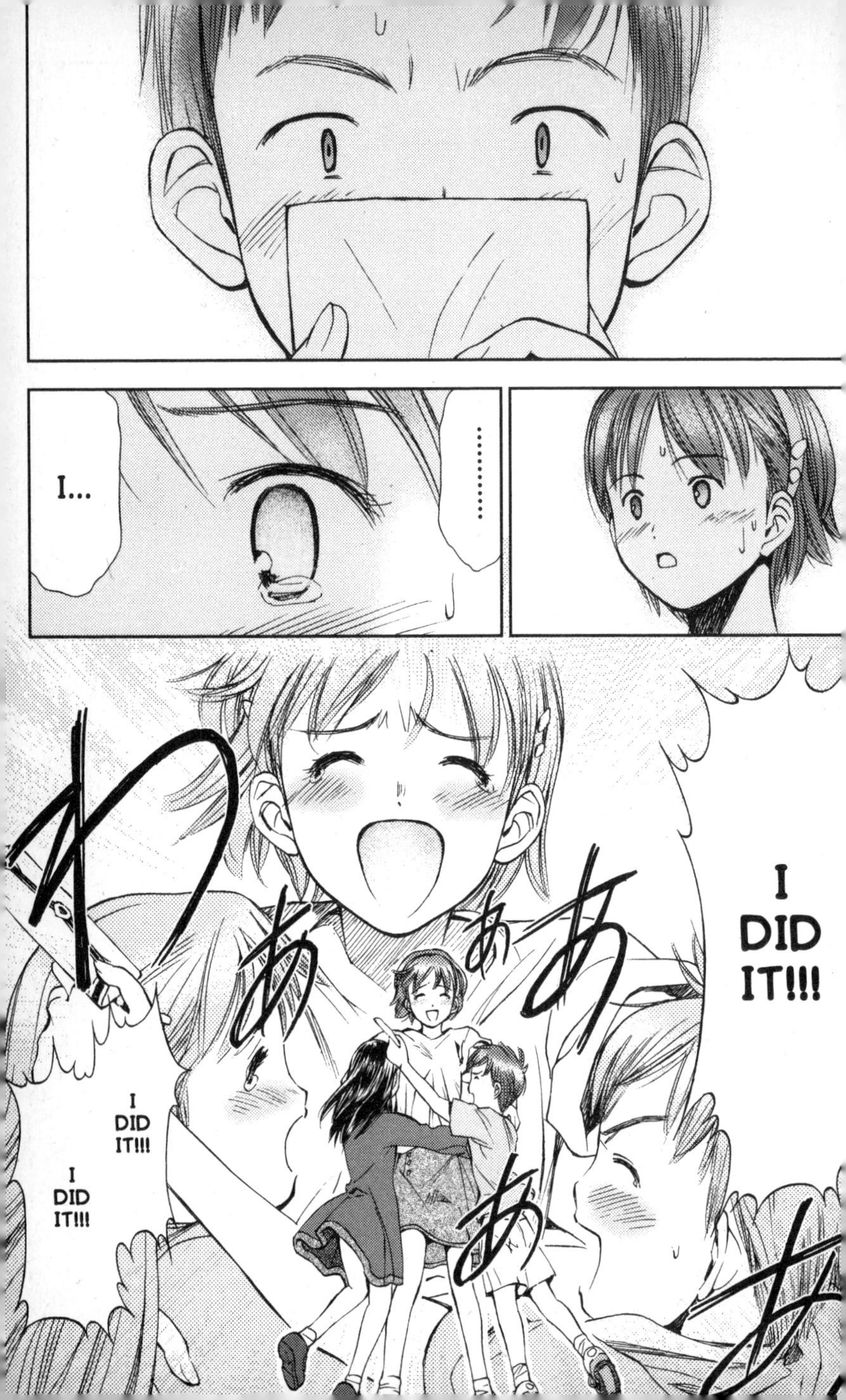
....
I...
I DID IT!!!
I DID IT!!!
I DID IT!!!

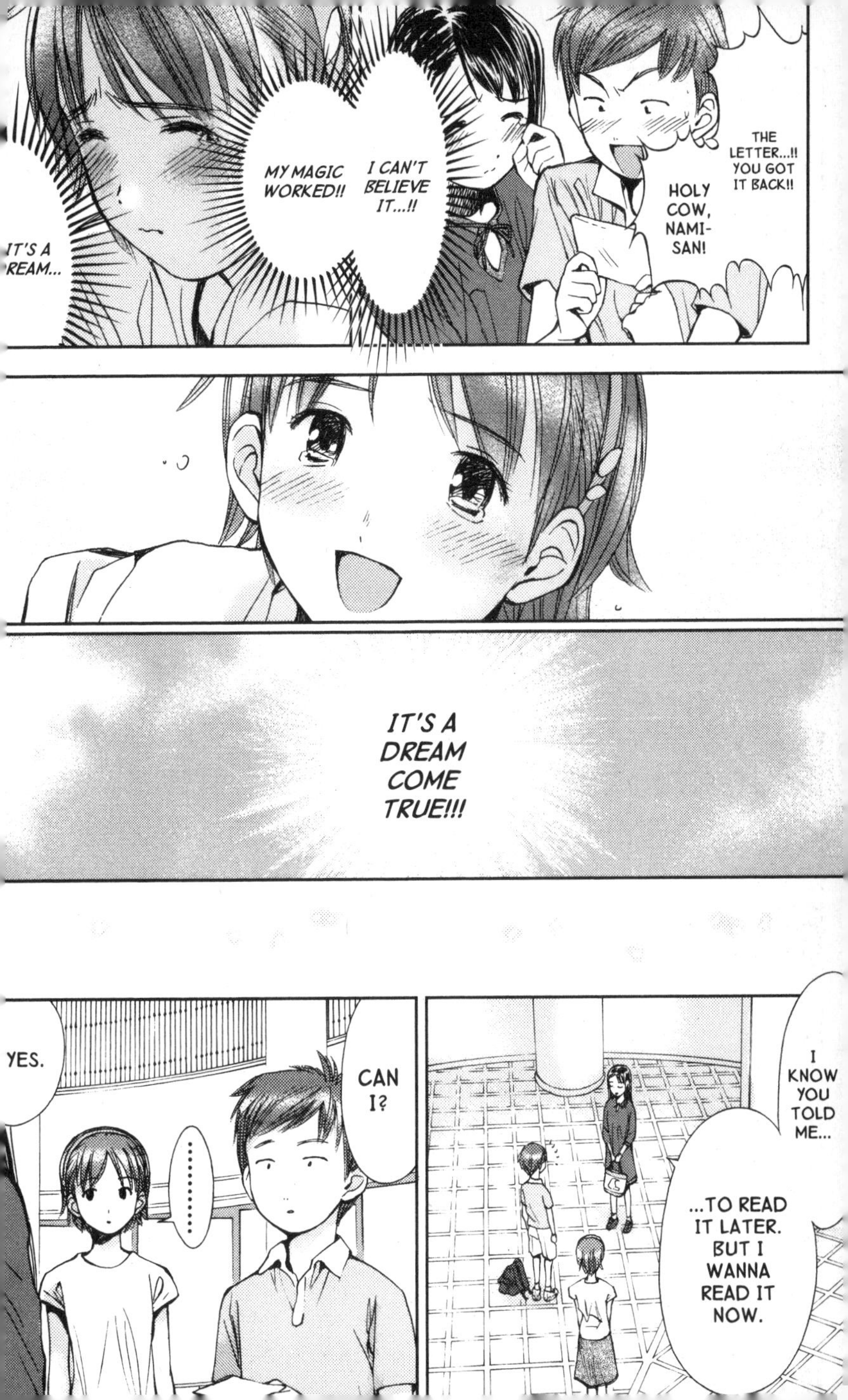
THE LETTER...!! YOU GOT IT BACK!!
HOLY COW, NAMI-SAN!
I CAN'T BELIEVE IT...!!
MY MAGIC WORKED!!
IT'S A REAM...
IT'S A DREAM COME TRUE!!!
I KNOW YOU TOLD ME...
...TO READ IT LATER. BUT I WANNA READ IT NOW.
CAN I?
....
YES.

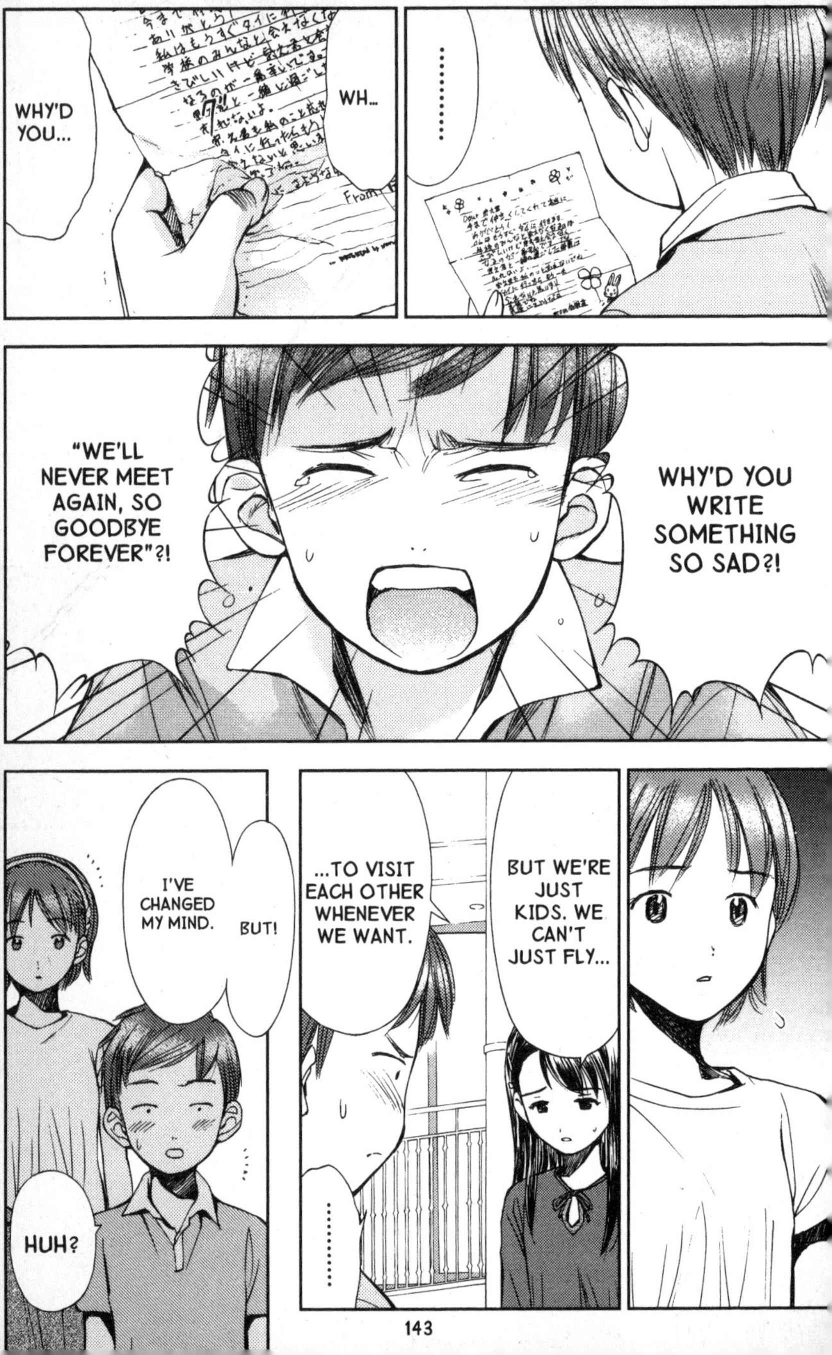
......
WH...
WHY'D YOU...
WHY'D YOU WRITE SOMETHING SO SAD?!
"WE'LL NEVER MEET AGAIN, SO GOODBYE FOREVER"?!
BUT WE'RE JUST KIDS. WE CAN'T JUST FLY...
...TO VISIT EACH OTHER WHENEVER WE WANT.
......
BUT!
I'VE CHANGED MY MIND.
HUH?

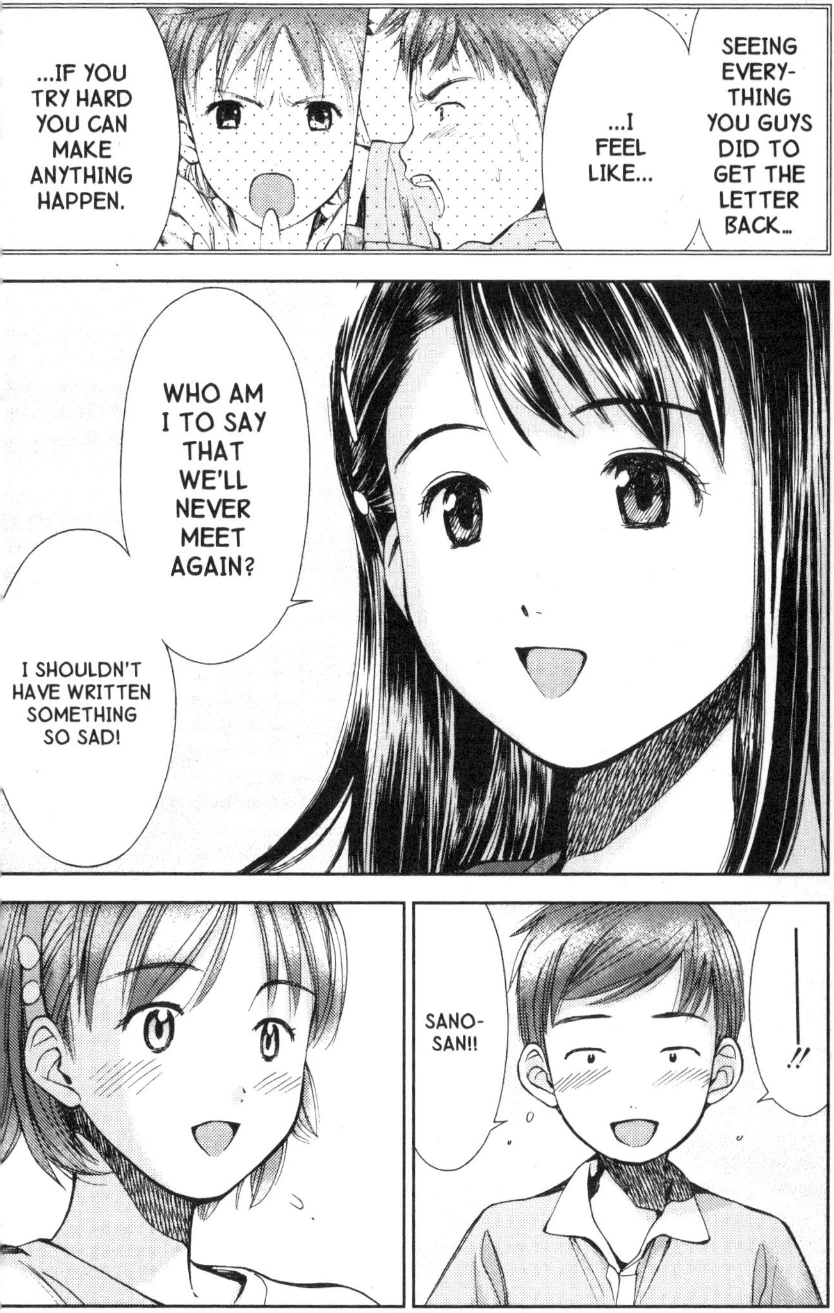
SEEING EVERY-THING YOU GUYS DID TO GET THE LETTER BACK...
...I FEEL LIKE...
...IF YOU TRY HARD YOU CAN MAKE ANYTHING HAPPEN.
WHO AM I TO SAY THAT WE'LL NEVER MEET AGAIN?
I SHOULDN'T HAVE WRITTEN SOMETHING SO SAD!
——!!
SANO-SAN!!

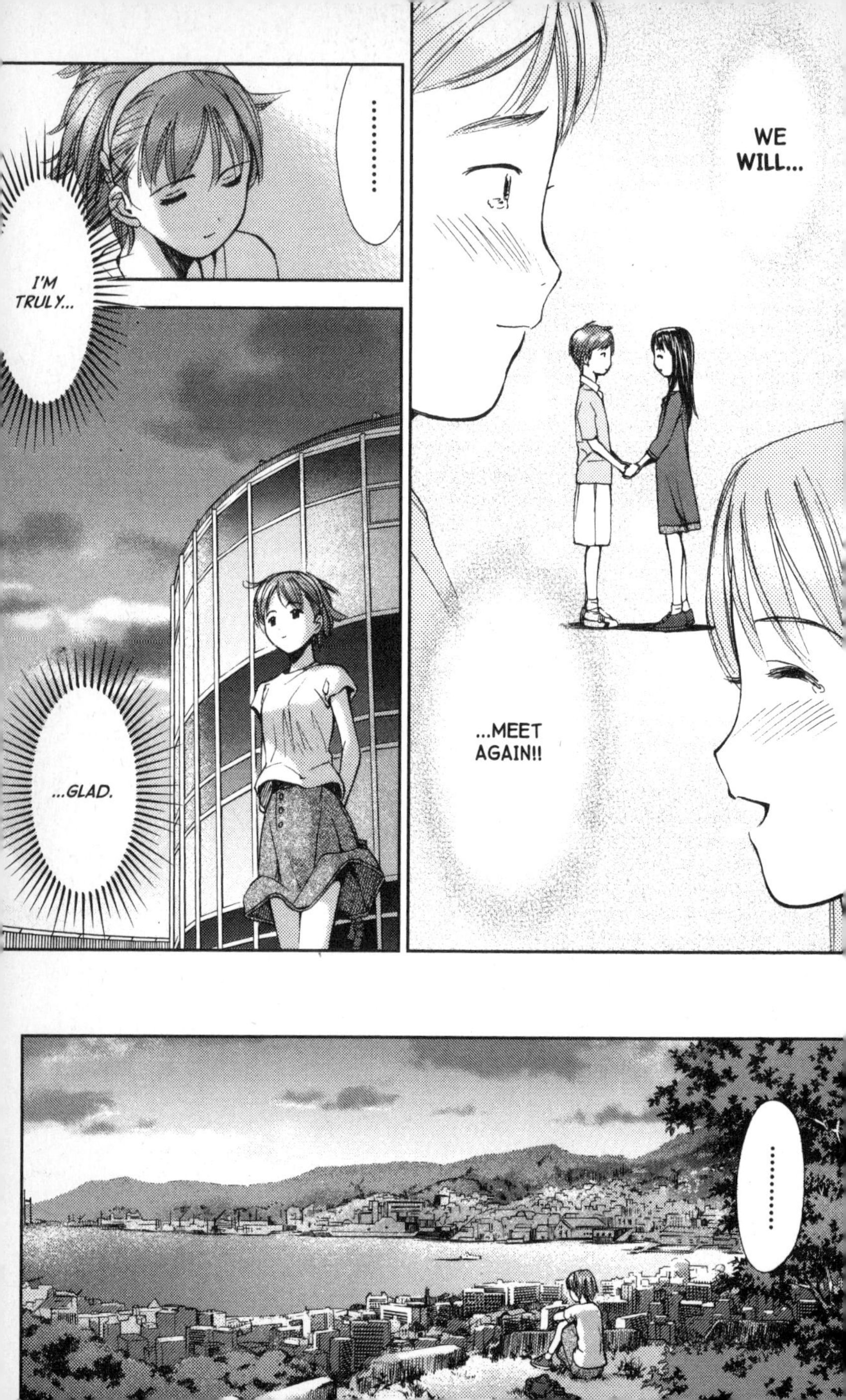
WE WILL...
...MEET AGAIN!!
....
I'M TRULY...
...GLAD.
....

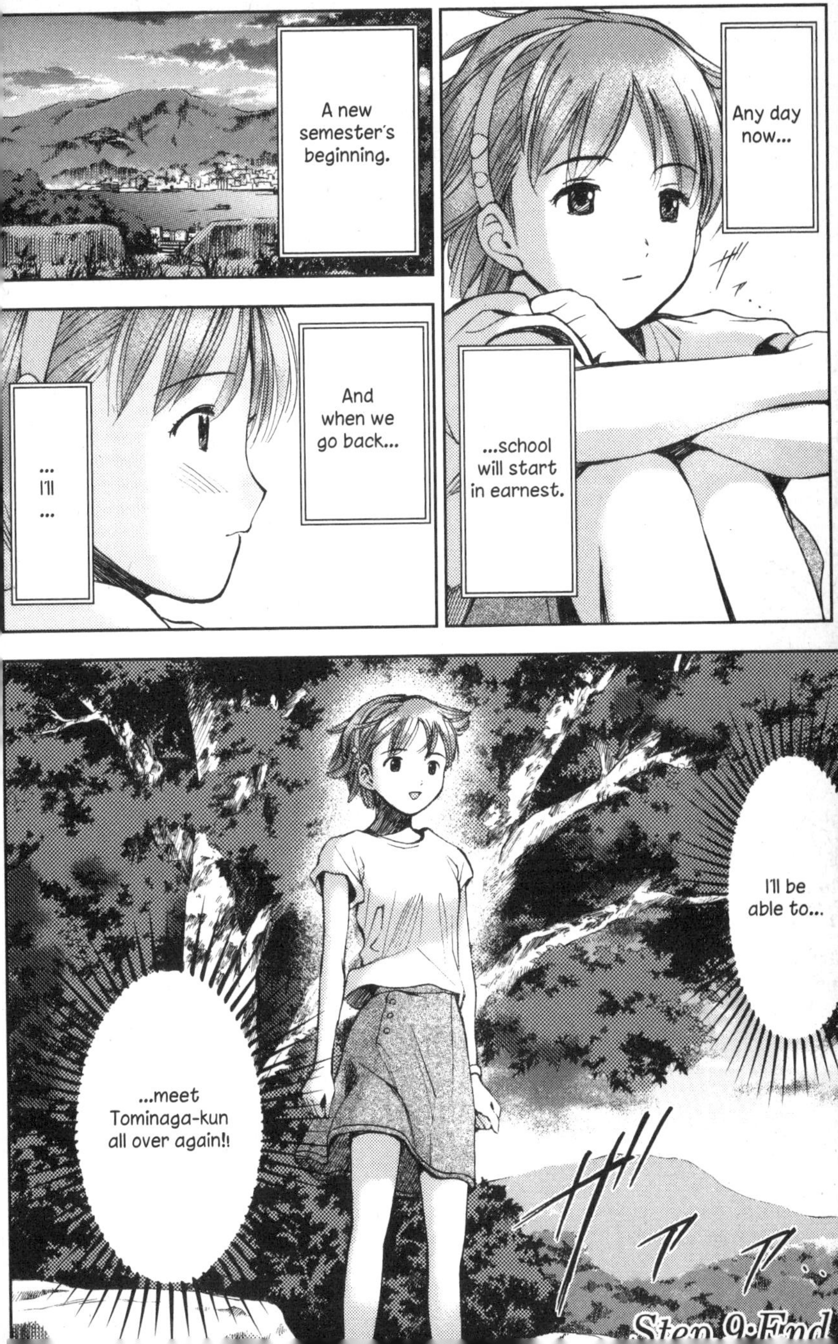
Any day now...
...school will start in earnest.
A new semester's beginning.
And when we go back...
...I'll...
I'll be able to...
...meet Tominaga-kun all over again!!
Step 9: End

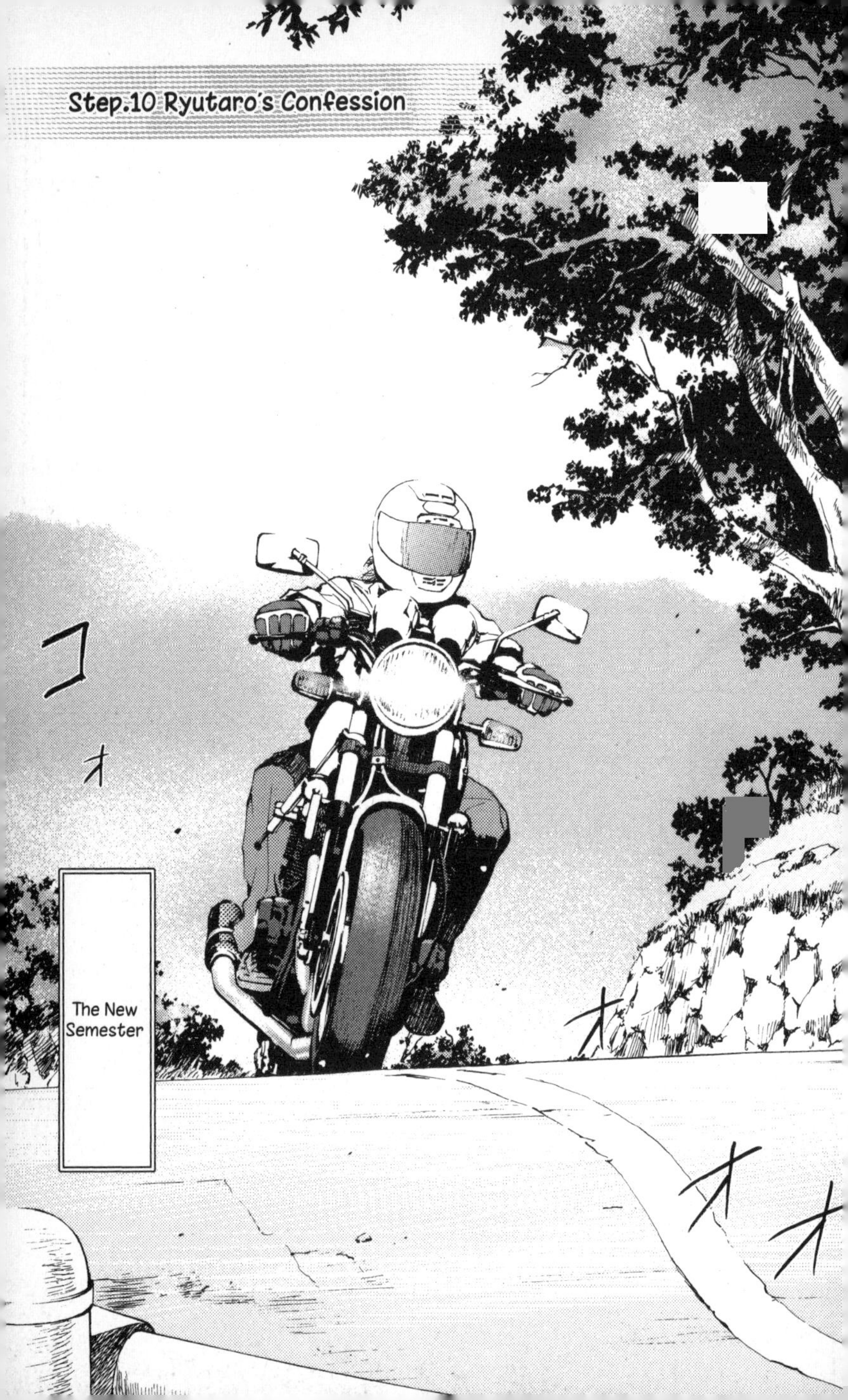
Step.10 Ryutaro's Confession
コ
オ
オ
オ
オ
The New Semester

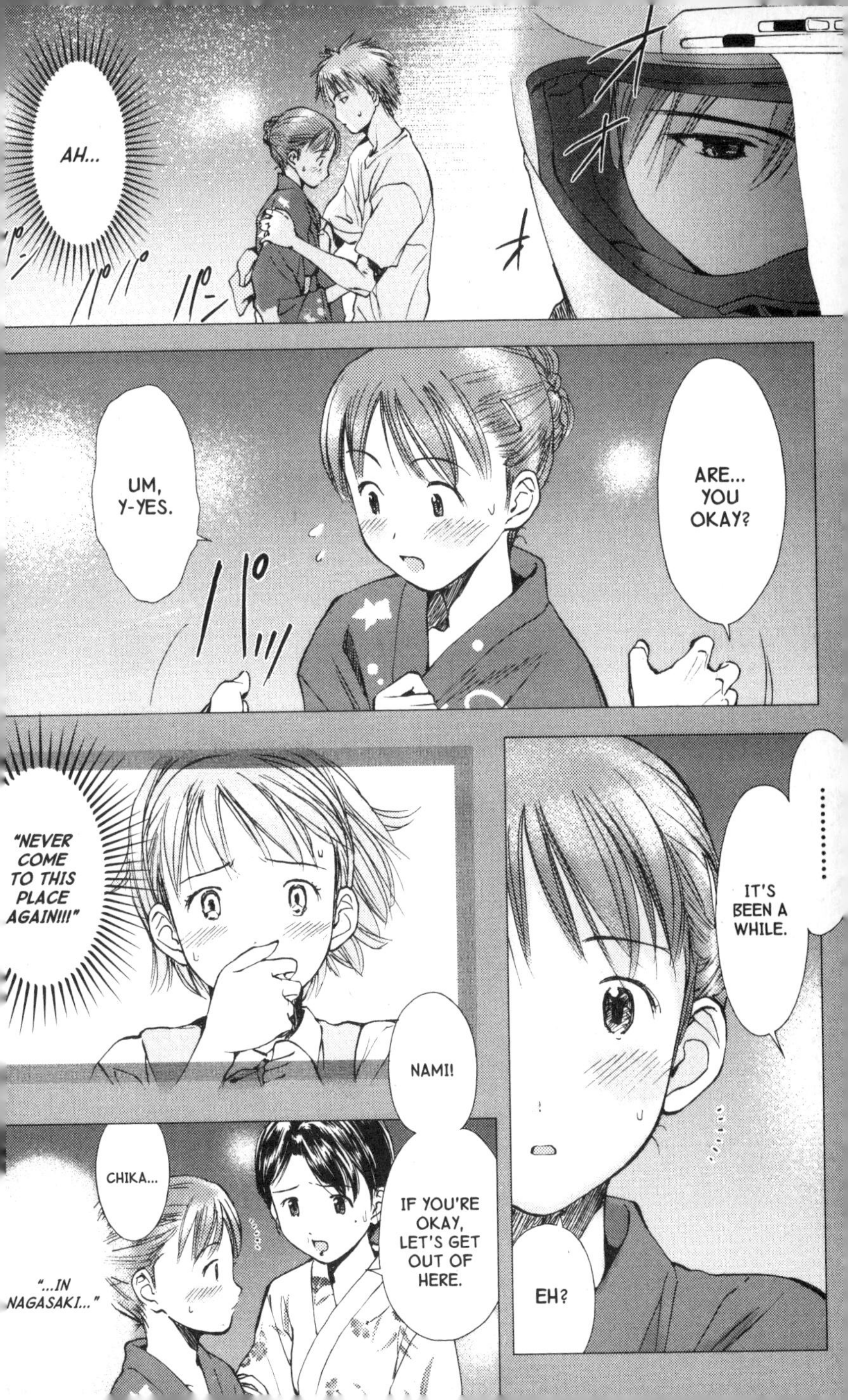
AH...
ARE... YOU OKAY?
UM, Y-YES.
......
IT'S BEEN A WHILE.
EH?
"NEVER COME TO THIS PLACE AGAIN!!!"
NAMI!
IF YOU'RE OKAY, LET'S GET OUT OF HERE.
CHIKA...
"...IN NAGASAKI..."

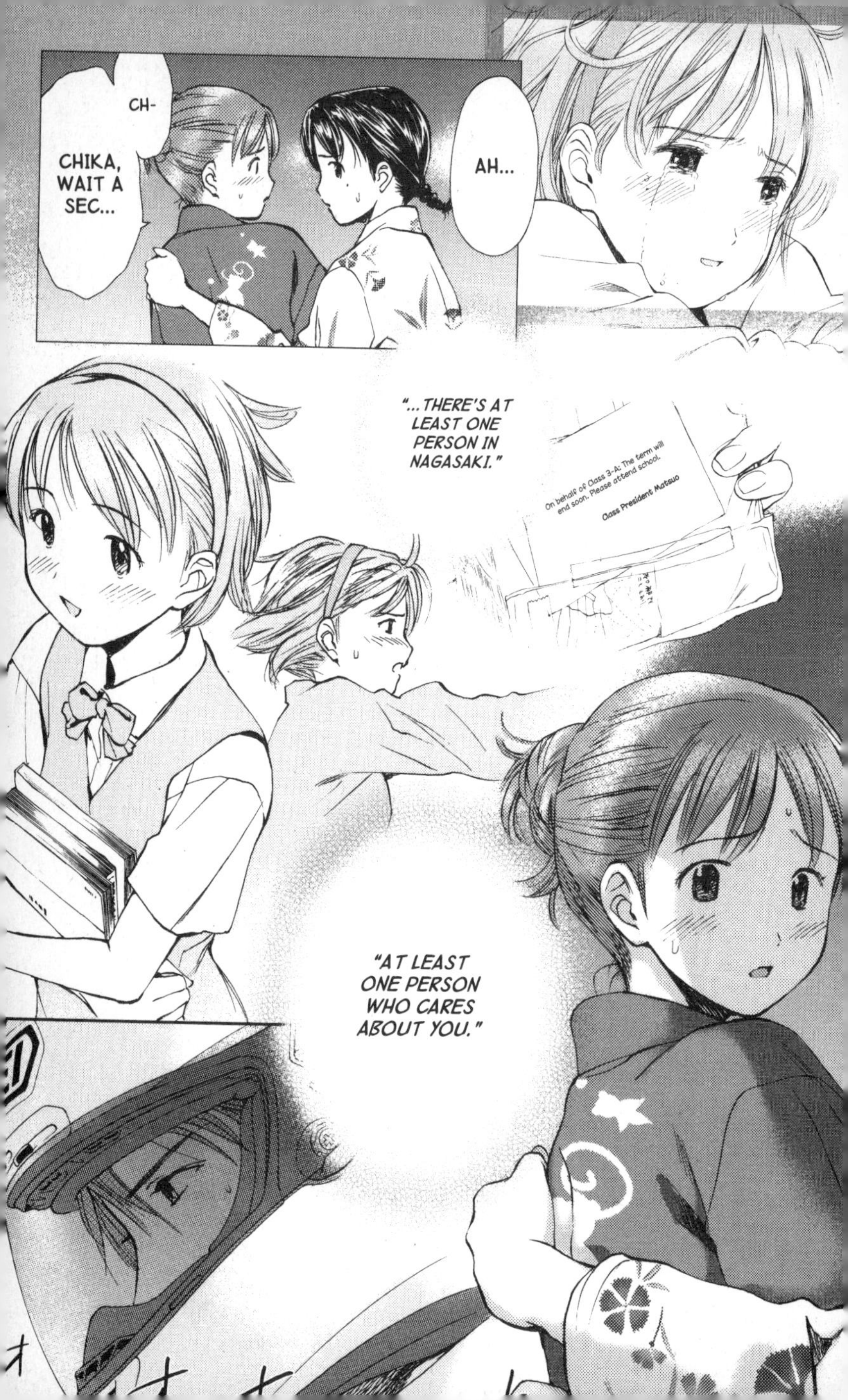
AH...
CH-
CHIKA, WAIT A SEC...
"...THERE'S AT LEAST ONE PERSON IN NAGASAKI."
On behalf of Class 3-A: The term will end soon. Please attend school.
Class President Matsuo
"AT LEAST ONE PERSON WHO CARES ABOUT YOU."

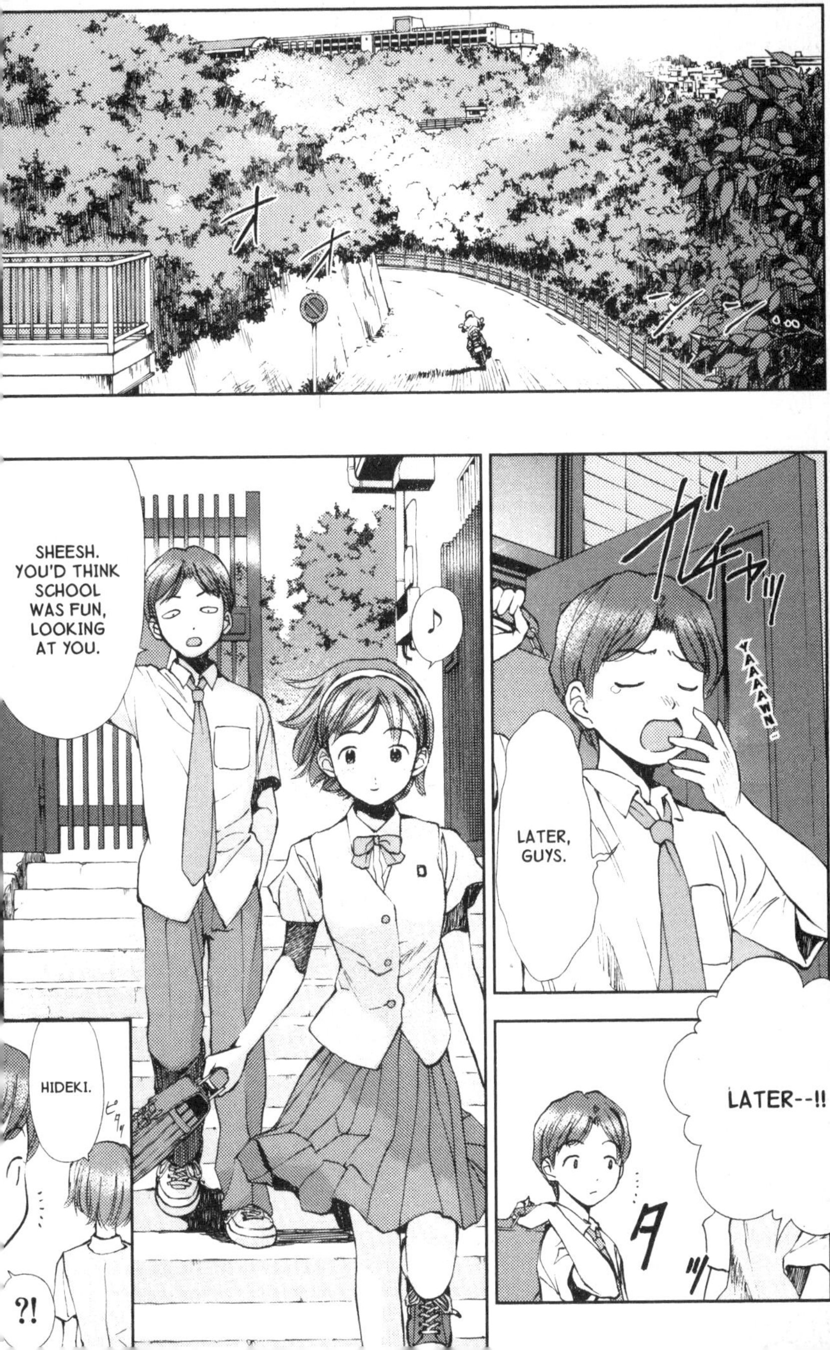
ガチャッ
YAAAAWN!!
LATER, GUYS.
LATER--!!
タッ
SHEESH. YOU'D THINK SCHOOL WAS FUN, LOOKING AT YOU.
♪
HIDEKI.
ピタッ
?!

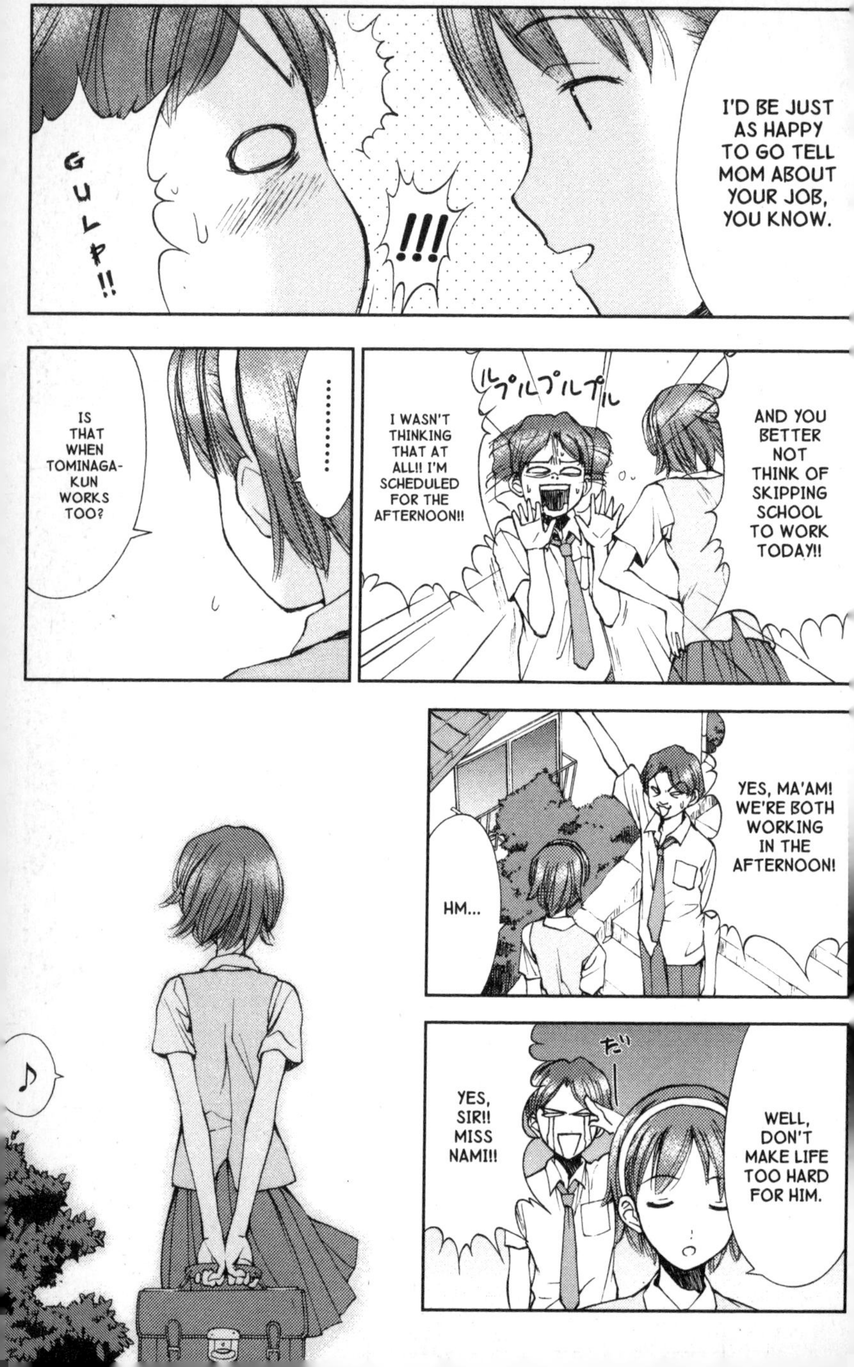

I'D BE JUST AS HAPPY TO GO TELL MOM ABOUT YOUR JOB, YOU KNOW.
!!!
GULP!!
AND YOU BETTER NOT THINK OF SKIPPING SCHOOL TO WORK TODAY!!
ルプルプルプル
I WASN'T THINKING THAT AT ALL!! I'M SCHEDULED FOR THE AFTERNOON!!
....
IS THAT WHEN TOMINAGA-KUN WORKS TOO?
YES, MA'AM! WE'RE BOTH WORKING IN THE AFTERNOON!
HM...
WELL, DON'T MAKE LIFE TOO HARD FOR HIM.
だー
YES, SIR!! MISS NAMI!!
♪

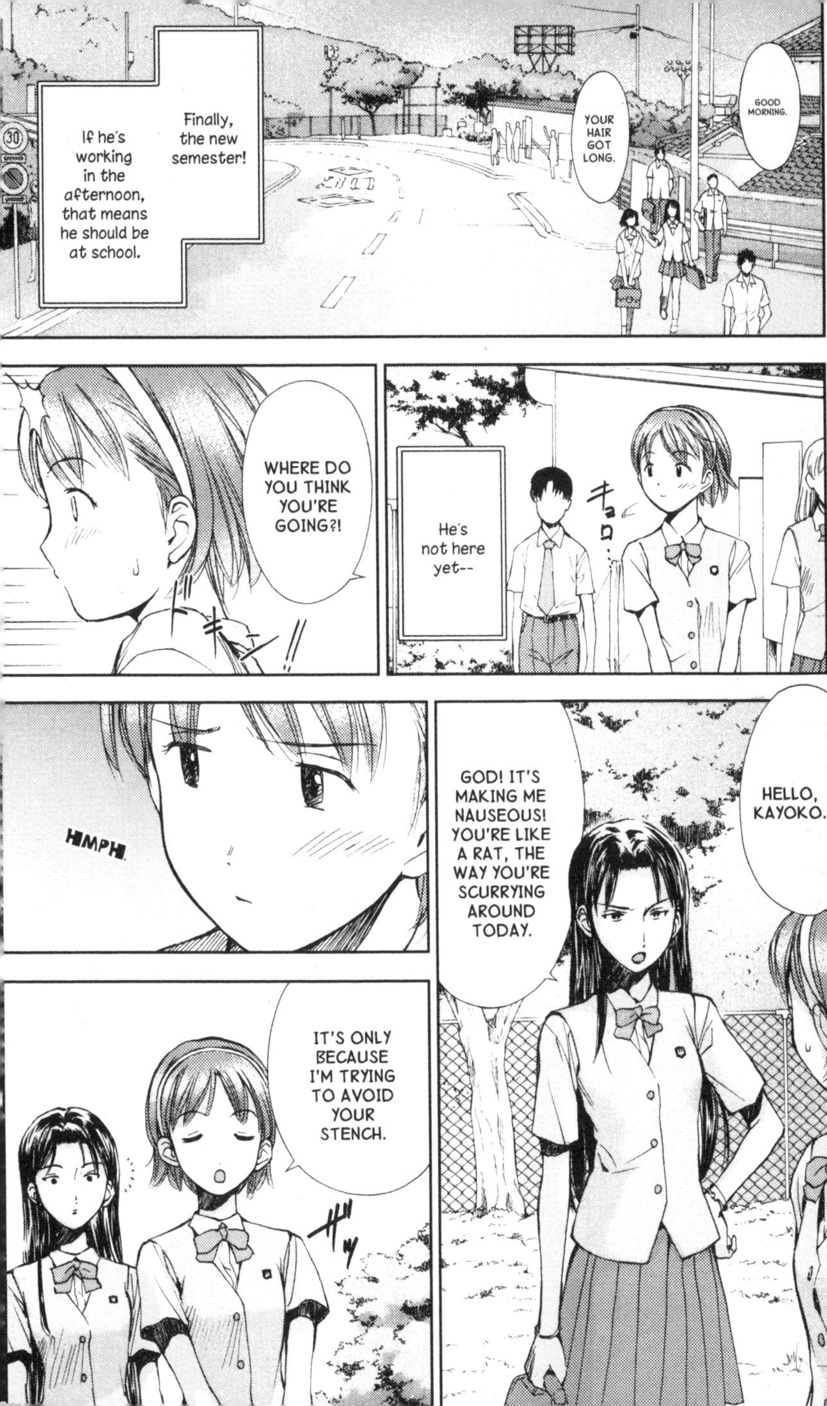
GOOD MORNING.
YOUR HAIR GOT LONG.
Finally, the new semester!
If he's working in the afternoon, that means he should be at school.
He's not here yet--
WHERE DO YOU THINK YOU'RE GOING?!
HELLO, KAYOKO.
GOD! IT'S MAKING ME NAUSEOUS! YOU'RE LIKE A RAT, THE WAY YOU'RE SCURRYING AROUND TODAY.
HMPH.
IT'S ONLY BECAUSE I'M TRYING TO AVOID YOUR STENCH.

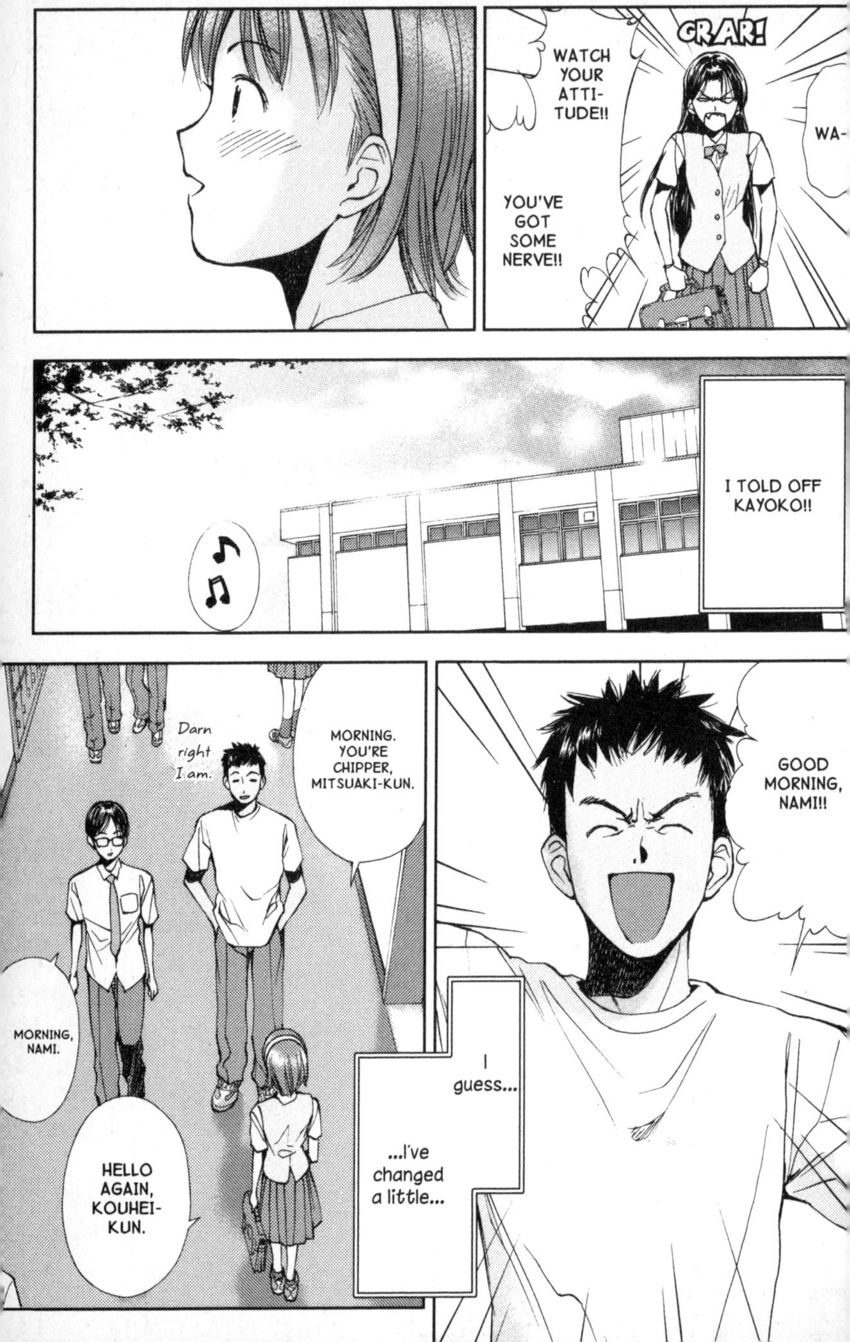
GRAR!
WA-
WATCH YOUR ATTITUDE!!
YOU'VE GOT SOME NERVE!!
I TOLD OFF KAYOKO!!
GOOD MORNING, NAMI!!
I guess...
...I've changed a little...
MORNING. YOU'RE CHIPPER, MITSUAKI-KUN.
Darn right I am.
MORNING, NAMI.
HELLO AGAIN, KOUHEI-KUN.

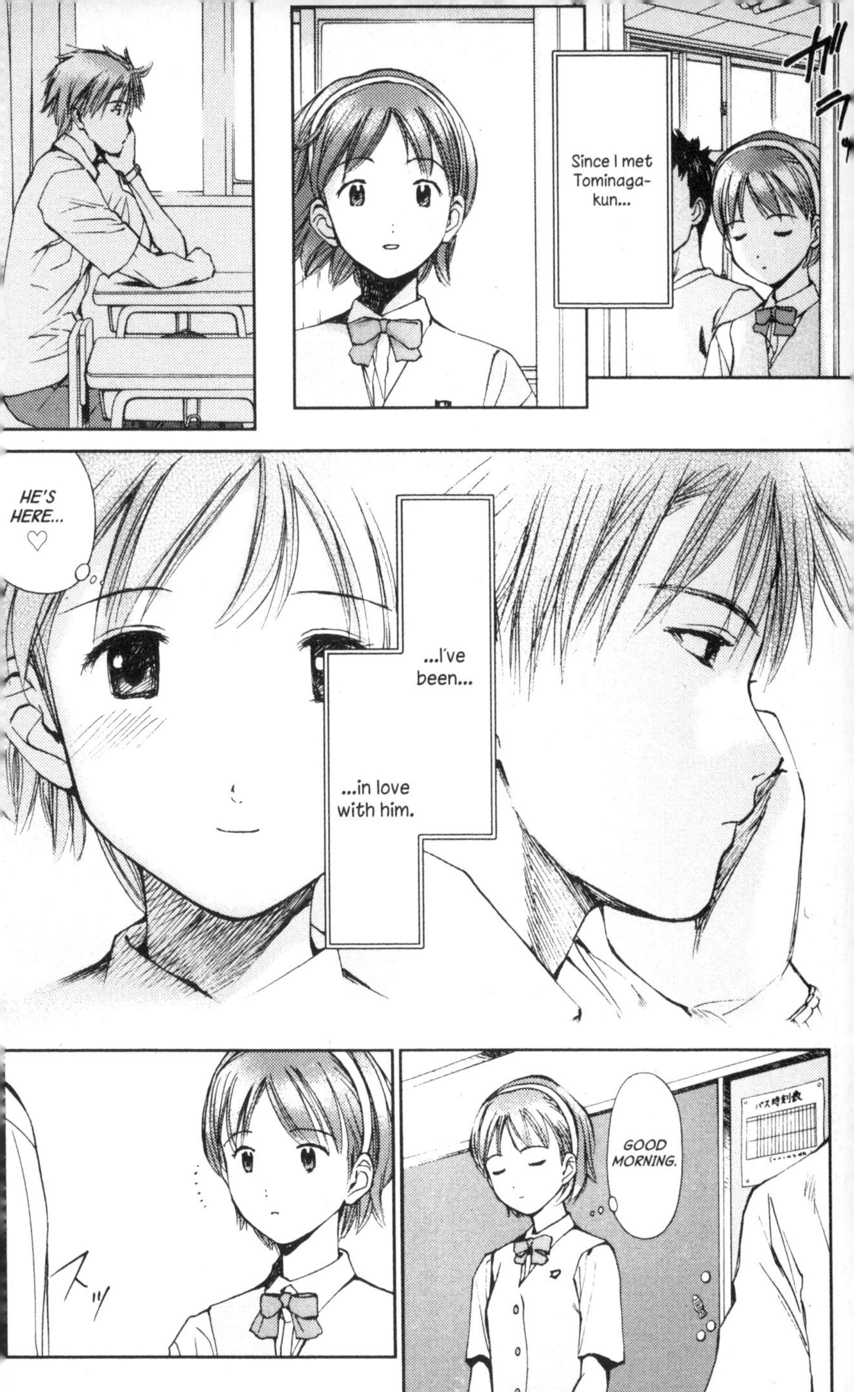
ガラッ
Since I met Tominaga-kun...
...I've been...
...in love with him.
HE'S HERE... ♡
バス時刻表
GOOD MORNING.
スッ

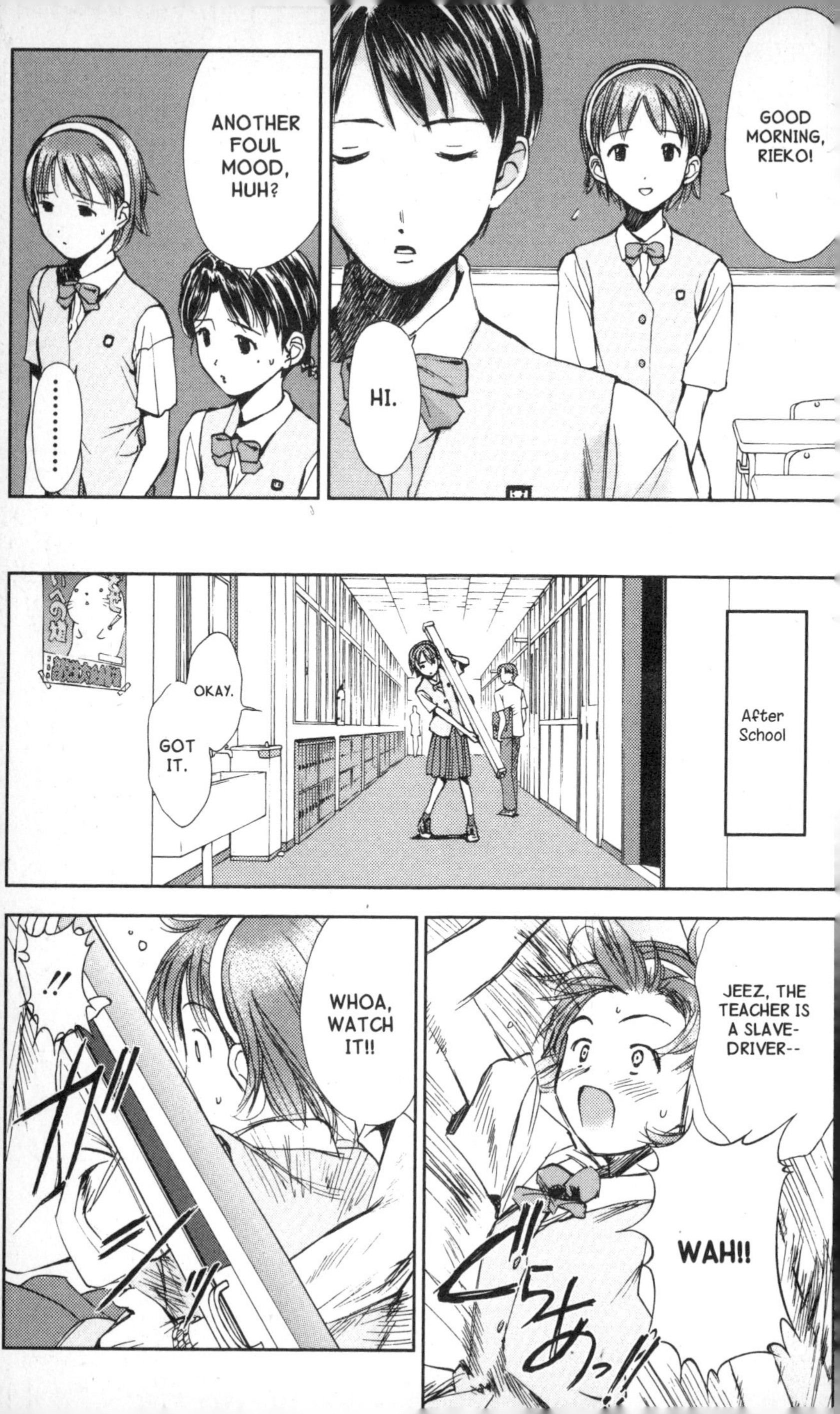
GOOD MORNING, RIEKO!
HI.
ANOTHER FOUL MOOD, HUH?
......
After School
OKAY.
GOT IT.
JEEZ, THE TEACHER IS A SLAVE-DRIVER--
WAH!!
ぐらあっ!!
!!
WHOA, WATCH IT!!
ガン

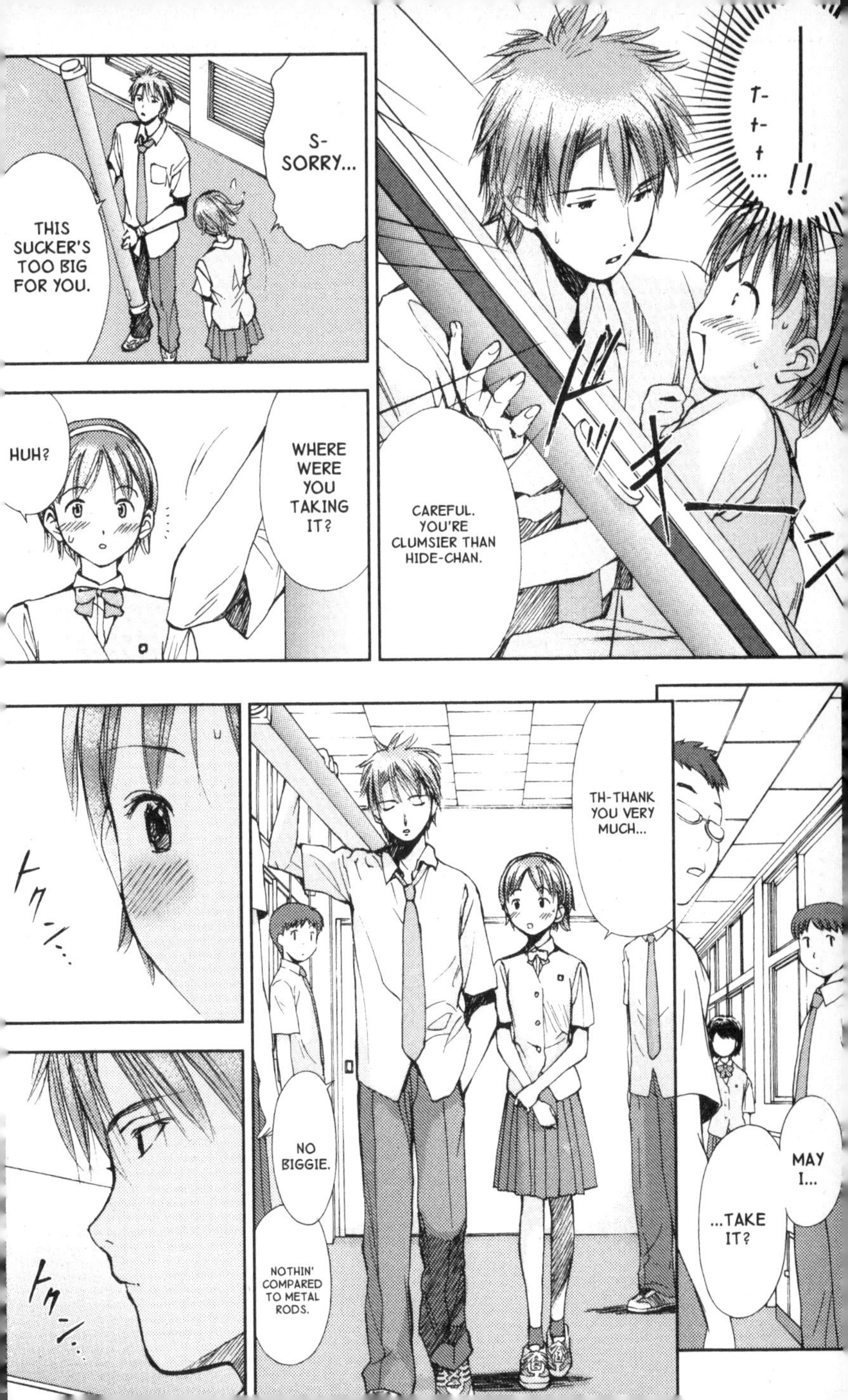
T- t- t...
!!
CAREFUL. YOU'RE CLUMSIER THAN HIDE-CHAN.
S-SORRY...
THIS SUCKER'S TOO BIG FOR YOU.
WHERE WERE YOU TAKING IT?
HUH?
MAY I...
...TAKE IT?
TH-THANK YOU VERY MUCH...
NO BIGGIE.
NOTHIN' COMPARED TO METAL RODS.

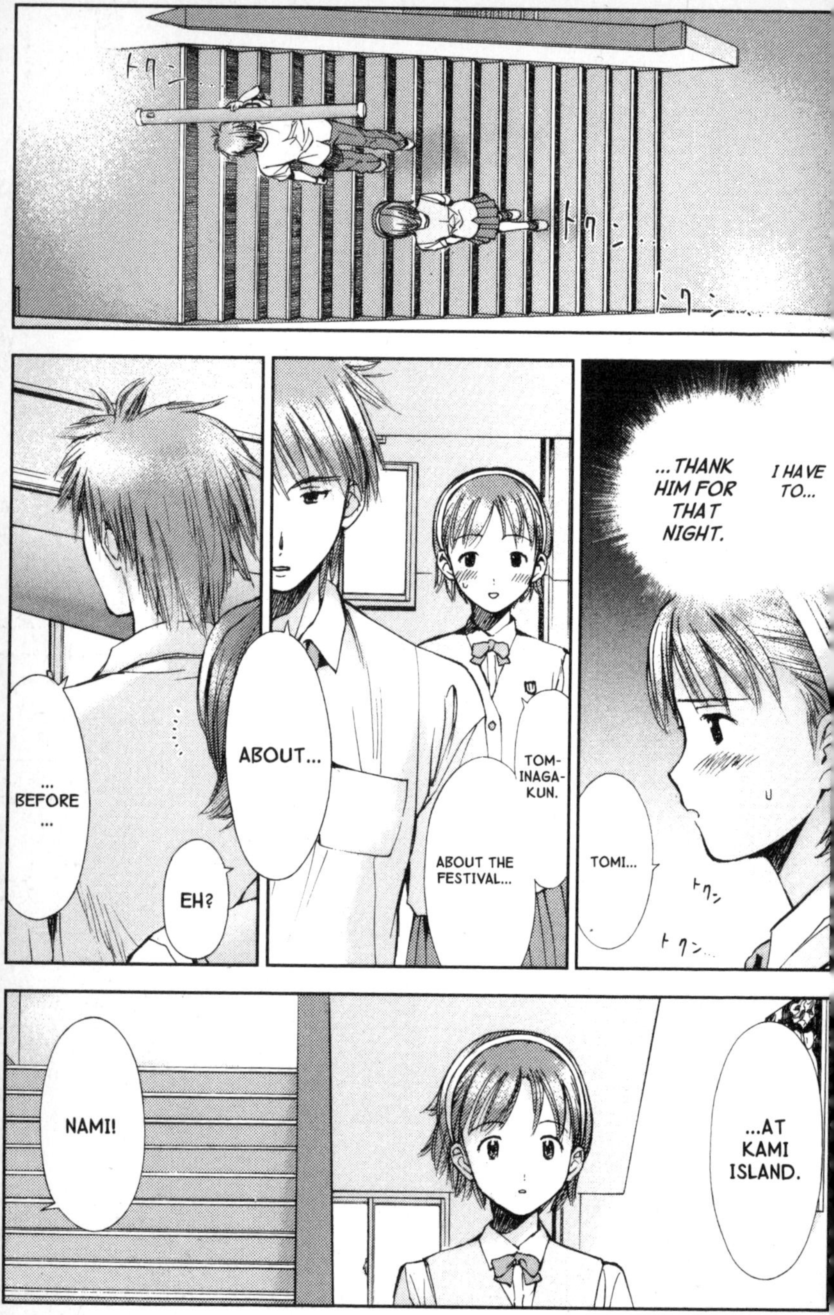
トクン…
トクン…
トクン…
I HAVE TO...
...THANK HIM FOR THAT NIGHT.
TOMI...
トクン
トクン…
TOM-INAGA-KUN.
ABOUT THE FESTIVAL...
ABOUT...
.....
...BEFORE...
EH?
...AT KAMI ISLAND.
NAMI!

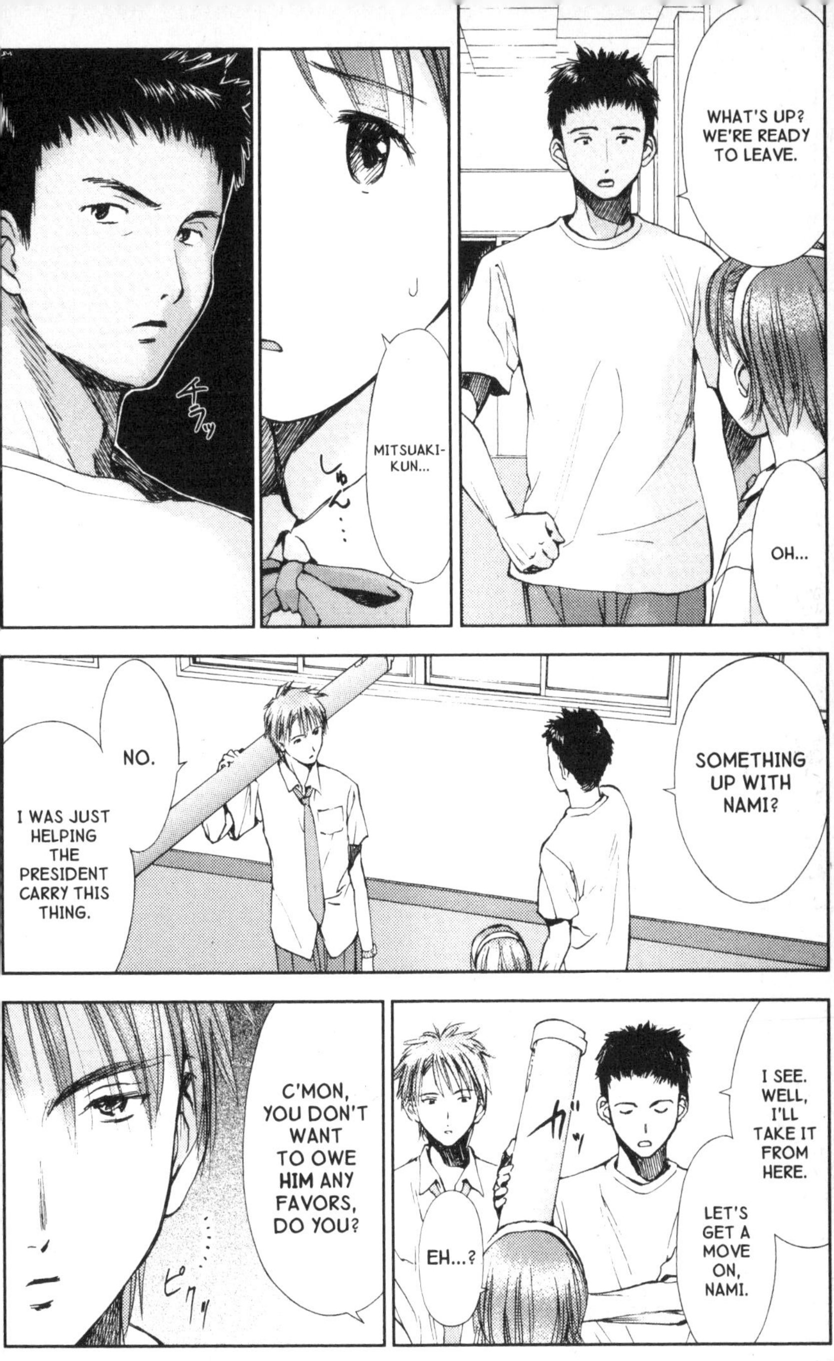
WHAT'S UP? WE'RE READY TO LEAVE.
OH...
MITSUAKI-KUN...
しゅん…
チラッ
SOMETHING UP WITH NAMI?
NO.
I WAS JUST HELPING THE PRESIDENT CARRY THIS THING.
I SEE. WELL, I'LL TAKE IT FROM HERE.
LET'S GET A MOVE ON, NAMI.
ガッ
EH...?
C'MON, YOU DON'T WANT TO OWE HIM ANY FAVORS, DO YOU?
......
ピクッ

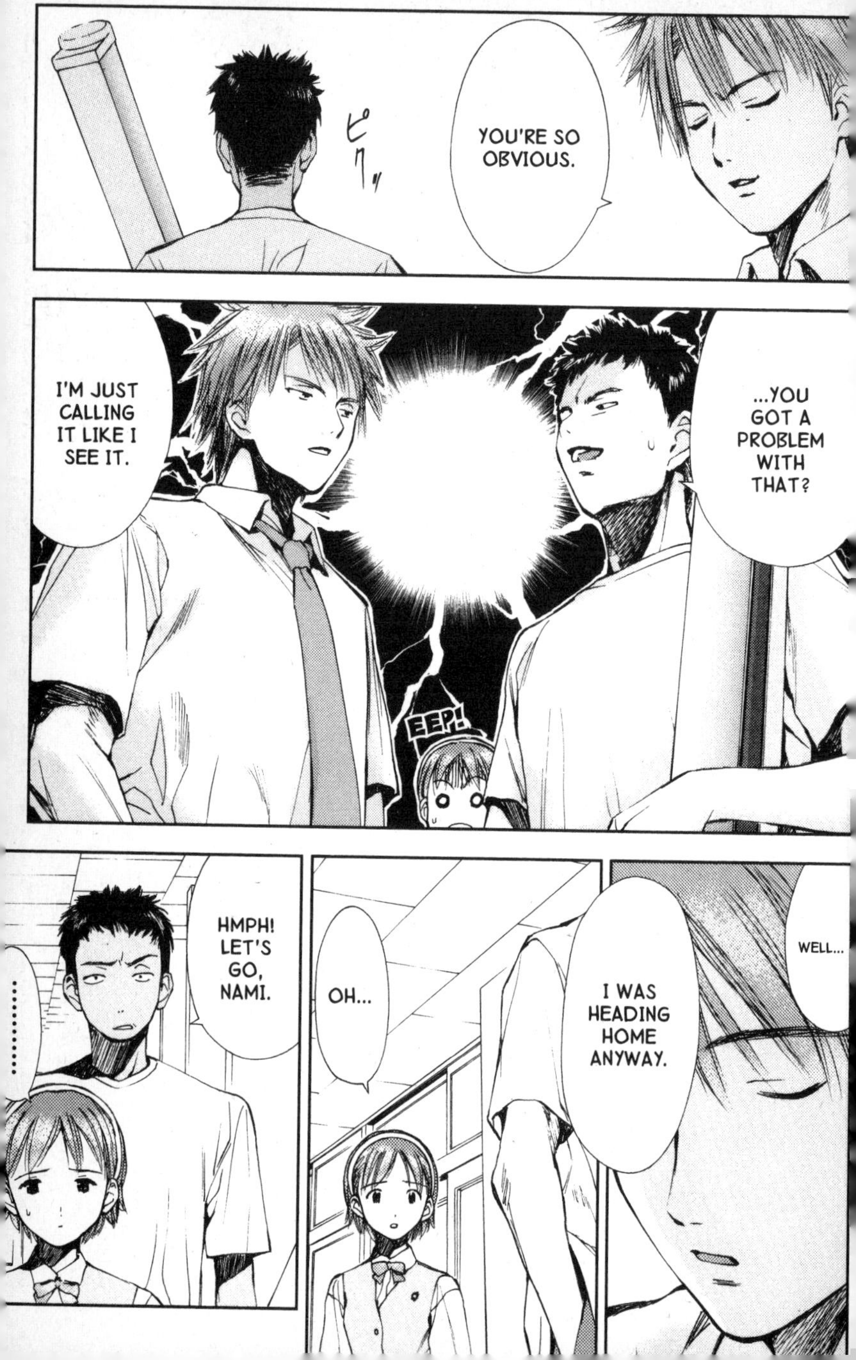
YOU'RE SO OBVIOUS.
ピクッ
...YOU GOT A PROBLEM WITH THAT?
I'M JUST CALLING IT LIKE I SEE IT.
EEP!
WELL...
I WAS HEADING HOME ANYWAY.
OH...
HMPH! LET'S GO, NAMI.
......

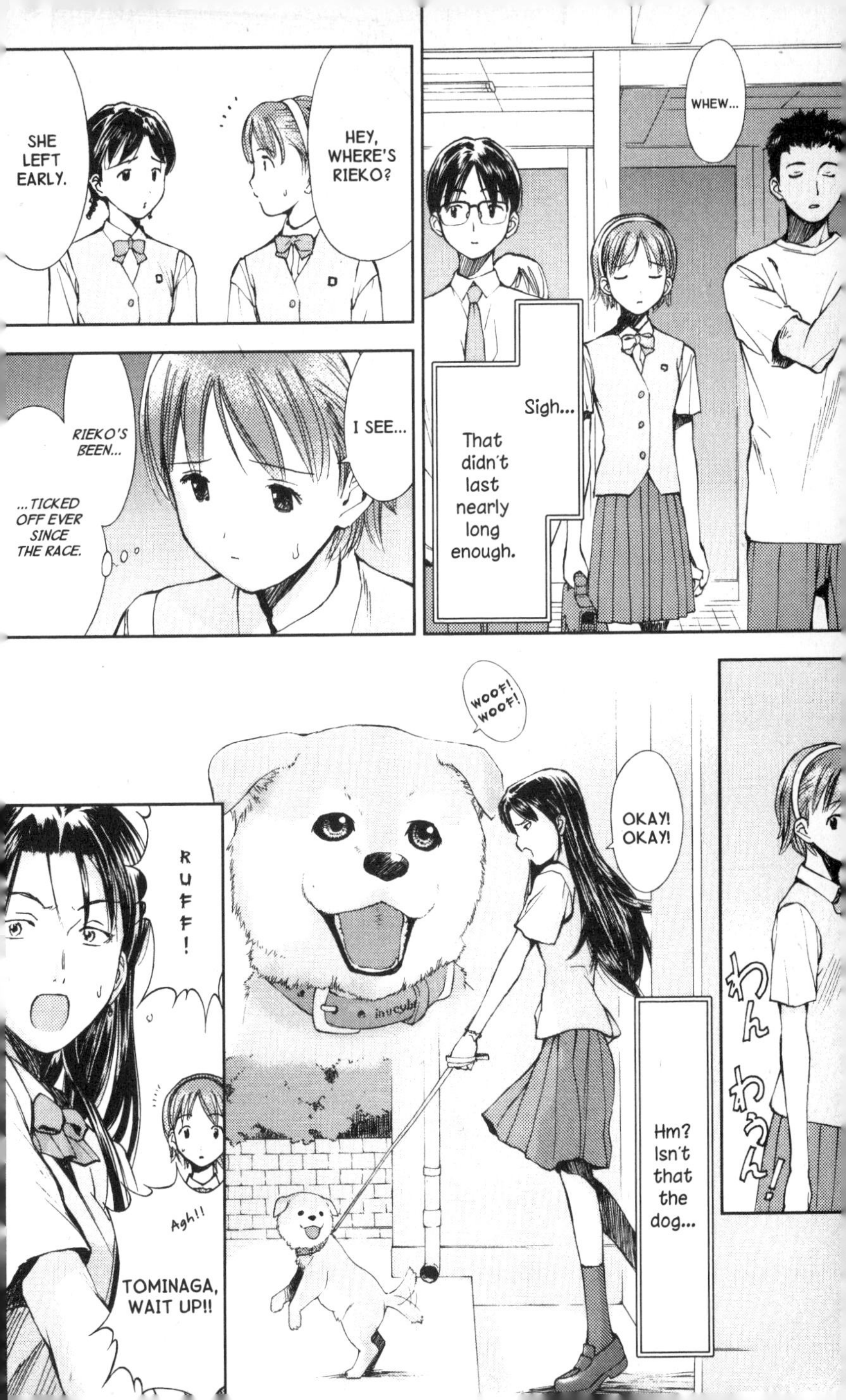
WHEW...
Sigh...
That didn't last nearly long enough.
HEY, WHERE'S RIEKO?
SHE LEFT EARLY.
I SEE...
RIEKO'S BEEN...
...TICKED OFF EVER SINCE THE RACE.
わん わうん!
WOOF! WOOF!
OKAY! OKAY!
Hm? Isn't that the dog...
RUFF!
Agh!!
TOMINAGA, WAIT UP!!

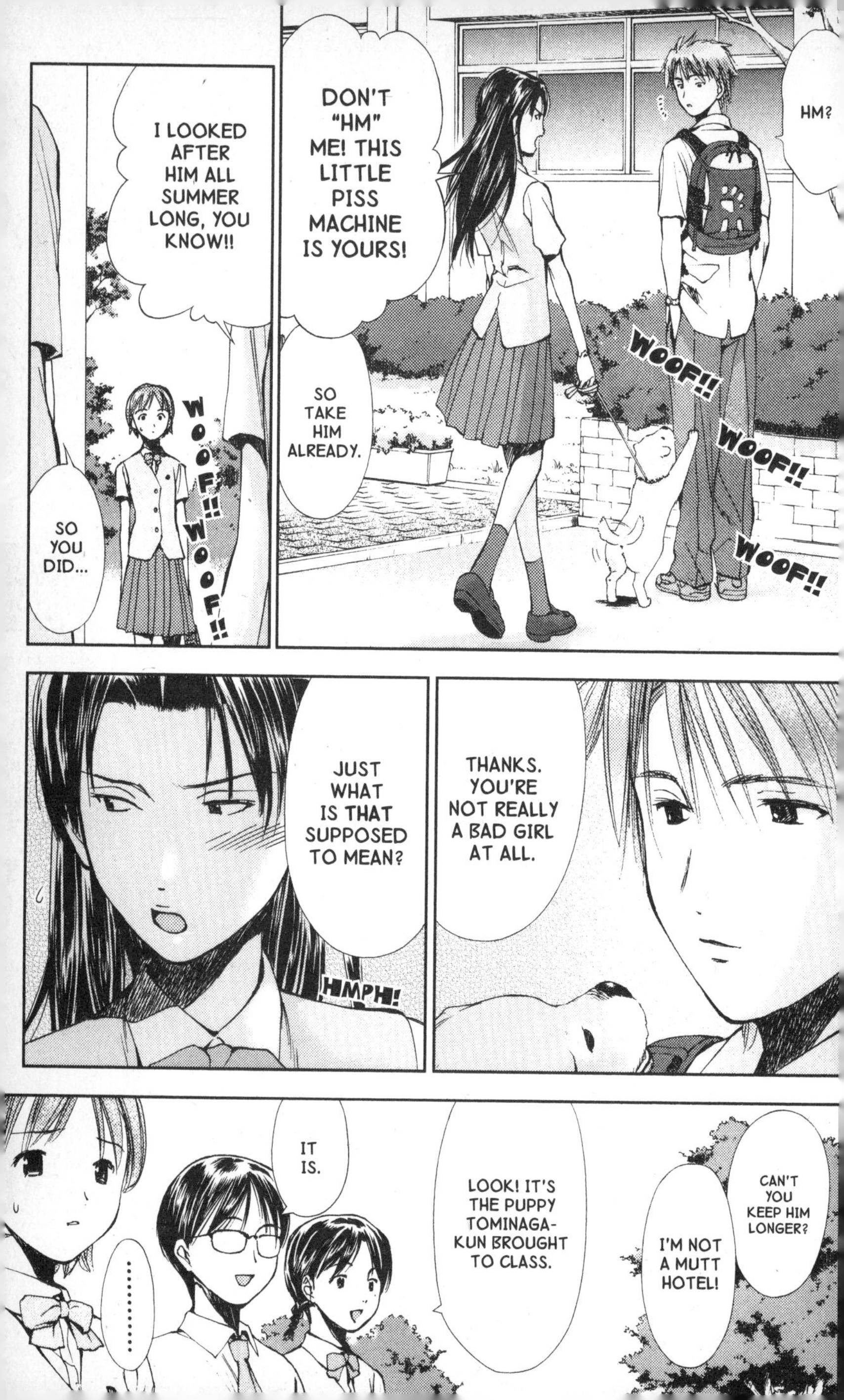
HM?
DON'T "HM" ME! THIS LITTLE PISS MACHINE IS YOURS!
SO TAKE HIM ALREADY.
WOOF!!
WOOF!!
WOOF!!
I LOOKED AFTER HIM ALL SUMMER LONG, YOU KNOW!!
WOOF!!
WOOF!!
SO YOU DID...
THANKS. YOU'RE NOT REALLY A BAD GIRL AT ALL.
JUST WHAT IS THAT SUPPOSED TO MEAN?
HMPH!
CAN'T YOU KEEP HIM LONGER?
I'M NOT A MUTT HOTEL!
LOOK! IT'S THE PUPPY TOMINAGA-KUN BROUGHT TO CLASS.
IT IS.
....

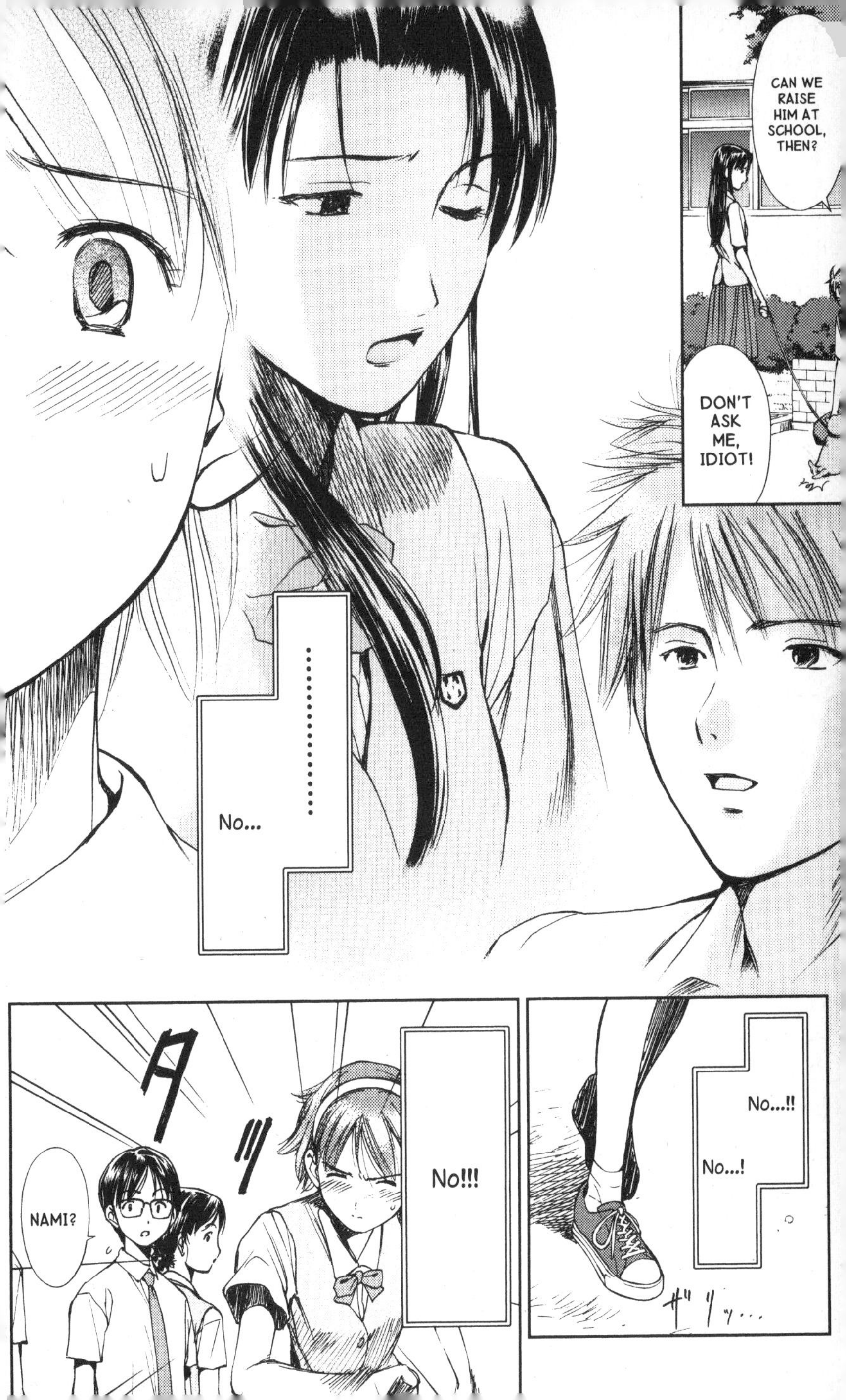
CAN WE RAISE HIM AT SCHOOL, THEN?
DON'T ASK ME, IDIOT!
......
No...
No...!!
No...!
ザリッ...
No!!!
タッ
NAMI?

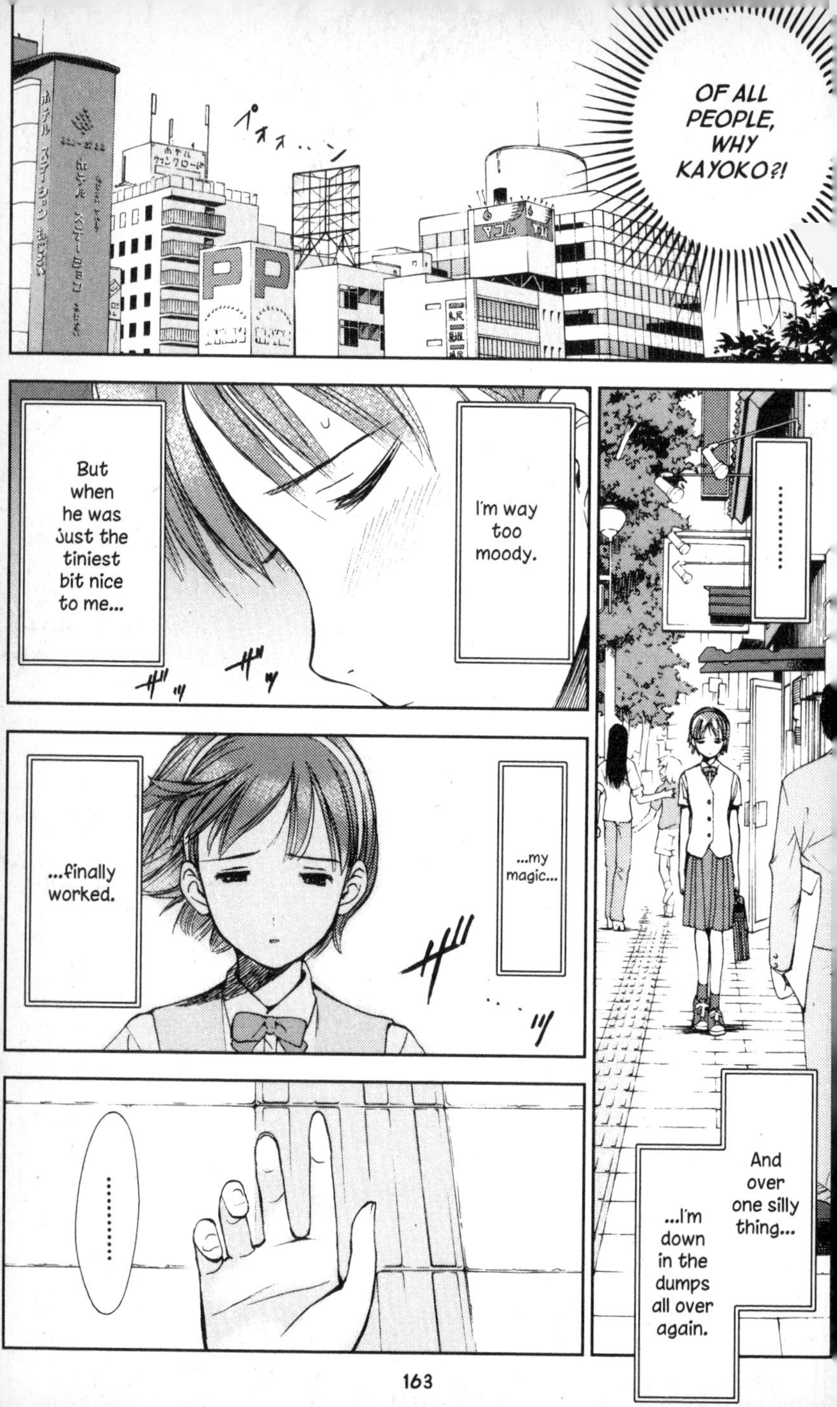

OF ALL PEOPLE, WHY KAYOKO?!
パオォ‥ン
......
And over one silly thing...
...I'm down in the dumps all over again.
I'm way too moody.
But when he was just the tiniest bit nice to me...
...my magic...
...finally worked.
......

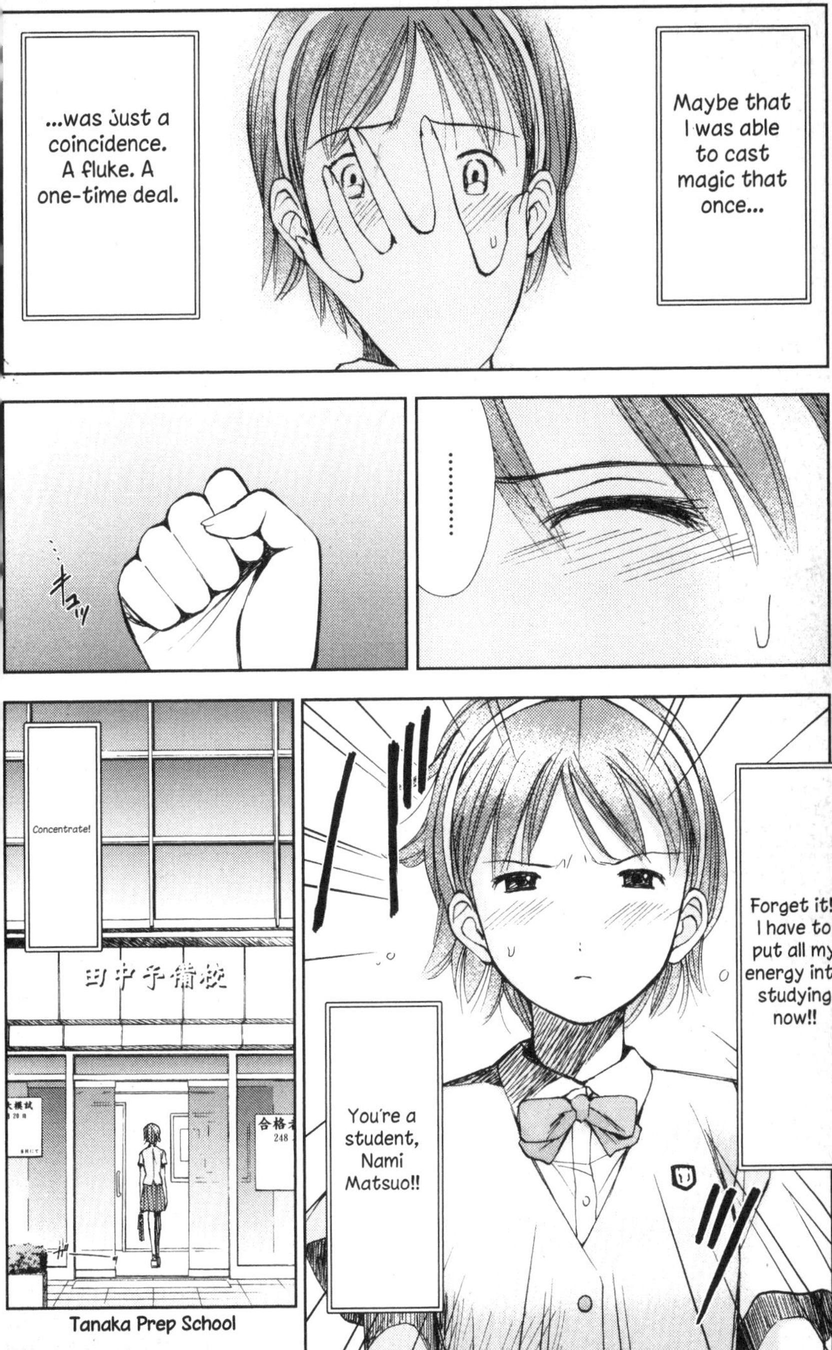
Maybe that I was able to cast magic that once...
...was just a coincidence. A fluke. A one-time deal.
....
Forget it!! I have to put all my energy into studying now!!
You're a student, Nami Matsuo!!
Concentrate!
田中予備校
合格者
248
Tanaka Prep School

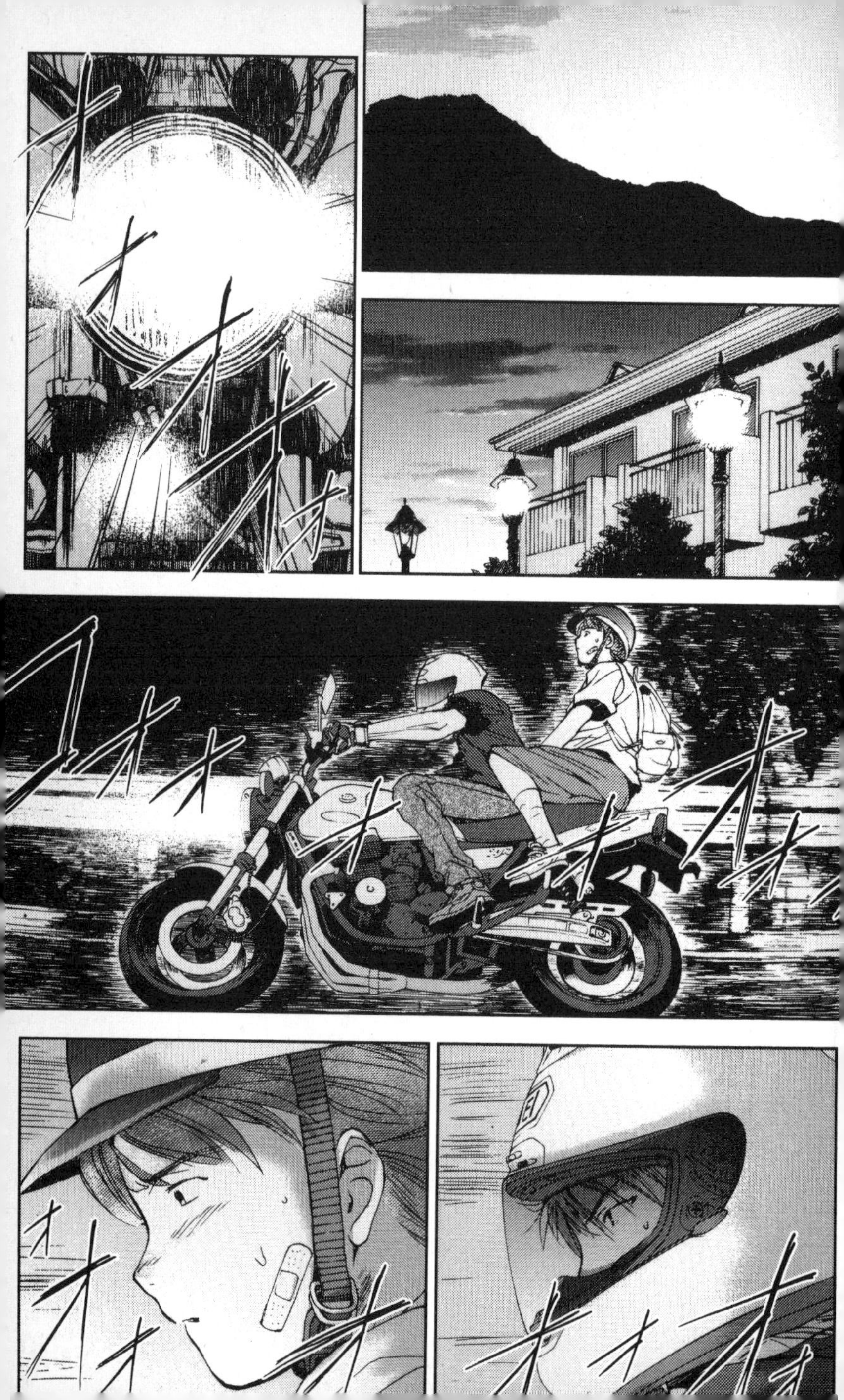

オオオオオオ
ゴオオオ
オオオ
オオオ
オオオオ

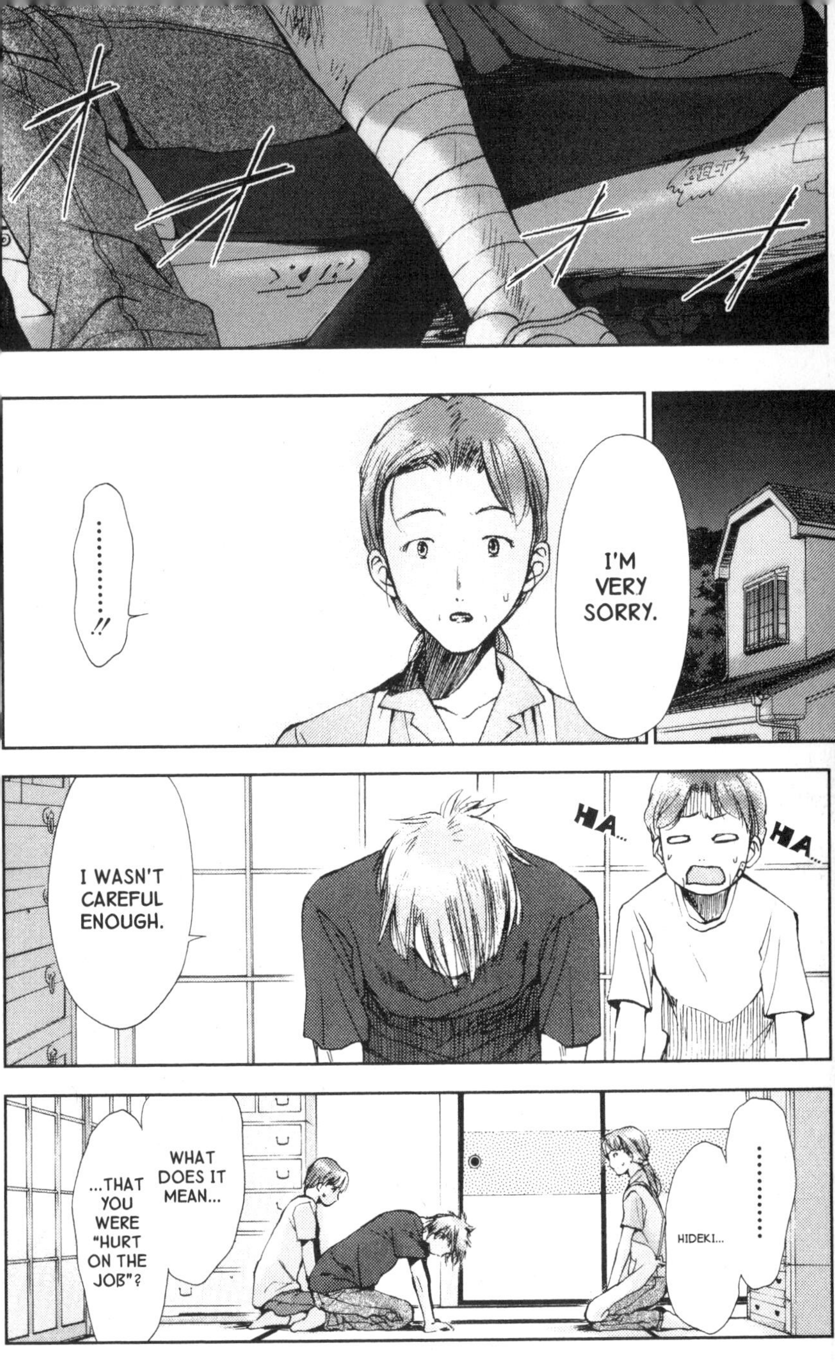

オオオオ
I'M VERY SORRY.
……!!
HA... HA...
I WASN'T CAREFUL ENOUGH.
……… HIDEKI...
WHAT DOES IT MEAN...
...THAT YOU WERE "HURT ON THE JOB"?

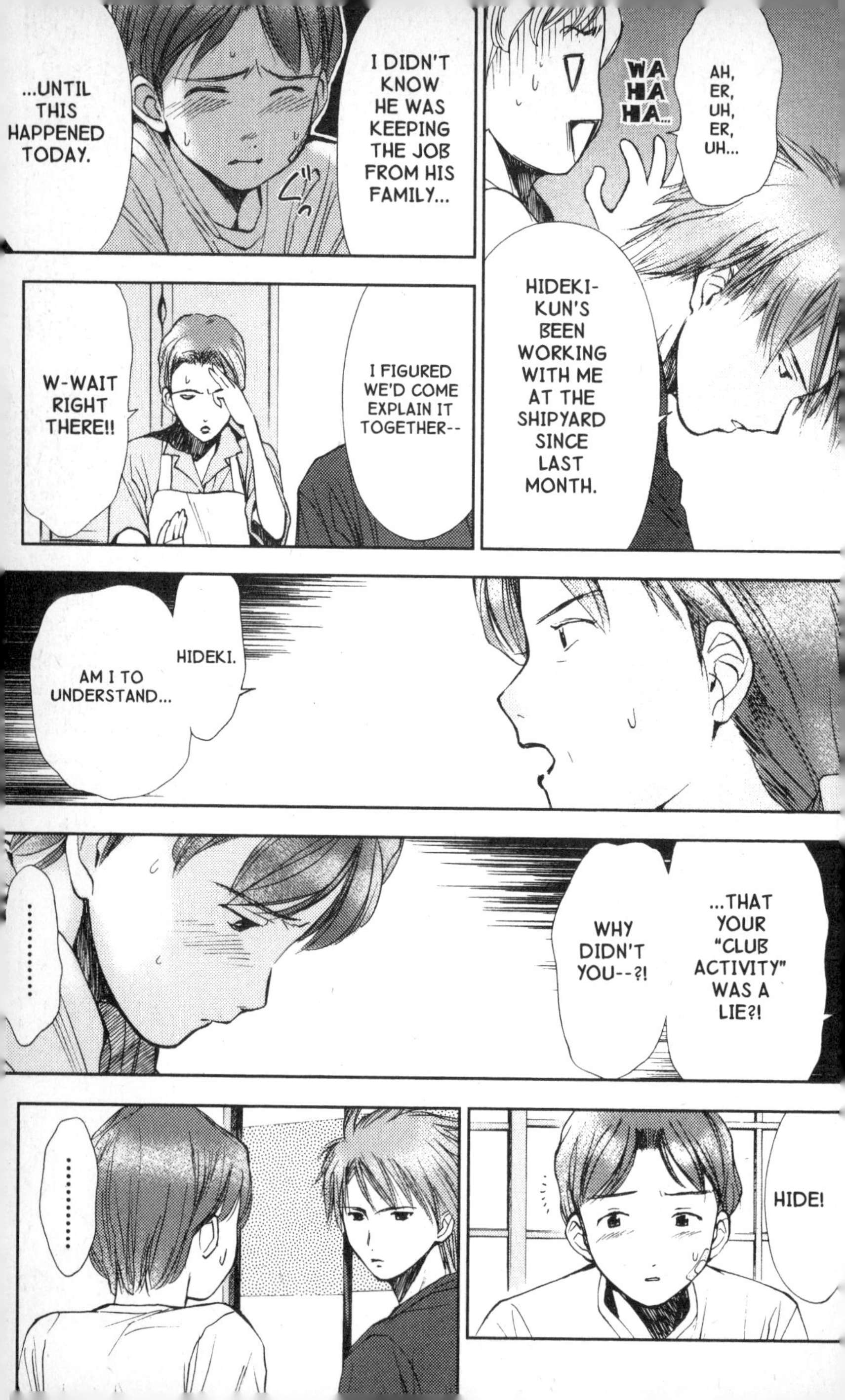
AH, ER, UH, ER, UH...
WA HA HA...
HIDEKI-KUN'S BEEN WORKING WITH ME AT THE SHIPYARD SINCE LAST MONTH.
I DIDN'T KNOW HE WAS KEEPING THE JOB FROM HIS FAMILY...
...UNTIL THIS HAPPENED TODAY.
I FIGURED WE'D COME EXPLAIN IT TOGETHER--
W-WAIT RIGHT THERE!!
HIDEKI.
AM I TO UNDERSTAND...
...THAT YOUR "CLUB ACTIVITY" WAS A LIE?!
WHY DIDN'T YOU--?!
....
HIDE!
...
....

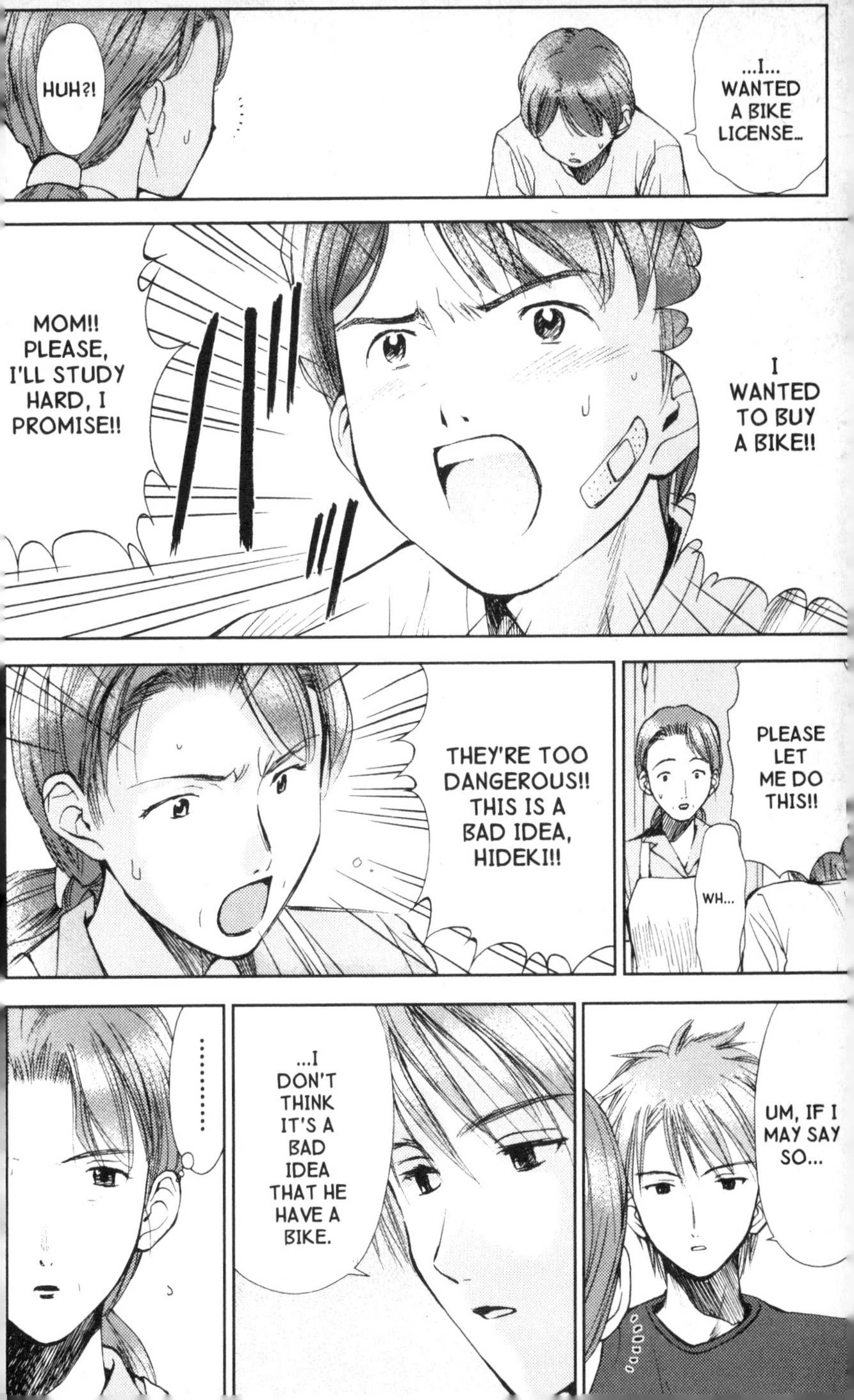
...I... WANTED A BIKE LICENSE...
HUH?!
I WANTED TO BUY A BIKE!!
MOM!! PLEASE, I'LL STUDY HARD, I PROMISE!!
PLEASE LET ME DO THIS!!
WH...
THEY'RE TOO DANGEROUS!! THIS IS A BAD IDEA, HIDEKI!!
UM, IF I MAY SAY SO...
...I DON'T THINK IT'S A BAD IDEA THAT HE HAVE A BIKE.
....

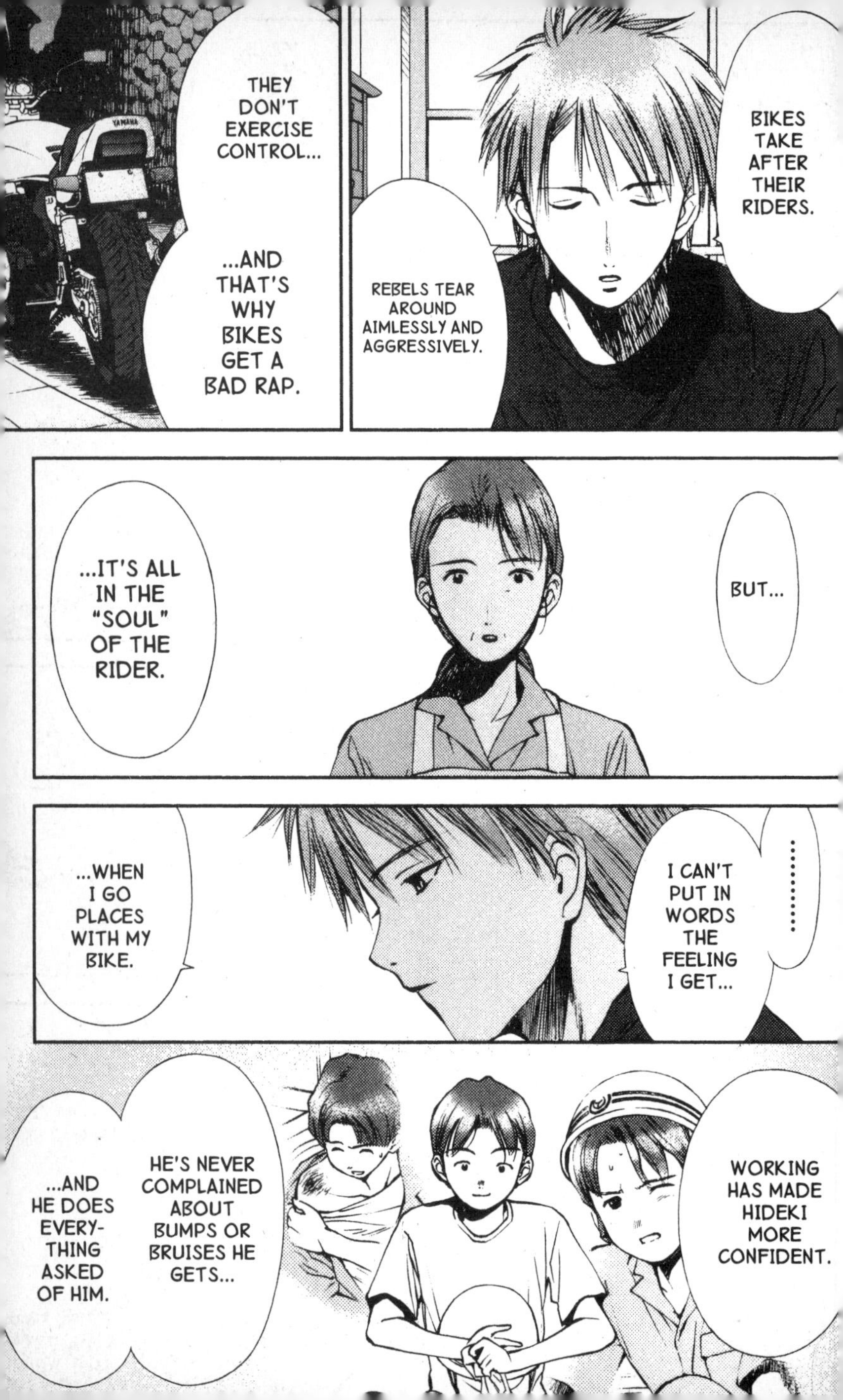
BIKES TAKE AFTER THEIR RIDERS.
REBELS TEAR AROUND AIMLESSLY AND AGGRESSIVELY.
THEY DON'T EXERCISE CONTROL...
...AND THAT'S WHY BIKES GET A BAD RAP.
BUT...
...IT'S ALL IN THE "SOUL" OF THE RIDER.
....
I CAN'T PUT IN WORDS THE FEELING I GET...
...WHEN I GO PLACES WITH MY BIKE.
WORKING HAS MADE HIDEKI MORE CONFIDENT.
HE'S NEVER COMPLAINED ABOUT BUMPS OR BRUISES HE GETS...
...AND HE DOES EVERY-THING ASKED OF HIM.

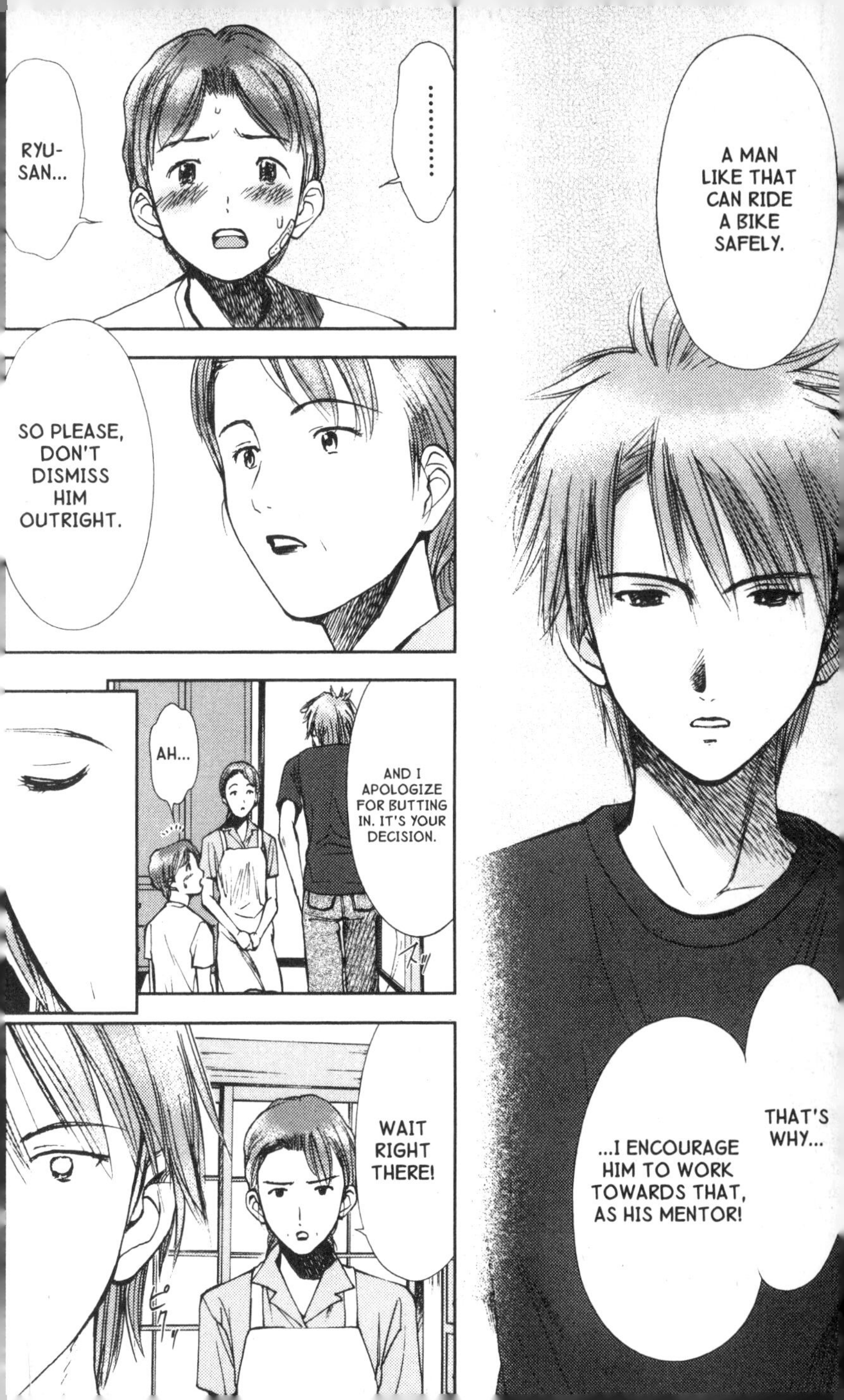
A MAN LIKE THAT CAN RIDE A BIKE SAFELY.
THAT'S WHY...
...I ENCOURAGE HIM TO WORK TOWARDS THAT, AS HIS MENTOR!
....
RYU-SAN...
SO PLEASE, DON'T DISMISS HIM OUTRIGHT.
AND I APOLOGIZE FOR BUTTING IN. IT'S YOUR DECISION.
AH...
WAIT RIGHT THERE!

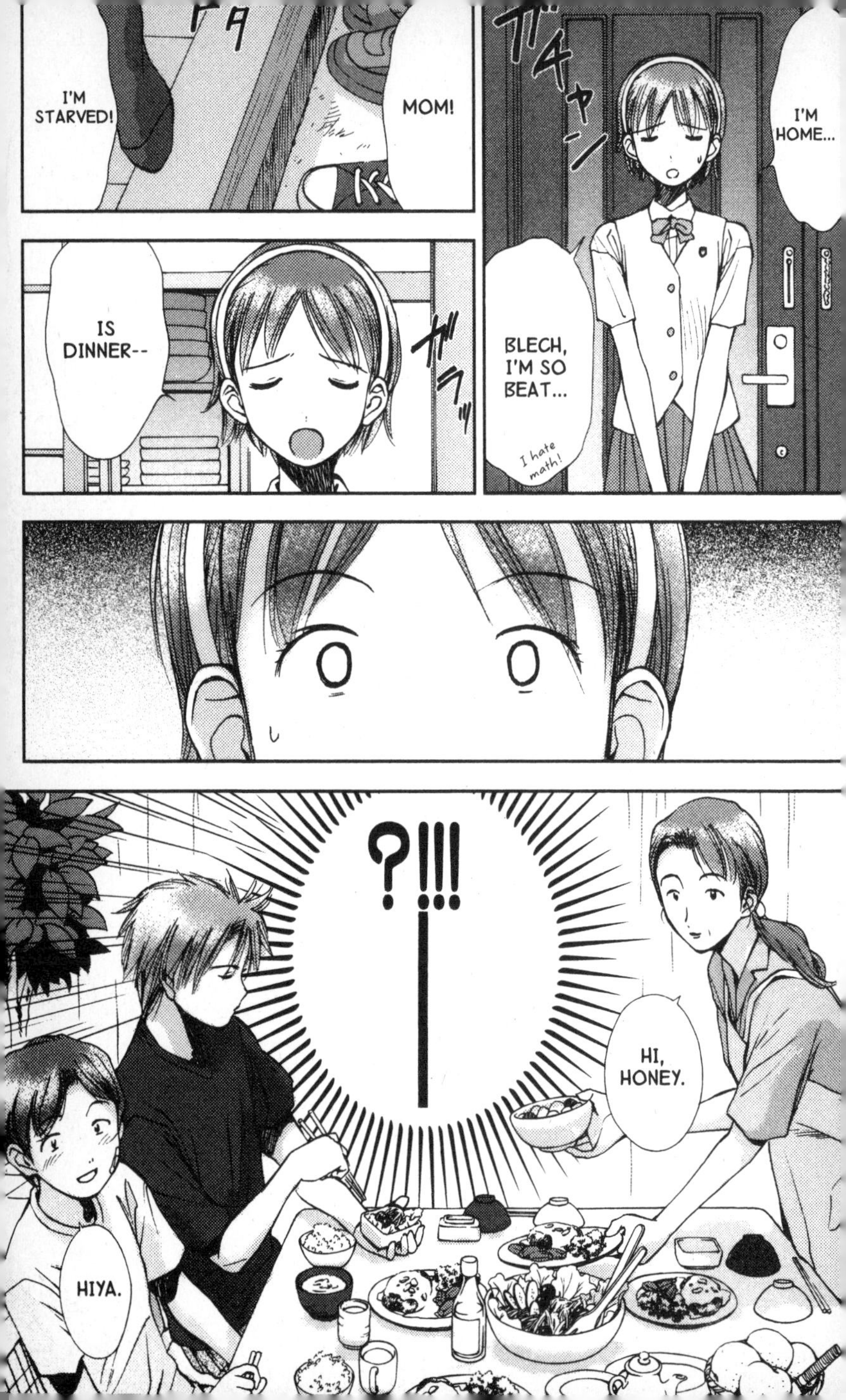
ガチャン
I'M HOME...
BLECH, I'M SO BEAT...
I hate math!
MOM!
I'M STARVED!
ガラッ
IS DINNER--
?!!!
HI, HONEY.
HIYA.

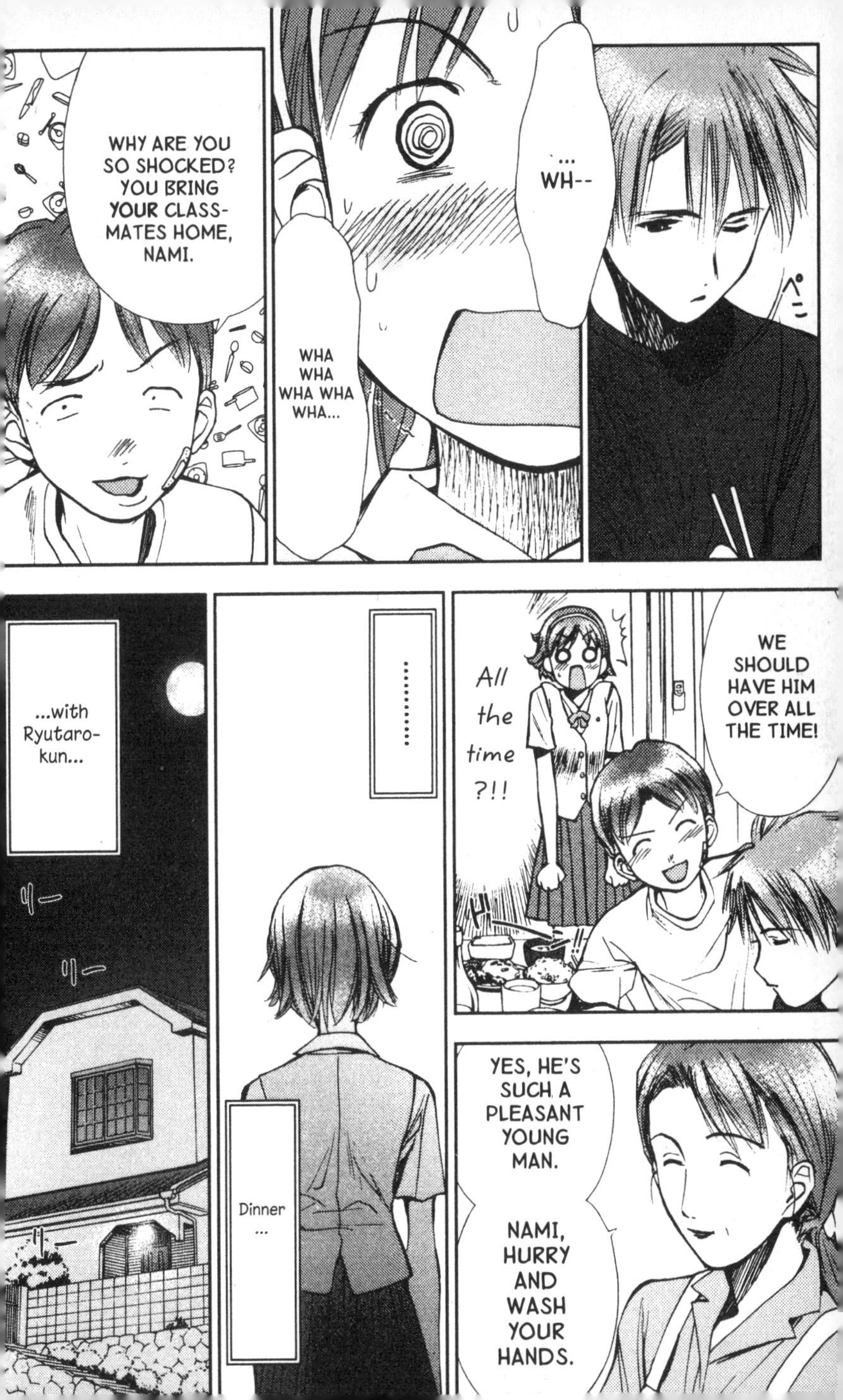
...
WH--
WHA WHA WHA WHA WHA...
WHY ARE YOU SO SHOCKED? YOU BRING YOUR CLASSMATES HOME, NAMI.
WE SHOULD HAVE HIM OVER ALL THE TIME!
All the time ?!!
YES, HE'S SUCH A PLEASANT YOUNG MAN.
NAMI, HURRY AND WASH YOUR HANDS.
....
Dinner ...
...with Ryutaro-kun...

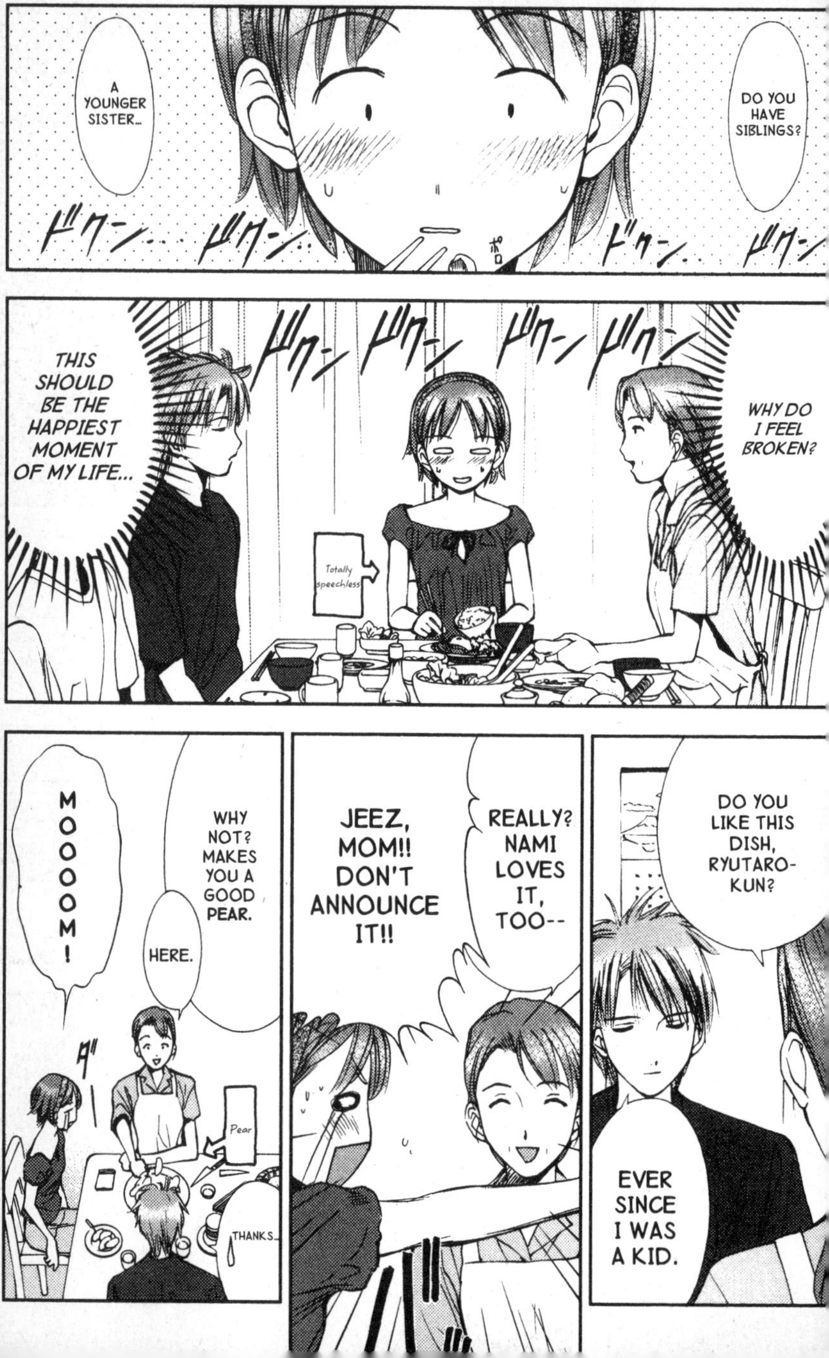
DO YOU HAVE SIBLINGS?
A YOUNGER SISTER...
ドクン… ドクン…
ポロ
WHY DO I FEEL BROKEN?
ドクン ドクン ドクン ドクン
Totally speechless
THIS SHOULD BE THE HAPPIEST MOMENT OF MY LIFE...
DO YOU LIKE THIS DISH, RYUTARO-KUN?
EVER SINCE I WAS A KID.
REALLY? NAMI LOVES IT, TOO--
JEEZ, MOM!! DON'T ANNOUNCE IT!!
WHY NOT? MAKES YOU A GOOD PEAR.
MOOOOOM!
HERE.
Pear
THANKS...

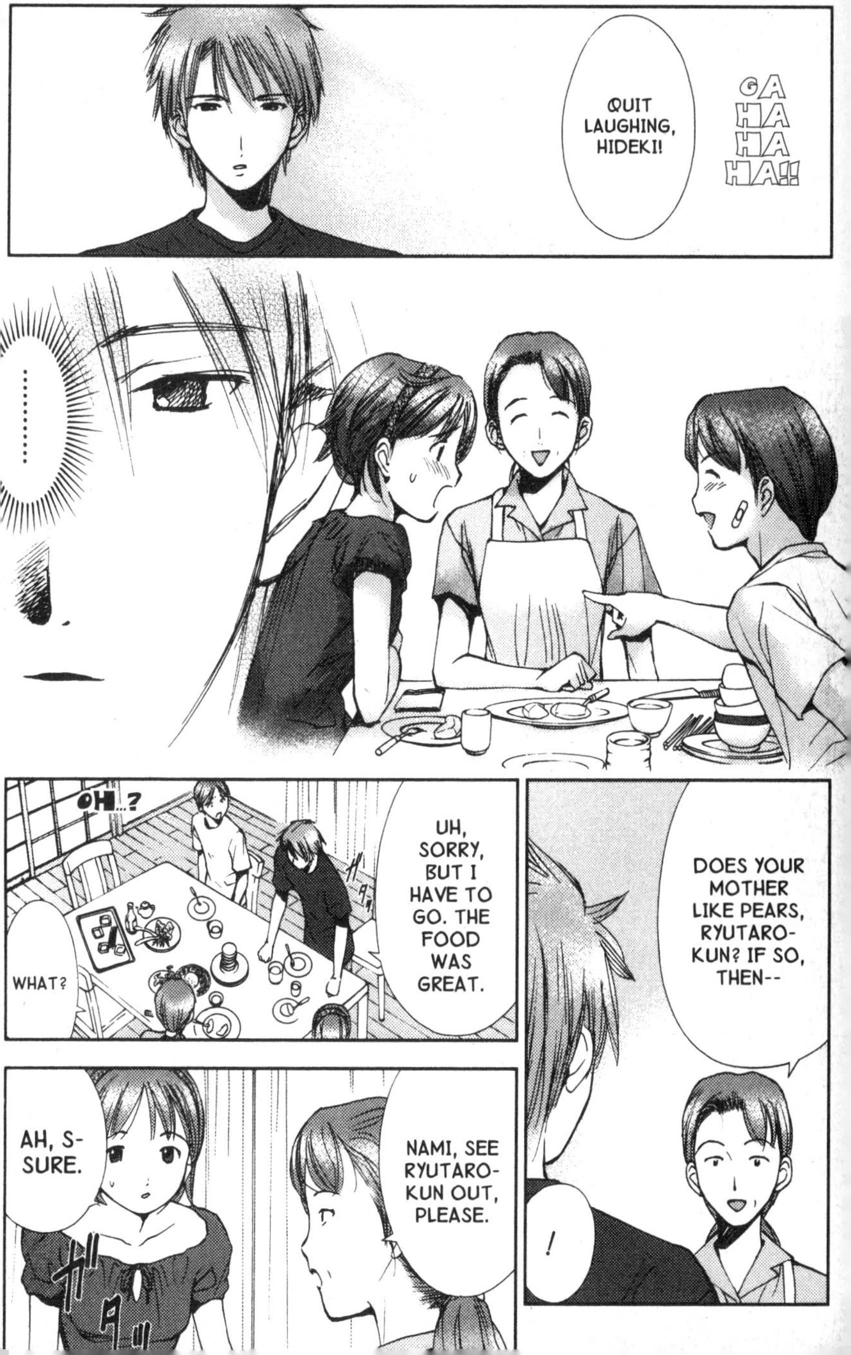
GAHAHAHA!!
QUIT LAUGHING, HIDEKI!
......
DOES YOUR MOTHER LIKE PEARS, RYUTARO-KUN? IF SO, THEN--
!
UH, SORRY, BUT I HAVE TO GO. THE FOOD WAS GREAT.
OH...?
WHAT?
NAMI, SEE RYUTARO-KUN OUT, PLEASE.
AH, S-SURE.

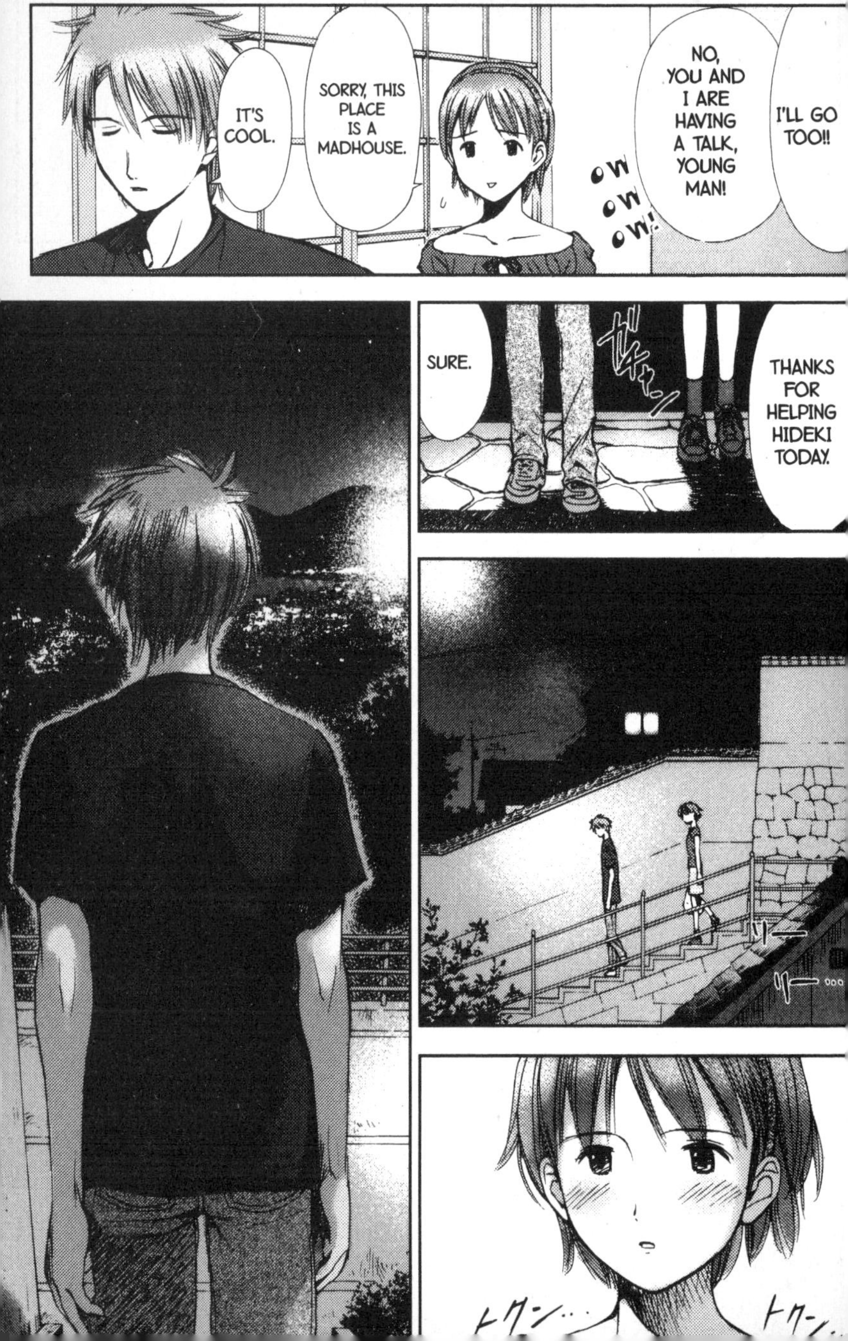
I'LL GO TOO!!
NO, YOU AND I ARE HAVING A TALK, YOUNG MAN!
OW OW OW!
SORRY, THIS PLACE IS A MADHOUSE.
IT'S COOL.
THANKS FOR HELPING HIDEKI TODAY.
ガチャン
SURE.
リー
リー…
トクン…
トクン…

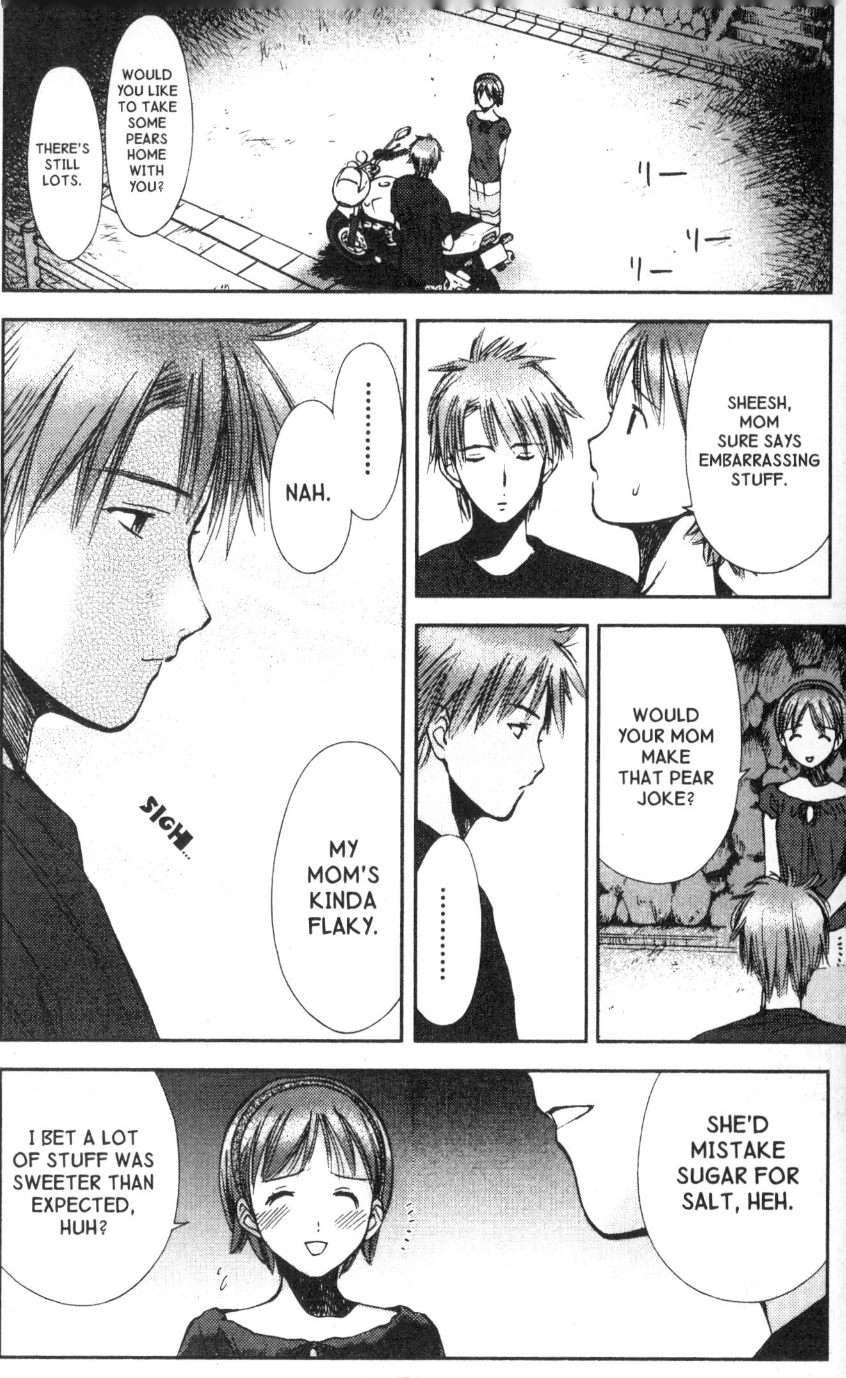
WOULD YOU LIKE TO TAKE SOME PEARS HOME WITH YOU?
THERE'S STILL LOTS.
リー
リー
リー
SHEESH, MOM SURE SAYS EMBARRASSING STUFF.
WOULD YOUR MOM MAKE THAT PEAR JOKE?
......
....
....
NAH.
SIGH...
MY MOM'S KINDA FLAKY.
SHE'D MISTAKE SUGAR FOR SALT, HEH.
I BET A LOT OF STUFF WAS SWEETER THAN EXPECTED, HUH?

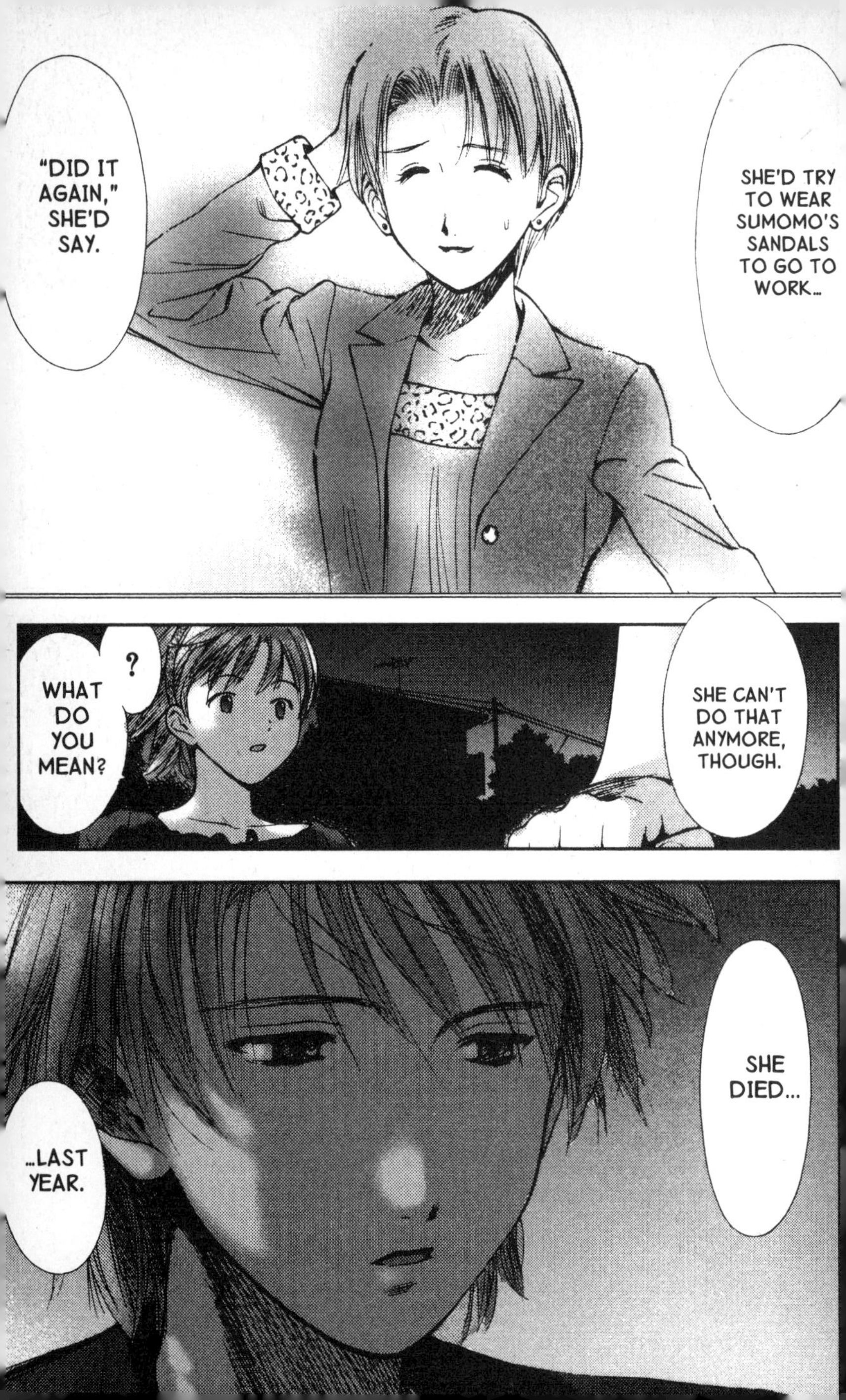
SHE'D TRY TO WEAR SUMOMO'S SANDALS TO GO TO WORK...
"DID IT AGAIN," SHE'D SAY.
SHE CAN'T DO THAT ANYMORE, THOUGH.
?
WHAT DO YOU MEAN?
SHE DIED...
...LAST YEAR.

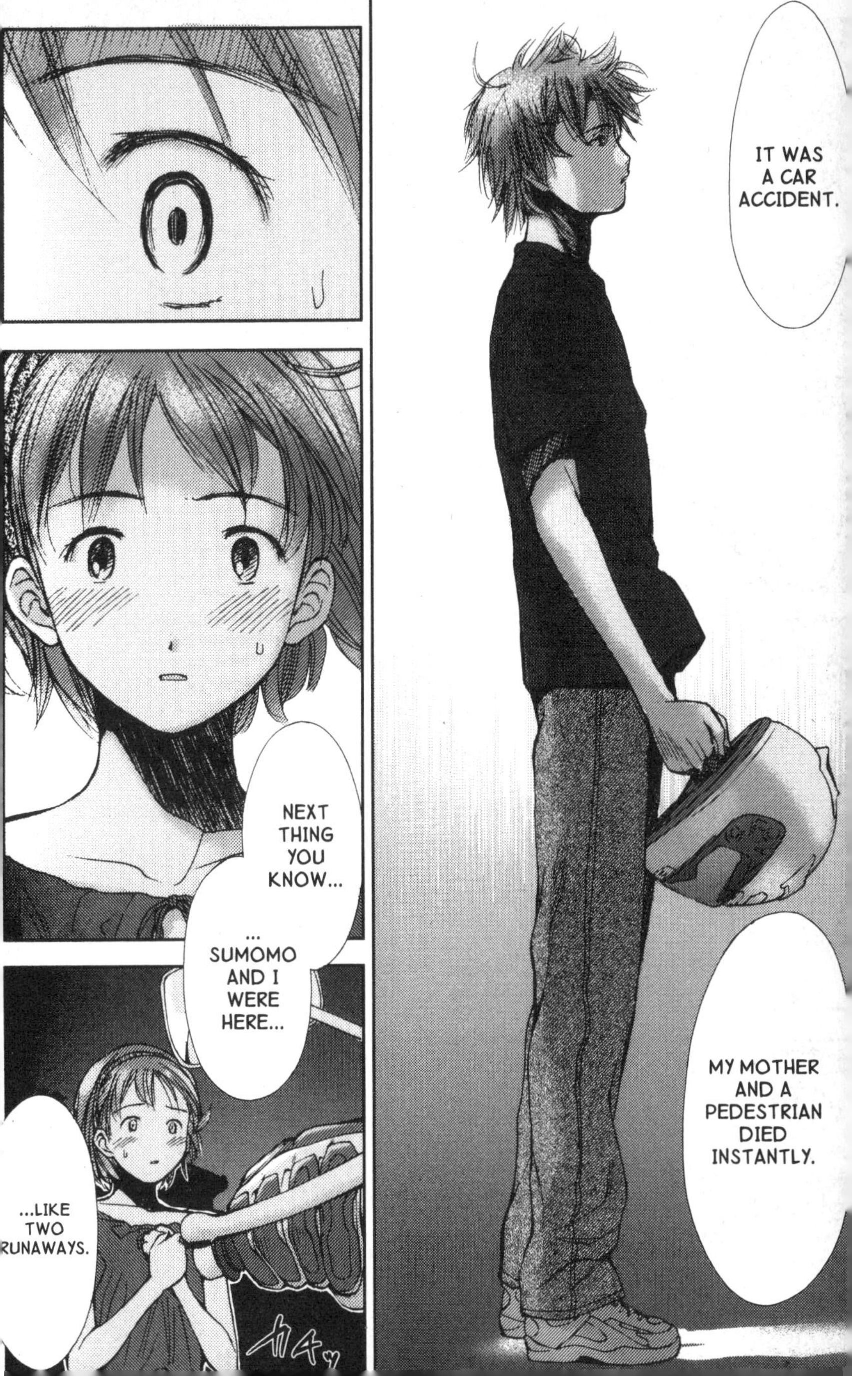
IT WAS A CAR ACCIDENT.
MY MOTHER AND A PEDESTRIAN DIED INSTANTLY.
NEXT THING YOU KNOW...
... SUMOMO AND I WERE HERE...
...LIKE TWO RUNAWAYS.
カチッ

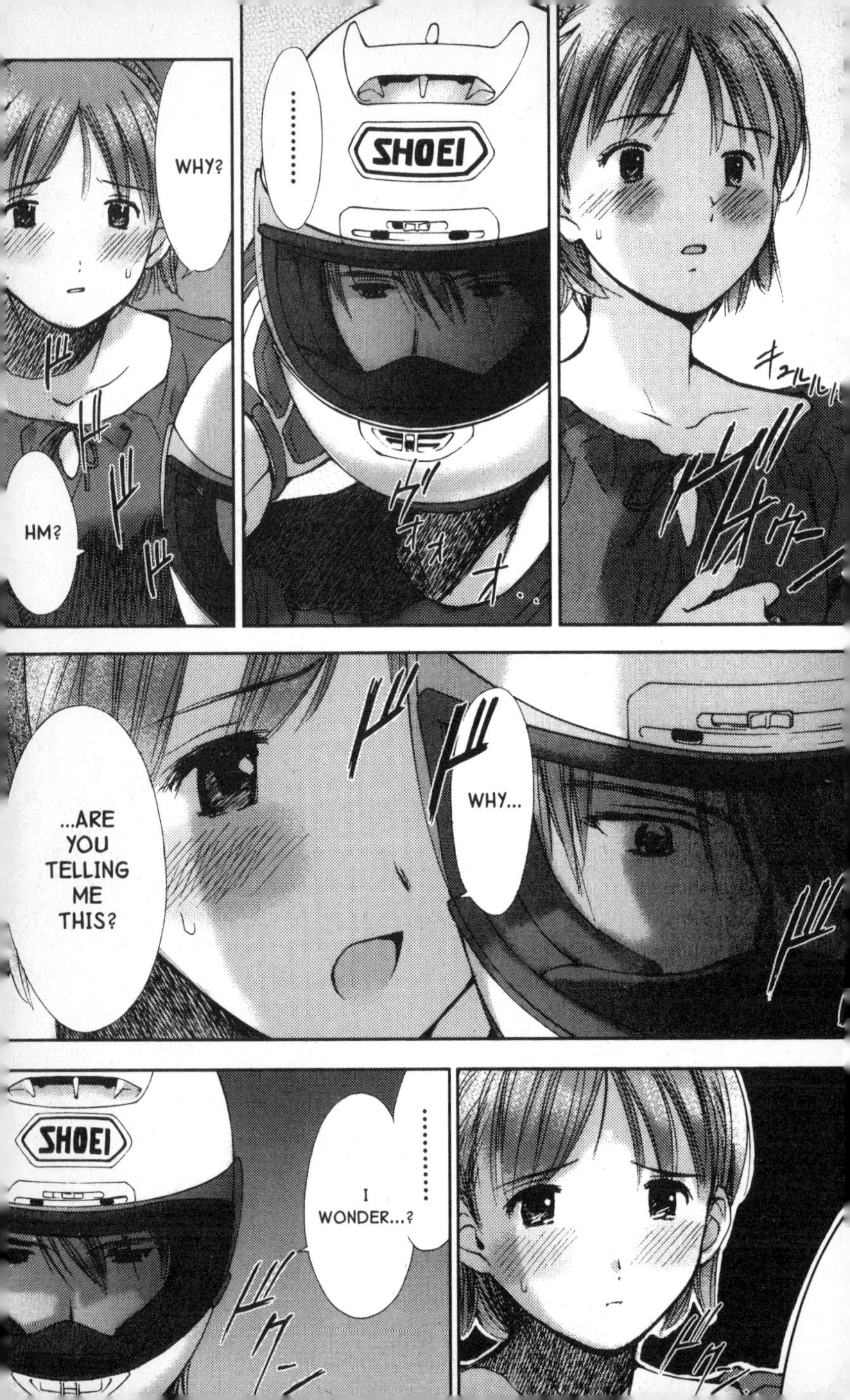

......
WHY?
HM?
WHY...
...ARE YOU TELLING ME THIS?
......
I WONDER...?

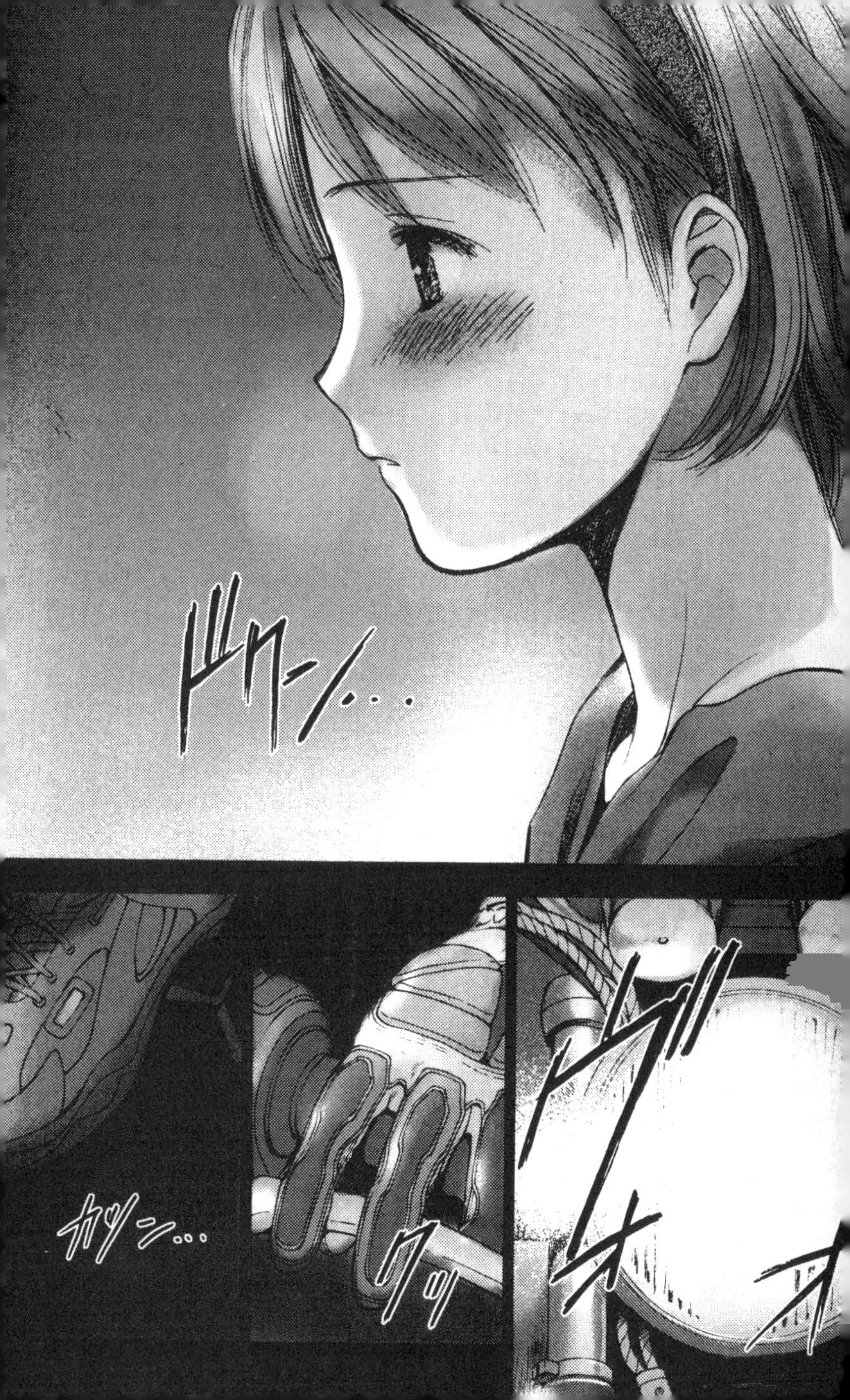
ドゥーン…
ドゥオオ
グッ
カツン…

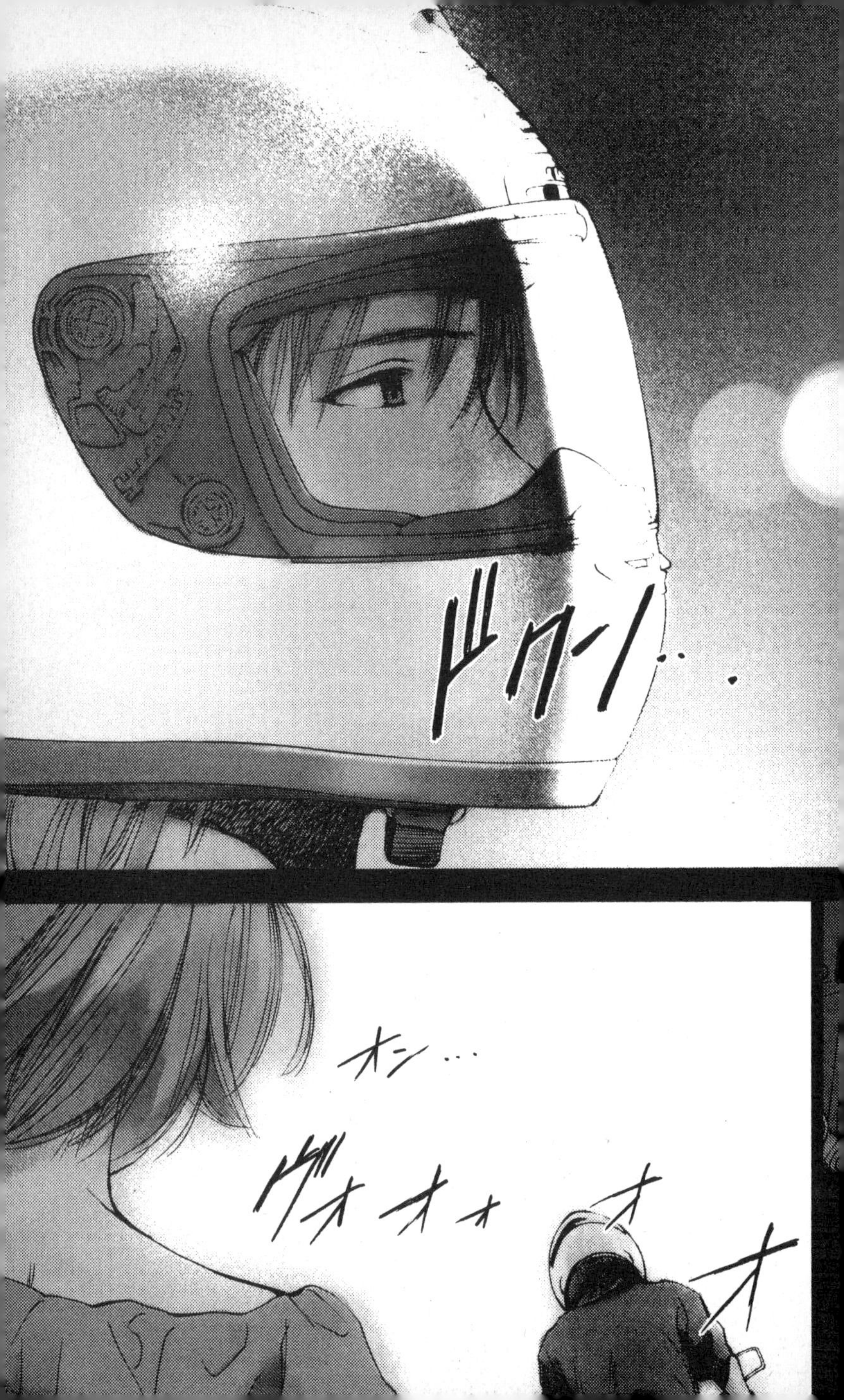
ドゥン‥.
オン…
ヴオオォオオ

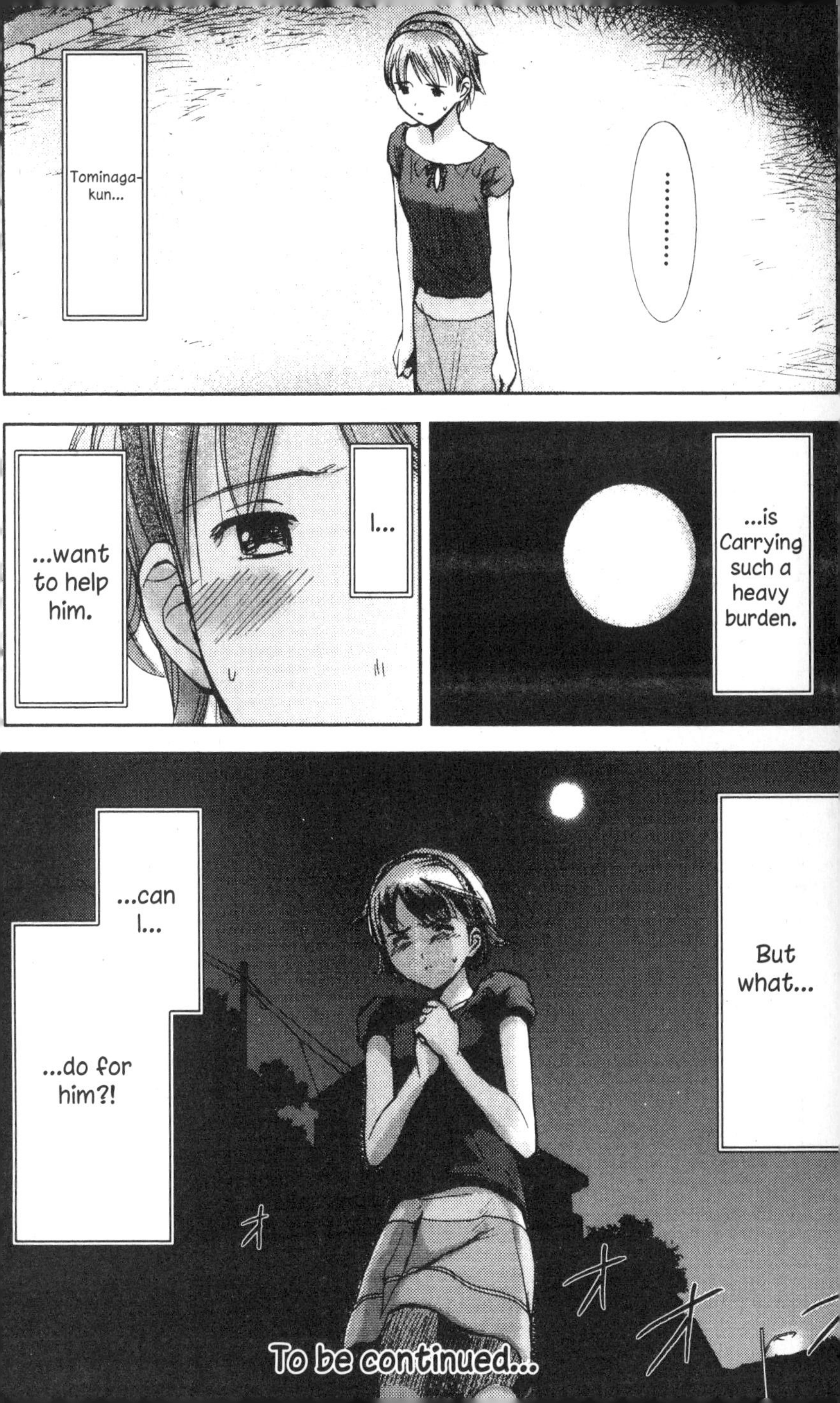
......
Tominaga-kun...
...is Carrying such a heavy burden.
I...
...want to help him.
But what...
...can I...
...do for him?!
オ
オ
オ
To be continued...

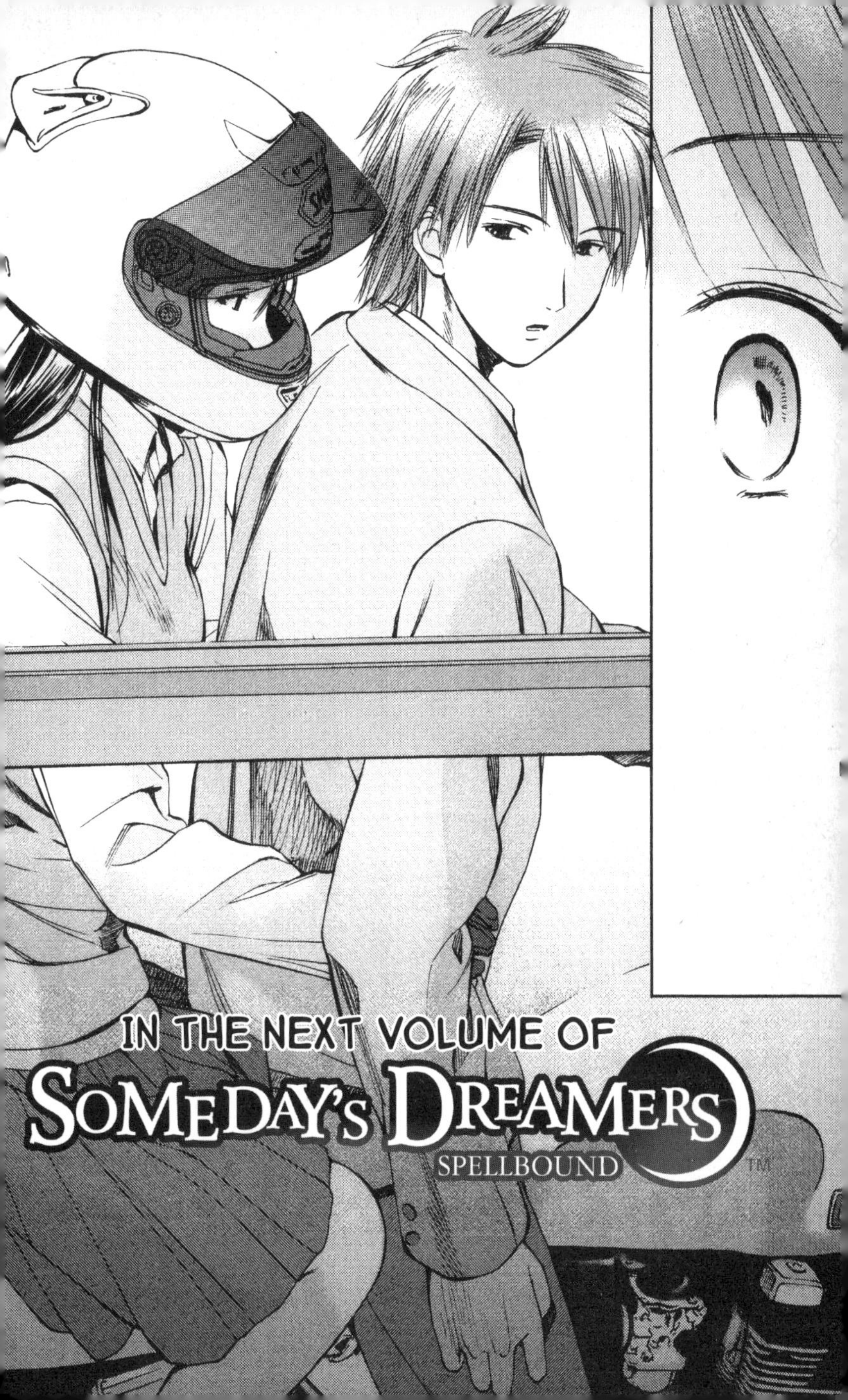
IN THE NEXT VOLUME OF
SOMEDAY'S DREAMERS
SPELLBOUND
TM

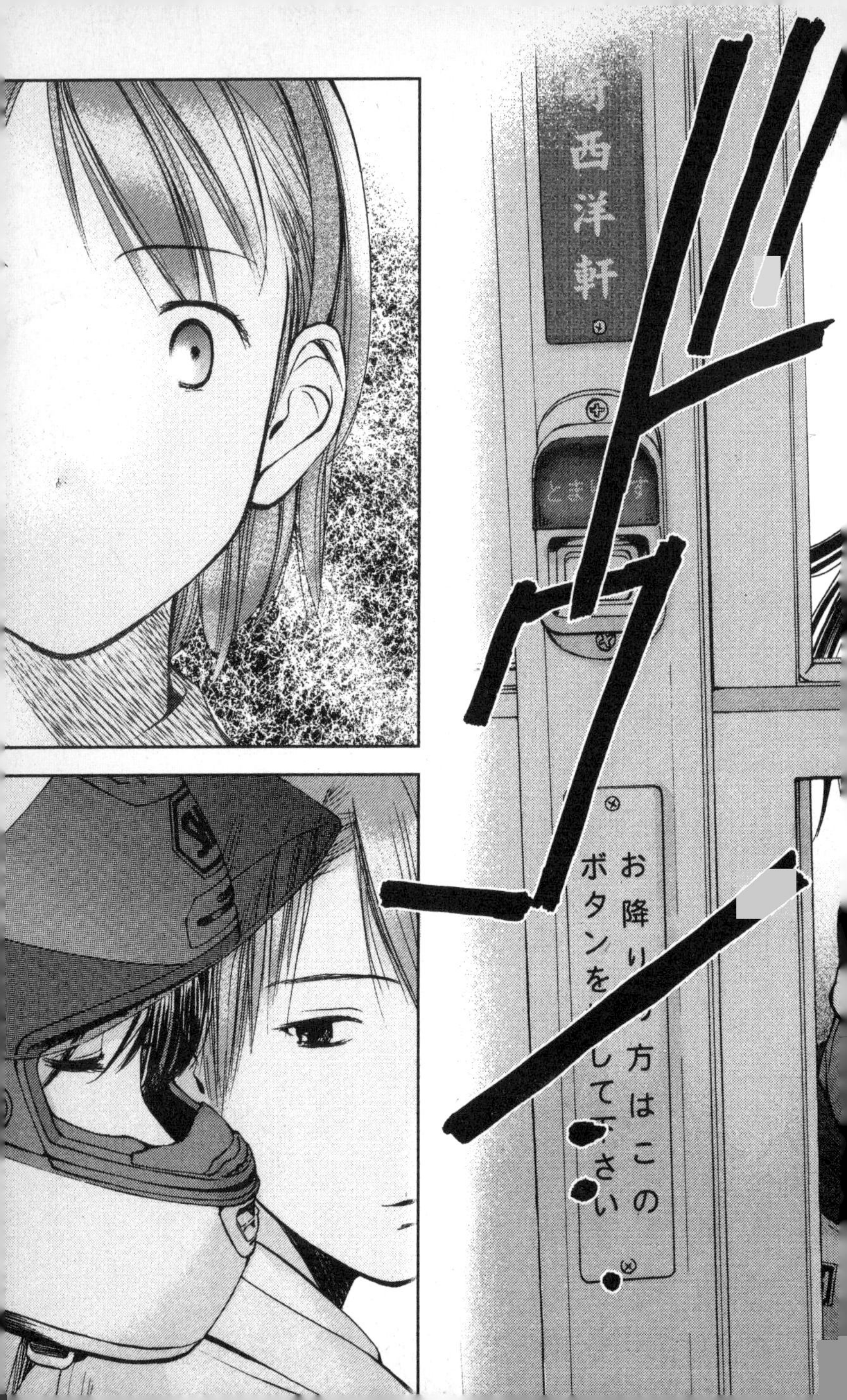
西洋軒
ドクン

SO YOU THINK YOU CAN RHYSMYTH?

RHYSMYTH™

As America's newest and most popular sport, Rhysmyth features one-on-one dance battles atop a hi-tech glass court grid. When the music hits, you and your opponent dance across a digital minefield for the glory of being the fastest, most accurate and stylish Rhysmyther. In steps clumsy high school student Elena looking for a little something extra to beef up her college apps. Now Elena is thrust into the fast-paced world of Rhysmyth, where getting your groove on can lead to rivalry and romance!

ROMANCE

T
TEEN
AGE 13+

Rhysmyth © Anthony Andora, Lincy Chan and TOKYOPOP Inc.

TOKYOPOP MANGA SUPPLEMENT

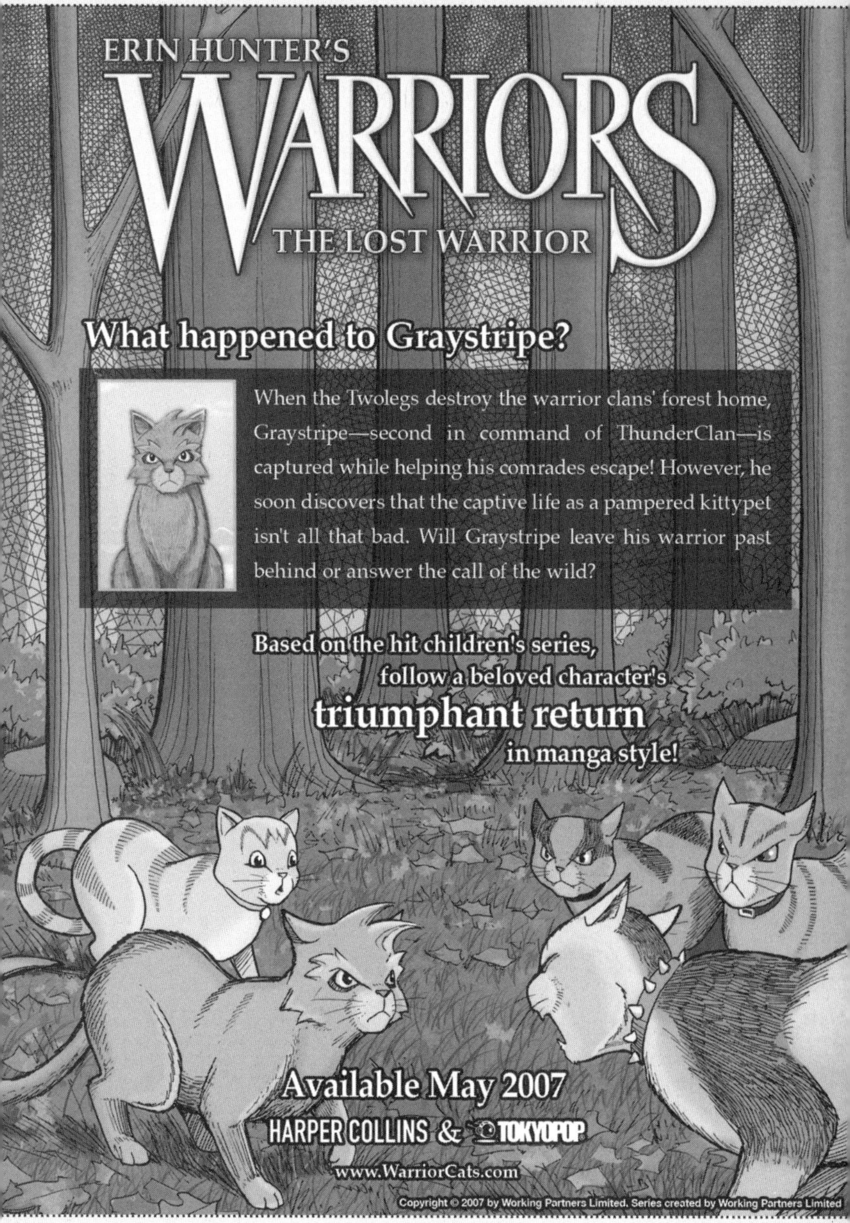
ERIN HUNTER'S
WARRIORS
THE LOST WARRIOR
What happened to Graystripe?
When the Twolegs destroy the warrior clans' forest home, Graystripe—second in command of ThunderClan—is captured while helping his comrades escape! However, he soon discovers that the captive life as a pampered kittypet isn't all that bad. Will Graystripe leave his warrior past behind or answer the call of the wild?
Based on the hit children's series, follow a beloved character's triumphant return in manga style!
Available May 2007
HARPER COLLINS & TOKYOPOP
www.WarriorCats.com
Copyright © 2007 by Working Partners Limited. Series created by Working Partners Limited

FOR MORE INFORMATION VISIT: WWW.TOKYOPOP.COM

STOP!

This is the back of the book.
You wouldn't want to spoil a great ending!

This book is printed "manga-style," in the authentic Japanese right-to-left format. Since none of the artwork has been flipped or altered, readers get to experience the story just as the creator intended. You've been asking for it, so TOKYOPOP® delivered: authentic, hot-off-the-press, and far more fun!

DIRECTIONS

1
2
3
4
5
6
7
8
9
10

If this is your first time reading manga-style, here's a quick guide to help you understand how it works.

It's easy... just start in the top right panel and follow the numbers. Have fun, and look for more 100% authentic manga from TOKYOPOP®!

THE MANGA REVOLUTION · LEADING · 漫画革命

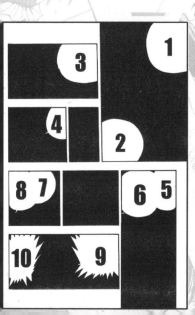

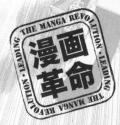